Empire of Refugees

EMPIRE OF REFUGEES

*North Caucasian Muslims
and the Late Ottoman State*

Vladimir Hamed-Troyansky

Stanford University Press
Stanford, California

Stanford University Press
Stanford, California

Studies of the Harriman Institute
Publication of this book is supported in part by the Harriman Institute at Columbia University.

Printed in the United States of America on acid-free, archival-quality paper

Library of Congress Cataloging-in-Publication Data
Names: Hamed-Troyansky, Vladimir, author.
Title: Empire of refugees : North Caucasian Muslims and the late Ottoman state / Vladimir Hamed-Troyansky.
Description: Stanford, California : Stanford University Press, 2024. | Includes bibliographical references and index.
Identifiers: LCCN 2023018074 (print) | LCCN 2023018075 (ebook) | ISBN 9781503636965 (hardcover) | ISBN 9781503637740 (paperback) | ISBN 9781503637757 (epub)
Subjects: LCSH: Refugees—Government policy—Turkey—History. | Refugees—Russia (Federation)—Caucasus, Northern—History. | Muslims—Russia (Federation)—Caucasus, Northern—History. | Caucasus, Northern (Russia)—Emigration and immigration—History. | Turkey—Emigration and immigration—History. | Turkey—History—Ottoman Empire, 1288-1918.
Classification: LCC HV640.4.T9 H36 2024 (print) | LCC HV640.4.T9 (ebook) | DDC 305.9/0691409561—dc23/eng/20230921
LC record available at https://lccn.loc.gov/2023018074
LC ebook record available at https://lccn.loc.gov/2023018075

Cover design: Gabriele Wilson
Cover art: Zaina F. El-Said, *Family Tree*, 2022, collage, 42 x 60 cm A2, Amman, Jordan

For Ronny

CONTENTS

ILLUSTRATIONS AND TABLES

TABLES

NOTES FOR THE READER

TRANSLITERATIONS

This book relies on many sources in Ottoman Turkish, Arabic, Russian, and Bulgarian. I transliterate Ottoman Turkish using Modern Turkish orthography, without diacritics. For Arabic, I adopt the transliteration system of the *International Journal of Middle East Studies*, marking ʿayn as ʿ and hamza as ʾ. For Russian and Bulgarian, I use the Library of Congress transliteration systems. Transliterations from Circassian (both Adyghe and Kabardian) are based on the romanization system adopted by the United States Board on Geographic Names and the (British) Permanent Committee on Geographical Names.

The names of less-known geographic localities are transliterated according to the rules outlined for modern Turkish, Arabic, and Russian: respectively, Pınarbaşı, Naʿur, and Temir-Khan-Shura. For the names of well-known locations, I use standard English spellings: for example, Istanbul not İstanbul, Amman not ʿAmman, Nalchik not Nal'chik.

MEASUREMENTS AND CURRENCY

Land Area

1 *dönüm* = 1,600 *arşın*

1 *dönüm* = 939.9 square meters = 10,117 square feet

1 acre = 4.31 *dönüm*

1 hectare = 10.64 *dönüm*

Volume and Weight (in wheat)

1 *kile* = 20 *okka*

1 *kile* = 25.66 kilograms = 56.6 pounds

1 *okka* = 1.28 kilograms = 2.8 pounds

1 *ṣāʿ* = 5.2–6.0 kilograms = 11.5–13.2 pounds

Currency

1 Ottoman lira = 100 *kuruş*

1 *kuruş* = 40 *para*

1 Russian ruble = 100 kopeks

ACKNOWLEDGMENTS

It takes a village to write a book, as the academic iteration of that saying goes. My village is approaching the size of a small town, and I am ever so grateful for that support.

This book is based on research in multiple places, learning different ways of record keeping, and speaking with many people, to whom this history is personal, raw, precious. My transnational fieldwork has only ever been possible thanks to the generosity of others. Many in the North Caucasian diaspora took a chance and shared with me, a stranger, their expertise, memories, and documents. In Jordan, I am indebted to Merissa Khurma and Yanal Ansouqa for welcoming me to their worlds and facilitating my interviews. Salim Khutat generously allowed me to use his family's letters and photographs to tell the incredible Ottoman history of the Khutat family in chapter 5. In Zarqa', Farid F. Sultan shared his Chechen community's letters and memoirs, and Adnan Younes Bazadugh welcomed me to his Circassian home–museum–research center. Isam Bino introduced me to the Chechen history of Sweileh, and Musa 'Ali Janib to the Circassian origins of Wadi al-Sir; and Faisal Habtoosh Khot and other Circassian elders sat down with me to share their families' recollections of founding Na'ur. I also thank Deeb Bashir Arslan; Mohammad Azoka; Majida Mufti Hilmi; Jamil Ishaqat; Amjad, Khaled, and Feridon Jaimoukha; Kamal Jalouqa; 'Omran Khamash; 'Awn Shawkat and Dina Janbek al-Khasawneh; Muhammad Khair Mamsir;

Mohydeen Quandour; Mohammad Kheir and Nart Pshegubj; Janset Berkok Shami; Dasi Amin Shamseddin; Nawriz Shapsough; Akram Qursha; and the Asendar, Janbek, Khurma, Mufti, and Qursha families.

In Turkey, Murat Papşu and Zeynel Abidin Besleney shared their vast knowledge of the Circassian diaspora's history and politics. For their friendship and guidance, I thank Elbruz Aksoy in Istanbul, Bislan Jalouqa in Ankara, Neslihan Kaplan in Kayseri, and Abidin İnci and his family, who hosted me in the magnificent mountain valley of Uzunyayla. Muhittin Ünal, Tsey Rengin Yurdakul, and Ebubekir Kızık facilitated my research in, respectively, Kafkas Araştırma Kültür ve Dayanışma Vakfı, Şamil Eğitim ve Kültür Vakfı, and Kafkas Vakfı. I also learned from Sevda Alankuş, Nihat Berzeg, Sefer Berzeg, Jade Cemre Erciyes, Erol Karayel, Kuban Kural, Ömer Aytek Kurmel, Ergün Özgür, Nefin Şakarcan, Metin Sönmez, and Rahmi Tuna.

In Russia, Vladimir Bobrovnikov warmly welcomed me at the Institute of Oriental Studies in Moscow. I also thank Alikber Alikberov, Yuri Anchabadze, Fasikh Baderkhan, Anastasia Ganich, Zaira Ibragimova, Madina Pashtova, Jamal Rakhaev, Mikhail Roshchin, Aleksandr Vasil'ev, and Ilya Zaytsev. In the North Caucasus, I had the good fortune of receiving advice from Anzor Kushkhabiev, Adam Gutov, and Murat Tabishev in Nalchik; Georgy Chochiev in Vladikavkaz; and Makhach Musaev, Shamil Shikhaliev, Amir Navruzov, Madina Abdulaeva, Amirkhan Magomeddadaev, and Magomedkhan Magomedkhanov in Makhachkala.

In Bulgaria, Margarita Dobreva patiently helped me to find my way through the largest Ottoman archive in the Balkans. Grigor Boykov, Petar Dobrev, Gergana Georgieva, Rossitsa Gradeva, Stoyanka Kenderova, and Ventsislav Muchinov generously gave their advice and expertise. I further extend my gratitude to every archivist and librarian, in every location during my research, who endured my queries, shared their knowledge, and brought out unending piles of documents. Without your work, this one would never exist.

For over a decade, Joel Beinin has been a wonderful friend and source of inspiration. He read many drafts and struck a beautiful balance between providing steady guidance and total freedom to explore, think, and craft. I now get to do daily what I love the most, and this is possible thanks to you, Joel. Ali Yaycıoğlu expanded my vision of the Ottoman world and its awe-inspiring mobility. He enthusiastically encouraged every archival adventure. Robert Crews reintroduced me to the Russian Empire, an empire that seemed equally familiar and foreign when looking at its southern borderlands. Norman Naimark made me think harder about how we write and what is at stake. Shahzad Bashir, Paula Findlen, Burcu Karahan, Nancy Kollmann, Martin Lewis, Khalid Obeid, Aron Rodrigue, Kären Wigen, and many others at Stanford University enriched this book in various ways.

Beautiful places and brilliant people helped to shape this work. This book was conceived in three magnificent cities: Istanbul, Amman, and Tbilisi. I first put the stories of remarkable individuals of this book on paper while living in northern California and doing regular Amtrak commutes between the Bay Area and the Sacramento Valley. Suad Joseph welcomed me to a vibrant community of Middle East scholars at the University of California, Davis, which I will always cherish. Baki Tezcan, Keith Watenpaugh, and Heghnar Zeitlian Watenpaugh provided great camaraderie. While on a research fellowship at Columbia University's Harriman Institute, I embarked on writing a transimperial history of migration, bridging scholarship on the Middle East, the Balkans, the Caucasus, and Russia, further buoyed by sparkling conversations with Catherine Evtuhov, Jane Burbank, Rashid Khalidi, Zachary Lockman, Mark Mazower, Elidor Mëhilli, and Larry Wolff. Writing continued in the Deep South, as I moved to Furman University in Greenville, South Carolina. There, in the stunning foothills of the Blue Ridge Mountains, I realized that my book captures the making of the Ottoman refugee regime. The manuscript took its final shape at the University of California, Santa Barbara. I am grateful for Sherene Seikaly, Adrienne Edgar, Anshu Malhotra, Bishnupriya Ghosh, Paul Amar, Charmaine Chua, Stephan Miescher, Dwight Reynolds, Shiva Balaghi, and other colleagues, with whom we are building vibrant Middle Eastern, migration, and global studies communities in an idyllic place between the Santa Ynez Mountains and the Pacific Ocean.

At UC Santa Barbara, with support from the UC Humanities Research Institute, I hosted a manuscript workshop. I am deeply grateful to Adrienne Edgar, Stacy Fahrenthold, Reşat Kasaba, and Michael Provence for their insightful feedback and for pushing me to redraft, deepen, and clarify. Sherene Seikaly provided invaluable suggestions and continues to model what intellectual generosity looks like. I benefited from feedback by Kristen Alff, Catherine Baylin Duryea, Basma Fahoum, and Rebecca Gruskin, my brilliant and beloved academic siblings, who witnessed every stage of this project; Rhiannon Dowling and Nana Osei-Opare, my daily writing partners through the pandemic; and Jacob Daniels, Jennifer Derr, Samuel Dolbee, Koji Hirata, and Michelle Lynn Kahn.

I thank Stanford University Press for turning this manuscript into a beautiful book. It has been a privilege working with Kate Wahl, Gigi Mark, Cat Ng Pavel, Athena Lakri, and the rest of the team. I owe a debt of gratitude to the peer reviewers. Bill Nelson produced beautiful maps. Zaina El-Said, whose art is inspired by Circassian heritage and whose family I met in Amman, kindly allowed her breathtaking work to be featured on the book cover.

Many scholars shared their advice, feedback, and friendship over the years. I thank Myriam Ababsa, Raouf Saʿd Abujaber, Patrick Adamiak, James Altman, Leyla Amzi-Erdoğdular, Alexander Balistreri, Nora Barakat, Timothy Blauvelt, Olga Borovaya, Fırat Bozçalı, Lâle Can, Dawn Chatty, John Colarusso, Camille Cole, Nazan Çiçek, Markian Dobczansky, Julia Elyachar, Tolga Esmer, Heather Ferguson, Sarah Fischer, Ella Fratantuono, Ryan Gingeras, Krista Goff, Chris Gratien, James Grehan, Zoe Griffith, David Gutman, Marwan Hanania, Peter Hill, Peter Holquist, Yasemin İpek, Aaron Jakes, Toby Jones, Eileen Kane, Cynthia Kaplan, Ceyda Karamürsel, Kemal Karpat, K. Mehmet Kentel, Akram Khater, Ilham Khuri-Makdisi, Masha Kirasirova, Hakan Kırımlı, Abdulhamit Kırmızı, Sandrine Kott, Selim Kuru, Jean-Michel Landry, Margaret Litvin, Anaïs Massot, Adam Mestyan, James Meyer, Eiji Miyazawa, Leslie Page Moch, Oktay Özel, Ramazan Hakkı Öztan, Uğur Zekeriya Peçe, Eda Pepi, Victor Petrov, Michael Reynolds, Laura Robson, Eugene Rogan, Sergey Salushchev, Cyrus Schayegh, Nir Shafir, Seteney Shami, Hind Abu al-Shaʿr, Lewis Siegelbaum, Will Smiley, Ulaş Sunata, Ronald Grigor Suny, Şölen Şanlı Vasquez, Tunç Şen, Philipp Ther, Ehud Toledano, Alexandre Toumarkine, Max Weiss, Amanda Wetsel, Benjamin Thomas White, Anna Whittington, and Sufian Zhemukhov.

The research and writing of this book were supported by the Social Science Research Council International Dissertation Research Fellowship, the American Council of Learned Societies and the Mellon Foundation Dissertation Completion Fellowship, and the National Endowment for the Humanities Summer Stipend. I further benefited from residential fellowships at the American Center for Oriental Research in Amman and the American Research Center in Sofia, and grants from the American Historical Association and the American Philosophical Society. Other financial support came from Stanford University's Department of History, Abbasi Program in Islamic Studies, Center for Russian, East European and Eurasian Studies, and Europe Center; Columbia University's Harriman Institute; and UC Santa Barbara's Academic Senate and Interdisciplinary Humanities Center.

My family and friends sustained me through the long years. My parents, with humor and a lot of heart, raised me through the Soviet collapse, the astonishingly difficult 1990s, and statelessness. My friends get all of the credit for getting me away from my desk to experience the world outside. This book is for Ronny, whose love and kindness are the greatest gifts.

Empire of Refugees

Map 1. **Ottoman Empire and the Caucasus, 1864.**

INTRODUCTION

ON A SCORCHING DAY in the late summer of 1863, fishermen in the Ottoman port of Trabzon, in the southeastern corner of the Black Sea, noticed several boats on the horizon. The boats carried Muslim refugees fleeing the Russian conquest of their lands in the Caucasus. Dehydrated and disoriented, Circassian families disembarked in the port. The next day, more boats sailed into the harbor. Dozens of boats kept arriving daily not only in Trabzon but also in Samsun and Sinop. By the end of autumn, Circassian refugees exceeded the resident population in Ottoman port cities on the Black Sea. Inns, schools, and mosques were filled to the brink, and refugees slept in covered bazaars, stables, and the streets. Deadly epidemics of typhus and smallpox broke out, devastating refugee communities. The ports in northern Anatolia started redirecting boats with refugees to Istanbul, Burgas and Varna (in Bulgaria), and Köstence (in Romania). The onset of winter did not stop the arrival of refugees, and the following year even more refugees disembarked on Ottoman shores. Between 1863 and 1865, up to half a million Circassians fled the Caucasus for the Ottoman Empire.[1] It was the largest refugee crisis that the Ottomans had experienced by then.

Migration from the Caucasus continued for the next half century. Abkhazians, Chechens, Ingush, Balkars, Karachays, Ossetians, Avars, Lezgins, and other Muslim communities left their native mountains. One constant in late Ottoman history was the continuous arrival of Muslim refugees from Russia.

1

While the earlier groups of refugees had fled an ethnic cleansing perpetrated by the Russian military in the North Caucasus, the latter parties were pushed out by Russia's new civil reforms and settler colonial policies. Between the 1850s and World War I, approximately a million North Caucasian Muslims had left the tsardom in what was one of the greatest displacements in Russian imperial history.

The Ottoman government maintained an open-door policy for North Caucasian refugees. They arrived when the Ottoman Empire was steadily losing territory and population in the Balkans and North Africa. Muslim refugees fit neatly into the Ottoman government's agenda to stem demographic decline, revitalize the economy, and solidify the imperial hold on far-flung provinces. Within two generations, North Caucasian refugees were resettled throughout the Ottoman Empire in the following fourteen countries today: Turkey, Syria, Jordan, Lebanon, Israel, Iraq, Georgia, Bulgaria, Romania, Serbia, Kosovo, Greece, Cyprus, and North Macedonia. The Ottomans considered settling Circassian refugees also in Albania, Bosnia, Montenegro, and Libya.[2] Temporary refugee camps existed in Palestine, and some North Caucasians moved, without Ottoman support, to Egypt.

The successive Muslim migrations turned the Ottoman state into an empire of refugees. In addition to North Caucasians, hundreds of thousands of Muslims from Crimea, the Balkans, the South Caucasus, and Crete, as well as smaller groups from North Africa, Central Asia, and Afghanistan, arrived in the Ottoman Empire as refugees. Many parts of the empire became a refugee country, where one was more likely to hear Circassian or Abkhazian than Turkish, Arabic, or Greek. The Ottoman Empire fashioned itself as a refuge for Muslims displaced in the age of European imperial conquest and colonialism. Meanwhile, the resettlement of Muslim refugees changed the empire from within and was a harbinger of population transfers and forced homogenization that befell the Middle East and the Balkans in the twentieth century.

EMPIRE AND REFUGEE RESETTLEMENT

Empire of Refugees is a history of migration that examines how North Caucasian refugees transformed the late Ottoman Empire and how the Ottomans managed Muslim refugee resettlement. This book advances several arguments. First, between 1860 and World War I, the Ottoman government had constructed a refugee regime, which coexisted with, but was distinct from, the Ottoman immigration system. The Ottoman Refugee Commission (Ott. Tur., Muhacirin Komisyonu), founded in 1860, implemented the refugee regime. The Commission was responsible for settling Muslim refugees from Russia, arriving in the aftermath of the Crimean War of 1853–56 and the Caucasus War of 1817–64, and Ottoman Muslims displaced during the Russo-Ottoman War of 1877–78, the Balkan Wars of 1912–13, and World War I. Having settled between three and five million Muslim refugees in total, the Commission presided over the demographic, economic, and social transformation of the remaining Ottoman territories, especially Anatolia. The Ottoman refugee regime built on the Ottoman Immigration Law of 1857, which had set the terms for immigration into the empire for anyone, irrespective of their faith, and the Land Code of 1858, governing land ownership and tenure. After the 1860s, the vast majority of immigrants in the Ottoman Empire were Muslim refugees. The Commission developed a set of additional policies and subsidies specific to refugee needs, inaugurating a regime of expectations—of protection and settlement by Muslim refugees and of obligations and loyalty by the Ottoman government.

The Ottoman refugee regime preceded and has a distinct genealogy from the contemporary international refugee regime. The modern refugee regime is a product of the United Nations and is anchored by the Convention Relating to the Status of Refugees, better known as the Refugee Convention of 1951. It has roots in the interwar era, when the League of Nations implemented ad hoc procedures to resolve refugee crises, arising out of the collapse of the Ottoman and Russian empires.[3] The legal status of a modern refugee is derived from one's citizenship in a nation-state. In recent years, historians demonstrated that the ideology of modern humanitarianism and such practices as population exchange, refugee transfer, and territorial partition, which were central to the interwar refugee regime, had roots in the Middle East.[4] Humanitarian crises in the post-Ottoman world defined global conversations about protecting refugees. This book suggests a further historiographical corrective. The nineteenth-century Ottoman Empire, struggling mightily with European annexations, created its own nonwestern and nonsecular system of categorizing, sheltering, and resettling refugees. The status of refugee, or muhajir, was based not on one's subjecthood or citizenship but on facing religious persecution and seeking refuge in the sultan-caliph's domains. A refugee being Muslim, while not a codified requirement, was an expectation and raison d'être of the Ottoman refugee regime.

Second, refugee resettlement accelerated the collapse of the empire in the Balkans and fortified Ottoman rule in the outlying regions of the Levant and Anatolia. Historians explain the disintegration of the Ottoman Empire by geopolitics, including European annexations throughout the nineteenth century and the empire's defeat in the Balkan Wars of 1912–13 and World War I, and by cultural forces, especially the sectarianism and nationalism that tore through the empire's social fabric.[5] By revisiting late Ottoman history through the prism of migration and political economy, I show that Muslim refugee resettlement had a profound impact on both the survival and the demise of the Ottoman Empire. Ottoman refugee resettlement was an ambitious project of the Azizian (1861–76) and Hamidian (1876–1908/9) governments. The Ottoman government expected Muslim refugees to become productive farmers. It happened for some but not all. The economic well-being of refugee communities depended on Ottoman support. That support could come in different forms: favorable legislation, free land, financial aid, roadway construction, and military backing. How much help the government provided and whether refugees could use it explain why refugee resettlement had vastly different outcomes throughout the empire.

This book examines refugee resettlement in three core parts of the Ottoman Empire: the Balkans, Anatolia, and the Levant. In the northern Balkans, the Ottoman government's settlement of Muslim refugees from Russia stoked anti-Ottoman sentiments among Balkan Christians. The lack of state funding for refugee households undermined the efficacy of the resettlement program and pushed some refugees toward banditry. The ensuing violence of Circassian gangs, especially against Christians, inflamed social tensions, leading up to the Bulgarian uprising of 1876 and the Russo-Ottoman War of 1877–78. The war ejected the Ottomans from half of their European territories, which they had held for over five centuries. Meanwhile in central Anatolia, Ottoman financial support for refugees was equally limited, but the government backed North Caucasians in their conflict over land with Turkic nomads. Refugee villages survived, well hidden among the mountains, yet their economies stagnated because of a lack of Ottoman infrastructure. In contrast, North Caucasian refugees in the Levant took advantage of Ottoman land reforms and the state-sponsored Hejaz Railway and built thriving villages on the edge of the desert. North Caucasian refugees founded three of the four largest cities in modern Jordan, including its capital city of Amman. The Ottoman government favored refugee farmers, and, through their settlements in the Levant and central Anatolia, it expanded authority into the sparsely settled parts of the empire.

The resettlement of Muslim refugees was key to the disintegration of the Ottoman Empire in several ways. Resettling Muslims from Russia strained Ottoman imperial and provincial budgets at a time of fiscal emergency. The Ottomans took out their first international loans during the Crimean War of 1853–56 and kept borrowing from European banks, in part to pay for the settlement of Muslim refugees. In 1875, the Ottoman state defaulted on its debts, which ushered in the European-controlled Ottoman Public Debt Administration, shrinking Ottoman sovereignty and fiscal control. Yet borrowing for refugee resettlement continued. Furthermore, the resettlement of Muslim refugees intensified intercommunal strife. In almost every place of settlement, refugees came into conflict with local populations over land. Those conflicts soured relations between North Caucasians and their settled and nomadic neighbors, whether Christian, Muslim, or Druze, while helping the Ottoman government to entrench a new land regime in its reformist drive to centralize the empire. Finally, after 1878, the resettlement of Muslim refugees went hand in hand with displacing and dispossessing Ottoman Christians. The Hamidian government altered demographic ratios on the margins of the empire to forestall further loss of territory. While the policies were not consistent and varied from region to region, the general message was clear. The government welcomed foreign Muslims and trusted them to become loyal subjects of the sultan at a time when it viewed its Christian subjects with suspicion. The resettlement of Muslim refugees lay at the heart of the Ottoman government's ambition to preserve the imperial project.

Third, Russia attempted to control Muslim migration to consolidate its authority over the Caucasus. Russia's migration policies in the Caucasus helped to manage its "Muslim empire," which stretched from Crimea and the Caucasus to the Volga region, through the Ural Mountains and into the

Kazakh steppe, Central Asia, and Siberia.[6] Muslims had long been Russia's second-largest religious community after Orthodox Christians. By World War I, the Russian tsar counted more Muslim subjects than the Ottoman sultan did. Russia's migration policies underwent a transformation. During the Caucasus War, the Russian government abetted, promoted, and sponsored Muslim emigration. Between 1862 and 1864, the tsarist military perpetrated ethnic cleansing, expelling western Circassians into the Ottoman Empire. After 1867, however, tsarist authorities changed course to discourage and restrict emigration as a way to keep their new Muslim subjects inside Russia. Simultaneously, after 1861, Russia vigorously opposed the return of North Caucasian refugees from the Ottoman Empire. Within the Caucasus, Russia pursued the policies of forced relocation of North Caucasians from highlands to lowlands and colonization of their territories by Cossacks and Christian peasants. Tsarist migration policies redrew the demographics of the North Caucasus and solidified Russia's control over its newest region near the borders of the Ottoman Empire and Iran. The North Caucasus is the tsarist empire's last major acquisition remaining within today's Russian Federation, unlike other non-Russian regions that had been annexed in the eighteenth and nineteenth centuries and have since become independent, including Poland, Finland, Ukraine, the Baltic states, the South Caucasus, and Central Asia.

Ottoman and Russian migration policies toward North Caucasian Muslims were starkly different, yet they pursued the same goal of consolidating imperial authority. The Ottoman policy was inclusive toward foreign Muslims because it benefited the Ottoman state. The government used refugees to increase the population of a shrinking empire, to bring unused land into cultivation, to rein in nomads, and to strengthen the empire's hold on Christian-majority frontier regions. The Russian government excluded those North Caucasian Muslims whom it perceived as opponents of Russian rule during and after the Caucasus War. Both empires developed a sectarian logic, equating one's religious identity with their loyalty to a co-religionist state. The Russians, who had a hard time conquering and suppressing rebellions in the North Caucasus, assumed that indigenous Muslims, especially those who had already left, would be loyal only to the sultan, not the tsar.

This transimperial history of migration explores how the Ottoman and

Russian governments tried to control mass movements of people and also how Muslim refugees responded to policies designed to limit their mobility. Refugees were not mere pawns, expelled and resettled at governments' will, but active agents of history. Most North Caucasians became farmers, transforming economies and landscapes of entire regions and shaping local forms of capital accumulation. Some refused to settle where the Ottoman government had sent them or abandoned their refugee villages. Many petitioned the government and litigated in courts, or joined the army or militias. North Caucasian refugees were transimperial subjects—not solely because they crossed borders but also because of the decisions they made in navigating their displacement and resettlement, negotiating with Russian or Ottoman authorities, and articulating their North Caucasian identity in exile.[7] They and their descendants helped to shape the history of the modern Middle East. Today, the Circassian diaspora in Turkey is estimated at between two and three million people and is the country's second largest non-Turkish minority after the Kurds. Up to 100,000 descendants of North Caucasian refugees live in Syria, 30,000 in Jordan, over 10,000 in Iraq, and 4,000 in Israel.[8]

MUSLIM REFUGEES WITHIN GLOBAL MIGRATION HISTORY

The migration and resettlement of North Caucasian Muslims were part of what is often called the first wave of globalization, between 1870 and 1914. Enabled by improvements in transoceanic transportation, migration in this period conjures images of mass voluntary immigration of Europeans to overseas colonies and nation-states. The proliferation of new forms of capitalism, agricultural expansion, and commodification of land accelerated the frontier settlement, mostly by white immigrants, in the Americas, southern Africa, and the Pacific region.[9] An inextricable, yet frequently omitted, part of this globalization was another migration—global displacement of indigenous communities, complete with the destruction of their landscapes, legal dispossession, and forced labor.[10] The late imperial era unleashed mass forced migration. The North Caucasians' migration was both of these stories. The Russian army displaced this Muslim community from its homeland, and Christian settlers took over its lands. Meanwhile, having arrived as refugees in the Ottoman Empire, North Caucasians soon became settlers themselves, occupying and working the land that had been claimed by other communities. North Caucasian refugees were victims of the expansion of the Russian imperial frontier southward, through conquest and settlement, and then also helped the Ottoman state to push its internal frontier into territories of nomadic communities on the empire's margins.[11]

The term that North Caucasian refugees used to describe themselves was *muhajir* (Ar., *muhājir*, pl. *muhājirūn*; Ott. Tur., *muhacir*, pl. *muhacirler*). The Arabic term *muhājir* is derived from *hijra*, which denotes the journey of the Prophet Muhammad from Mecca to Yathrib (Medina) in 622 CE. The Prophet Muhammad's companions who undertook this journey to preserve their nascent religious movement were the first muhajirs. Throughout Islamic history, Muslim communities that had left, or been expelled from, their homelands used this term in emulation of the Prophet's companions. By the nineteenth century, the term acquired anticolonial and anti-imperialist sentiments, as many regions across the Muslim world were occupied by the European empires. The flight of Muslims for refuge in the Ottoman Empire, the world's strongest sovereign Muslim state and the seat of the caliph, acutely reverberated throughout the Caucasus, the Balkans, North Africa, and beyond. The present-day translations of *refugee* in Turkish, Arabic, and Russian are, respectively, *mülteci*, *lāji'*, and *bezhenets*. None of these terms were commonly used to refer to North Caucasians between the 1850s and World War I. I will use *muhajir* throughout the book as well as the terms *refugee*, *immigrant*, and *emigrant*, which all capture different aspects of what being a muhajir entailed, when discussing relevant stages of muhajirs' experiences.

The English-language term *refugee* came into popular usage in the aftermath of the collapse of the Ottoman and Russian empires. Previously used to refer to religious and political exiles, it then described Armenian survivors of the genocide and refugees of the Russian civil war who were stranded away from their homeland, stateless, and increasingly seen as a global responsibility.[12] It was defined in the United Nations Refugee Convention of 1951 as someone who, "owing to well-founded fear of being persecuted for reasons of race, religion, nationality, membership of a particular social group or political opinion, is outside the country of his nationality and is unable or, owing to such fear, is unwilling to avail himself of the protection of that country" or "unable or, owing to such fear, is unwilling to return to it."[13]

The terms *muhajir* and *hijra* defined how the Ottoman state conceived of Muslim refugee migration and resettlement and how North Caucasians perceived their displacement. They challenge the artificial distinction between forced and voluntary migration, still prevalent in the study of global migration. Hijra is not only a religious concept but also a distinct type of global migration that draws its legitimacy and language from early Islamic history and comprises different kinds of Muslim displacement, including ones caused by imperial conquest, ethnic cleansing, and partitions over the past two centuries. The North Caucasian hijra stemmed from Russia's expulsions of Muslims from the Caucasus but also encompassed emigration as a way to escape poverty and to live under the rule of a Muslim sovereign.

In recent decades, historians have demonstrated astounding mobility between the Ottoman and Russian empires. Muslim pilgrims from Russia and its protectorates in Central Asia made an annual hajj, or pilgrimage, to the holy cities of Mecca and Medina, where some stayed as long-term residents.[14] Intellectuals from Istanbul, Crimea, Kazan, and Bukhara traveled widely within the Turkic world, which spanned the two empires.[15] The two governments captured and exchanged prisoners of war.[16] In the Danubian borderlands, Bulgarian, Gagauz, Ukrainian, and Moldavian peasants crossed the Russo-Ottoman border back and forth, fleeing epidemics and tax collectors, and, in the Caucasus borderlands, Armenian, Greek, and Laz villagers and Kurdish and Turkic nomads traversed the porous frontier along with their herds and contraband goods.[17] *Empire of Refugees* focuses on the final half century of the autocratic empires of the Romanovs and Ottomans, when transborder migration increased dramatically. The Russo-Ottoman borderlands were being remade through displacement, and most migrants crossing the border were refugees.

The North Caucasian refugee migration was part of mass population displacements in late Ottoman history. Lord Curzon, Britain's foreign secretary, famously referred to demographic changes in the Balkans in the early twentieth century as the "unmixing of peoples," a phrase that later became associated with international negotiations over post-Ottoman demographics in Lausanne in 1923.[18] That unmixing, which homogenized the maps of modern-day Turkey, Greece, and Bulgaria, is remembered as the apotheosis of ethnic nationalism, although it also had a significant religious component.

The religious "unmixing" of communities in the Russo-Ottoman borderlands had begun earlier. Since the late eighteenth century, Muslims from
Russia had been fleeing to the Ottoman Empire, while Ottoman Armenians,
Greeks, and Bulgarians had been emigrating to the tsarist Caucasus, Crimea,
and Bessarabia.[19] The displacements of Muslims and Christians evidenced
gradual sectarianization in the Russo-Ottoman borderlands, whereby one's
religious identity became the basis for one's political identity. The religious
sorting in the nineteenth-century borderlands laid the groundwork for more
comprehensive, demographic engineering, justified in ethnonational terms
in the early twentieth century.[20] The migration of North Caucasian Muslims was a turning point in the history of displacement in the Middle East
and Eastern Europe. The expulsion of most western Circassians from the
Caucasus, followed by their resettlement throughout the Ottoman domains,
confirmed a dangerous idea that a modern state could swiftly move a large
population elsewhere for its benefit. This book excavates the origins of state-
managed population transfer, which would soon be implemented for different ends, including in the 1923 Greek-Turkish population exchange and
Stalin's deportations of Chechens, Ingush, Karachays, and Balkars from the
Caucasus in the 1940s.

Muslim hijra to the Ottoman Empire occurred alongside two other migrations. Their terminology draws on the same Arabic root (h–j–r). The first
one was the emigration of Ottoman subjects from the Levant to the mahjar,
as diasporic lands were known to Arabic speakers. Between 1880 and 1914,
about half a million Lebanese and Syrians—mostly Christians but also Jews,
Druze, and Muslims—emigrated to South and North America.[21] As foreign Muslims fled for refuge in the Ottoman Empire, many Ottoman non-
Muslims sought to escape poverty and discrimination at home. The second
migration was tahjīr, or tehcir when transliterated from Ottoman Turkish,
used to describe deportations by the Ottoman government of Ottoman
Greeks in 1914 and Armenians and Assyrians in 1915. The ethnic cleansing,
and eventually genocide, of Anatolia's Christians was unfolding parallel to
the immigration of Muslims. Those were mutually reinforcing processes in
the state-driven overhaul of Anatolia's demographics, homogenizing it as a
Muslim land, soon to be reimagined as a Turkish one.

The displacement of Muslims from the Caucasus proceeded apace with the Jewish exodus from the Pale of Settlement, in the territories of Poland, Ukraine, Belarus, Moldova, Lithuania, Latvia, and Russia. As with the Crimean Tatars and Circassians in previous generations, discriminatory policies and violence, culminating in pogroms, drove out Jewish communities. Between 1881 and 1914, about 1.5 million Jews emigrated, primarily to the United States, but several tens of thousands made their way to Ottoman Palestine, forming the bulk of early Zionist immigrants of the modern *aliyah*, or migration to Palestine.[22] The Jewish aliyah holds many parallels to the Muslim hijra in the specific directionality and religious mandate of emigration as well as in their origins in persecution and mass flight.

North Caucasian refugees included both free and enslaved people, and their migration transformed late Ottoman slavery in many ways. Circassian, Abkhazian, and Georgian slaves had long been trafficked to the slave markets of Istanbul and Cairo, where they were sold into elite urban households, including the Ottoman imperial harem.[23] By the mid-nineteenth century, the Black Sea slave trade was all but gone, and new slaves from the Caucasus were few in the Middle East. The mass arrival of North Caucasian refugees in the 1860s changed that. The Caucasus communities had practiced various forms of bondage, rooted in household and agricultural servitude. Many upper-status muhajirs brought with them their serfs and slaves. The sudden supply of thousands of enslaved Circassians bloated the Ottoman and Egyptian slave markets and depressed prices, making Circassian slaves more accessible to a greater range of urban households and significantly hampering abolitionist efforts in the Middle East.[24] Moreover, North Caucasian forms of slavery were transplanted into the Ottoman countryside, where many muhajirs continued to be owned by other muhajirs.[25] For many North Caucasian Muslims, their resettlement in the Ottoman domains meant their continued enslavement.

WRITING A HISTORY OF REFUGEE MIGRATION

Muslim refugees from the North Caucasus are the main subjects in this book. The North Caucasus, a mountainous region between the Black Sea and the Caspian Sea, sustains remarkable ethnic and linguistic diversity. By the mid-nineteenth century, the region was home to several dozen ethnic groups. Much of the indigenous Muslim population in the region spoke Northwest

Caucasian and Northeast Caucasian languages, which are unrelated to their neighbors' languages, such as Russian, Armenian, and Persian (of the Indo-European language family); Turkish and Azerbaijani (of the Turkic language family); and Georgian (of the Kartvelian language family, endemic to the South Caucasus). The tenth-century Arab historian and geographer al-Mas'udi aptly called the Caucasus the "mountain of tongues."[26] The region's rugged terrain ensured spectacular isolation of many villages, proliferating languages and dialects spoken nowhere else.

In the western Caucasus, specifically on the Black Sea coast and in the fertile Kuban region, lived Circassians, Abazins, and Abkhazians (see map 2), who spoke closely related but mutually unintelligible Northwest Caucasian languages. Circassians, or the *Adyghe* in their native language, were divided into twelve communities: Abzakh, Bzhedugh, Hatuqwai, Mamkhlegh, Natukhai, Temirgoi, Yegeruqwai, Zhaney, Shapsugh, Ubykh, Besleney, and Kabardian, each with its own dialect.[27] The first ten communities, the western Circassians, were the ones who bore the brunt of the expulsions in the early 1860s, and their descendants form the majority of the North Caucasian diaspora in the Middle East today. To the south of western Circassians, along the Black Sea coast leading toward Georgia, lived Abazins and Abkhazians, whose diaspora is collectively known as *Abaza* in the Middle East. Moving eastward along the northern slopes of the Caucasus Mountains, through mountain ridges and valleys, one could find six large communities: Turkic-speaking Balkars and Karachays; Kabardians, or eastern Circassians; Ossetians, speaking an Iranian (Indo-European) language; and the closely related Ingush and Chechens, speaking Northeast Caucasian languages. In the Northeast Caucasus, where the mountains slowly descend toward the Caspian Sea and the Nogai steppe, lies Dagestan. If *Circassian*, *Chechen*, and *Ossetian* are terms for ethnic groups, *Dagestani* is a multiethnic regional designation. Dagestan, or the "land of mountains," is home to over thirty ethnic groups. Many of them, including Avars, Dargins, Lezgins, Laks, Tabasarans, and Tsakhurs, speak Northeast Caucasian languages, and others, like Nogai Tatars and Kumyks, speak Turkic languages. Most North Caucasian languages did not have a written tradition in the nineteenth century. The dominant literary language among Muslim communities in the region had been Arabic, despite not being native to anyone in the Caucasus, and many elites

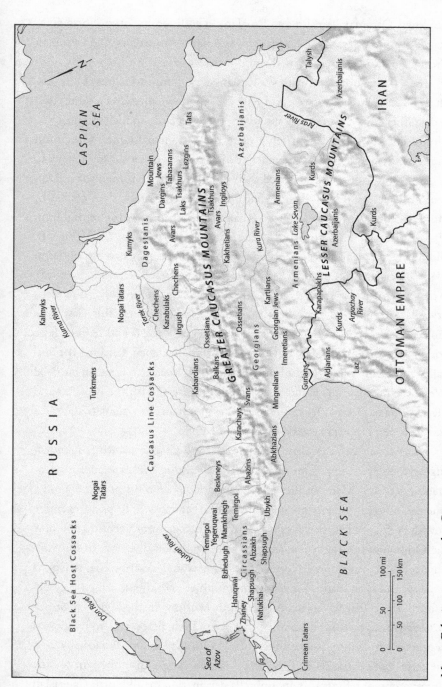

Map 2. Ethnic groups in the Caucasus, c. 1850.

also knew Ottoman Turkish and Russian. In addition to native North Caucasian communities, many Russians, Ukrainians, Armenians, and Ottoman Greeks settled in the region by the mid-nineteenth century.

The vast majority of North Caucasians were Sunni Muslims. Only Abkhazia, Kabarda, and Ossetia had native Orthodox Christian communities, and southern Dagestan was home to Shi'i Azerbaijanis and Mountain Jews. Almost all North Caucasian refugees to the Ottoman Empire were Sunni Muslims. By no means was the practice of Islam homogeneous in the region. Some Muslim communities traced their origins to the Arab conquest of Derbent in Dagestan in the seventh century. Others embraced Islam gradually, through contacts with the Crimean Khanate, the Ottoman Empire, and Iran. The anti-Russian resistance and the spread of Sufi orders in the eighteenth and nineteenth centuries accelerated the conversion of many communities to Islam, especially in the Northwest Caucasus. A common refrain in literature is that when Circassians arrived in the Ottoman Empire their Muslim identity was still new and less salient than their Circassianness. This view risks projecting ideals of twentieth-century secular intellectuals and reifies a false notion that there is a specific way to be a Muslim, or a good Muslim. The muhajirs' faith, while certainly only one part of their identity, played an outsized role in their displacement and resettlement because of what the Russians and the Ottomans made of it, and it also helped muhajirs to articulate their loss and their place in history and in their new empire.

I collectively describe these refugees as *North Caucasians*, while acknowledging that they came from vastly different cultural backgrounds and geographic settings. Many studies of migration focus on a single ethnic group, whereas my approach is purposefully multiethnic, as it helps to examine how the refugee identity was constructed in the nineteenth century and how the Ottomans and the Russians managed population diversity. In the mid-nineteenth century, most North Caucasians would describe themselves as *Muslims* and then identify specific communities and kins to which they belonged. The tsarist government referred to Muslims in the region as *mountaineers* (Rus., *gortsy*), an identity that was Orientalized and romanticized in nineteenth-century Russian literature.[28] Ottoman authorities usually used the term *Circassians* (Tur., *Çerkesler*; Ar., *Sharākisa*), an ethnonym for the largest group of refugees, as an umbrella designation for all North Caucasian

Muslims. Only in the early twentieth century did diasporic intellectuals in Istanbul popularize the idea of a multiethnic North Caucasian identity, based on their origins in the same region. I further include Muslim refugees from Abkhazia and the Zaqatala region, south of the Caucasus Mountains, who emigrated to the Ottoman Empire alongside their kin communities from the north. In this book, you will meet many western Circassians, Abkhazians, Kabardians, Chechens, and Dagestanis, who, in that order, formed the largest muhajir communities from the Caucasus in the Middle East. Wherever possible, I will identify ethnic and subethnic identities of refugees.

This book builds on the rich scholarship that has situated Muslim refugee migration within the broader Ottoman and Middle Eastern history. Kemal H. Karpat stressed the importance of Muslim migrations in Islamicizing and Turkifying Anatolia.[29] Muslim refugees were long presented as perpetrators

Figure 1. **Circassians in Istanbul.**

Photograph by Abdullah Frères, between 1880 and 1900. Library of Congress, Prints and Photographs Division. LC-DIG-ppmsca-03805.

of violence, especially in the post-1878 Balkan historiographies, or as victims of European nationalism and imperialism in Turkish scholarship.[30] The latter approach has occasionally veered toward minimizing, or even denying, the Ottoman genocide of Christians during World War I, as if the suffering of one community justifies or explains the horrors that the state would inflict on another.[31] In recent decades, historians have scrutinized the work of the Ottoman Refugee Commission and the impact of global capitalism on Ottoman settlement policies.[32] Reşat Kasaba placed nineteenth-century refugees into the longer narrative of Ottoman history, wherein the government managed its "moveable empire" by increasingly suppressing nomad, migrant, and refugee mobility.[33] Meanwhile, Dawn Chatty found the arrival of Muslim refugees from the Caucasus and the Balkans as a starting point in the history of mass displacement in the modern Middle East, preceding that of Armenians, Palestinians, Jews, Kurds, Iraqis, and Syrians.[34]

Refugee migration from the North Caucasus, despite being among the largest displacements in Middle Eastern and Russian history, did not attract scholarly interest until the late twentieth century. In the North Caucasian diaspora, research on Ottoman resettlement long faced both institutional and self-imposed censorship.[35] For much of Turkey's republican era, North Caucasians had to be careful not to draw attention to their non-Turkishness. Beginning in the late 1980s, Turkish historians, including many of North Caucasian descent, published works that delved into the geography and demographics of North Caucasian resettlement, based on Ottoman documents.[36] To challenge the common perception among the Turkish public that the Circassian leadership was disloyal to Mustafa Kemal's cause in the 1920s, several works emphasized contributions of refugee communities to the Turkish National Movement.[37] Similarly, North Caucasian writers in the Arab world proceeded cautiously, careful to center the commitment of their non-Arab minorities to the Syrian and Jordanian nation-states and to popular pan-Arab causes, such as Palestinian liberation.[38] In recent decades, Turkish and Jordanian scholars produced pathbreaking work on the complexity of North Caucasian identities in the contemporary Middle East.[39]

In the Soviet Union, discussion of tsarist-era displacements of North Caucasians, although not entirely taboo, was not welcomed. It challenged the Soviet narrative of "brotherhood of nations" and risked reopening old wounds in a region brutalized by Stalin's deportations of entire ethnic groups during World War II. The glasnost of the late 1980s blew the lid off, allowing scholars to mine Russian archives and to share their findings in the 1990s and 2000s.[40] The Russian-language monographs, mostly published in the autonomous North Caucasus republics, focused on migrations of specific ethnic groups— Circassians,[41] Karachays and Balkars,[42] Chechens,[43] and Dagestanis[44]—and included a few overviews of the multiethnic diaspora in the Middle East.[45] By and large, the existing historical scholarship in Turkish, Arabic, and Russian prioritizes the early stages of migration: displacement from the Caucasus, arrival in the Ottoman Empire, and settlement by the Ottoman Refugee Commission. This book brings scholarship in Turkish, Russian, and Arabic in conversation with each other, while focusing on migration from the entire North Caucasus region between the 1850s and World War I and on what happened after refugee settlement in the Ottoman Empire.

Empire of Refugees is based on extensive research in over twenty public and private archives, primarily in Turkey, Jordan, Bulgaria, Georgia, the United Kingdom, and Russia, including the autonomous North Caucasus republics of Kabardino-Balkaria, North Ossetia-Alania, and Dagestan, as well as in Romania, Armenia, Azerbaijan, and the United States. It adopts top-down and bottom-up approaches to migration to explore different facets of refugeedom, or how refugees have experienced their displacement.[46] This is a history of how the Ottoman and Russian empires managed migration, for which I use a wide variety of state-produced evidence: on the Ottoman side, documentation by the government in Istanbul and provincial (*vilayet*), subprovincial (*sancak*), and district (*kaza*) authorities, and on the Russian side, correspondence between the administration of the Caucasus Viceroy in Tiflis (now Tbilisi, Georgia) and North Caucasus provincial (*oblast'*) and district (*okrug*) authorities. To examine the political economy of refugee re-settlement, I draw data from different types of Ottoman registers that have recorded the population, land allotments, financial aid, and tax payments of refugee communities, as well as from shari'a court records. During my fieldwork, I was fortunate to gain access to a full set of Ottoman land records for the Amman region, under the purview of Jordan's Ministry of the Interior; minute provincial data on refugee resettlement on the Black Sea coast of Bulgaria and Romania, preserved in yet uncatalogued boxes in Bulgaria's

National Library in Sofia; and documents of the Ottoman Refugee Commission, only recently made available at the Ottoman Archives in Istanbul. This book further relies on Russian and British consular records; travel accounts of European and American visitors to the Ottoman Empire; and newspapers in Ottoman Turkish, Russian, and Bulgarian.

This is equally a social history of migration, exploring how refugees challenged the two empires and built anew. Refugees often appear silent in the imperial archive: their individualities sacrificed for collective generalizations and their predicament summarized by officials in how they understood it.[47] The resettlement authorities' efficiency depended on reducing refugees to numbers in their paperwork: how many arrived and therefore how much land to allot and how many oxen to distribute and coffins to make. I use several types of evidence to bring out refugees' migration experiences. First, I collected dozens of private letters that muhajirs wrote to their families, within the Ottoman domains and across the Ottoman-Russian border, in Ottoman Turkish and Arabic. Some of these letters have been preserved in archives in Nalchik, Vladikavkaz, and Tbilisi. I searched for the rare letters in private hands through communal listservs and by word of mouth and am very grateful to families who shared with me copies from their private collections in Amman and Zarqa' in Jordan and Kizilyurt in Dagestan.[48] Private letters, which muhajirs did not intend for the authorities to see, reveal how they sought to improve their lot in the Ottoman Empire and preserve ties with their families in the Caucasus.[49] Second, I examined petitions that North Caucasians sent to Ottoman and Russian authorities. These documents, while carefully crafted by their writers and curated by the state, testify to refugees' most urgent needs during their migration and resettlement and their expectations from the two empires. Petitions varied widely: from individual complaints to communal requests on behalf of hundreds of refugees, and, depending on their content, soliciting justice from the sovereign, the government, or local officials. Finally, I interviewed forty descendants of North Caucasian refugees in Jordan and Turkey about how their families remember Ottoman resettlement, and their recollections richly supplement the archival findings about their communities' histories.

STRUCTURE OF THE BOOK

Empire of Refugees is divided into three parts, each representing a specific stage in the refugees' journey. Part I, "Refugee Migration," provides a bird's-eye overview of displacement from the Caucasus and immigration in the Ottoman Empire in the late imperial era. Chapter 1 examines what led to mass expulsions and emigration of Muslims from the North Caucasus to the Ottoman Empire between the 1850s and World War I. It traces the evolution of Russia's emigration policies for Muslims. Chapter 2 investigates what happened to North Caucasian refugees when they arrived in the Ottoman domains. I demonstrate how, over the years, the Ottoman Refugee Commission built up a refugee regime that guaranteed admission to displaced Muslims. It remained a state agency, and its settlement of muhajirs increasingly reflected the Ottoman government's political objectives.

Part II, "Refugee Resettlement," zooms into the Ottoman resettlement of North Caucasians in the Balkans, the Levant, and Anatolia. Within those regions, I focus on provinces that accepted the highest numbers of refugees, respectively the provinces of Danube, Damascus, and Sivas. Chapter 3 explores the resettlement in the northern Balkans, particularly the steppe region of Dobruja, now split between Bulgaria and Romania. Between 1860 and 1878, it was a bustling Circassian and Abkhazian refugee country, but, without sufficient support, refugee economies floundered in these northernmost districts of the Ottoman Empire. During the Russo-Ottoman War of 1877–78, almost all North Caucasians fled the Balkans with the retreating Ottoman army, prohibited to return by the victorious Balkan national governments. Chapter 4 follows some expellees from the Balkans across the Aegean and Eastern Mediterranean, via port cities in Lebanon and Palestine, to arid Transjordan, where Circassians and Chechens founded refugee villages. In what became the Ottomans' southernmost region of refugee resettlement, muhajirs invested in real estate, traded with bedouin, and attracted Syrian and Palestinian merchants to the booming village of Amman, founded in 1878. Chapter 5 moves to the snowy mountain valley of Uzunyayla in central Anatolia, where refugees from different ethnic groups built their own Little Caucasus between 1860 and World War I. This chapter traces the remarkable history of the Circassian Khutat family, who had been searching for an ideal place to settle in the Ottoman Empire.

Part III, "Diaspora and Return," examines how North Caucasians navigated their lives between the Ottoman and Russian empires. Chapter 6 explores how muhajirs forged the North Caucasian diaspora. By the early twentieth century, muhajir intellectuals in Istanbul published the first Circassian-language newspaper, established the first Circassian schools, and tried articulating what it meant to be Circassian, North Caucasian, Muslim, and Ottoman. They also engaged in a transimperial debate about Muslim emigration from Russia and whether it should continue. Chapter 7 brings the book full circle by tracing the little-known history of Muslim return migration from the Ottoman Empire to Russia. The tsarist army instituted a ban on the return of North Caucasians, which was never rescinded and, in new iterations, continued into the Soviet and post-Soviet eras. Yet despite Russian and Ottoman opposition to return migration, about 40,000 Chechen, Abkhazian, and other refugees clandestinely returned to the Caucasus.

Part I

REFUGEE MIGRATION

ONE

MUSLIM MIGRATIONS FROM THE NORTH CAUCASUS

IN 1910, AHMED BIN SALTMURAD BIN TAMBULAT, a Chechen living in the Russian Empire's Dagestan Province, wrote a letter in Arabic to his cousin Kerim-Sultan. Kerim-Sultan had emigrated to the Ottoman Empire a few years earlier, and his family in Russia grew worried after not having heard from him. Ahmed wrote that he had searched for news from his beloved cousin "for weeks, months, years, for some time, and always" and implored him to get in touch with his relatives in the Caucasus. "Does one forget about the loved ones, and can one's spirit rest before the family reunites again," Ahmed rhetorically asked Kerim-Sultan. He sealed the letter but did not know where to send it. He entrusted the letter, with no address on it, to a caravan of Chechen pilgrims going on the hajj, instructing them to ask around if anyone in the Ottoman Empire knew of Kerim-Sultan from the village of Keshen-Evla.[1]

Ahmed's plan might seem far-fetched, but within a few months the pilgrims found Kerim-Sultan. Pilgrims traveled through many North Caucasian refugee villages on their way to Mecca. At their last stop in the Chechen village of Zarqa' in Ottoman Transjordan, Kerim-Sultan came out to greet them and recognized that the letter was meant for him. From then on, Kerim-

Sultan and his family in the Caucasus used the hajj to send letters to each other. Chechen pilgrims would deliver letters from the Caucasus on their way to Mecca and collect Kerim-Sultan's responses on their way back.[2] The following year, Kerim-Sultan received a letter from his brother, Hajj Janʿaq. His brother wished to conduct what he called a "white hijra" (Ar., *al-hijra al-baydāʾ*). His village elders, however, cautioned against emigration, as it was unlikely that those leaving Russia could ever return. Hajj Janʿaq's father-in-law refused to let his daughter follow her husband and become a refugee. Hajj Janʿaq considered the "honorable hijra" (Ar., *al-hijra al-gharrāʾ*) to be his religious duty and sought to join his brother in the Ottoman Empire.[3] Kerim-Sultan encouraged his brother to emigrate and to urge others to leave the Caucasus and become muhajirs. He offered to write to those who were hesitant about conducting hijra and promised that muhajirs would be content and taken care of in exile.[4] This chapter examines what led Kerim-Sultan and other North Caucasians to move to the Ottoman Empire between the 1850s and World War I.

Approximately a million North Caucasians, including Circassians, Abkhazians, Ossetians, Chechens, Ingush, and Avars, left Russia for the Ottoman Empire. This displacement came as a result of Russia's military strategy during the Caucasus War, which ended in 1864, and civil reforms in the ensuing decades. Russia adjusted its migration policies to consolidate its authority in the Caucasus. Between 1862 and 1864, the Russian military carried out ethnic cleansing in the Northwest Caucasus, expelling up to half a million western Circassians. The government encouraged and sponsored the mass relocation of Circassians to lowlands and then to the Ottoman Empire. After 1867, tsarist authorities changed course and sought to prevent Muslim emigration, creating administrative obstacles to their departure. Concurrently, the government banned the return of North Caucasians from the Ottoman Empire, aspiring to establish better control over migration across the Russo-Ottoman border.[5]

Many displaced Muslims regarded their emigration to the Ottoman Empire as hijra. Hijra constitutes a distinct type of international migration that was specific to the Muslim world in the nineteenth and twentieth centuries. Hijra drew on venerated accounts of refugee migration throughout Islamic history but was also a decidedly modern, late imperial phenomenon.

Hijra encompasses the types of migrations that rarely come together. Most muhajirs fled to the Ottoman Empire to escape ethnic cleansing or the loss of land and forcible resettlement in the lowlands. Some were taken to the Ottoman Empire against their will in continued enslavement to their masters. Others undertook hijra to preserve their faith and ways of life, considering it to be their religious obligation. Muslim migrations from Russia, although drawing on a rich tapestry of reasons to leave the Caucasus, were never voluntary. Voluntary migration is hardly possible in wartime, let alone amid targeted expulsion or under foreign rule, which many perceive as occupation.

RUSSIAN CONQUEST OF THE NORTH CAUCASUS

The displacement of Muslims from the North Caucasus was not inevitable. Starting in the sixteenth century, Russia had been expanding southward and eastward and absorbed many Muslim communities in the Volga region, the Ural Mountains, and western Siberia. In the late eighteenth century, Catherine the Great presented herself as a protector of Islam. Her male successors upheld the claim that the Russian sovereign guaranteed freedoms of his Muslim subjects.[6] Yet the conquest of the North Caucasus ended in an ethnic cleansing of Muslim communities. Russia's violent counterinsurgency and postwar reforms sparked mass Muslim migrations to the Ottoman Empire.

Russia's drive toward the warm Black and Caspian Seas started with Muscovy's conquest of the khanates of Kazan in 1552 and Astrakhan in 1556. The annexation of the khanates placed Muscovy close to the Ottoman borders, foreshadowing the Russo-Ottoman rivalry that would span twelve wars over almost 350 years. These wars took place in 1568–70 (Astrakhan Campaign), 1677–81, 1686–1700 (Wars of the Holy League), 1710–11 (Prut River Campaign), 1735–39, 1768–74, 1787–91, 1806–12, 1828–29, 1853–56 (Crimean War), 1877–78, and 1914–17/18 (World War I). The war of 1768–74 ended with the Ottoman defeat, commencing the "Eastern Question," which was a euphemism for a series of decisions that the European Powers would make about the future of Ottoman territories.[7] It also accelerated Russia's expansion into the Caucasus. The Treaty of Küçük Kaynarca of 1774 ended the Ottomans' protectorate over the Crimean Khanate, one of the last vestiges of the Mongol Empire. In 1783, Russia annexed Crimea, Taman, and the right-bank Kuban region, extending its southern border in the Northwest Caucasus to the

Kuban River, beyond which lay western Circassian territories. The Treaty of
Küçük Kaynarca also affirmed Russia's sovereignty over Kabarda, an eastern
Circassian region in the Northcentral Caucasus. The Kabarda plateaus provided the Russian army a way into the Darial Gorge, a critical pass through
the mighty Caucasus Mountains into Georgia and, from there, via the Armenian and Kurdish highlands, to the Ottoman and Qajar domains. The only
other land routes from Russia to the Middle East were around the mountains,
down the Circassian and Abkhazian coast on the Black Sea or the Dagestani
coast near Derbent on the Caspian Sea, neither of which were territories that
Russia controlled then.

Shortly after Küçük Kaynarca, Russia expanded beyond the Caucasus
Mountains into a region that had been historically contested between the
Ottoman and Iranian empires. By the late eighteenth century, the Qajars
claimed sovereignty over all Christian principalities and Muslim khanates
on the southern slopes of the mountains. The Russians first established a
protectorate over the eastern Georgian kingdom of Kartli-Kakheti in 1783
and then annexed it in 1801. In the following decade, Russia occupied the
western Georgian kingdom of Imereti and the principalities of Guria, Me-
grelia, and Abkhazia, as well as the Muslim khanates of Ganja, Karabakh,
Shaki, Shirvan, Quba, Baku, and Derbent farther east. The Qajars grudg-
ingly acknowledged Russian suzerainty over these territories in the Treaty of
Gulistan of 1813. The next war with Iran ended in Russia's annexation of the
khanates of Erivan, Nakhichevan, and Talysh, which was confirmed in the
Treaty of Turkmenchay of 1828. Russia then reimagined these heterogeneous
territories as a single region, Transcaucasia, which later became the South
Caucasus. Over the twentieth century, these lands would be homogenized
into Georgia, Armenia, and Azerbaijan.[8]

Following the consolidation of tsarist rule in the South Caucasus, the
Russian government focused on the mountainous areas to the north that
remained outside its control. By then, Russia had erected a line of fortresses
and settlements cutting deep into the North Caucasus, but most Muslim
communities living around these colonial outposts retained their autonomy.[9]
The Russian government demanded their submission after branding some
of them as rebels who had previously claimed and then denounced Russian
subjecthood, or in retaliation after some mountaineers attacked Russian set-

tlements. A series of Russian military operations against the last independent Muslim communities in the mountains entered Russian and western historical literature as the Caucasus War (1817–64) and is occasionally described, especially within the North Caucasian diaspora, as the Russo-Circassian War (1763–1864).[10]

The Russian expansion prompted the formation of two new Muslim states in the North Caucasus. The first one was the Caucasus Imamate, between 1828 and 1859, which comprised territories in Chechnya and northern Dagestan. The establishment of the Imamate marked a milestone in the political history of the Caucasus. Muslim khanates and village confederations had previously based their legitimacy on dynastic genealogy and often sought patronage of nearby Iran or the Ottoman Empire. The Imamate was a centralized state that rooted its legitimacy in an anticolonial struggle against Russia and strict adherence to shari'a law, forming part of the global Muslim reaction against European imperialism. It drew its vocabulary and inspiration from early Islamic conquests and relied heavily on Sufi and messianic movements, similar to Mahdist uprisings in Sudan and northern Nigeria against Britain and in northern Cameroon against Germany, the Dipanagara revolt in Java against the Netherlands, and the revolts of the Sufi orders, the Qadiriyya in Algeria against France and the Senusiyya in Libya against Italy in the long nineteenth century.[11] The imams declared a *ghaza* and a *jihād*, both of which could be interpreted as "holy war" against non-Muslims, and for several decades fought Russia.[12] The third imam, Shamil (r. 1834–59), styled himself an *amīr al-mu'minīn,* or "commander of the faithful," a term previously reserved for caliphs, and sent deputies throughout the mountains to foster anti-Russian alliances.[13] Shamil surrendered to the tsarist troops in 1859, which put an end to the most serious challenge to Russia's expansion in the Caucasus or elsewhere in its Muslim borderlands.[14]

The second new state was Circassia, founded by western Circassians as a federative republic in 1861. Until the eighteenth century, Circassian communities occasionally paid tribute to the Crimean Khanate and the Ottoman Empire, but neither of them ever fully controlled those territories. In the 1830s, several Circassian communities attempted to establish a confederation and were aided in their efforts by the maverick Scottish diplomat David Urquhart, who lobbied British authorities to support an independent Circassia.[15]

Between 1848 and 1859, many Circassians united under the leadership of Mu-hammad Amin, a deputy of the Caucasus Imamate.[16] In June 1861, Circassian notables established a *mejlis*, a "great and free assembly," on the Sochi River and drafted a constitution.[17] Their proclamation of the republic was the final attempt by western Circassians to preserve their autonomy, when the rest of the Caucasus had been absorbed into Russia. The mejlis sent deputies to Istanbul and London to request international recognition, in coordination with the Circassian committees established there and with Polish revolution-aries in exile.[18] In June 1862, Russian troops burned down the building of the mejlis.[19] The mejlis then reconvened in exile in Istanbul's Tophane neighbor-hood. The mejlis sent a proclamation back to Circassia, encouraging remain-ing fighters to resist Russian troops.[20] The Circassian elites rightfully judged the Europeans' support to be critical in their bid for sovereignty. In preceding decades, Greece, Serbia, and Montenegro used the Eastern Question to their advantage, securing European support to win independence from, or auton-omy within, the Ottoman Empire. However, unlike the Balkan countries, Muslim Circassia was virtually unknown to the Europeans, had no history of independence or even political unity, did not control its claimed territories, and was at war with Russia, which surrounded it on all sides. Its short state-hood was a testament to the diplomatic acumen of the Circassian elites but came too late in the Caucasus War to be viable.

After the defeat of the Imamate in 1859, the Russian army focused on breaking the resistance of Circassian communities. By then, Russia had been fighting the Circassians for almost a century, ever since the establishment of the first Russian fort in Kabarda in 1763. The value of the Northwest Cauca-sus for Russia lay in its geography. The Circassian coast presented the fastest route from southern Russia to Georgia, already within the tsardom. In the 1830s and 1840s, Russia built up fortified settlements along the Circassian coast. Russia then suffered a humiliating defeat to Britain, France, and the Ottoman Empire in the Crimean War of 1853–56. It had to evacuate its garri-sons from much of the Circassian coast in 1854. The Crimean War impressed on Russia that Britain posed a serious threat in the Black Sea. Russia's first priority after the war was to reclaim its control of the coastline to prevent any potential military support, from Britain or the Ottoman Empire, to Cir-cassians. The forested slopes of the Northwest Caucasus proved particularly challenging for the Russian army to conquer. From that terrain, Circassians waged fairly successful guerrilla warfare, thwarting tsarist military's advancement down the coast and, from the Russian perspective, threatening the security of agricultural settlements in the fertile Kuban River plain to the north.[21]

To complete the conquest of the Northwest Caucasus, the Russian military devised a new strategy: not merely to subdue a native population by force of arms, as it did to many Muslim communities in the region, but to expel and resettle it elsewhere to minimize further resistance. In 1857, Dmitrii Miliutin, the chief of staff to Aleksandr Bariatinskii, the commander of Russia's Caucasus Army, first suggested that "pushing out and resettling mountaineers is meant not as a *means* to cleanse the land, which is allegedly insufficient for new Cossack settlements, but on the contrary as the *objective* whereby the land held by the enemy would be settled with a Russian people and the hostile indigenous population would be reduced in numbers" (emphasis in the original).[22] Miliutin, a former professor at the General Staff Academy and founder of military statistics in Russia, advocated for the expulsion of Circassians and their replacement with a loyal settler population to transform the entire population of the region, which would be described by historians as "population politics," "social alchemy," or demographic engineering.[23] In 1860, Nikolai Evdokimov, a new commander of the Caucasus Army in Kuban Province, formally proposed to expel western Circassians from their mountains and to force them either to settle behind Cossack stations in the lowlands or to leave for the Ottoman Empire. Miliutin, who would become Russia's minister of war in 1861, and Bariatinskii supported the motion, which passed in May 1862.[24]

The North Caucasian migration to the Ottoman Empire can be divided into distinct periods: 1850s–1862, 1863–64, 1865–78, and in the post-1878 era.[25] During the first stage of migration, up to 150,000 Circassians and Nogai Tatars emigrated amid the escalating violence of the Caucasus War.[26] In this period, the tsarist government abetted the emigration of Muslims from the North Caucasus. Russian generals regarded local Muslims as a potentially disloyal population and encouraged the flight of Nogai Tatars and Circassians to the Ottoman Empire, viewing Muslim emigration as a welcome and cheap way to "pacify" the Caucasus. In 1860, Mikhail Loris-Melikov, a Russian general who would later be appointed as the governor of Terek Province, traveled to

Istanbul to negotiate the Ottoman resettlement of Circassians. The Porte (Ottoman government) agreed to accept 40,000–50,000 muhajirs over a period of several years.[27] Refugee numbers exceeded this figure shortly thereafter, but this deal remains the only confirmed Russo-Ottoman agreement concerning western Circassian refugees and had never been renegotiated.

The Russian army implemented a scorched-earth approach to hasten the expulsions. Between 1862 and 1864, the military burned down dozens of Circassian villages and destroyed harvests and fields to prevent survivors from coming back. The detailed Russian military reports relay the systematic destruction of Circassian villages.[28] Evdokimov's troops took prisoners or massacred those who did not abandon their burning villages.[29] One by one, entire Circassian communities—Shapsughs, Temirgois, Natukhais, and Abzakhs—were pushed out of their villages in the mountains toward the Black Sea coast. Some were forcibly resettled in the lowlands around the Kuban River, where they were interspersed among Cossack settlements for easier control.[30] In 1864, the General Staff of the Caucasus Army reaffirmed that "the indispensable condition to end the war in the Caucasus must be the complete cleansing of the Black Sea coast from its insubordinate population."[31] Not all Circassians came into direct contact with the Russian troops. A string of Circassian defeats led to the collapse of morale across the mountains, and the panic set in. Many Circassians heard of a mass slaughter of their kin farther north and abandoned their villages because of fear of what might happen to them should they stay. This anticipatory refugee movement, or flight out of fear, between 1863 and 1864 almost completely emptied the forested mountains of the Northwest Caucasus, which was precisely the goal of disproportionate state violence against Circassian communities.[32] By the end of the Caucasus War, up to half a million western Circassians, or about 90 percent of the entire population, left for the Ottoman Empire.[33]

Today, the Circassian diaspora uses the Turkish terms *büyük göç* (great migration), *sürgün* (banishment), and *soykırım* (genocide); the Arabic term *tahjīr* (displacement); and increasingly the Ubykh term *Tsitsekun* (killing of people) to describe its displacement.[34] In recent decades, Circassian organizations within Russia and in the Middle East diaspora have called for the recognition of massacres and expulsions in the Northwest Caucasus in 1863–64 as a genocide.[35]

Figure 2. **Circassian displacement in Russian art.**
The Abandonment of the Village by the Mountaineers as the Russian Troops Approach (1872)
by Pyotr Gruzinsky, a Russian painter who witnessed the flight of Circassians in 1864.

Between 1862 and 1864, the Russian government partially funded the
forced relocation of Circassians to the Ottoman Empire. In 1862, it established the Commission for Resettlement of Mountaineers to Turkey (Rus.,
Komissiia po delu o pereselenii gortsev v Turtsiiu). This agency paid for Russian, Ottoman, Greek, Ionian, British, and Romanian boats to take Circassians from Russia's Black Sea ports of Anapa, Taman, Tuapse, Sochi, and
Konstantinovskoe (Novorossiysk) to the Ottoman ports of Trabzon, Samsun,
and Sinop. The Russian government spent 289,678 rubles 17 kopeks on the
transfer, or removal, of western Circassians in 1863 and 1864.[36]

The Circassians' flight became a full-blown humanitarian crisis. Several
hundreds of thousands of refugees huddled on the coast between modern-day
Anapa and Sochi, which is known today as the Russian Riviera. According
to eyewitnesses, the boats designed for several dozen people were routinely

overloaded with up to 400 refugees.[37] One Circassian refugee, Nuri, later recalled his journey from Russia to the Ottoman Empire: "We were thrown into boats like dogs; suffocating, hungry, and tattered, we expected to die there."[38] Many died of hunger and disease during this voyage, and many overloaded boats sank. An eyewitness wrote of the Circassians who arrived on three boats in Cyprus in October 1864, "It was one of the saddest sights that could be imagined to see these wretched creatures landing, after having been crowded to so cruel an excess in these small vessels for more than two months, without even standing room. . . . For three days previous to their arrival they had been without water. Of the 2,700 Circassian refugees packed into three brigs, 1,300 were dead by the time they reached Cyprus, and 900 "were more dead than alive."[39] By all accounts, the chaotic evacuation led to a staggering death count, with anywhere between a third and a half of refugees dying at sea or shortly after their arrival in Ottoman ports.[40] Most North Caucasians in the Middle East today trace their ancestry to those refugees who had boarded boats on the Circassian coast and survived their harrowing journey.

The expulsions were not a byproduct of war but a deliberate choice. The massacres and expulsions of Circassians constituted an ethnic cleansing in the sense that the Russian military targeted a specific ethnic group for near total expulsion. Ethnic cleansing is the systematic removal of a population to achieve cultural homogeneity, as typically demanded by an exclusivist ethnic or religious nationalist ideology. Imperial Russia's ethnic cleansing of Circassians in the 1860s had a similar end result to ethnic cleansing by the twentieth-century nation-states, which were motivated primarily by nationalism. Tsarist expulsions resulted in demographic homogenization and population replacement in parts of the Northwest Caucasus, as largely Slavic colonists took the lands of western Circassians. Russia's decision to expel was grounded in military strategy to secure control over the Northwest Caucasus. The Russian military chose to violently remove a population that had resisted Russian advances the most and could undermine Russia's control of its new frontier region.[41] At the same time, the Circassians' identity was not irrelevant to their being targeted for expulsions. Russia expelled this community not because they were Circassians or Muslims per se but because tsarist generals believed that their Muslim identity and connections to the Ottoman Empire made them an unreliable frontier population. The perception of Muslim Circassians as untrustworthy subjects was rooted in Russian nationalism, which permeated tsarist bureaucrats' thinking on who belonged fully, partially, or not at all in the Russian state.

On May 21, 1864, the Russian military celebrated the official end of the war. Since then, territories lying between Circassia and Dagestan were molded into a single administrative region, now known as the North Caucasus. The conquest of the entire Caucasus, which Russia governed as a viceroyalty with the seat in Tiflis, expanded the geography and cultural reach of Russia's Muslim domains and provided Russia with direct access to the Middle East.[42] It also forced many Muslim communities out of the Caucasus Mountains, creating a large refugee diaspora scattered from the central Balkans to southern Kurdistan.

MUSLIM EMIGRATION UNDER RUSSIAN RULE

Muslim emigration from Russia began as soon as Russia acquired its first Muslim populations. Following tsarist conquests of Kazan and Astrakhan in the 1550s, many Volga Tatars left for the Ottoman Empire.[43] The slow emigration of Tatar communities of the Volga region, the Urals, and Siberia continued throughout the remainder of Russian imperial rule. Muslim emigration became a mass phenomenon after Russia's annexation of Crimea in 1783, when between 150,000 and 200,000 Crimean Tatars fled to the Ottoman Empire.[44] In 1856–62, about 200,000 Crimean Tatars left for the Ottoman Balkans and Anatolia.[45] Up to 18,000 Crimean Tatars emigrated in 1874–75 and the early 1890s.[46] Many Adjarians (Muslim Georgians), Laz, Karapapakhs, Turkmens, Meskhetian Turks, and Kurds from western regions of the South Caucasus left for the Ottoman Empire in the aftermath of the Russo-Ottoman wars of 1828–29 and 1877–78.[47] For example, the number of Muslims in the khanate of Erivan declined from 87,000 to just over 50,000 shortly after Russia's conquest in 1828.[48] After Russia's annexation of the Ottoman districts of Batum, Kars, and Ardahan in 1878, some 74,000 Turks, Kurds, Karapapakhs, and Turkmens, or 73 percent of the population of Kars and Ardahan, left for the Ottoman Empire by 1880; many returned later.[49] Central Asian Muslims also emigrated to the Ottoman Empire, Iran, and China's Xinjiang province.[50]

The emigration of Russia's Muslims proceeded alongside the immigration of Ottoman Christians in Russia. After Catherine the Great's manifestos of 1762 and 1763, which invited foreigners to settle in Russia, Ottoman Greeks and Slavs had been slowly migrating to southern Ukraine. By 1812, around 87,000 Ottoman Bulgarians moved to the Danubian Principalities of Moldavia and Wallachia, and in 1828–34 over 100,000 more Bulgarians immigrated in the Danubian Principalities and Russia's Bessarabia.[51] Many of them later moved to Crimea. Meanwhile, many Christians had been emigrating from Ottoman Anatolia and Kurdistan to the Caucasus. About 84,000 Ottoman Armenians and Greeks moved to Russia's South Caucasus provinces after the Russo-Ottoman War of 1828–29.[52] Some 85,000 Ottoman Armenians arrived after the Russo-Ottoman War of 1877–78, and up to 300,000 more arrived after the Hamidian massacres of 1894–96.[53] Approximately 40,000 Ottoman Greeks arrived after 1878.[54]

Migrations of Christians and Muslims in opposite directions evidenced a new relationship between one's faith and subjecthood that had been taking shape between the shores of the Aegean, Black, and Caspian Seas. Starting in the late eighteenth century, frontier communities sought protection by their co-religionist state, and religious difference was increasingly seen as justification for violence and reason for migration in the Russo-Ottoman borderlands. These migrations reinforced the notion that Muslims would want to be in the domains of an Ottoman sultan-caliph, and Christians longed to live under a Russian tsar. The gradual religious homogenization in the Russo-Ottoman borderlands was an early stage of ethnic homogenization, which would result in ethnic cleansing and population transfers in the early twentieth century.

The Russo-Ottoman migrations generated the idea of a population exchange. Most of these migrations were spurred by the Russo-Ottoman wars and occurred shortly after the end of hostilities. Beginning in the early nineteenth century, every peace treaty concluding a Russo-Ottoman war included articles regulating transfers of frontier populations that had already left or considered leaving for another empire.[55] Those state-sanctioned migrations in the borderlands entered popular imagination as permission for Ottoman Christians to move to the tsardom and for Russian Muslims to move to the sultanate.[56] By the 1860s, many frontier populations and foreign observers viewed mass migrations as a "population exchange" between the Ottoman and Russian empires.[57] As early as 1861, rumors circulated in northern Bulgaria that Circassian and Nogai Tatar refugees would replace the Bulgarians, who had already been steadily emigrating to Russia.[58] The rumor was deemed serious enough for the office of the grand vizier to order district governors in the Balkans to reassure local residents that all rumors of an exchange (Ott. Tur., *mübadele*) were false and that the sultan was committed to protecting his Bulgarian subjects.[59] Likewise, many Muslims in the Caucasus believed that the Russian government allowed Muslim emigration from the Caucasus, based on its agreement with the Ottoman government, despite tsarist officials' denial of such an agreement.[60] Saint Petersburg and Istanbul did not exercise control over the timing and scale of Russo-Ottoman migrations, which largely happened without their authorization. However, while the two governments never affirmed migrations of Russian Muslims to the Ottoman Empire and of Ottoman Christians to Russia as a population exchange, the outcomes of those migrations served their interests.

Russia's governance in the Caucasus Viceroyalty was an uneasy equilibrium between civil and military authorities. After the end of the Caucasus War, the government reorganized the region into governorates (*guberniia*), provinces (*oblast'*), and districts (*okrug*), with varying degrees of oversight from the viceroy's administration in Tiflis and the Russian military. While much of the South Caucasus was governed directly by civil authorities, most territories of North Caucasian Muslims came under military-civil administration, under the purview of the Caucasus Mountain Administration, also in Tiflis.[61] This mixed system of administration held many parallels to French governance in Algeria and British rule in India, which to some extent inspired Russian administrators in the Caucasus.[62] It allowed a certain degree of indirect rule and elevated customary law in governing Muslim communities in the region. This model was at its strongest in Dagestan and was less consistently applied in the Northwest and Northcentral Caucasus, where it gave way to direct civil rule in the 1870s and then military rule in the 1880s.[63] The overall objective of tsarist rule in the Caucasus after 1864 was to speed up the integration of this culturally heterogeneous region into Russia, which necessitated extensive administrative, economic, and legal reforms.

Muslim emigration from the North Caucasus did not cease with the end of the Caucasus War. After 1864, North Caucasian Muslims, who by then were Russian subjects, continued emigrating to the Ottoman domains. This emigration lasted through the final decades of Russian rule and was remarkably comprehensive, cutting across ethnolinguistic and social lines. Kabardians, Abkhazians, Ossetians, Chechens, Ingush, Avars, Kumyks, Karachays, Balkars, and others were moving to the Ottoman Empire. Sometimes entire villages and, more commonly, individual families or single men, either poor or of means, petitioned tsarist authorities to allow them to leave Russia or asked Ottoman authorities to intercede on their behalf.[64] So did many Turkic-speaking Muslims of the South Caucasus.[65]

Many Muslims emigrated because of Russia's land reforms in the 1860s, which reorganized land ownership and taxation in the Caucasus. The reforms limited the amount of land that private landowners could hold and redistributed some of the confiscated land among landless peasants. In the Caucasus, the government's objectives were not so much to empower landless Muslims but to standardize the fragmented land tenure system, opening the region to mass colonization and breaking the power of the old elites, so that the government could mold its own clients in the region.[66]

Muslim emigration followed two other kinds of migration, both of which the Russian government mandated as part of its land reforms. The first one was the forced resettlement of Muslim communities from highlands to lowlands. During the war, the military required Muslims to relocate to lowlands, which were often swampy and malarial, as a punishment. The civil authorities continued the same policy after the war, ostensibly under economic pretexts.[67] The government confiscated lands that many Kabardian, Ossetian, and Chechen villages had used as communal pastures and merged their villages. For example, in 1865–67, ninety-three villages in Greater Kabarda were forcibly reorganized into thirty-three, and twenty-five villages in Lesser Kabarda into nine.[68] These forcible relocations resembled the Ottoman sedentarization of nomads in central Anatolia and Kurdistan, which was unfolding in the same period.[69]

The second type of migration was mass colonization of the Caucasus by Christian settlers. The earlier groups of colonists near the North Caucasus were Cossacks of the Don (1570), Terek (1577), Kuban (1696), Astrakhan (1750), Black Sea (1787), Azov (1832), and Caucasus Line (1832) hosts, an ethnically heterogeneous frontier force that helped to push Russia's southern border for centuries. Russia accelerated the construction of Cossack settlements during the Caucasus War. For example, between 1861 and 1864, 111 new Cossack settlements appeared in western Circassia.[70] The next group of settlers were the newly emancipated landless peasants of southern Russia, whom the government encouraged to take up free land in the fertile plains of the Kuban and the Terek, the two largest rivers in the North Caucasus. By 1897, Slavic colonists comprised 91 percent of the population in Kuban Province, which incorporated western Circassia, and 34 percent in Terek Province, which included territories of Kabardians, Ossetians, Ingush, and Chechens.[71] Kuban Province, in particular, became the empire's premier agricultural region, ensconced in the modern Russian psyche as the "breadbasket of Russia." In addition to Russian and Ukrainian settlers, smaller German, Polish, Belarusian, Moldavian, Czech, Estonian, Latvian, Lithuanian, Bulgarian, and Ottoman Greek and Armenian communities arrived in the North Caucasus in the late tsarist period.[72] The government expected Christian settlers to become a successful agricultural population and a loyal one in a Muslim-majority region near the Ottoman and Iranian borders.

The categories of faith and ethnicity informed Russia's colonization strategy in the Caucasus.[73] Religious identity was the most important category in shaping Russia's migration policies in the region. The tsarist government perceived one's faith to likely determine their loyalty to the empire. In Russia's religious hierarchy, Orthodox Christians occupied the top position, followed by other Christians, then by Muslims and Jews, and then by all others.[74] In the tsarist Caucasus, most emigrants were Muslims and most immigrants were Christians. Ethnicity had been entangled with faith and political loyalty in Imperial Russia and grew in importance over time.[75] Already in 1864, several months after the end of the war, Baron Aleksandr Nikolai, chief of the civil administration in the Caucasus, wrote that "without doubt, for governing purposes, the best thing would be to settle the newly acquired region exclusively with the Russian people [Rus., *russkaia narodnost'*]."[76] Because there were not enough potential Russian settlers, Nikolai recommended other groups in the following order: Georgians (i.e., Russians' co-religionists within the empire), Montenegrins and Nekrasov Cossacks (Orthodox Slavs in the Ottoman Empire), Trabzon Greeks (Orthodox non-Slavs in the Ottoman Empire), and only then foreign non-Orthodox Christians.[77] Tsarist officials wanted their frontier subjects to be loyal, or obedient to Russian rule, and ascribed the notion of loyalty most easily to those of Russian ethnicity and Orthodox faith. After the Russo-Ottoman War of 1877–78, the Caucasus authorities openly stated that allowing mass immigration of Ottoman Greeks and Armenians in the South Caucasus had been a mistake because they were not a trustworthy frontier population. Instead, authorities advocated the immigration of as many "Russian elements" as possible into Russia's newest territories in the Caucasus.[78] Likewise, by 1893, Russian military officials insisted on colonizing the lands of Terek Province, vacated by emigrating Muslims, with "exclusively Russian settlers."[79] The Russian government's preferred population in the Caucasus was never in doubt—Russian-speaking settlers, faithful to Orthodoxy and the tsar.

The Russian government categorized any Muslim leaving for the Ottoman Empire as *pereselenets* (migrant, resettler), a broad term that covered anyone who moved elsewhere for permanent settlement, also encompassing Greek and Armenian immigrants from the Ottoman Empire and Slavic peasants moving to the Caucasus. Tsarist authorities often used the term *mukhadzhir* (Russian rendering of *muhajir*), which was the preferred term of North Caucasians themselves, and occasionally *emigrant*. The government did not use *bezhenets*, the modern Russian term for refugee, for North Caucasians at the time; that term gained prominence only in the early twentieth century and was typically used to describe Christian, and not Muslim, subjects of the Russian and Ottoman empires.[80]

Tsarist abolition of slavery accelerated Muslim emigration. By the mid-nineteenth century, many communities living between the coasts of the Black and the Caspian Seas practiced slavery. North Caucasian slavery was a multitiered institution. The terms of enslavement and forced labor could vary within the same village, ranging from fixed-term household servitude, akin to Russian serfdom, to hereditary agricultural bondage, similar to Caribbean plantation slavery. For example, in western Circassia an unfree person belonged to one of three groups: *unauty*, mostly women who had no right to hold property and could be separated from their family and sold at their holder's whim; *pshitli*, who had limited property rights and were obligated to pay levies and do agricultural service for their masters; or *ogi*, a transitional stage to freedpersons, who were exempt from land service and served as guardsmen for their masters.[81] While most unfree people in the North Caucasus belonged to the same ethnic and religious group as their masters, small groups originated outside the region, namely Russian prisoners of war and enslaved Africans whom Ottoman slave traders sold as far north as Abkhazia and Kabarda.[82] Slaveholders were also an eclectic group, ranging from Kabardian princes to Abkhazian *ankhaiu* peasants, who themselves were in economic and social bondage to their notables.[83]

Russia's abolitionism in the North Caucasus was not driven by humanitarian ideals. As part of tsarist land reforms, abolition was meant to standardize local institutions of land ownership and labor and make them legible to new Russian administrators. Tsarist abolitionism in the Caucasus came on the heels of the Emancipation Manifesto of 1861, which freed Russian serfs, or unfree peasants who were legally attached to the land, on private estates. Slavery in Russia proper was abolished in 1723, but the institution of serfdom denied basic freedoms to over a third of Russia's population.[84] Although the Emancipation Manifesto did not extend to the Caucasus, the formal abolition of serfdom in Russia allowed the Caucasus authorities to push ahead with their own reforms. The Russian government enacted abolitionist legislation in the South Caucasus governorates of Tiflis in 1864, Kutais between 1866 and 1871, and Baku and Erivan in 1870. In the North Caucasus, the government abolished slavery in Terek Province in 1864–67, including among Terek Cossacks in 1864, in Kabarda in 1866, and in Ossetia, Chechnya, Ingushetia, and Kumykia in 1867; in Dagestan Province in 1867; in Kuban Province in 1868; and in Sukhum Department (Abkhazia) in 1870.[85] The Russian government proceeded gradually to secure the support of North Caucasian elites, whom it consulted when drafting abolitionist legislation. Tsarist authorities made a series of abolitionist deals throughout the region, whereby new cases of enslavement were outlawed but existing slaveholding temporarily remained legal. Slaveholders were required to liberate their slaves after a certain number of years in servitude and were compensated by the state or could set them free sooner in exchange for a manumission payment by enslaved persons.[86]

Russia's abolition of North Caucasian slavery in the 1860s prompted many slaveholders to emigrate to the Ottoman Empire and take their slaves with them. Abolitionism provoked resistance among many slaveholding families, especially in Kabarda, Abkhazia, and Ossetia, who interpreted abolitionism as part of Russia's wider assault on their social institutions.[87] We do not know how many North Caucasians left as slaves because refugee communities rarely disclosed to Ottoman authorities who among them was unfree. One Ottoman report suggests that more than 150,000 Circassian muhajirs were enslaved.[88] Foreign consuls corroborated the extent of enslavement through their local informants. Reportedly, some refugee villages near Edirne in eastern Thrace had five slaves to one free person, and in the Kahramanmaraş area in southeastern Anatolia more than half of muhajirs in Kabardian villages were enslaved.[89] This final transfer of enslaved North Caucasians to the Middle East coincided with the voyages of the last ships carrying enslaved Africans to the Americas.[90]

North Caucasian insurgency against Russian rule led to new rounds of displacement. After the end of the Caucasus War, the Russian government suppressed a string of uprisings in Chechnya (1864), Abkhazia (1864, 1866), Zaqatala District (1863, 1869–70), western Circassia/Kuban (1870), and Dagestan (1866, 1871).[91] The first major uprising occurred in Chechnya in 1864, when followers of the Qadiriyya Sufi order protested the imprisonment of their shaykh Kunta Hajji.[92] Following the suppression of the uprising, the Russian government secured the Ottomans' agreement to resettle Kunta Hajji's followers and others who wished to emigrate, which was the second and final formal Russo-Ottoman agreement—after the one in 1860—on the population transfer of North Caucasian Muslims.[93] In 1865, Musa Kundukhov, a Muslim Ossetian general in the Russian army, organized the emigration of 23,057 Muslims, mostly Chechens and some Ingush, Karabulaks,[94] Ossetians, and Kabardians.[95] Another large revolt, known as the Lykhny rebellion, occurred in Abkhazia in 1866 in response to the impending land reform and the abolition of slavery. About a quarter of Abkhazia's population participated in the rebellion, making it the largest anti-abolitionist revolt in the Caucasus.[96] The uprising led to the emigration of 19,342 Muslim Abkhazians to the Ottoman Empire in 1867.[97] Finally, in 1877, a series of revolts in support of the Ottoman Empire in the Russo-Ottoman War of 1877–78 broke out in Abkhazia, Chechnya, and Dagestan. The suppression of those revolts led to the emigration of 30,000–50,000 Abkhazians and smaller groups of Chechens and Dagestanis.[98]

Social pressure played a massive role in the emigration of free Muslims of a lower social status. The elites of the Northwest and Northcentral Caucasus, who had the most to lose from tsarist reforms, often persuaded or coerced their peasants to emigrate with them. In the Ottoman Empire, they surrounded themselves with their kinsfolk and usually retained a high social status. The emigration with their kin and upper-status patrons allowed poorer North Caucasians to preserve their social networks and community, even if it meant separation from their homeland. In this fashion, entire Kabardian and Ossetian villages followed their notables to the Ottoman Empire. Ossetian notables Ahmet Tsalikov and Alimurza Abisalov, Shapsugh Temirkhan Shipshev, and Kabardian Fitsa Abdrakhmanov, who all were in tsarist military or civil service, led large emigrating parties of their kinsfolk out of Russia. The ʿulama, or Muslim religious elites, occasionally led the emigrating parties of Kabardians, Shapsughs, Bzhedughs, and Karachays.[99]

In later decades, many Muslims left the Caucasus because they thought that the government might further infringe on Muslims' freedoms. Tsarist reforms had transformed the daily lives of many North Caucasians, who had to traverse Cossack settlements to reach each other's villages and experienced heavy state oversight of their mosques, madrasas, and courts.[100] The anxiety that the worst was yet to come instigated new rounds of North Caucasian emigration. In rare surviving testimonies, emigrants expressed fear that, with time, the government would impose additional taxes on them, force them to educate their children only in Russian, give local women in marriage to Russians, and even convert everyone to Christianity.[101] Some Kabardians believed that those who die on Russian-occupied soil would not be able to enter paradise and that cholera epidemics were Allah's punishment for not emigrating to the Ottoman Empire.[102]

One anonymous Dagestani muhajir, before leaving for the Ottoman Empire, left the following open letter, which illustrates such worries. This message, written in Arabic, was secretly copied and passed on as a chain letter before it was discovered and confiscated by the Russian police:

> I leave Dagestan forever because of my disdain for it. How can I not abandon Dagestan and not leave for Istanbul, when [it is] the latter [that] has faith? In Dagestan . . . [people] do not distinguish anymore between what is permitted and what is prohibited. . . . Whoever stays here will regret it later

and turn into Russians. . . . Heavy taxes will be imposed, and bad times will come. . . . Those who live with the Russians drink wine. Whoever stays here will be in hell forever. Dagestanis, let's go to the Ottoman state! Do you remember what happened to Kazan Tatars? Your turn is coming, and you will be recruited as soldiers, and Allah will reproach you for that in the afterlife. Do not stay here, true Muslims. Pack your bags, and may Allah help you in your journey![103]

Conscription was a persistent fear of many North Caucasian Muslims. Many believed that the introduction of conscription in Russia in 1874 meant that Russia's Muslim subjects, who had been exempted until then, would be drafted into the military. Many non-Muslim families also dreaded military service—a fear that transferred seamlessly into the Soviet and post-1991 eras—but the Muslim subjects of the tsar had a culturally specific concern, namely that their sons would be forced to eat pork in the army, as Russians do.[104] Notably, many other imperial subjects feared conscription introduced by their rapidly centralizing nineteenth-century states. Egyptian peasants were terrified of being drafted into Muhammad 'Ali's army, and some maimed themselves to avoid conscription, while many Ottoman Christians preferred to continue paying additional taxes than to serve in the Ottoman army, for which they were eligible after 1856.[105]

The Russian approach to Muslim emigration changed after the end of the Caucasus War. In late 1864, the Russian government banned the emigration of Circassians from Kuban Province to the Ottoman Empire, extending the ban in 1867 for other Muslims in the North Caucasus.[106] The new policy followed a similar one toward Crimean Tatars, whose emigration Russia restricted after 1860. The government tried to prevent the Crimean flight to maintain a large tax base and labor force.[107] Likewise, in the Caucasus, civil authorities were concerned about the long-term costs of emigration, which hindered "the fastest development of the region."[108] Many Slavic peasants and Cossacks, who had arrived as colonists to take the place of Circassians and Chechens, had trouble adapting to terrace farming and to growing grapes and mulberry trees. Their settlements were economically failing.[109] In these circumstances, the loss of Muslim farmers to emigration spelled the collapse of local agriculture and tax revenue for generations to come. The state rhetoric on emigration changed: during the Caucasus War, Muslim refugees were imagined as rebels and religious fanatics who could never be redeemed as loyal tsarist subjects; after 1864, prospective Muslim emigrants were seen as peasants who were misled by Ottoman propaganda and whom the government should persuade to remain and be productive Russian subjects.[110]

The Russian government did not separate application procedures for Muslim emigration and pilgrimage. Both prospective emigrants and pilgrims had to request a Russian passport (*zagranichnyi pasport*), which allowed one to exit and return to Russia within six months to a year.[111] After May 1861, the authorities in the Caucasus stamped emigrant passports with the note "leaving for resettlement," turning them into exit-only documents.[112] Many muhajirs, however, would not reveal their intention to emigrate and applied for passports as pilgrims because that gave them six months to a year to change their mind and return to the Caucasus. By the early 1870s, Russian authorities in the North Caucasus were split between those in favor of allowing Muslim emigration and those who opposed it.[113] Meanwhile, local officials received hundreds of petitions from Muslim residents requesting permission to emigrate to the Ottoman Empire. The Russian governor of Kuban Province wrote in 1872 that "all mountaineers, with fairly few exceptions, were ready to immediately move to Turkey if they were allowed to do so."[114]

In 1872, the Caucasus Viceroyalty relaxed its ban on travel to the Ottoman Empire, allowing temporary leave to the Ottoman Empire for the hajj. The authorities no longer accepted petitions requesting to emigrate, but they knew that many applicants for the hajj did not intend to ever return to Russia. The government, however, raised the bar for an applicant to qualify for an exit passport. According to the new instructions, a Muslim resident wishing to conduct a pilgrimage needed to submit an individual petition, demonstrate sufficient funds for the journey and the upkeep of their family while they were away, pay the prohibitively high fee of 70 rubles as a deposit in lieu of advance taxes, and secure a statement from their village administration testifying that the applicant had no debts and was not under criminal investigation or on trial. Petitioners were not allowed to sell their property before obtaining formal permission to leave, which was granted at the discretion of their provincial governor.[115] Caucasus authorities eased the total ban on emigration for Muslims in 1876 and removed it altogether in 1885. Threshold requirements to receive permission to emigrate were high: a prospective emigrant had to secure the written approval of two-thirds of their village and of the Ottoman government for their emigration.[116]

Russia's restrictions on Muslim emigration after the Caucasus War supported its overall goal to solidify its rule in the Caucasus. The government discouraged mass Muslim emigration but provided a legal way to emigrate for those Muslims who were adamantly opposed to staying. The onerous and expensive procedure to leave Russia suppressed the number of formal applications and fueled unauthorized emigration to the Ottoman Empire. Between the late 1860s and World War I, most Muslims emigrated without informing the tsarist government.[117] At their own pace, muhajirs settled their affairs, said their goodbyes, and then crossed the Russo-Ottoman border in the dead of night.

Russia prohibited the return of North Caucasian refugees from the Ottoman Empire. In June 1861, the Caucasus Army enacted a ban on readmitting most North Caucasian Muslims.[118] Requests to return, submitted by muhajirs to Russian consuls in the Ottoman Empire, were to be denied and visas not issued. The admission of those who presented themselves to tsarist officials on the Russo-Ottoman border hinged on their carrying a Russian passport. Those returning without a passport were to be deported. Returnees who carried a Russian passport were not guaranteed readmittance either: they were to be denied entry if they had overstayed in the Ottoman Empire and returned with an expired Russian passport; if their passport was issued for an entire household and not its individual members, which had been a practice by some local authorities;[119] or if their passport had the special exit stamp "leaving for resettlement."[120] Even those who returned with an unexpired passport but who had previously sold their property in the Caucasus, which the authorities interpreted as an intention to emigrate, were to be denied readmittance to the Caucasus and instead resettled in the distant Orenburg Governorate or territories of the Ural Cossack Host.[121] In practice, very few returnees had in their possession unexpired Russian passports. The procedure of a formal application to exit Russia was not properly communicated to all Muslim residents, and, according to the regulations of March 1861, military authorities were not to issue passports to those mountaineers who wished to emigrate to the Ottoman Empire.[122] Moreover, most muhajirs were western Circassians, many of whom had departed from territories that had not been controlled by Russia in the early 1860s, and no authority in sight could issue them passports at the time. The official ban on the return of North Caucasian Muslims remained in place through the end of imperial rule.[123]

Russia's ban on the return of North Caucasian Muslims after 1861 and restrictions on emigration after 1867 complemented each other. They meant to keep North Caucasian Muslim populations, which had now resided within the Russian and Ottoman empires, separate from each other to prevent the exchange of ideas that could challenge Russian authority in the Caucasus. The Russian government grew increasingly paranoid that North Caucasian returnees could be Ottoman emissaries who would sway local Muslim populations to either emigrate to the Ottoman Empire or rise up against tsarist rule.[124] The ban had further underlined the tenuous position of Muslims still residing in the Caucasus. The tsar's newest Muslim subjects faced restrictions on their mobility in and out of Russia. The government's ban on return sent an unequivocal message to local Muslims that, were they to leave the Caucasus, the road home would be closed because the Russian state did not want them. Russia's policies were similar to Ottoman ones toward Armenians. The Ottoman government banned Armenian emigration in 1888 because it feared that Armenians would be exposed to revolutionary ideas overseas and bring them home. For that very reason, in 1893, the Porte also barred Armenians from returning to the Ottoman Empire.[125]

The Russian government denaturalized Muslim emigrants. Denaturalization, or the revocation of subjecthood, was rare in the Russian Empire.[126] The tsarist government never developed legislation recognizing Russian subjects' right to emigrate or leave Russian subjecthood but claimed the authority to denaturalize Russian subjects for serious crimes, such as treason. In practice, tsarist authorities rarely denaturalized Russia's emigrants, who were presumed to remain Russian subjects. Thus, ethnic Russians and Germans who returned to Russia after their emigration to the United States commonly resumed their Russian subjecthood.[127] Ottoman Greeks and Armenians who had acquired Russian subjecthood through Russian consuls retained it and even passed it on to their children while never stepping outside the Ottoman Empire.[128] By the second half of the nineteenth century, the tsarist government stopped extending such continuity of subjecthood to non-Christians, frequently disavowing its Jewish and Muslim emigrants. For example, the government allowed Jewish and Crimean Tatar communities to emigrate only if they signed statements consenting to being "eternally banned" from returning to the Russian Empire. This pledge of nonreturn, not asked of Slavic emigrants, amounted to "compulsory denaturalization."[129]

North Caucasian Muslims who received tsarist permission for emigration had their subjecthood abrogated soon after their departure.[130] They were expunged from their community's membership list, losing the right of residence; their state-allotted land was returned to their community's land grant or was distributed to retired Russian soldiers or colonists from interior Russian provinces; and they lost the right to return to Russia under any circumstances.[131] The tsarist government denaturalized North Caucasian muhajirs who emigrated without authorization by regarding them as Ottoman subjects. This policy was evident when muhajirs were trying to return to Russia from the Ottoman Empire. Russia's authorities operated on the assumption that North Caucasians who arrived at the border without a Russian passport or with an expired one had already become Ottoman subjects.[132] According to Russia's penal code, entering the subjecthood of another empire was punishable by the "eternal expulsion from the state's domains" or, should they attempt to return to Russia, exile in Siberia.[133] The tsarist government's presumption of North Caucasian returnees' Ottoman subjecthood led to retroactive denaturalization.

Russia's denaturalization of North Caucasian muhajirs underscores the intentionality of Russia's emigration policies. Denaturalization was an exception to Russia's long-standing strategy to extend its extraterritoriality on Ottoman soil through Russian subjects. In the late Ottoman era, foreign powers secured capitulations, including broad exemptions from Ottoman law for their subjects. As James H. Meyer and Lâle Can demonstrated, Muslim migrants from Russia often invoked tsarist subjecthood to claim Russian diplomatic protection and exemption from Ottoman law when it suited them.[134] The Russian government routinely claimed jurisdiction in the Ottoman domains over migrants with varying claims to Russian subjecthood, from Cossack fugitives to Bukharan emigrants.[135] It also provided protection and intervened on behalf of North Caucasian pilgrims.[136] North Caucasian muhajirs, or any North Caucasians suspected of having settled in the Ottoman Empire, however, were one group—and by far the largest—that the Russian government almost never claimed as Russian subjects. Tsarist authorities viewed them as Russia's former and denaturalized subjects.[137]

Denaturalization as a tool of war and nation building became more common in the interwar era. Between 1921 and 1923, Soviet authorities denaturalized former tsarist subjects who resided outside the Soviet Union.[138] That rendered hundreds of thousands of Russian, Ukrainian, and other refugees stateless, prompting the League of Nations to focus its refugee efforts on the issue of statelessness and eventually create the Nansen passports, the first internationally recognized refugee travel documents. Interwar nation-states also widely practiced denationalization, especially against ethnic and religious minorities inside or outside their national borders, which, in the words of Hannah Arendt, became a "powerful weapon of totalitarian politics."[139] Some of the more egregious examples include Turkey's denationalization of overseas Armenians in 1927; Nazi Germany's revocation of German Jews' citizenship between 1933 and 1935; and anti-Jewish denationalization legislation in Poland, Romania, and Hungary in 1938.[140]

Russia's migration policies in the Caucasus were consistent in their exclusion. The government permanently excluded from Russia those whom it perceived as an unreliable frontier population, either because they resisted initial conquest, waged anticolonial struggle, or emigrated without authorization. North Caucasian Muslims were disproportionately targeted for exclusion. Russia's migration policies toward local Muslims aided the empire's expansion and were driven by the insecurity of tsarist rule in the Caucasus. It was the most difficult region for Russia to conquer and then to keep. Policies on Muslim mobility in the Caucasus resembled those in another frontier region, Crimea, but were much more restrictive than those in Russia's interior provinces in the Volga region, the Urals, and Siberia.[141] Where in Russia Muslims lived shaped their ability to emigrate, return, or keep their subjecthood.

After the Russo-Ottoman War of 1877–78, emigration from the North Caucasus subsided to a few thousand people per year. In this period, many Muslims left Russia to reunite with their muhajir families or to seek better opportunities in the Ottoman Empire. New generations of North Caucasian Muslims followed in the footsteps of their friends and relatives and typically moved to Ottoman villages with their ethnic brethren. New rounds of migration by western Circassians, Karachays, Balkars, Kabardians, Chechens,

Ingush, Avars, Dargins, Kumyks, Lezgins, and Laks occurred in 1884–87, 1890–91, 1895, 1900–1902, 1904–6, and 1912.[142] This gradual emigration from the North Caucasus to Anatolia and Syria continued into the 1920s, after the two empires ceased to exist.

The estimates of the numbers of North Caucasian refugees vary widely. The lowest number, or the starting point of any estimate, was given by Adolf P. Berzhe, a Russian Orientalist scholar and head of the Caucasus Archaeographic Commission. He tallied up the Russian military's data to count 493,194 North Caucasians, mostly western Circassians, who left Russia between 1858 and 1865. Berzhe himself considered that number to be a significant undercount.[143] On the receiving side, Salaheddin Bey, an Ottoman official in charge of counting immigrants, estimated that, between 1855 and 1866, 1,008,000 Muslims from the Caucasus and Crimea had arrived, of which 595,000 settled in the European provinces and 413,000 in Anatolia.[144] The highest number was suggested by Sultan Devlet-Giray, a Circassian historian in tsarist Russia, who estimated that 3,097,949 North Caucasian Muslims left for the Ottoman Empire in 1816–1910, including around 2,750,000 Circassians who were allegedly present in the Ottoman Empire by 1910.[145]

Likely over a million Muslims left the North Caucasus in 1858–1914. The estimate is for first-generation muhajirs who were born in the Caucasus and were expelled into or emigrated to the Ottoman Empire (see table 1).[146] Because of high mortality rates, especially during the first Circassian refugee crisis, in 1863–65, fewer than a million refugees lived to be resettled in the Ottoman Empire.[147] The precise numbers are impossible to calculate. The Russian government undercounted during the wartime chaos in 1863–64 and 1877–78. The Ottoman authorities never produced a complete tally of immigrants in all of their provinces. Nor could either government perform a comprehensive count because parts of migration were invisible to the authorities. The Russian government recorded numbers of only those Muslims who boarded the boats that it had commissioned; all refugees who hired private boats to take them off the Circassian coast were not included in the statistics.[148] After 1864, the Russian authorities knew only of those emigrants who formally notified them of their departure, which was a minority. As for the Ottoman count, upper-status North Caucasians who did not require financial aid from the state would not necessarily appear in population registers

Ethnic Group	Peak of Migration	Estimates
Western Circassians *Abzakh, Bzhedugh, Hatuqwai,* *Mamkhlegh, Natukhai,* *Temirgoi, Yegeruqwai, Zhaney,* *Shapsugh, and Ubykh*	1858–64	464,093–812,933
Eastern Circassians *Kabardians and Besleneys*	1860–61, 1890, 1895	64,000
Abkhazians and Abazins	1859–64, 1867, 1877	70,000–145,000
Nogai Tatars	1858–64	30,650–70,000
Karachays and Balkars	1884–87, 1893, 1905–06	10,000–15,756
Chechens and Ingush	1865, 1904–06, 1912	40,000–45,000
Ossetians	1860–61, 1865	5,000–10,000
Dagestanis	1877	20,000–25,000
Total		**703,743–1,187,689**

Table 1. **North Caucasian refugees, 1858–1914.**

as muhajirs. The post-Soviet conflicts aggravated our access to precious evidence. The historical archive of Abkhazia burned down amid the Georgian-Abkhazian conflict in 1992, and most holdings of the historical archive of Chechnya and Ingushetia were destroyed during the Chechen Wars of 1994–96 and 1999–2000. Archival dispossession only solidifies the erasure of generations that are no longer there.

NORTH CAUCASIAN HIJRA

Many North Caucasian Muslims viewed their migration to the Ottoman Empire as hijra. The ʿulama often taught that it was a religious duty of Muslims who found themselves in *dār al-ḥarb* (the "domain of war") to move to *dār al-islām* (the "domain of Islam"). Many heeded that call. As early as 1860, one Hajj Biy-Sultan, who had emigrated from Kabarda to the Ottoman

Empire, circulated the following appeal, in Arabic, among his Kabardian kin: "May Almighty Allah save you from what you would otherwise regret. All Circassians are heading to the Ottoman state, whereas you are staying with the infidels. . . . If you live by shariʿa law and follow all that is prescribed by the Prophet, you must immediately leave for the Ottoman state."[149]

For most North Caucasians, hijra provided the vocabulary to describe and make sense of their displacement. By performing hijra and becoming muhajirs, these Muslims placed their traumatic experiences within the revered narratives of Islamic history. After having lost their country, they conducted a journey that generations of Muslims, including the Prophet himself, made before them. Hijra promised a sense of belonging to a larger Muslim community, as thousands of other Muslims had been expelled from their ancestral territories and sought refuge in the Ottoman Empire. Hijra also offered refugees a way to speak to Ottoman officials and their new Muslim neighbors, who would have sympathy for them because they were muhajirs and became refugees in a foreign land because of their Muslim identity. The language of hijra fit both the circumstances and the needs of those who had been displaced. While evoking the sacrifices of Muslim refugees of the past, hijra captured the contemporary injustice done to the new muhajirs, the honor of their tragic journeys, and a new beginning in the Ottoman Empire.

Not all muhajirs thought of their migration to the Ottoman Empire in religious terms. Western Circassians, who were violently displaced in the early 1860s, were certainly not emigrating for religious reasons. Yet even many Circassians, especially in later Ottoman generations, remembered their displacement as *hijra* because the term covered various reasons why Muslims would leave their homeland and seek refuge elsewhere. By the nineteenth century, hijra, or refugees' choice to express their migration as such, had everything to do with Islam but not necessarily with religiosity.

The idea of Muslim migration to the Ottoman Empire as hijra faded away in the twentieth century in both diasporic literature and academic scholarship.[150] Soviet historians of the Caucasus, writing in a scholarly environment critical of religious causation, were averse to explaining migrations as motivated by faith. It had to be about the brutality of tsarism and the exploitation of mountaineers by their overlords. North Caucasian writers in the diaspora

likewise treaded carefully. The immigration of their minority communities
on account of Islam did not exactly fit into the newly secular narratives of
Turkish, Syrian, and Jordanian nations. Finally, contemporary diasporic activists rightly emphasize the violence during the expulsions of 1863–64, and
the idea of hijra, purportedly a voluntary aspiration, might seem incompati-
ble with an ethnic cleansing or a genocide. As this book shows, this is not the
case. Neither was the North Caucasian hijra voluntary, nor does it exclude
nonreligious reasons to migrate.

The North Caucasian hijra drew on a rich legacy of migration within the
Caucasus itself. Before the mass exodus to the Ottoman Empire began, Muslims who resisted Russian rule would conduct hijra within the mountains.
North Caucasians applied the term *hijra* to at least three localized migrations
in the nineteenth century. First, in the early nineteenth century many Kabardians fled the Russian annexation of Kabarda for the still independent
western Circassian territories. Known in literature as "free" or "fugitive" Kabardians (*khadzhrety*, derived from *hijra*), they settled in the lowlands on the
left bank of the Kuban River. Most of them would leave for the Ottoman
Empire together with western Circassians in the early 1860s.[151] Second, the
leadership of the Caucasus Imamate encouraged North Caucasian Muslims
to leave Russian-held territories and move to their state so they could live
under Muslim rule and shariʿa law. In the 1840s and 1850s, many Muslims
arrived in the Imamate as muhajirs, and many of them continued their hijra
to the Ottoman Empire after the Imamate collapsed.[152] Finally, the leaders of
the uprisings of 1877 in Chechnya and Dagestan also called on North Caucasian Muslims to join them as muhajirs in the territories briefly recaptured
from Russia. After tsarist authorities suppressed the uprisings, many rebels
fled to the Ottoman Empire or were exiled to Siberia.[153] Those intra-Caucasus
migrations popularized the concept of hijra as a form of anticolonial resistance. Hijra to the Ottoman Empire was not the first displacement for many
North Caucasian Muslims. Many muhajirs were refugees before they left the
Caucasus.

The direction of the hijra out of the North Caucasus was almost exclusively to the Ottoman Empire. The reasons for that were the proximity of
the Ottoman border and the shared Sunni heritage, as well as a rich history

tying the Caucasus to Anatolia. North Caucasian communities long lived
in the outer reaches of the Ottoman Empire, and their cultural awareness
of the Ottoman world vitalized the nineteenth-century migrations. For
those from the western slopes of the Caucasus, the Mediterranean world
was the terminus of the centuries-long slave trade. Circassian slaves gave
rise to an entire Mamluk dynasty that ruled Egypt between 1382 and 1517
and to generations of Ottoman governors in North Africa and Syria. Seven
of the last eight Ottoman sultans were born to a Circassian, Abkhazian, or
Georgian slave. The white slave trade wove the eastern shores of the Black
Sea into Ottoman history. For Northeast Caucasians, the Ottoman lands
were a cherished destination for their learned men. Dagestan, in particular,
was well integrated into intellectual networks of the Muslim world, and it
was a long-standing tradition of Dagestani ʿulama to seek religious and legal
office on a far larger Ottoman job market. In the last decades of Ottoman
rule, the ʿulama of Dagestani origin could be found in some of the highest-
ranking positions in the empire, such as the grand mufti (*şeyhülislam*) and
chief judge (*kazasker*) of Anatolia.[154]

The North Caucasian hijra was also tightly connected to the hajj. The
two are very different types of migration in principle: the hajj, the fifth pillar
of Islam, constitutes a voluntary time-limited journey, whereas hijra was a
permanent relocation born of persecution. The hajj, however, was the primary
source of information about the Ottoman Empire for those who considered
emigration. Those North Caucasian Muslims who traveled to Hejaz by sea
did so via Istanbul and Jeddah, and those who journeyed by land made multiple stops on their way, including in Kars, Erzurum, Diyarbakır, Aleppo,
Damascus, and Jerusalem.[155] Pilgrims' experiences of visiting holy shrines
and Sufi lodges and their interactions with like-minded hajjis shaped popular perceptions in the Caucasus of the Ottoman state as a righteous Sunni
caliphate. Many hajjis spoke highly of the Ottomans when they returned to
their mountainous villages, and, for some, the hajj influenced their decision
to conduct hijra.[156] For many, the hajj and hijra were part of the same physical
journey. Those who were issued a temporary Russian passport for the hajj
used their allotted leave of six months to a year to contemplate whether to
remain in the Ottoman Empire and to become Ottoman subjects. For ex-

ample, Kerim-Sultan, the Chechen muhajir whose story opened this chapter, had relatives who left for the Ottoman Empire as pilgrims. They stayed in Mecca for several decades as *mücavirin* (long-term pious residents of the holy cities of Mecca and Medina) and then joined Kerim-Sultan in Transjordan as muhajirs.[157] The North Caucasian hijra also changed the hajj. Mass migrations of Russia's Muslims mapped the Caucasus onto the Middle East, with hundreds of Circassian, Chechen, Avar, and Ossetian villages dotting the landscapes of Anatolia, Kurdistan, and Syria. The hajj for many Russian Muslims became more than a religious journey, however treasured that spiritual experience was. The hajj, as Kerim-Sultan's letters attested, was a journey across the expanded North Caucasian world. Pilgrims traveled from one muhajir village to another, seeing old relations, sharing the news from the tsarist Caucasus, and learning about muhajirs' lives as Ottoman subjects.

Many North Caucasians long regarded the Ottomans' "well-protected domains" to be a place of refuge. They imagined the Ottoman sultan-caliph to be a just Islamic ruler who protected Muslims inside and outside of his realm. This perception may have come from emissaries whom the Ottoman government had purportedly sent to propagandize emigration, but it also drew on sentiments long present in the Caucasus.[158] Even before mass displacement in the 1860s, Abkhazian Muslims had been emigrating to the Ottoman Empire in small groups in 1810, 1821, 1824, 1829–30, 1837, 1840–41, and 1854.[159] Likewise, elites from the Northeast Caucasus, including Imam Shamil's spiritual mentor Jamal al-Din al-Ghazi-Ghumuqi, fled Russia's defeat of the Caucasus Imamate in 1859 to the Ottoman state, where they received houses and annual salaries and had their children enrolled in the empire's best educational institutions.[160] North Caucasians expected the Ottoman government to be as welcoming to them in their time of need.

The earlier and limited familiarity with the Ottoman Empire explains why, at the early stages of migration, many Circassians called their migration, in their native language, *Istambylakw'ä* (*ИстамбылакӀуэ*, "exodus to Istanbul").[161] Much of what they knew about the empire was tied to its shining imperial capital. Muhajir expectations were usually dashed shortly after arrival. One folk song, collected by ethnographers in a Kabardian village near

Bursa in northwestern Anatolia retells muhajirs' heartbreak over losing their homeland and disappointment with their new home:

> *The Circassian banner, oh misfortune,*
> *Flutters in the wind.*
> *May Allah the great reunite us!*
> *We are going, and going,*
> *We are moving to Istanbul,*
> *Oh misfortune!*
>
> *The Istanbul houses are multistory houses,*
> *They grind flour on lower floors.*
> *For we are muhajirs.*
>
> *These villages, where we arrive,*
> *What are these villages?*
> *They wear wide-leg pants, oh misfortune.*
> *Their hats are round and ugly.*
> *For we are muhajirs. . . .*
>
> *Oh, the cursed road to Istanbul,*
> *How curved it is.*
> *Our one homeland, oh misfortune,*
> *We are leaving behind.*
> *We are going, and going,*
> *We are moving to Istanbul. . . .*
>
> *Oh, the muhajir elder, oh misfortune,*
> *With a white beard.*
> *Our muhajir affairs*
> *Do not leave to the mercy of the fate.*
> *We are going, and going,*
> *We are moving to Istanbul,*
> *Oh misfortune!*[62]

The Kabardian song captures the anguish of a long journey and fears of what lay ahead. Hijra included not only the act of migration but also that of resettlement. The next chapter tells what awaited muhajirs in the Ottoman Empire: how the Ottoman government constructed a refugee regime to accommodate incoming Muslims from Russia and how muhajirs fit into the Ottoman designs to preserve the empire.

TWO

OTTOMAN REFUGEE REGIME

IN AUGUST 1902, SEVERAL DOZEN MEN rode into the town of Pasinler near Erzurum in eastern Anatolia. The men represented the most prominent households of their kin and arrived at a meeting of a *khasa*, or Circassian council, to discuss the plight of their people who were temporarily settled in surrounding villages. After hours of deliberation, the Circassian elders agreed on the text of the petition, which they sent as a telegram to Istanbul. The petition read:

> Nine months ago, together with 700 households, we have taken refuge in the land of the compassionate Sultan to preserve our Muslim faith. We were settled in Pasinler, where we have been destitute. Our food rations were suspended after only four months, and many of our children died of hunger, while others remain sick. For the permanent place of settlement, the local governor wishes to send us to Bitlis, and the provincial governor of Syria wishes to settle us among some ruins. Because we have relatives who had previously emigrated to Syria, we beg you, in the name of Islam and justice, to free us, your poor subjects, from poverty and misery and to allow us to settle in Syria.[1]

The Ottoman Refugee Commission, a state agency in charge of settling new migrants, received this petition, written in Ottoman Turkish. The government previously hoped to find agricultural land to settle these refugees in the provinces of Van or Bitlis, near the Iranian borders, or maybe in Bursa in northwestern Anatolia. But the Circassians resisted being sent to those places and had already dispatched their own envoys to search for empty farmland in Syria, which was farther away and would require a costly relocation. The Commission, after consulting the office of the grand vizier, agreed to transport over 3,000 muhajirs from Pasinler to the Black Sea port of Trabzon and from there, by steamship, to the Mediterranean port of Beirut, as long as the Circassians would pay their own way.[2] They would then be free to move to the already existing Circassian villages in the hinterland of Syria and Transjordan. This refugee petition highlights several critical issues in Ottoman refugee resettlement: the scarcity of free agricultural land, a chronic insufficiency of funds, and the urgency to act amid a humanitarian crisis. It also demonstrates that muhajirs were not passive players in their traumatic journey, as they are often portrayed. They wrote petitions to Istanbul, lobbied local powerholders, and scouted out the land, doing everything in their power to better the terms of their settlement in their new empire.

This chapter examines how, why, and where the Ottomans had been settling North Caucasian muhajirs. Since the late 1850s, the Ottoman government had accepted several million immigrants from the Caucasus, the Balkans, Crimea, North Africa, and the Aegean islands. The Ottomans were not alone in settling masses of immigrants. Russia, the United States, Canada, Australia, and other states were also moving millions of newcomers to colonize their frontier territories. The defining characteristic of Ottoman resettlement was that most immigrants to the Ottoman Empire were refugees. The continuous arrival of Muslim refugees from Russia drove the evolution of Ottoman migration and resettlement policies.

After 1860, the Ottoman government had developed a refugee regime. A refugee regime is a set of principles, norms, and procedures governing the acceptance and resettlement of refugees. It is typically viewed as a product of the post–World War II international system. Yet, in the second half of the nineteenth century, an Islamic empire resisting European territorial conquests built a regime that provided refuge, protections, and aid for refugees, with its own channels of communication among state and nonstate actors and refugees themselves. It was a refugee regime that emerged in response to European imperialism.

This chapter retraces Ottoman history since the 1850s through the lens of refugee resettlement. In this period, the resettlement of Muslim refugees, itself a symptom of the shrinkage of the Ottoman world, was a burden, a duty, and a tool of the imperial government. The Ottoman government conceived of refugee resettlement as a way to centralize its authority and to strengthen the empire. In the aftermath of the Russo-Ottoman War of 1877–78, the Ottomans used refugees to change demographics on the empire's margins. By the time of World War I, the government's humanitarian commitment to alleviate the suffering of Muslim communities coalesced with its resolve to annihilate others.

OTTOMAN IMMIGRATION SYSTEM

The Ottoman government had long maintained an open-door policy for immigrants, irrespective of their faith, who were willing to pledge loyalty to the sultan and become his taxpaying subjects. The Ottoman Empire welcomed Jews who had been expelled from Spain in 1492, Sicily in 1493, Portugal in 1497, and Naples in 1510. The Ottomans settled Sephardi and Italian Jews primarily in Istanbul and the empire's Adriatic and Aegean ports, including Salonica.[3] In later centuries, the Ottomans accepted various Christian and Jewish communities fleeing the Russian and Habsburg domains. For example, Russia's Old Believers and Zaporozhian Cossacks had been crossing the Danube and settling in the Ottoman Balkans throughout the eighteenth and early nineteenth centuries.[4] Before the mid-nineteenth century, immigration proceeded on an ad hoc basis, with the Ottoman government offering separate deals to incoming communities. Local authorities had been in charge of settling immigrants.

The impetus for a comprehensive immigration reform came during the Crimean War of 1853–56. During the war, Crimea's Tatar, German, and Jewish communities started leaving for the Ottoman Empire.[5] Municipal and district officials in the Ottoman Balkans took charge in resettling these groups, aided by the Ministry of Trade and, in the case of refugees stranded in Istanbul, by the Ministry of Police and Istanbul's municipal administration.[6] The arrival of thousands of refugees had strained the infrastructure in the northern Balkans and the imperial capital, pushing the Ottoman government toward new legislation and a centralized administration for resettlement.

In 1857, the government issued the Immigration Law (Muhacirin Kanun-namesi), which became the cornerstone of the late Ottoman immigration legislation. The Ottomans' first comprehensive immigration act fit neatly into the ambitious Tanzimat reforms, between 1839 and 1876, designed to preserve and strengthen the Ottoman state.[7] In its landmark act, the government guaranteed all immigrants free plots of agricultural land (Article 4) and an exemption from taxes (Article 5) and military service (Article 6) for six years in the Balkans or for twelve years in Anatolia. Although spurred by the ongoing humanitarian crisis in Crimea, the Immigration Law pursued a long-term agenda. Its architects envisioned a bright future, when farmers from Europe would want to move to the sultan's thriving domains and make the Ottoman steppes and highlands bloom. The Ottomans published the text of the law in European journals, where it attracted some interest from potential Maltese, Irish, Swiss, Prussian, Alsatian, Tuscan, and Bessarabian German immigrants.[8] Even some farmers from the U.S. South enthusiastically inquired, through the Ottoman consul in New York, about the possibility of becoming Ottoman subjects and expanding their cotton-growing business into Ottoman Syria.[9]

The Ottoman Land Code (Kanun-i Arazi) of 1858 complemented the Ottoman Immigration Law. The new land code redefined relations between Ottoman subjects and their property and between the state and its rural populations. The land code divided all land in the empire into five categories: *miri* (state lands), *mülk* (freehold or privately owned property), *vakıf* or *mevkufe* (charitable endowments), *metruke* (land for public use), and *mevat* (dead lands).[10] The categories themselves were not new, but, by standardizing them, the land code provided a centralized framework governing land ownership that better suited the needs of the expanding Ottoman and global markets. The goals of the new legislation were to increase tax payments into the imperial treasury and to open new areas for economic development. The Land Code of 1858 was among the most enduring legacies of the empire, as it laid the groundwork for land legislation in Turkey and Ottoman successor states in the Balkans and the Arab world.

The Land Code proved particularly favorable to the settlement of immigrants. The government used the legislation to reassert state ownership of all *miri* land. Ottoman farmers had the right of *tasarruf*, or usufruct: they could cultivate and derive profit from the land in exchange for tax payments. Under certain conditions, they could inherit and sell the usufruct, but they did not have legal ownership of the land (Article 3). The government could abrogate one's usufruct rights if they did not till the land or did not pay taxes for three years (Article 68). The land code also eroded communal rights to the land, whether of settled or nomadic communities, prioritizing individual over collective rights (Article 8). As land pressure increased and the available fertile land became a prized commodity in the empire, the land code offered the government a legal way to dispense land in favor of muhajirs.

The new Ottoman immigration system was similar to those of Russia, the United States, and other countries that looked for "pioneers" to settle their sprawling frontier territories. In the second half of the nineteenth century, the global expansion of capitalism and the transportation revolution enabled the modern state to colonize its own territories faster, which in turn necessitated new legislation that would be favorable to immigrant farmers. Thus, Russia's Resettlement Law of 1889 guaranteed free land to all who wished to move to the tsar's vast empire in southern Russia, Central Asia, and Siberia. Similar to the Ottoman Immigration Law, Russia's Resettlement Law made a distinction between the Asian and European parts of the empire, providing more generous exemptions to settlers who moved to less desirable destinations east of the Ural Mountains. In Russia's European provinces, peasants rented the allotted land for six to twelve years before they received a permanent deed on the land and were exempt from taxation and conscription for two years. In the Asian provinces, settlers received immediate usufruct rights on the land, were exempt from conscription and taxation for three years, and could claim tax discounts for three additional years.[11]

Across the ocean, the government of the United States passed a series of Homestead Acts, between 1862 and 1930, to encourage the establishment of farming settlements, mostly west of the Mississippi River. The Homestead Acts disproportionately favored white settlers, many of whom were recent arrivals from Europe. Similar to immigrants in the Ottoman Empire, homesteaders in the United States needed to demonstrate commitment to their allotted land to secure full rights of land tenure. Thus, the act of 1862 granted a deed of title to free public domain, up to 160 acres, to a male or female "head of a family" who resided on the land for at least five years and improved the land through farming.[12]

Following the enactment of the Ottoman Immigration Law of 1857, the humanitarian crisis on Russia's Black Sea coast worsened. Many more refugees left Crimea and the Caucasus for the Ottoman Empire. In 1860, the Ottoman government created the Refugee Commission to handle the traffic of incoming Muslims from Russia. This state agency was called *Muhacirin Komisyonu* in Ottoman Turkish, which can be translated as "Immigrant," or "Migrant," or "Refugee" Commission. I prefer the latter because the Commission worked primarily with refugees. The agency's primary duties included registering muhajirs at their port of arrival, securing temporary accommodation for them, and arranging transport to their final places of residence.[13] The newly established Commission faced a test when the arrival of Circassian refugees overwhelmed Ottoman ports on the Black Sea.

FIRST CIRCASSIAN REFUGEE CRISIS, 1863–65

The expulsions of Circassians from Russia became the Ottomans' largest humanitarian crisis in the nineteenth century. Up to half a million Circassians left the Caucasus for the Ottoman shores in a matter of two years.[14] The Ottoman ports on the Black Sea were ill-equipped to handle daily arrivals of destitute refugees who had lost their homeland and loved ones and urgently required housing, food, water, and medicine to survive. Municipal authorities moved many refugees into makeshift camps, such as those in Akçakale and Sarıdere near Trabzon, with thousands of tents sprawling on the beach away from the ports. Epidemics of typhus and smallpox soon broke out among refugee populations. By December 1863, forty to sixty muhajirs were dying daily in Trabzon, a city of about 56,000 people.[15] Unauthorized burials, often on the beach, led to new rounds of disease and death. By May 1864, the daily death rate in Trabzon reached 120–150 people. In fear of contagion, bakeries in the city shut down, leading to the scarcity of bread, which meant more deaths from starvation.[16] By June 1864, 180–250 people were dying daily in Trabzon, which by then hosted 63,190 muhajirs. Meanwhile, over 110,000 refugees stayed in the environs of Samsun, where 200 people were dying daily.[17] The Ottoman chief sanitary inspector Barozzi, who visited Samsun a month earlier, wrote, "Everywhere you meet with the sick, the dying and the dead; on the threshold of gates, in front of shops, in the middle of streets, in the squares, in the gardens, at the foot of trees. Every dwelling, every corner of streets, every spot occupied by the immigrants, has become a hotbed of infection."[18] Many Circassian refugees were redirected from Trabzon, Samsun, and Istanbul to Ottoman ports in the Balkans, which also did poorly. In June 1864, Varna hosted about 70,000–80,000 refugees, all starving because of a breakdown in bread supply.[19]

The Circassian refugee crisis of 1863–65 pushed the Refugee Commission to become more efficient in registering, settling, moving, feeding, clothing, treating, and burying refugees. The discrepancy between the Immigration Law and the reality of Ottoman immigration was glaring. The Ottoman immigration legislation was designed for farmers who were willing to move to the empire and invest their capital in a homestead. The needs of refugees were drastically different from those of the voluntary immigrants that the Immigration Law had envisioned. Circassian refugees were survivors of ethnic cleansing and a harrowing journey across the sea. They could not bring cattle or household items on their boats. Most arrived penniless and severely sick and required immediate support.

To alleviate the refugee crisis, the Refugee Commission built on the existing immigration legislation and expanded its provision of aid. The Commission extended the exemption from military service for muhajirs to twenty-five years.[20] In addition to the core guarantees of free land and exemptions inherent in the Immigration Law, the Commission provided certain subsidies. In the first years since their arrival, many muhajirs received a cash allowance of 15 kuruş per adult and 7.5 kuruş per child a month, or its equivalent in wheat, considered essential for their survival.[21] When muhajirs were permanently settled on the land, local authorities pledged a one-time gift of draft cattle, ideally, a pair of oxen per household, as well as crop seeds and farming tools. The funding for the subsidies came out of the Commission's budget and provincial treasuries and was highly irregular. The Commission had always struggled to deliver sufficient aid to refugees.

OTTOMAN REFUGEE REGIME

Successive rounds of Muslim emigration from Russia prompted the formation of the Ottoman refugee regime, which had operated from 1860 until the
end of the empire. This regime guaranteed protections for Muslim refugees
entering the Ottoman domains, notably admission, resettlement, and Ottoman subjecthood. The Immigration Law of 1857 and the Land Code of 1858
formed its legislative basis. The Refugee Commission, in its several iterations,
was the chief actor in the refugee regime, but the regime encompassed the
work of the Ottoman ministries of interior, finance, trade and agriculture,
public education, public works, forestry, and charitable endowments, as well
as regional resettlement committees. The regime was one of expectations: it
created expectations by Ottoman officials of what refugee resettlement should
entail and how it would be supported by Istanbul, as well as expectations of
refuge and aid by Muslims living on the frontiers of the Ottoman world.

The legal notion of a refugee as a person fleeing wartime violence and
deserving of political protections abroad dates to the aftermath of World War
I. In 1921, the League of Nations appointed Fridtjof Nansen, a Norwegian
polar explorer and humanitarian, as the first high commissioner for refugees.
He was charged with resolving the status of Russian and Armenian refugees who were left stateless after the collapse of the Russian and Ottoman
empires.[22] The Nansen International Office for Refugees (1930–39), based in
Geneva, continued providing relief for refugees, primarily from Europe.[23]
Its responsibilities were inherited by the United Nations Relief and Reha-
bilitation Administration (1943–47), the International Refugee Organization
(1946–52), and the United Nations High Commissioner for Refugees (1950–).
In 1951, the United Nations adopted the Refugee Convention, which outlines
basic protections for refugees, as guaranteed by the Convention's signatories.[24] Since the onset of the contemporary refugee regime, the notion of a
refugee, as commonly understood in the west, has been tied to one's belonging to a nation-state.[25]

In contrast, the Ottoman refugee regime was based around the concept
of muhajir. *Hijra*, or Muslim emigration, was both its rationale and justification. The idea that religious persecution drove millions of Ottoman and
foreign Muslims into Anatolia and Syria, and that the Ottoman state was
required to protect Muslims, was the ideological core of the Ottoman refu-

gee regime. The Ottomans generally embraced the responsibility to protect and to offer permanent refuge to those who asked for it. The government accepted virtually all Muslim refugees who had entered the Ottoman domains. Similar to the contemporary refugee regime, the Ottoman one emerged in response to devastating wars and insufficient infrastructure to handle mass resettlement of refugees.

The Ottoman refugee regime was a product of rapid shrinkage of the Ottoman world, which was accompanied by mass refugee migrations. In the Ottoman house of cards, Greece was the first territory to secede and gain sovereignty. Shortly after Greece won its war of independence between 1821 and 1829, France occupied Algeria in 1830. The Ottomans then lost control over Egypt, Serbia, and the Danubian Principalities. The Russo-Ottoman War of 1877–78 marked the most devastating territorial loss in Ottoman history. The Ottoman government was forced to recognize the independence of Serbia, Montenegro, and Romania and the autonomy of Bulgaria. After the war, the European Powers openly scrambled for Ottoman territories. The Ottoman Empire lost Cyprus to Britain in 1878, Tunisia to France in 1881, Egypt to Britain in 1882, Bosnia and Herzegovina to Austria-Hungary in 1908 (de facto in 1878), Eastern Rumelia to Bulgaria in 1908 (de facto in 1885), Libya to Italy in 1911, the Dodecanese islands to Italy in 1912, and Crete to Greece in 1913 (de facto in 1908). The Balkan Wars of 1912–13 ended in the Ottoman loss of Albania, Kosovo, and Macedonia, with eastern Thrace holding out as the last Ottoman territory to the west of the Bosphorus. Within less than a century, the Ottoman Empire had lost all of its territories in Africa and nearly all of its territories in Europe.

Military defeats forced many Muslim communities to seek safety in the remaining Ottoman territories. Up to 400,000 Crimean Tatars left the Russian Empire after 1783, and approximately a million North Caucasians followed suit after 1858.[26] The war of 1877–78 displaced about 515,000 Muslims from Bulgaria and 60,000 Muslims from Russian-occupied Kars, Ardahan, and Batum in eastern Anatolia.[27] The imposition of foreign rule sparked prolonged Muslim emigration, similar to what happened in Russia's North Caucasus. Another half a million Muslims arrived in the Ottoman Empire by the end of the century, including 239,335 Muslims from Bulgaria in 1880–1900.[28] Some 45,000 more Muslims left Bulgaria in 1900–1912.[29] At least 42,000

Muslims left Thessaly, and at least 45,000 Muslims departed from Crete in 1881–1911.[30] Up to 150,000 Bosnian Muslims fled Habsburg occupation to the Ottoman Empire in 1878–1918.[31] During the wars of 1912–13, about 440,000 Ottoman Muslims fled Macedonia and western Thrace.[32] Overall, between the end of the Crimean War of 1853–56 and the outbreak of World War I, at least 2.5 million Muslims, most of whom were Ottoman and Russian subjects, fled to Ottoman Anatolia and Syria.[33]

In a reverse process, the Ottoman Empire was losing its Christian subjects to emigration. In the first half of the nineteenth century, up to 200,000 Bulgarians left for the Danubian Principalities and Russia's Bessarabia and Crimea. Between 1828 and 1896, up to half a million Armenians moved to Russia's Caucasus, and so did tens of thousands of Greeks and Assyrians.[34] Between 1875 and 1878, over 250,000 Orthodox Christians fled Ottoman Bosnia for the Habsburg Empire.[35] Meanwhile, Armenians and Levantine Christians had been moving to the Americas. Between 1885 and 1915, at least 65,000 Armenians departed for the United States and several thousand for Canada.[36] Between 1880 and 1914, about half a million Lebanese and Syrians, mostly Christians, made home in the *mahjar*, or diasporic lands. The largest destinations for Levantine emigrants were Brazil, Argentina, and the United States.[37]

In the age of consecutive territorial losses, the resettlement of Muslim refugees became critical to the Ottoman image and legitimacy. The Ottoman Empire remained the strongest sovereign Muslim state and the last globally recognized caliphate. Since the sixteenth century, the reigning Ottoman sultan held the title of caliph, a successor to the Prophet Muhammad and the leader of the Muslim community. The sultan's claim of the caliphal title was substantiated by the Ottoman dynasty's control of the holiest sites in both Sunni and Shi'i Islam—Mecca, Medina, Jerusalem, Damascus, Karbala, and Najaf—and organization of the annual hajj. Yet Ottoman rulers had not actively promoted themselves as caliphs outside Ottoman borders after the seventeenth century.[38] Only after the disastrous war of 1877–78 did Sultan Abdülhamid II revive the rhetoric of the caliphate and proclaim himself a protector of all, not just Ottoman, Muslims. The Ottomans found that, in the age of European imperialism, the idea of a global caliphate was in popular demand throughout the Muslim world, from French-occupied West Africa to

the Dutch colonies in Southeast Asia, and especially among Russia's Muslim
subjects in the Caucasus and Central Asia and Britain's Muslim subjects in
India.[39] Remarkably, the Ottoman Empire, at its weakest point regionally,
enjoyed the strongest display of its soft cultural power globally and, in short
time, became a power held in the highest esteem in many parts of the Muslim
world.[40] The idea of the caliphate was also important internally as a way to
raise the morale of the Ottoman Muslim public after a string of defeats. This is
where hijra and caliphate reinforced each other. As caliphs, Ottoman sultans
could not refuse to accept Muslim refugees without damage to the legitimacy
of the caliphate. The caliphate's reputation came to rest on the resettlement of
Muslims who fled the displacement and dispossession by European empires.
The generosity toward Muslim refugees became a way to shore up the Ottomans' internal and external image as benevolent protectors of Islam.

The Ottoman Refugee Commission evolved from an ad hoc agency, established in 1860, to a permanent directorate by World War I. Shortly after
the first Circassian refugee crisis, in 1863–65, the Ottoman government dissolved the Refugee Commission (Muhacirin Komisyonu, 1860–65), assuming that Muslim emigration from Russia would cease. Eight months later, the
government reinstated the agency as the Refugee Administration (Muhacirin
İdaresi, 1866–75), because tens of thousands of Chechen and Abkhazian refugees needed to be settled. Following the outbreak of the Russo-Ottoman War
of 1877–78, the agency was reestablished as the General Refugee Commission
(Umum Muhacirin Komisyonu, 1877–78) and then the Refugee Commission
General Administration (İdare-i Umumiye-i Muhacirin Komisyonu, 1878–
94). The agency was reorganized after the Ottoman-Greek War of 1897 as the
High Refugee Commission (Muhacirin Komisyon-ı Alisi, 1897–98) and then
the Commission for Muslim Refugees (Muhacirin-i İslamiye Komisyonu,
1899–1908).[41] Following the Young Turk Revolution of 1908, the new government abolished the agency, with its functions transferred to the Ministry of
the Interior. During the First Balkan War of 1912–13, the government reinstated it and expanded its mandate as the Directorate for the Settlement of
Tribes and Refugees (İskan-ı Aşair ve Muhacirin Müdüriyeti, 1913–16) and
then the General Directorate for Tribes and Refugees (Aşair ve Muhacirin
Müdüriyet-i Umumiyesi, 1916–22).[42] In addition to the general commission,

the Ottoman government authorized several ad hoc agencies to resettle refugees of the Italo-Ottoman War of 1911–12 and the Ottoman-Bulgarian population exchange in 1913.[43]

The Refugee Commission generated an elaborate bureaucracy that entrenched the refugee regime. The Commission was based in Istanbul and established branches in port cities, such as Trabzon and Samsun, and centers of refugee-heavy provinces, such as Sivas.[44] It built on the Immigration Law of 1857 to issue directives customized for different provinces and in response to evolving logistical challenges and budget constraints.[45] The Commission's budget was always small, accounting for a fraction of resettlement-related costs, with most expenses coming out of the budgets of imperial ministries, provincial administrations, and local municipalities. The Commission routinely sent out inspectors throughout the empire to count and register refugees and to coordinate resettlement efforts. Refugee resettlement, as an administrative process, expanded through all levels of Ottoman bureaucracy and required input from thousands of Ottoman officials: provincial, subprovincial, and district governors, treasurers, public housing administrators, and port authorities. In 1888, the government required every Ottoman province to have its own refugee resettlement committee, with subcommittees on subprovincial and district levels. Elected councillors and even members of the public served on those many committees.[46] The logistics of resettlement trickled down from the imperial capital to the smallest districts, making refugee migration a local issue for everyone; when the Refugee Commission in Istanbul discussed the arrival of another thousand refugees, local committees in Pristina and Kars worked on settling individual families.

The chief duty of the Refugee Commission was to move refugees from Ottoman cities and resettle them in the countryside. To accomplish that, the authorities needed to locate sufficient agricultural land for settlement. Provincial governors created land committees, which collected detailed information about arable land that could be reassigned to muhajirs or land that could be reclaimed from nature. In the process, the authorities were surveying and demarcating territory, establishing a record of land purchase and usage, and verifying who had been paying taxes on the land. The resettlement of thousands of muhajirs produced new knowledge about the land and people who lived on it. Through refugee resettlement, the officials in Istanbul were learning about their own empire.

The Ottoman refugee regime created expectations among Muslim populations throughout Eastern Europe, Western Asia, and North Africa that they could find refuge and be welcomed in the Ottoman Empire. Who else would protect Muslims who had lost their homeland to, and had been brutalized by, Christian armies if not the Muslim sultan? For example, many Muslims in the Caucasus knew that thousands of their kinsfolk made a life for themselves in the Ottoman domains and that the government gave them free land, and they anticipated similar treatment.[47] The Russo-Ottoman border in the South Caucasus was notoriously porous, and, throughout the late imperial period, pilgrims, merchants, and smugglers were traversing the two realms carrying news back and forth. Muhajirs, especially those whose families remained in Kabarda, Chechnya, and Dagestan, sent letters describing their lives in the Ottoman Empire and urging their loved ones to emigrate.[48]

Refugees actively communicated with the Refugee Commission by sending petitions. Petitioning the sultan was a time-honored Ottoman tradition, and, over the centuries, complaints (*şikayet*) and petitions (*arzuhal*) evolved into a distinct genre of Ottoman writing.[49] Muhajirs eagerly embraced the art of petitioning. Refugees wrote to district and provincial officials, especially on matters related to their financial aid and land allotments, and to the Refugee Commission, the grand vizier, and the sultan himself when they believed that local officials were unresponsive to their requests. Muhajirs often hired professional petitioners to compose the text of the petition in Ottoman Turkish. At an early stage of resettlement, the North Caucasian ʿulama, as the most educated members of refugee communities, would write petitions in Arabic. Petitions could be individual or communal. Communal petitions, signed by male heads of households, supposedly amplified the importance of muhajirs' requests in the eyes of the authorities. For example, the petition from Circassians in Pasinler that opened this chapter claimed to represent 700 households, or several thousand refugees. The telegraph, which became common by the early twentieth century, further proliferated the volume of petitions, as refugees could communicate their requests with greater speed. The culture of petitioning reinforced the refugee regime, particularly refugee expectations of their orderly settlement and aid, which often remained insufficient. The regime allowed space for interaction and negotiation, giving muhajirs hope that they could better their lot and that the authorities were listening to them.

The refugee regime both nourished and was nourished by the culture of charity. If there was something that we could call Ottoman humanitarianism, it was most explicit in the Ottoman society's provision of aid to Muslim muhajirs.[50] From the onset of Circassian displacement, the governments of Sultan Abdülmecid I (r. 1839–61) and Sultan Abdülaziz (r. 1861–76) cultivated broad public support for refugee resettlement. In 1860, the government instructed provincial, subprovincial, and district governors to circulate a call for charity toward Circassian and Nogai Tatar muhajirs throughout the empire.[51] The royal family led by example, donating 800,000 kuruş for resettlement, and the sultan's court collected 100,000 kuruş.[52] In 1864, Hoşyar Kadın, the Circassian mother of Isma'il Pasha of Egypt, donated 300,000 kuruş to Circassian refugee relief; one of the khedive's wives, 150,000 kuruş; the Ottoman grand mufti, 25,000 kuruş; and several 'ulama, 15,000 kuruş.[53] The massive fundraising operation in the Ottoman Empire, in which the old Ottoman-Circassian elites were actively involved, also spurred a fundraising campaign in London, with the establishment of the Circassian Aid Committee in 1864. The organization held among its members former British diplomats in the Ottoman Empire and Russia. It distributed collected funds among Circassian refugees in Istanbul.[54]

The government of Sultan Abdülhamid II (r. 1876–1909) promoted charity for Muslim refugees as both a religious obligation of good Muslims and a patriotic duty of good Ottoman subjects.[55] The Ottoman elites donated money for the resettlement of muhajirs to fulfill their charitable responsibility and to demonstrate their commitment to the imperial cause. Ordinary Ottoman subjects, Muslims and non-Muslims, also donated money, provisions, and their labor for the resettlement of North Caucasian refugees. Some aid was certainly coerced by provincial officials, but much was genuine charity. In 1897, the government instituted a new stamp for official correspondence and a lottery, the proceeds from which went to refugee aid. These fundraising initiatives were meant to instill in the general public the sense of collective duty toward refugees.[56]

During the Russo-Ottoman War of 1877–78, several semi- and nongovernmental organizations provided refugee relief. The Refugee Charity Commission (Muhacirin İane Komisyonu), founded in 1877 as part of Istanbul's municipal administration, fundraised for refugee relief. The Refugee Aid Society (Muhacirine Muavenet Cemiyeti) was established in 1878 by members of the first Ottoman parliament and then gradually merged into the Refugee Commission. It sent aid workers to help refugees at Istanbul's Sirkeci pier. In 1878, foreign diplomats established the International Committee for Refugee Assistance, which was chaired by an Austro-Hungarian consul and included twelve European consuls and foreign reporters, merchants, and bankers who resided in the Ottoman Empire.[57] Finally, the Ottoman Red Crescent, founded in 1868, contributed significant humanitarian relief. During the wars of 1912–13, the Red Crescent set up soup kitchens and hospitals for refugees and carried out mass vaccination campaigns against chickenpox.[58]

The Ottoman refugee regime came with a new form of legal identification. Previously, the Ottomans categorized their subjects by faith, residence, or tribal affiliation. *Muhajir* became a new administrative category that applied to all refugees who had registered with the Commission.[59] The government typically specified their regional origin, for example Kars muhajirs or Cretan muhajirs, or their ethnicity, for example Circassian muhajirs or Laz muhajirs. The government often determined the type of settlement based on muhajirs' cultural background, skills, and characteristics ascribed to them.[60] The authorities used *muhajir* as a separate administrative category partly to denote the newcomers' exemptions and subsidies. For example, population registers compiled for taxation purposes could list residents in four columns: Muslims, Christians, Jews, and muhajirs. The term *muhajir* even led to a counter-term: the "old communities" (*ahali-i kadime*), which the authorities applied to native populations in provinces with many refugees. The status of *muhajir* outgrew its utilitarian purpose and lasted beyond the expiration of one's exemptions. The authorities had referred to some communities as muhajirs for decades. Likewise, Muslim refugees readily used this term imbued with a powerful religious and historical legacy. Muhajir became a social identity in its own right, especially in places where refugees formed a community conspicuously distinct from host populations. Throughout the Ottoman and post-Ottoman world, second- and third-generation North Caucasian, Bosnian, Bulgarian, and Cretan Muslims proudly called themselves muhajirs.

The Ottoman refugee regime coexisted with the immigration system. The immigration of non-Muslims proceeded throughout the late Ottoman era, although in small numbers. For example, groups of Austrian and German immigrants arrived in the 1860s and 1870s.[61] At the time, *muhacir* was the main term in Ottoman Turkish to describe a migrant, but Ottoman authorities used it to refer primarily to Muslim refugees. The standard Ottoman practice in describing non-Muslim immigrants was to refer to their national origin or faith. The Ottomans governed their Christian and Jewish communities through the millet system, a patchwork of political and cultural autonomies for non-Muslim subjects, which was fully institutionalized only in the nineteenth century.[62] Correspondingly, Ottoman officials categorized non-Muslim immigrants according to their faith and the millet that they would join in the empire.[63]

The core Ottoman legislation on immigration, dating back to the late 1850s, did not distinguish between non-Muslim immigrants and Muslim refugees, which is why Ottoman migration policies have traditionally been studied as one, if highly fragmented, system.[64] The distinctions emerged as the refugee regime evolved. The immigration of non-Muslims, and the award of free land to them, depended on prior negotiations of the terms of their settlement with the Ottoman government. For example, in 1864, the Ottoman government declined the immigration of Swiss farmers because it was overwhelmed by the first Circassian refugee crisis.[65] Those non-Muslims who arrived without prior authorization from the Ottoman government could not benefit from the Ottoman Immigration Law of 1857. Non-Muslim immigrants also relied on their own organizations for assistance. A notable example is the private Jewish Colonization Association, founded in 1891, which helped Jewish immigrants to establish agricultural settlements in Ottoman Palestine and Anatolia. Headquartered in London, it set up an office in Istanbul in 1910 to aid Jewish immigration from Russia.[66] In contrast, the arrival of Muslim refugees was more haphazard and unplanned, but they were all but guaranteed admission and were settled by the Ottoman Refugee Commission, which provided additional refugee-only subsidies.

Muhajirs had a straightforward path to naturalization as Ottoman subjects. According to the Law of Ottoman Nationality (Tabiiyet-i Osmaniye Kanunnamesi) of 1869, foreign subjects could obtain Ottoman nationality after having lived in the Ottoman domains for five consecutive years (Article 3).[67] The notions of nationality and citizenship had not been fully elaborated and extricated from subjecthood in the Ottoman Empire or, for that matter, in Russia.[68] For the purposes of naturalization and border crossing, they were the same. To naturalize refugees, the Ottoman government applied the Immigration Law of 1857, which specified that muhajirs must take an oath of allegiance to the sultan before receiving any benefits from the state (Article 1). Refugees needed help from the state soon after their arrival; hence, they were effectively treated as Ottoman subjects the moment they registered with the Refugee Commission and received their first benefits. Furthermore, the Ottoman government wished to prevent muhajirs from ever claiming Russian subjecthood to avoid Russia's interference in its resettlement affairs and to forestall return migration. Neither the Ottomans nor the Russians allowed dual subjecthood. In the 1860s, most muhajirs arrived without any Russian documents, and the Ottoman government assumed them to not have been Russian subjects or to be denaturalized ones. Those who arrived with limited-term Russian passports usually had their passports confiscated by the Refugee Commission before resettlement and admission into Ottoman subjecthood.[69] By the early twentieth century, the Ottoman government routinely insisted that Muslims obtain Ottoman visas prior to their departure from Russia.[70] In practice, Muslims from Russia continued to be accepted and registered by the Refugee Commission, regardless of their documentation.[71]

GEOGRAPHY OF RESETTLEMENT

The Ottoman government opened up much of the empire to refugee resettlement. North Caucasian muhajirs moved into every province in Anatolia, the Balkans, the Levant, and Iraq. The geographic exceptions to their resettlement were few. The Ottomans did not send muhajirs to Yemen, Tunisia, or Libya, likely because of the high transportation costs and the environmental conditions that the mountaineers were unlikely to survive.[72] The Porte settled relatively few North Caucasians in Lebanon and Palestine, which were governed under the special administrative status of mutasarrifate, respectively of Mount Lebanon (after 1861) and Jerusalem (after 1872), to avoid European diplomats protesting the burden of Muslim refugees on local Christian populations.[73] Ottoman authorities generally avoided sending North Caucasians to eastern Anatolia, as Russia insisted on not settling muhajirs close to its borders.[74]

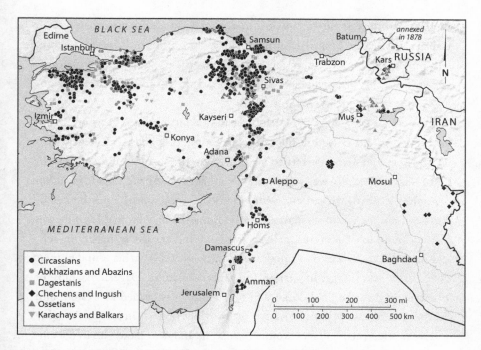

Map 3. **North Caucasian villages in Anatolia, the Levant, and Iraq.**

Map 3 illustrates the geography of North Caucasian refugee resettlement in Ottoman Anatolia, the Levant, and Iraq. Every dot represents a village founded by muhajirs between the late 1850s and 1914. This map is based on my archival research and also builds on the painstaking work of North Caucasian scholars and activists who generously shared with me their lists of villages or made their data publicly available.[75] The map shows over 1,100 villages, including at least 706 Circassian (western and eastern), 199 Abkhazian and Abazin, 98 Dagestani, 54 Chechen and Ingush, 43 Ossetian, and 24 Karachay and Balkar villages. About a hundred of those villages are ethnically mixed, shared by several North Caucasian communities; over the years, many became home to Turkish, Arab, and Kurdish residents too. These are villages that survived into the twentieth century. Many others failed or were abandoned in the late Ottoman era. For example, before 1878, North Caucasians lived in several hundred villages in the Balkans, spread north from Salonica to Macedonia, Kosovo, and southern Serbia and then east across

Bulgaria. In the last fifty years of Ottoman rule, in addition to these North Caucasian villages, hundreds of new villages of Crimean, Bosnian, Cretan, and Bulgarian Muslims sprang up along river valleys, on mountain plateaus, and in the ruins of abandoned desert cities. They turned the Ottoman domains into an empire of refugees.

The ethnic geography of North Caucasian resettlement reflects when and how refugees had arrived in the Ottoman Empire. By and large, new groups of refugees requested to be settled near their co-ethnic communities. Western Circassians, especially well represented by Shapsugh, Abzakh, and Natukhai communities, came by sea and were resettled throughout the northern Balkans and northern and western Anatolia. Kabardians, who had lived deeper in the Caucasus Mountains, arrived overland and settled primarily in central Anatolia and the Syrian interior. Abkhazians and Abazins founded their own closely knit villages in western and central Anatolia. Dagestanis, most of whom arrived in the final decades of the empire, also settled in western and central Anatolia. Ossetians moved to the province of Sivas in central Anatolia and set up clusters of villages around Sarıkamış and near Lake Van in the empire's east. Chechens settled in central Anatolia, Kurdistan, and Transjordan. Turkic-speaking Karachays and Balkars established villages in western and central Anatolia.

The original intention of the Ottoman government was to build model settlements for muhajirs. The authorities approved the first model village in Mecidiye (now Medgidia, Romania) for Crimean Tatars in 1856 and planned to construct more across the empire.[76] These preplanned villages and towns would have wide streets, tidy houses, schools, and mosques in each neighborhood. The model settlements, like the empire's newest populations, were meant to represent a new, modern Ottoman state.[77] The idea of model settlements was in vogue at the time. Muhammad 'Ali's dynasty was busy building model villages for Egyptian peasants.[78] In the Ottoman case, model settlements came out of the same assumption that undergirded the Immigration Law of 1857, namely that immigration would be voluntary and orderly. The high numbers of refugees and a lack of funding led the Ottomans to abandon the idea of model settlements in the 1860s. Very few North Caucasian muhajirs moved into villages that had been designed or built in advance for them.[79]

The Ottoman government developed three models of resettlement for

Muslim refugees. These models differed in how much freedom refugees enjoyed in selecting their settlement locations. The first model was direct settlement by the Refugee Commission, in coordination with provincial and district officials, and allowed little input from refugees as to where they wanted to go. The Ottomans followed this heavy-handed approach during the first Circassian refugee crisis, in 1863–65, to deal with a massive number of refugees whom the government needed to resettle expeditiously. Most refugees who ended up in the Balkans had been settled under this model, as described in chapter 3. Some muhajirs were directed to empty areas to establish new villages, but most moved into the already existing Muslim or Christian villages.[80] The second model was semidirect settlement, wherein the government identified regions with sufficient agricultural land, and refugees had some freedom to choose locations for their villages. This model was implemented, for example, across the Levant after the second Circassian refugee crisis, in 1878–80, as elaborated in chapter 4. Under this model, muhajirs typically established clusters of monoethnic villages next to each other; mixed settlements, especially with non-Muslims, were rare. The third model was the most flexible one and involved a negotiation between refugees and the government. This model was characteristic of migrations before 1860 and after 1880, when the state could accommodate requests of smaller groups of incoming refugees. This model of resettlement also appealed to upper-status muhajirs, who had the means to wait and the confidence to make demands from the state about their future. The Khutat family, as revealed in chapter 5, negotiated with the authorities and relocated several times in search of an ideal settlement.

OTTOMAN RESETTLEMENT STRATEGY

The geography of Muslim resettlement was not random because the refugee regime served the needs of the Ottoman government. Between the late 1850s and World War I, the Ottoman government pursued several long-term objectives, which occasionally overlapped. The government was not the sole or uniform agent in the resettlement process. The Refugee Commission, its regional branches, provincial and district governors, and muhajir leadership all haggled over places of settlement.

In the late 1850s to the mid-1860s, the Ottoman government did not have a "master plan" as to where to resettle muhajirs. The government was scrambling to respond to daily arrivals of thousands of Crimeans and Circassians and an escalating humanitarian disaster in the Black Sea ports. The guiding principles of resettlement were an availability of land and expediency, namely how quickly and how cheaply the refugees could be moved from the coast to interior districts. This is why the majority of Circassian refugees who had arrived in boats by 1864 settled in coastal areas (between Ordu and Sinop, Sulina and Burgas, and Istanbul and Çanakkale) and adjacent interior areas (the provinces of Trabzon, Sivas, Kastamonu, Hüdavendigar, and Aydın in Anatolia and the provinces of Salonica, Edirne, and Danube in the Balkans). Most of those areas were predominantly Muslim, while the southern districts of Danube Province had a Bulgarian majority and the provinces of Edirne, Salonica, and Aydın had large Greek and Bulgarian populations.

The Ottoman government's primary resettlement objective was economic. The tsar's rebels were meant to become the sultan's peasants and boost the empire's agriculture. This general and relatively vague agenda underlaid refugee resettlement throughout the late Ottoman period.[81] The government invested an enormous amount of money into resettlement. Between 1856 and 1862, expenses for resettling Crimean and Nogai Tatar and Circassian refugees may have reached 700 million kuruş, including at least 200 million kuruş for shipping expenses, which roughly correlates to the Ottoman budget deficit at the time.[82] These massive expenses predated the peak of Circassian migration in 1863–64. The Ottoman government borrowed money for refugee-related expenditure at a time of severe fiscal crises, expecting muhajirs to be a long-term investment. Muhajirs would cultivate wheat, barley, and corn, and, with time, export their agricultural surplus, start growing cash crops, and pay taxes to the state.

The economic objective is accentuated by the rural nature of resettlement. The government discouraged North Caucasians from moving into Ottoman cities. To qualify for subsidies, one needed to register with the Commission, which then settled muhajirs almost exclusively in the countryside, legally tying them to their new land. According to the Ottoman Immigration Law of 1857, muhajirs could sell their land plots or, to be precise, the usufruct on the state-owned land only after having tilled the land for twenty years (Article 8). The requirement was lowered to ten years in 1887.[83] Leaving the land before the prescribed term resulted in the government's appropriation of the land, along with all buildings on it, and the cessation of all subsidies and exemptions (Article 9). Some upper-status North Caucasians with independent wealth moved to Ottoman cities, forfeiting all exemptions and subsidies guaranteed through the Ottoman refugee regime. The government also required muhajirs, as other Ottoman subjects, to apply for *mürur tezkeresi*, or documents of passage, to leave their district and travel within the empire.[84] The predominantly rural and agricultural resettlement, with limitations on mobility, was a distinctive feature of the Ottoman refugee regime.

Under the dual framework of the Immigration Law of 1857 and the Land Code of 1858, the government committed to giving muhajirs empty lands (*arazi-i haliye*) for free. This land typically included arable land in the *miri* category, but it was rarely fertile land and was meant to be improved through muhajir labor. Muhajirs sometimes received land in the *mevat* category, which denoted "dead," agriculturally unusable land. The government would assign muhajirs *mevat* plots precisely so that muhajirs would drain the swamps or irrigate arid lands, thus reclaiming new arable land for the empire and boosting regional economies.[85] The main value of muhajirs in this resettlement objective was their physical labor.

This ambitious project of reinvigorating Ottoman economy through refugee resettlement did not work as well as the government had hoped it would. Many mountaineers never worked in agriculture, and those who did were used to growing specific crops at a higher elevation. Turning almost everyone into farmers and expecting them to succeed in their new environments, including wetlands and semideserts, was always a tall order. Furthermore, the chronic underfunding of the Refugee Commission and the mismanagement of existing funds did not allow many refugee villages to reach their full economic potential. In 1866, six-year tax exemptions in the Balkans were reduced to three-year ones.[86] In 1875, the Ottoman government declared a default on its massive debt and subsequently diminished contingent subsidies in financial aid. By 1878, muhajirs arriving in Anatolia received exemptions from military service for twenty-five years and from taxation for ten years. In 1889, the exemptions were reduced to, respectively, six and two years.[87] By the end of the Ottoman era, few North Caucasian villages produced cash crops, generated a surplus of cereals for export, or paid their tax obligations in full.

The Ottoman government's second resettlement objective was to bring nomadic territories under state control. Starting in the 1860s, the government had settled North Caucasians near nomads' lands and along traditional nomadic routes. For the Ottomans, the lands inhabited by Turkic and Kurdish nomads, Arab bedouin, and the Druze were part of their internal frontier, which they could not quite control.[88] The settlement of muhajirs necessitated surveying the land, building roads, and bringing state officials and tax collectors there. The muhajirs were expected to keep nomadic populations in check and improve security in these outlying regions, which would in turn attract new immigrants and bring more lands under cultivation.[89] The Ottoman authorities readily used refugees as settlers to extend Ottoman sovereignty in the empire's remote provinces.[90] Confronted with massive territorial losses, the Ottoman government was increasingly concerned about territoriality and sought a greater control over the empire's land, resources, and people.[91] By standing their ground against nomads, refugees helped to solidify the government's hold over Ottoman territories. The chief value of muhajirs in this resettlement strategy was their fighting capability. The government occasionally placed North Caucasians to guard the external frontiers, too, to deter foreign military incursions, for example, along Ottoman borders with Serbia and Russian-held Bessarabia.[92] In the empire's final decades, the Ottoman government may have thought of North Caucasians in the Levant as their line of defense against potential Arab uprisings, or at least this is how Russian and British diplomats understood the Ottoman resettlement strategy.[93]

The settlement of muhajirs on nomadic territories was also part of the Ottoman "civilizing mission." Refugee farmers were supposed to transform not only nomads' lands but also nomads' behavior. As European governments were disparaging the Ottoman Empire for being backward and uncivilized, urban Ottoman administrators adopted the same patronizing rhetoric toward its nonsettled and semi-settled populations.[94] "Civilizing" nomadic populations meant sedentarizing and taxing them. The resettlement of Muslim refugees accelerated that process. For example, in Transjordan the risk of losing their land to muhajirs prompted the bedouin to formally register their land with state land registry offices, till the land, and pay tax on it.

The resettlement strategy that pitted Muslim refugees against nomads can be traced on the map of refugee villages (map 3). By the 1880s, the "muhajir belt" had stretched through the Ottoman provinces of Trabzon, Sivas, Adana, Aleppo, and Damascus. It included several hundred villages, which ran in the north-south line from Samsun on the Black Sea coast, through Amasya and Tokat, to the Uzunyayla plateau, down to the Mediterranean coast near Adana, then east toward Aleppo, and down through Hama and Homs toward the Golan Heights and Amman.[95] In many areas, the land-tilling, armed muhajirs formed a physical buffer between the settled populations and nomads. In the Levant, the muhajir belt had a clear environmental dimension, too: muhajirs settled near precious wells on the western edge of the Syrian desert. Their lands separated the fertile lands of Levantine peasants to the west from the arid desert of bedouin to the east.

The idea of moving populations to specific locations for the benefit of the state was not new in Ottoman history. Muslim refugee resettlement in the nineteenth century built on older Ottoman practices. One of them was *sürgün*, or forced relocation of sedentary and nomadic communities, which the Ottoman government used to colonize parts of the Balkans and Anatolia in the early Ottoman centuries. Those subjected to *sürgün* were exempted from taxes for two years.[96] When the Ottomans took Constantinople in 1453, they had repopulated it with Christian, Muslim, and Jewish communities through *sürgün*.[97] The meaning of *sürgün* has evolved since then. In modern Turkish, *sürgün* denotes "banishment" or "exile." Many Circassians in Turkey refer to the expulsions of 1863–64 from the Caucasus as a *sürgün*.[98] Another Ottoman practice was *derbend*, or the settlement of nomadic communities along roads and mountain passes. For bringing security to those areas, the nomads would receive salaries and be exempt from taxation.[99] Likewise, nineteenth-century muhajirs were expected to protect the empire's infrastructure, typically against the nomads. The arrival of refugees broadly coincided with the construction of railways throughout the empire. Notably, the very first model refugee settlement of Mecidiye lay on the first completed Ottoman railway, connecting Köstence and Boğazköy (Cernavodă, Romania).[100] As railways, paired with telegraph lines, stretched for hundreds of miles through sparsely populated territories, the government placed refugee villages along the railways so that muhajirs could protect them against nomadic raids and rural banditry. The Refugee Commission helped to set up muhajir villages along the Anatolian Railway, the empire's busiest railway, which connected Istanbul to Ankara in 1892 and to Konya in 1896. Along its route 30,000 muhajirs were settled, and some of them worked on constructing the railway.[101] Likewise, the Hejaz Railway, which connected Damascus to Medina by 1908, went through several Circassian and Chechen villages. The North Caucasian gendarmerie, or *zaptiye*, were tasked with protecting the northern section of the railway.[102]

The defeat in the Russo-Ottoman War of 1877–78 changed how the Ottoman government perceived the empire's demographics. After the war, the Ottomans were compelled to sign two humiliating treaties with Russia, first the Treaty of San Stefano in March 1878 and, following its revision by the European Powers, the Treaty of Berlin in July 1878. The two treaties entrenched ethnoreligious demographics as a legitimizing principle of statehood and border delineation in the Balkans.[103] Pained negotiations with the Europeans affirmed to the Ottomans the importance of counting people to stake out territorial claims. The Ottoman government was used to conducting population surveys for taxation purposes, but a demographic census now emerged as a powerful tool of foreign policy and military strategy.[104] The new Balkan nation-states, backed by the European empires, claimed territory based on the language and faith of people inhabiting those lands, and the Ottoman government started collecting various data on its frontier populations.

The final Ottoman resettlement objective was sectarian. While glimpses of sectarian designs flashed in Ottoman Cilicia and Bulgaria even earlier, the sectarian rationale in resettlement became a comprehensive strategy during the Hamidian rule.[105] The mass arrival of Muslim refugees from the Balkans allowed the Ottomans to put the lessons of 1878 into practice, altering demographic ratios in frontier regions. After 1878, the Ottoman government strategically settled many muhajirs in provinces with large non-Muslim populations. By changing demographic ratios in favor of Muslims, the Hamidian government sought to prevent territorial losses and counter any future claims by irredentist movements.[106] In this resettlement strategy, the value of muhajirs was their Muslim identity, which the government regarded as a guarantee of their loyalty to the Ottoman state. Thus, the government settled muhajirs along the Dardanelles and on the eastern side of the Sea of Marmara to reduce the Greeks' share of population on western Anatolia's coastline.[107] Likewise, many muhajirs were directed to villages around Istanbul in order to guarantee a Muslim majority in the vicinity of the imperial capital, which itself became a Muslim-majority city only in the 1880s, or over four centuries after the Ottoman conquest in 1453.[108]

While the Treaty of Berlin of 1878 impressed on the Ottomans the political value of demography in frontier provinces, it placed constraints on where the Ottomans could settle incoming Muslim refugees for that very reason. The Ottoman government was forced to agree "not to employ irregular troops, such as Bashi-Bazouks and Circassians, in the garrisons at frontiers" of the newly created province of Eastern Rumelia (Article 15). The Porte was also urged to implement reforms "in the provinces inhabited by Armenians" and to guarantee their security "against the Circassians and the Kurds" (Article 61). This stipulation effectively cautioned the Ottoman government against directing new groups of North Caucasian muhajirs to the "six Armenian provinces" (Vilayat-ı Sitte) in the empire's east. The treaty implied that Russia and other European Powers considered Muslims, and especially Muslim refugees, to be a threat to non-Muslims, an idea that lived on within and beyond Ottoman borders after 1878.[109] Nevertheless, the Ottoman government quietly settled some North Caucasian muhajirs near Armenian communities to increase the share of Muslim population in those areas: for example, near Erzurum in 1894 and around Muş in 1902 and 1906.[110]

Between 1878 and 1908, the Ottoman government positioned the Ottoman Empire as a refuge for Muslims persecuted in neighboring countries. The Porte stressed that it was the sultan-caliph's responsibility to protect fellow Muslims from injustice. For example, a palace report in 1884 proclaimed that Muslim muhajirs were "taking refuge under the protection of the exalted Caliph. In this way, the people of Islam are drawn under the royal wings."[111] In 1887, the government criticized injustices that Muslims faced in neighboring states and called on Muslims to move to the Ottoman Empire. It noted that it was the Ottoman state's "sacred duty" to accept Muslims who faced oppression under foreign rule in the Balkans.[112] The rhetoric of the Hamidian government was different from the Tanzimat-era Immigration Law of 1857, which invited all and any immigrants regardless of their creed. Thirty years later, the government explicitly courted Muslims.

The Ottoman government's policies toward Jewish immigration illustrate the gap between the refugee regime for Muslims and the immigration system for non-Muslims. While foreign Muslims were welcome in the Ottoman state, the Hamidian regime tightened its policies for non-Muslims wishing to immigrate. By the 1880s, Zionist leaders attempted to negotiate with the Ottoman authorities the immigration of Jews fleeing pogroms in Russia. As early as 1881, the Ottoman government objected to mass Jewish immigration in Palestine.[113] In a series of decrees in 1884, 1887, and 1888, the Ottoman government reaffirmed its commitment to accept immigrants but ruled out compact settlement of the same community in one region.[114] In practice, those pronouncements referred to Palestine, as Russian Jews continued arriving in the empire.[115] The Ottoman authorities likely sought to prevent the emergence of a new national question, akin to the Bulgarian or Armenian ones, and one that would likewise enjoy European support and invite foreign interference in governing the Levant.[116] The difference in treating Muslim and non-Muslim migrants came down to preserving Ottoman rule and the empire's territorial integrity. The Ottoman government could use the arrival of Muslim refugees to reinforce imperial rule in multiple ways. In contrast, by the late nineteenth century, the mass immigration of non-Muslims was politically fraught and could jeopardize Ottoman sovereignty.

The Ottoman Empire had never been more Muslim than in its final decades. Despite the empire's loss of half of its territories in Europe, the Ottoman population increased by 40 percent, from 19.9 to 27.3 million, between 1875 and 1895.[117] The Muslim population grew faster than the Christian one, in part thanks to incoming Muslim refugees. The Muslim share of the empire's population rose from 60 percent in the 1820s to 68 percent in the 1870s, to 76 percent in the 1890s, and to 81 percent in 1914.[118] This demographic change led to an ideological shift in how Ottoman officials thought about the empire's population. The Ottoman subjects of Christian and Jewish faith were becoming "minorities," whereas those of Muslim faith a "majority," both of which were new ways to conceive of the empire's subjects.[119] The empire's Muslim population was now a central building block for the new Ottoman nation. Likewise, Anatolia was being reimagined as the Muslim homeland and cultural core of the Ottoman Empire.[120]

Religion was a central category in the Ottoman refugee regime. The Ottoman open-door policy for Muslim refugees was consistent over the years because of the Ottoman state's self-vision as a refuge for Muslims. For North

Caucasians, their Muslim identity also helped them to integrate in Ottoman society. Ethnically and linguistically distinct from their host communities, North Caucasians relied on their faith to relate to and be accepted by other Ottoman Muslims. By the 1900s and 1910s, ethnicity became another way to categorize difference in the Ottoman Empire. Previously championed by Ottoman non-Muslims, it gained traction among the empire's Muslim elites. Many Ottoman Muslim intellectuals now viewed the Turkish identity as a foundation for the national one. Most notably, the Committee of Union and Progress (CUP), a secret revolutionary organization that instigated the Young Turk Revolution of 1908, espoused commitments to both Islam and Turkism, or Turkish nationalism.[121] The CUP—whose four founders were two Kurds, an Albanian, and a Circassian—aimed first and foremost to preserve the Ottoman state.[122] For many Ottoman revolutionaries, Turkism was an effective domestic propaganda tool. Similarly, Pan-Islamism and Pan-Turkism, or movements for the political unity of, respectively, Muslims and Turkic people, were propaganda tools of Ottoman foreign policy.[123]

The Ottoman refugee regime facilitated an increasing overlap between Islam and Turkishness. After 1878, most muhajirs were Turkish-speaking Muslims from the Balkans. North Caucasian muhajirs, understandably, would have been excluded from the notion of Turkishness, were it solely based on language. But the categories of Muslim, Turkish, and Ottoman were intricately intertwined throughout the last Ottoman decades. What mattered the most to Ottoman authorities was that North Caucasians were not implicated in others' ethnoseparatist movements, which made their allegiance to the state all the more valuable. By the 1910s, many early Turkish nationalists were of Circassian and Abkhazian origin.

Administrative categories of migration evolved in the late Ottoman era. By the late nineteenth century, Ottoman bureaucrats sometimes used the term *muhacir* for non-Muslims.[124] Another migration term was *mülteci*, which the Ottomans had used for political exiles, including non-Muslims, such as Polish and Hungarian revolutionaries who arrived in the Ottoman Empire after the suppressed European uprisings of 1848.[125] Its administrative usage, like that of *muhacir*, changed over time, and officials employed it to describe various migrants. In 1913, the Ottoman government clarified that the distinction between *muhacir* and *mülteci* was in how one's nationality was disavowed.[126] *Mülteci* referred to those who applied for Ottoman naturalization while still holding foreign nationality. *Muhacir* described those who arrived in the Ottoman domains with their nationality canceled by their former state.[127] Under this new administrative definition, *muhacir* continued to be applied to Muslim refugees from the Russian Empire because they were correctly assumed to be denaturalized Russian subjects.[128] The Ottoman officialdom was embracing evolving international norms on immigration, wherein one's migrant status was determined by one's individual nationality, not collective belonging to a religious community.

The Balkan Wars of 1912–13, which all but ejected the Ottomans from the Balkans, reaffirmed the primacy of demography in contesting frontier regions.[129] The Ottoman government insisted that new Muslim refugees from the Balkans settle around Edirne in eastern Thrace and not move to Anatolia, in order to prop up the Muslim majority in this remaining Ottoman sliver of land in Europe.[130] The Ottoman defeat in the Balkan Wars further stoked anti-European and anti-Christian sentiments among the ruling elites and helped to increase support for the CUP. The CUP led a coup in January 1913 and then suppressed its opposition after the assassination of its grand vizier in June 1913.

Under the leadership of the Three Pashas in 1913–18, the CUP engaged in explicit demographic engineering throughout the empire.[131] The resettlement of Muslim refugees featured heavily in the CUP's strategy. In 1913, the CUP adopted new immigration regulations and reestablished the Refugee Commission as the Directorate for the Settlement of Tribes and Refugees. This well-resourced organization coordinated the twin tasks of resettling refugees and forcibly sedentarizing nomads, and also gathered intelligence on various ethnic and religious communities in Ottoman Anatolia. It used these data to determine where to settle Muslim refugees and nomads.[132] The CUP further relied on *Teşkilat-ı Mahsusa* (Ott. Tur. for "special organization"), a clandestine unit established in 1913. The organization prepared logistics for deporting Ottoman Armenians. It recruited from various Muslim groups, with North Caucasian muhajirs well represented among its command and rank-and-file agents.[133]

In 1915, the CUP enacted the Relocation and Resettlement Law (*Sevk ve İskan Kanunu*, better known as *Tehcir Kanunu*), which provided a legal framework for deporting Ottoman Christians. In the ensuing genocide, the Ottoman government annihilated up to 1.5 million Armenians, and several hundred thousand Greeks and Assyrians.[134] Imperial troops, paramilitary forces, and many Ottoman Muslim citizens were responsible for the violence. North Caucasian gangs in the east committed their share of atrocities: for example, Circassian bandits massacred Armenian deportees in Diyarbakır, and Chechen muhajirs around Ra's al-'Ayn killed Armenians in desert detention camps.[135]

The processes of *hijra/hicret* and *tahjīr/tehcir* complemented each other. Today, ethnic cleansing and refugee relief are imagined as polar opposites: one is a war crime by a regime gone bad, and the other is a humanitarian good provided by charitable benefactors. In reality, they often overlap. In the 1910s, the displacement and dispossession of Christians and the immigration and resettlement of Muslim refugees were two sides of the same coin.[136] Between 1914 and 1916, the CUP evolved the legal notion of *emval-i metruke*, or abandoned property, to appropriate lands and buildings left by deported Ottoman Christians for their eventual transfer to others.[137] Many Ottoman Armenians, Greeks, and Assyrians were deported to be murdered, and Ottoman Muslims, whether muhajirs from the Balkans or internally displaced Turks and Kurds, settled in their place and took up their houses, fields, and pastures.[138] Ethnic cleansing and refugee relief, specifically refugee resettlement, came together by design in the last, and the worst, Ottoman decade.

Starting in the late 1850s, the Ottoman government had built up an immigration system and a refugee regime. The chief executor of the regime, the Refugee Commission, became one of the world's largest refugee resettlement agencies. Its work certainly made life more bearable for several million destitute refugees. Refugee resettlement was both a product and a tool of transition from the imperial order to the national order, which entailed ethnic and religious homogenization. As an arm of the Hamidian regime and then the CUP dictatorship, the Commission was a driver of the empire's demographic transformation. By World War I, the refugee resettlement policy had become one of the most potent mechanisms to Islamize, and, in the case of muhajirs from the Balkans and Crete, also Turkify Ottoman Anatolia.[139]

The Ottoman refugee regime ended with the collapse of the empire after

World War I. As Muslim refugees of the late Ottoman era became part of the Turkish nation and several Arab nations, new terminology set in. The terms *hicret/hijra* and *muhacir/muhājir* were secularized in common parlance. Most speakers of Turkish and Arabic would translate them today as "immigration" and "immigrant." Instead, *mülteci* and *lāji'* became the preferred terms for "refugee" in, respectively, Turkish and Arabic. These terms, with no significant religious baggage, better fit the vocabulary of the new era. So did the Turkish-language neologism *göçmen*, "emigrant" or "immigrant," which is commonly used to describe North Caucasians in Turkish scholarship.

The legacy of the Ottoman refugee regime runs deep in the contemporary Middle East. The Refugee Commission and various actors involved in the Ottoman refugee regime had built up an enormous amount of practical knowledge about how to move people around. This expertise in population transfer did not disappear when the empire ceased to exist. The new nation-states, including Turkey, Bulgaria, Greece, and mandatory Syria, Lebanon, Palestine, Iraq, and Transjordan, inherited Ottoman administrators, their land registers and maps, and procedures for managing population migrations. This knowledge was put to use, as post-Ottoman national governments started exchanging populations across the Aegean, resettling survivors of the genocide, relocating nomads to the lowlands, and building sprawling suburbs for rural migrants.

Part II

REFUGEE RESETTLEMENT

THREE

INEQUALITY AND SECTARIAN VIOLENCE IN THE BALKANS

IN 1874, AUTHORITIES in the subprovince of Tulça, which lay in the Danubian delta in the northernmost corner of the Ottoman Empire, received a petition from the Circassian Ishak Efendi. In his letter, he rebuked Ottoman authorities for their failure to provide relief and asked for help:

> I am a Circassian muhajir and, a year ago, moved to the village of Gölbaşı, in Mecidiye District [now in Romania]. Since my arrival, I have not received a thing from the authorities. I was not given a house, or an ox, or agricultural land. I could not collect harvest from the land. I repeatedly asked for a cash stipend, grain, and oxen to provide for my five children but received nothing. Without a house, I do not know where we will live this winter. I beg the authorities to give me, your humble servant, a house, a pair of oxen, and a plot of land.[1]

Ishak Efendi felt that the Ottoman government did not live up to its promise of free land and subsidies for muhajirs. He lacked shelter, provision, and security to plan a future for his family. Ishak's sentiments reverberated throughout the Balkans. In the first two decades of resettlement, Circassian and Abkhazian refugees inundated local administrations with complaints about the shortcomings of Ottoman resettlement. The authorities should have recognized muhajirs' petitions as distress signals. How refugees coped in their new environments had major repercussions for the economy and stability of their host regions and, as it turned out, the territorial integrity of the Ottoman state.

In the 1860s, over 300,000 North Caucasians had arrived in the Ottoman Balkans. For most refugees, that settlement was short-lived. After the Russo-Ottoman War of 1877–78, almost all North Caucasians were expelled from the northern Balkans. They fled with the retreating Ottoman army and were barred from returning to the territories now controlled by the Bulgarian, Romanian, and Serbian governments. This chapter investigates how the resettlement of muhajirs had been implemented in the northern Balkans in the 1860s and how it ran into trouble by the 1870s. It draws on rich quantitative data on refugee villages from Danube Province, especially its northeastern region of Dobruja, which was among the empire's densest areas of refugee resettlement. Muhajirs were not mere pawns of the Ottoman state. The rare surviving petitions testify that muhajirs criticized what they perceived to be the government's indifference to their grievances and fought for economic justice. Furthermore, muhajir conflicts were not solely with other communities. The Ottoman resettlement bred conflict within North Caucasian communities themselves, as it created inequality through uneven land distribution, empowered new refugee elites, and entrenched Circassian slavery.

Refugee migration allows us to reexamine the collapse of Ottoman rule in Europe. Historians make sense of the events leading to the independence of the Balkan nation-states through two main narratives. First is the national struggle of Christian communities against Ottoman rule. The earlier Serbian uprisings in 1804–13 and 1815–17, the Greek revolution in 1821–29, and the uprisings in Herzegovina in 1875–78 and Bulgaria in 1876 are key moments on a timeline culminating in the independence and restoration of Christian kingdoms in the Balkans. Second is the Eastern Question, which was one of many "questions" in nineteenth-century European politics, pertaining to Ottoman territorial integrity and sovereignty.[2] Russia's steady expansion southward and European diplomacy ensured the victory of Balkan national movements. This chapter approaches the end of Ottoman rule in the Balkans through the prism of Muslim refugee resettlement. Muhajirs were critical to the Ottomans' unsuccessful attempt to hold onto the Balkans. The Ottoman government expected to strengthen its positions in the Balkans through the resettlement of North Caucasians. In 1876, Circassian militias helped to suppress the Bulgarian uprising and perpetrated violence against local Christians. This chapter asks why that happened and explores the economic foundation of sectarian conflict in the Ottoman Balkans, specifically the post-1858 commodification of land, which intensified conflicts over land and resources.[3] By sectarianism, I mean primarily the acts of violence between different communities that were expressed in ethnic or religious terms.

The Ottoman resettlement of Muslim refugees hastened the demise of Ottoman rule in the northern Balkans. First, insufficient allotments of land and financial aid in the 1860s set the Ottoman refugee resettlement project on the wrong footing. It arrested the economic development of muhajir villages, while aggrieving local communities whose lands the state had seized and assigned to muhajirs. Second, a combination of local, Ottoman, and global economic developments in the 1870s threw thousands of refugee households into poverty. As a result, some muhajirs turned to banditry or joined the Ottoman gendarmerie and irregular troops as a means to survive. Finally, the Ottoman government's brutal suppression of the Bulgarian national movement, especially by refugee militias, unraveled intercommunal relations in the region, leading to violent clashes between Muslims and Christians in 1876–78. Ultimately, the insufficient Ottoman support for refugee resettlement expedited the end of nearly five centuries of Ottoman rule.

REFUGEE RESETTLEMENT IN THE BALKANS

During the first Circassian refugee crisis, in 1863–65, the Ottoman government settled about half of all muhajirs in the Ottoman Balkans. The provinces of Danube, Edirne, Salonica, and Prizren all accepted Circassian refugees.[4] Danube Province soon emerged as a primary destination for Muslims from Russia (see map 4).[5] By the 1860s, Danube Province, which stretched from Niş in southern Serbia across western and northern Bulgaria and toward the Danubian delta, was a premier agricultural region. It supplied the empire with grain, corn, grapes, cotton, and livestock. It was also well positioned to reap trade benefits in the age of railways and steamships. Danube Province was close to both Istanbul and Russia's Odessa (now Odesa, Ukraine) through its

Black Sea ports of Varna and Köstence (Constanţa), and its merchants could reach deep into the Balkans through its Danubian ports of Tulça (Tulcea), Silistre (Silistra), Rusçuk (Ruse), and Vidin.

The first Circassian refugees started arriving in the ports of Varna and Köstence in early 1863, and their immigration continued into the 1870s. Abkhazians arrived after the failed uprising of 1866. By 1867, about 150,000 western Circassians—mainly Shapsughs, Ubykhs, Bzhedughs, and Abzakhs—and 8,000 Abkhazians had settled in the province.[6] Within Danube Province, most refugees settled in subprovinces on the Ottoman border with the de facto independent principality of Serbia and the Romanian United Principalities (1862–66; after 1866, Romania). The Ottomans directed many Circassians to the frontier subprovinces of Rusçuk (Ruse) in

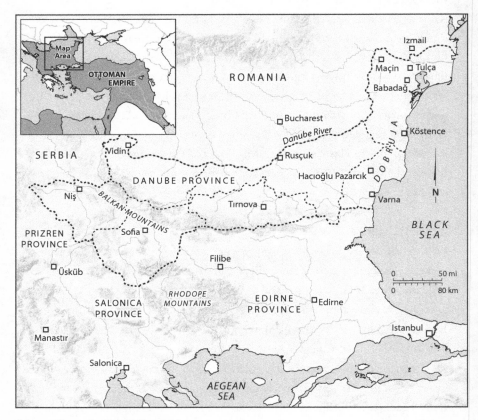

Map 4. **Danube Province, 1867.**

the north and Varna and Tulça in the northeast, which already had Muslim majorities, and of Vidin in the northwest and Niş in the west, which had Christian majorities. In 1874, the overall population of Danube Province was about 60 percent Christian and 40 percent Muslim. By some estimates, in 1860–77, Circassians were the fourth largest group within the borders of modern-day Bulgaria after Bulgarians, Turks (or Turkish-speaking Muslims), and Crimean Tatars.[7]

North Caucasian refugees arrived in the Balkans at a critical time, when many local Christians supported autonomy or outright independence from the Ottoman Empire. For many Balkan Christians, muhajirs were a foreign element imposed on them by Istanbul to increase the Muslim population, whose very presence was an affront to their political aspirations. The Danubian authorities settling many refugees in the subprovinces of Vidin and Niş near the Serbian border further affirmed European observers' suspicions that the Ottomans were using refugee resettlement as an anti–pan-Slavic strategy. The Russian consul in Varna wrote that, with the settlement of Circassians, the Ottomans pursued a goal of "paralyzing any movement of Slavs toward liberation and independence."[8] In a similar vein, Felix Kanitz, an Austro-Hungarian scholar who did extensive fieldwork in the region, believed that "the Circassians were meant to advance the Muslim and Albanian settlement, from east to west, like a 'living frontier' or a 'military belt,' that would separate Christian Bulgarians from their Serb brethren."[9]

Most North Caucasians settled in Danube Province during the governorship of Ahmed Şefik Midhat Pasha, a prominent Tanzimat statesman, in 1864–68.[10] The Danubian authorities initially planned to let muhajirs establish their own villages. However, the government could rarely cobble together sufficiently large land grants for new villages. They started settling muhajirs into already existing villages, which was cheaper and faster than creating new ones.[11] The authorities preferred to place North Caucasian muhajirs with other Muslim communities in order to minimize potential tensions between refugees and local residents. For example, in the district of Hacıoğlu Pazarcık (now Dobrich, Bulgaria) in southern Dobruja, muhajirs constituted 24 percent of the population; they inhabited seventy-eight out of one hundred eight villages, sharing fifty villages with other Muslims (Turks, Crimean Tatars, and Roma), twenty villages with Muslims and Christians, and only three villages solely with Christians (Bulgarians). Five villages had a muhajir-only population.[12] Interspersing refugees with other communities, but with a preference for Muslim neighbors, was common throughout the Ottoman Balkans.[13]

The migration took a severe toll on North Caucasian communities. By the time the Ottoman government conducted population surveys of refugees, muhajir households numbered three or four people on average, which was smaller than a typical Ottoman household of five or a Northwest Caucasian household of six.[14] Refugee communities had fewer children and skewed gender ratios. Men vastly outnumbered women, with anywhere between 114 and 134 men per 100 women.[15] What these data obscure are loss and survival. Every stage of refugee migration was accompanied by death. Thousands of muhajirs perished during their expulsion from the Caucasus on the dangerous journey across the Black Sea and while waiting for months in disease-ridden refugee camps in Ottoman ports. Women and children were particularly vulnerable. When refugees finally arrived in their new villages in the Ottoman hinterland, many found their land to be of poor quality. Then, while mourning the loss of their homeland and loved ones, muhajirs, who arrived with no agricultural tools and no farm animals, had to learn how to grow local and perhaps unfamiliar cereals and vegetables in a new soil and a new climate. They needed to learn quickly enough, because one lost harvest could lead to their starvation the following winter. In their first years in the Ottoman Empire, entire villages of refugees perished of famine and disease. Most people who show up in Ottoman sources and whose voices appear in this book were survivors. Seeing them as such helps to better understand refugee histories in the Ottoman Empire.

The migration had also altered the internal politics of North Caucasian communities. The Ottoman authorities broke up large refugee communities into smaller groups and placed them into mixed villages primarily because of the scarcity of land. That also undermined the power of muhajirs' old elites. The decline of Circassian aristocracy had already been underway. Some notables lost credibility when they joined the Russians, and others were dispossessed or perished during the Caucasus War. Many notables escaped to the Ottoman Empire, wherein the wealthiest Circassians preferred residence in Istanbul, not the countryside. By the 1860s, most Circassian refugees were physically separated from their princely families and old chieftains, which meant that they found themselves in the Ottoman Empire without their traditional leadership.

The new refugee elites slowly emerged through the Ottoman institution of village councils, which were created through the Provincial Reform Law (Vilayet Nizamnamesi) of 1864. The governor of Danube Province, Midhat Pasha, was the chief architect of this landmark Tanzimat legislation, which standardized administrative divisions throughout the empire. It enshrined an Ottoman province (*vilayet*) as the highest-level regional unit, further subdivided into subprovinces (*sancak*) and districts (*kaza*), which were ruled by their respective governors: a *vali*, a *mutasarrıf,* and a *kaymakam*. Various political offices were similarly replicated through multiple tiers of governance. The reform, while ensuring state centralization through the direct appointment of high-ranking officials from Istanbul, fostered communal participation through an elaborate system of elected councils. The Provincial Reform Law stipulated that villages, which were the lowest-level administrative units in the empire, were to be governed by elected councils, chaired by a village headman (*muhtar*). These councils would aid higher-level district and subprovincial authorities in tax collection and law enforcement.[16] Village councils embodied the Tanzimat spirit of expanding popular participation in governance. Throughout the empire, tens of thousands of elected village representatives negotiated with Ottoman authorities and staked out local demands. Village councils played a particularly important role in the refugee resettlement process. Serving as interlocutors between the government and refugee communities, they drew up village population lists, upon the basis of which the Refugee Commission dispensed financial aid, cereals, and farm animals. The councils also exercised authority in allotting assigned land to new residents and distributing subsidies. They managed the construction of village mosques, schools, and public fountains and made decisions about communal farming. The most prominent muhajir families, many of whom were lesser notables back in the Caucasus, sought election to village councils. In the first decades of North Caucasian resettlement, village headmen and councillors effectively served as leaders of their refugee communities.

TROUBLES IN THE 1860s

The government's public forecast on refugee economies was optimistic. In April 1866, the official provincial newspaper, *Tuna* (Ottoman Turkish for Danube), reported that, in the previous year, Circassian muhajirs in the Danubian northeastern districts produced more crops than they needed to sustain themselves.[17] Such news aimed to foster public goodwill and sympathy toward muhajirs amid continuing refugee migration. It was also a falsehood. By then, many muhajirs had been reaping their first harvest or had not even been allotted land plots. Nor could the authorities estimate refugees' agricultural output, as such data would only appear in tithe tax registers, and muhajirs did not start paying taxes until later. In reality, throughout the 1860s, refugees largely relied on state subsidies.

The chief problem in Ottoman refugee resettlement was the limited availability of land. The Ottoman Land Code of 1858 stipulated that a muhajir household was entitled to one *çiftlik*, or a tract of land that requires a pair of oxen (*çift*) to work it. A *çiftlik* measured 70–80 dönüm (16–19 acres) of fertile land, or over 100 dönüm (23 acres) of land of medium productivity, or over 130 dönüm (30 acres) of arid or marshy land.[18] For the next half a century, regional land committees would aspire to those numbers in their allotments of land to refugees. The actual size of allotted land depended on the availability of free land and was typically lower than what the Land Code prescribed.

Throughout the 1860s and 1870s, the Ottoman government appears to have believed that the empire had plenty of uncultivated land, and it was a matter of finding and assigning that land to muhajirs.[19] Local authorities rarely shared the central government's optimism about how much free land they had at their disposal. The most fertile land was typically claimed and in cultivation, whereas the unallotted land that the government could immediately disperse to muhajirs lay in swamps, mountains, or deserts. Some of that land could be made fertile, but it would require bone-breaking labor from refugees. The government could also reclaim the *miri* land that had not been cultivated and for which taxes had not been paid in the previous three years. By doing so, the Ottomans made the land of decent quality available to muhajirs, while aggrieving local villagers who had claimed the land as theirs.

The region of Dobruja, in the utmost north of the Ottoman Empire, provides a good example of how land allotment proceeded in practice. Dobruja was split into the subprovinces of Tulça and Varna, the borders of which correspond to modern-day northern Dobruja in Romania and southern Dobruja in Bulgaria. Unlike much of Danube Province, Dobruja was a steppe region, a western end of the Eurasian steppe stretching from Mongolia and Manchuria. Situated in the borderlands between the Ottoman and Russian empires, Dobruja had long been a transit zone for migrants moving in either direction. In 1858, its population was 30 percent Turkish-speaking, 23 percent Wallachian, and 14 percent each Crimean Tatar and Bulgarian, with the rest being Roma, Jews, Armenians, and emigrant communities of Cossacks, Lipovans, Molokans, Ukrainians, and Germans from Russia.[20] After the Crimean War of 1853–56, over 120,000 Crimean Tatar refugees had settled in Ottoman Bulgaria, most of them in Dobruja.[21] Local authorities raised the alarm in 1860, warning that Dobruja could accommodate no more than 20,000 new immigrants.[22] Yet Crimean immigration continued into the early 1860s, and in 1863–65 about 20,000–30,000 Circassian and Abkhazian refugees arrived in Dobruja. Conflicts over land proliferated in the region. Local resettlement officials had to lower the size of land allotments to 60 dönüm per household, regardless of soil quality, which was below the minimum numbers promised in the Ottoman Land Code. Muhajirs knew of this reduced target and repeatedly asked for 60 dönüm of land in their petitions, but even that number proved a difficult goal, and thousands of muhajirs never received a promised land allotment.[23]

In 1873, Ottoman authorities in northwestern Dobruja were untangling a web of complaints from Circassian residents of three villages in the district of Maçin, a hilly area nestled in the last loop of the Danube before it flows into the Black Sea. The first village, Balabanca (pronounced Balabanja), was largely Turkish-speaking, and its first Circassian refugees arrived around 1864. Twenty-six muhajir households received free agricultural carts and tools, including plows, axes, and hoes, and fourteen oxen for them to share.[24] The land that the government gave them was insufficient for agriculture or pasture. The muhajirs took the initiative and, through their labor, opened up new "watered lands" on the slopes of the Maçin Mountains, which allowed them to claim a little over 60 dönüm per household by the 1870s.[25] The village became a prominent center of Circassian life in the region. In 1871, Ottoman authorities appointed a Circassian muhajir as an imam and a schoolteacher, who was tasked with teaching the local community to read and write in Ottoman Turkish.[26]

The neighboring village of Tsiganka accepted two groups of Circassian muhajirs. Its earliest muhajirs arrived together with others who settled in Balabanca. Tsiganka used to be inhabited by Ukrainian peasants who had fled serfdom in Russia but returned home after the tsarist abolition of serfdom in 1861.[27] The Circassians likely moved into abandoned Ukrainian houses. Local Ottoman authorities issued land, tools, and sixteen oxen to share among twenty-eight Circassian households.[28] A new group of Circassians arrived in Tsiganka in 1867, likely relocating from a previous settlement where the Ottoman government could not give them enough land; this kind of internal migration by muhajirs in search of land was common throughout the Balkans, to the displeasure of the Ottoman authorities, who could not do much about it. The land around Tsiganka was scarce, and forty-one new Circassian households were allotted, on average, only 40 dönüm. The village, surrounded by mountains, lacked adjacent space to expand its arable land.[29] The district authorities then offered Tsiganka's new Circassian residents a meadow lying between the villages of Tsiganka and Balabanca. However, it turned out that the Circassians of Balabanca already claimed usufruct rights to it, having privately purchased parts of the meadow in previous years.[30] Circassians of Balabanca, with title deeds in hand, opposed any attempt to confiscate or reallot their land. Tsiganka's new Circassian residents then searched for land in another direction. In the vicinity of Tsiganka lay the semiabandoned village of Tainca, whose Crimean Tatar population had arrived twenty years earlier and whose settlement failed. The new Circassian immigrants asked the government to assign them some of the land of that village.[31]

A third village, Cafarka (pronounced Jafarka), welcomed its first Circassian refugees in 1870. This mixed village had a Muslim neighborhood, where Circassians moved in, as well as a Christian one, populated by immigrant farmers from the Russian Empire. Like every village, this one also faced a shortage of land. District authorities, probably under the assumption that Circassians of Balabanca had sufficient land, reapportioned 800 dönüm from that village to the village of Cafarka. Circassians of Cafarka occupied at least 250 dönüm of that land and started cultivating it.[32] The Balabanca village council then complained to the Tulça subprovincial authorities about the infringement of their usufruct rights, which they could prove through their title deeds.[33] Negotiations between Circassian communities in the two villages ensued through the 1870s, while Circassians in the region continued developing and purchasing additional land to make up for their insufficient original allotments. As late as 1877, Circassians purchased 410 dönüm of the Karapelid meadowland near the three villages for 2,780 kuruş.[34]

The story of land contestation in the three Dobrujan villages illustrates several consequences of refugee resettlement. In the aftermath of refugee arrival, the ownership of usufruct rights became the most contentious rural issue throughout the Ottoman Empire. Good agricultural land, with fertile soil and access to water, was scarce everywhere. In hundreds of districts, North Caucasian muhajirs clashed over land with others—settled farmers and pastoralists; Christians, Muslims, and Druze; and Turkish, Greek, Bulgarian, Serbian, Armenian, Kurdish, and Arabic speakers.[35] The scholarship often focuses on conflicts between different communities because those had a "national" or "sectarian" dimension, but land in the late Ottoman era was also very much disputed within the same communities, including among refugees. Muhajirs who arrived later were typically assigned less land than muhajirs before them, which led to intracommunal grievances. Muhajirs showed tremendous initiative in their search for new land: they moved around, leaving behind places where they were not given sufficient land, and scouted out uncultivated fields and forests to clear and create arable land. Furthermore, they accepted the arbitration of local Ottoman authorities in resolving their legal disputes over land and actively petitioned their district and subprovincial officials. For people who recently arrived in the empire and had little experience with Ottoman bureaucracy, the North Caucasians quickly grasped the power of petitioning. Through their complaints, drafted by professional Ottoman scribes, they kept pressure on the Ottomans to deliver the bare minimum to which they were entitled as muhajirs. Finally, muhajirs embraced the tenets of the Ottoman Land Code of 1858, whereby land was held in individual usage and needed to be properly registered. Muhajir success in legally contesting the land typically came down to whether they had title deeds to prove that the land had already been registered in their name.

Title deeds (tapu), which were small sheets of paper issued by the newly created institution of land registries, epitomized protracted battles over land

and the entrenchment of the post-1858 Ottoman land regime. These documents specified the exact size and borders of every land plot to the usufruct of which one was entitled. After 1858, individuals held on to their original title deeds, whereas the government preserved their duplicates in provincial land registries. Muhajirs, unlike other Ottoman subjects, were first issued temporary title deeds, and only upon the payment of tithe for ten years could they claim permanent ones. Yet amid the chaos of refugee resettlement in the 1860s, not all muhajirs received their temporary deeds. Nor did their neighboring communities always hold updated title deeds for their land, because that required submitting written evidence of their land usage and tax payments. This all set up the empire's rural population for a torrent of litigation over land. By the 1870s, refugees commonly complained in their petitions that they were not issued *tapu* "in hand" and asked local authorities for physical copies of these documents.[36] In the final decades of Ottoman rule in the Balkans and the Middle East, a title deed was a farmer's most precious possession, an ultimate insurance of their right to till and derive profit from their land.[37]

Land scarcity was even more pronounced in other parts of Danube Province. For example, in northwestern Bulgaria in the district of Rahova (Oryahovo), Circassians in five of six refugee villages, for which we have data, received a median of 30 dönüm per household; the sixth village received a median of 50 dönüm per household. In the neighboring district of İvraca (Vratsa), the median distribution for three refugee villages was only 15–24 dönüm per household.[38] The insufficient land allotment exacerbated the poverty of North Caucasian refugees, who had already been the most economically insecure community in the region.

Circassian slavery further aggravated inequality within refugee communities. In the 1860s, many muhajirs brought their slaves with them to the Ottoman Empire. Slavery was a racialized multitiered institution in the Ottoman Empire. Slaves from the Caucasus traditionally occupied the top position in the Ottoman hierarchy, which privileged whiteness. Slave merchants had long trafficked Circassian, Abkhazian, and Georgian youth to urban slave markets of the Eastern Mediterranean, where girls were purchased for harems and boys for palace and military service. Most white slaves ended up in servitude in urban households and harems. For a select few, slavery was an engine of remarkable social mobility, as they became *valis* (governors), viziers (ministers), *hasekis* (favorite concubines), and *valide sultans* (mothers of sultans).[39] Those pathways were generally closed to black slaves.[40] By the nineteenth century, white slavery of Ottoman harems achieved global recognition, as British Romantic authors and American traveling circuses popularized the "Circassian beauty," a feminine ideal steeped in Orientalism and premised on a woman's submission to her man/sultan.[41] Meanwhile, the westerners' exposure to Circassian slaves in elite households produced a perception that Circassian harem slavery, erroneously used as a stand-in for Ottoman slavery in general, was a more benign form of global slavery, especially when compared to plantation slavery in the Americas. Ottoman anti-abolitionists also actively promoted that idea.[42] Slavery in the Ottoman Empire, in its many forms, was brutal, exploitative, and dehumanizing, as elsewhere.

The Circassian refugee crisis of 1863–65 reinforced the institution of Ottoman slavery. By the mid-nineteenth century, the Ottoman supply of white slaves was reduced to a trickle because the old Crimean and Circassian slavers' economy was destroyed after Russia had annexed the northern shores of the Black Sea. Meanwhile, Ottoman abolitionism was slowly gaining strength, inspired by the Tanzimat reforms and British pressure on the Porte to suppress slave trade. The Ottomans eventually abolished slave trade, if not ownership, in a series of edicts: the sale of Circassian and Georgian slaves was prohibited in 1854–55, and that of African slaves was prohibited in 1857. The arrival of Circassian refugees in the early 1860s thwarted abolitionist efforts in the Ottoman Empire because it restored the supply of white slaves.[43] Many destitute muhajirs resorted to selling their slaves and, reportedly, their own children to survive. The ports of Trabzon, Samsun, and Istanbul and refugee camps in their vicinity became hubs for illegal slave trade.[44] The sudden oversupply led to the collapse of prices in the Ottoman slave market. White slaves, who had previously commanded high prices, were now within reach of many urban households throughout the empire. Reportedly, in 1862–64, a Circassian child was sold for only 2.5–5 Ottoman liras in Varna.[45] The British vice-consul in Edirne reported that provincial notables in the area "have replenished their households" with Circassian girls at the cost of 6 Ottoman liras each.[46] The governor of Trabzon, in June 1865 alone, sent 130 enslaved Circassian women to Istanbul as gifts to various dignitaries at the palace.[47]

After the 1860s, the ownership of Circassian slaves became more common throughout the empire, with ever more households invested in preserving the institution of Ottoman slavery.

If the refugee crisis of 1863–65 had bolstered the Ottoman institution of urban household Circassian slavery, the resettlement of muhajirs introduced the North Caucasian institution of agricultural Circassian slavery to the Ottoman countryside. The resettlement process empowered Circassian slaveholders. The Ottoman government reaffirmed Circassian slaves as property of their Circassian lords because it was unwilling to alienate refugee notables, whose cooperation it required during resettlement.[48] The Ottoman legal system did not recognize distinctions between different categories of bondage in North Caucasian communities. The only legal category available for enslaved North Caucasians was *köle*, or slave.[49] At the same time, as far as the government was concerned, all Circassian slaves were also muhajirs, just like their masters, who had sought refuge in the Ottoman domains. As muhajirs, they were entitled to free land, tax exemptions, and subsidies from the government. This legal tension between the *muhajir* and *köle* statuses was never resolved. In practice, enslaved muhajirs could not enjoy the full privileges of their Ottoman subjecthood or the muhajir benefits to which they were entitled. Through the institution of village councils, Circassian slaveholders had free rein on the allotment of land and distribution of aid. Circassian notables registered land that was earmarked for other muhajirs, especially slaves, in their own name, leaving slave families landless.[50] They further benefited from the free labor of their slaves who were forced to till their land.

Migration between the two empires proliferated unfreedom. Russia's expulsion of Circassians in the 1860s reinforced Ottoman slavery. In parallel, in the late eighteenth century, as Will Smiley demonstrated, the Ottomans' consent to return Russian fugitives had reinforced Russian serfdom.[51] The two empires' policies on North Caucasian slavery seem drastically different, yet, similar to their migration policies, they served the same goal of strengthening imperial rule. Russia abolished slavery in the Caucasus to advance its comprehensive land reforms and remake the region's weakened Muslim notables into its clients. The Ottoman government, by preserving Circassian slavery, empowered Circassian slaveholders, which ensured the loyalty of its new refugee elites.

Many slaves resisted exploitation by their Circassian masters. In January 1877, seven Circassian notables—Musa, Mehmet, Süleyman, Mehmet ʿAli, Kanhat, Idris, and ʿOsman—sent a collective petition to the subprovincial governor of Tulça. They complained that three slaves of Mehmet in the village of Urum Bey in Hırsova District (now Hârşova, Romania) had refused to obey their master. Following their example, two other slaves belonging to Mehmet ʿAli in the same village also refused to do household service. That group of slaves, whom the petitioners called the "disobedient mischief makers," started inciting other slaves in neighboring districts. The notables asked the governor to intervene and punish the slaves to set an example for others.[52] A month later, two of the notables sent another petition to the governor. They reported that the local gendarmerie had confiscated weapons from their slaves but did not arrest them. The slaveholders complained that their slaves' resistance to their enslavement was "against their customs" and repeated their demand to have their insubordinate slaves arrested to serve as a deterrent to others.[53]

Slave revolts exposed a fissure in a refugee regime in which some refugees were slaves. Circassian muhajir slaveholders regarded the Ottoman state as a guarantor of their property rights because Circassian slavery remained legal in the empire. Meanwhile, Circassian muhajir slaves viewed the Ottoman state as the ultimate arbiter of Islamic justice, whose protection they sought as Muslims, muhajirs, and Ottoman subjects. In 1871, Circassians in Mecidiye District rebelled against their masters who "kept [them] in a state of serfdom, made [them] work without wages, beaten and sold." Slaves appealed to the Ottoman authorities for justice, stating that they would rather return under Russian rule than live in the servitude of their masters.[54] During another revolt in eastern Thrace in 1873, a group of slaves rebelled when they found out that slave trade had been outlawed in the Ottoman Empire, assuming that they could legally challenge their slave status.[55] The Ottoman government navigated disputes between Circassian masters and slaves with caution. Its goal was to keep the order in the countryside, while preserving its authority among its new refugee populations. The government often attempted to defuse slave rebellions by negotiating manumission certificates (*mükatebe*), which slaves had to purchase from their enslavers. The price of freedom was often out of reach for slaves who had already been cheated out of land by their

masters, or it led them into lifelong debt to the same masters.[56] For many
Circassians, Ottoman resettlement meant the continuation of their bondage,
merely on the other side of the Black Sea.

ECONOMIC FAILURE IN THE 1870s

A decade into Circassian resettlement, crime spiked in the Ottoman countryside, and refugees were blamed for it. Most crimes were economic in nature,
like thefts of horses, cattle, and sheep, which signaled that refugee economies
were faltering. Isolated incidents of theft increasingly gave way to organized
raids, smuggling, and highway robbery. Traveling through parts of the countryside in the northern Balkans was no longer safe. A British vice-consul in
Edirne, when describing ongoing banditry, called Circassians "children of
the devil," which probably captured the sentiments of many locals.[57] Likewise, newspapers lamented the detrimental effect of refugee resettlement.
By 1878, about 80 percent of all references to Circassians in the Bulgarian-
language press were related to refugee offenses against local populations.[58]
Newspapers helped to shape the Bulgarian Christians' perception of Muslim
refugee resettlement as a threat to their safety.

The very word *Çerkes*, an ethnonym for Circassian communities that the
Ottomans applied to all North Caucasians, began to be associated with banditry. The traditional Circassian male costume, featuring a wide-sleeve goat-
hair cloak, a rifle slung across the shoulder, and a saber by the belt, became
a highwayman fixture in popular imagination. The stereotype of who a Circassian was had changed for the Ottoman public. Being Circassian had once
meant being of slave origin, often part of the harem, military, or administrative elite, and an urban resident, but by the 1870s it meant being a refugee
bandit in the countryside.[59] Throughout the final decades of the empire, provincial authorities would send panicked letters to Istanbul about "Circassian
gangs" roaming the roads, although the communal identity of gang members
was not always verified. Refugee bandits were a symptom of broader economic
decline in the Ottoman countryside. Many nonrefugee Muslims and Christians were also driven into gangs because of poverty.[60] Nevertheless, refugees
were an easy target to blame, and their economic woes were arresting.

The refugee economies were failing for four interrelated reasons. First,
the global demand for Ottoman grain declined in the 1870s. When North

Caucasians started arriving in the empire, the Ottoman government had every reason to prioritize cereal production in its long-term economic strategy. The European demand for Ottoman grain increased significantly during the Crimean War of 1853–56, as grain exports from Russia fell. Unfortunately for the Ottomans, the rapid expansion of U.S. grain production after the U.S. Civil War of 1861–65 and the opening of the Suez Canal in 1869 led to the arrival of cheaper grain from the United States, India, and Australia on European markets. The ensuing Long Depression of 1873–96 suppressed global prices for grain. These economic developments were acutely felt in agriculture-heavy Danube Province. For example, exports of grain through the port of Varna grew steadily through the early 1860s but dropped by 56 percent in 1868–69 and by 36 percent in 1869–70. Grain exports then stagnated through the 1870s and never returned to the volume from 1864.[61] The decline in the global demand for, and price of, grain directly hit Ottoman imperial and provincial treasuries and muhajir households that bartered their surplus of cereals for other foodstuffs.

Second, a massive drought hit the Balkans in 1872–73. Many refugee villages that had already struggled lost their harvest and, because of either famine or epidemic disease, their cattle, which led to more starvation and misery.[62] The drought in the Balkans coincided with the drought in Anatolia in 1872–75, and the collapsing harvests exacerbated the empire's financial woes.[63]

Third, the Ottoman Empire struggled to pay its mounting debt to European states. After the Crimean War, the Ottoman government borrowed heavily to pay for the resettlement of Crimean and North Caucasian refugees. With new lines of credit readily available in banks in London, Paris, and Vienna, the Ottomans continued to borrow cash to repay old debts and fund various modernization projects. The pace of borrowing was unsustainable. Between 1869 and 1875, the Ottoman government took out more in loans than its entire projected revenue for that period.[64] In 1875, the Porte declared a sovereign default on its loan repayments. When muhajirs needed help from the state the most, the Ottoman government, on the brink of bankruptcy, not only could not expand social welfare programs but also was phasing out monthly cash and grain stipends to muhajirs, with the exception of the poorest and disabled refugees.[65]

Finally, the six-year tax exemptions for Circassian muhajirs in the Balkans were set to expire in the late 1860s to early 1870s. Most refugee villages were in no position to start paying their full dues amid deteriorating economic conditions and dwindling subsidies in the 1870s. Throughout the Balkans, muhajirs were falling short on their payments. By 1877, refugee communities had been paying little tax proportionate to their population.[66]

Muhajirs' underwhelming tax payments are important because the government had envisioned that muhajir taxes would eventually offset the costs of refugee resettlement. In Danube Province, as elsewhere in the empire, a substantial portion of local tax payments remained in the region so that they could be efficiently reallocated to local low-income communities. For example, subsidies in wheat, barley, and sheep for Circassian muhajirs in the district of Hacıoğlu Pazarcık came out of local tax payments in kind in the neighboring districts of Balçık and Mangalya.[67] Likewise, taxes collected in cash from Crimean Tatar muhajirs who had arrived in the 1850s often paid for the resettlement of Circassian muhajirs in the 1860s, whose projected tax payments in the 1870s were to fund subsidies for new muhajirs.[68] Any leak in this tax pipeline, as happened in the 1870s, reduced district funding for welfare programs and hurt local communities and economies.

Refugee taxes were also earmarked to subsidize infrastructure in their villages. Muhajir tax payments were deposited separately with the Refugee Commission and the Public Benefits Bank.[69] Village tax accounts with the Commission were meant to fund the construction of schools, hospitals, and mosques for refugees and salaries of schoolteachers.[70] In many villages, however, muhajir tax payments were minimal, which jeopardized the underfunded Commission's ability to pay for the development of refugee villages. Likewise, muhajirs had limited capacity to contribute to the Public Benefits Bank, which was an agricultural credit cooperative that provided farmers with low-interest loans in cash, farm animals, and seeds. The bank was created by Midhat Pasha in 1863 and was among the world's first rural credit unions.[71] Many muhajirs took out loans from the Public Benefits Bank to pay their new tax obligations to the state rather than invest in agriculture, which drove muhajir households into a debt cycle and deeper into poverty.[72]

The deterioration of refugee economies widened the chasm between them and other communities. Babadağ District in central Dobruja provides a good example. In the hilly environs of Babadağ, muhajirs cultivated wheat, rye, barley, corn, millet, beans, and lentils and grew pear, wild apricot, and plum trees. Ottoman tax and population registers from the district offer insight into how unequal the distribution of wealth was. In the 1870s, Ottoman communities paid several major taxes: a tithe (*öşür vergisi*) of 10 percent, a property tax (*emlak vergisi*) of 4 percent, a profit tax (*temettüat vergisi*) of 3 percent, and an income tax (*irad vergisi*) of 4 percent.[73] Circassian muhajirs had not paid a profit tax and an income tax by 1877. Their tithe and property tax payments, however, paint a bleak picture. The amount of the tithe depended on the size of the harvest, which broadly reflected the land's quality, acreage, and water access, as well as the availability of human and animal labor. The property tax was based on the government-set cadastral value of the land, which largely corresponded to its size and location. In 1873, the average tithe paid by an able-bodied adult male in the Babadağ countryside was 70 kuruş. The wealthiest community were German immigrants, whose men paid on average 108 kuruş, whereas Circassian refugees were the poorest, paying 36 kuruş. Likewise, the value of Circassians' land was about three times lower than that of German, Bulgarian, and Turkish farmers in the area (see table 2). The inequality was even more pronounced in Babadağ itself, a small town noted for the tomb of its thirteenth-century founder, Turkoman dervish Sarı Saltuk. Circassians established three neighborhoods in Babadağ. Their neighborhoods were the poorest, with the average property value almost twelve times lower than that in Turkish neighborhoods (see table 3).

Few muhajir villages around Babadağ were economically self-sufficient. In 1876, the subprovincial authorities in Tulça received a communal petition requesting aid from the village of Vefikiye. Vefikiye was the largest Circassian village in Babadağ District and one of the largest in the northern Balkans. Its village council informed the authorities that the refugee population had run out of bread and was starving. The muhajirs asked the district for 300 kile (16,971 pounds) of millet, which they pledged to repay after the next harvest.[74] North Caucasian communities in other villages sent similar distress requests for basic foodstuffs.[75]

The situation in other parts of Danube Province, where muhajirs received less land than in Dobruja, was even worse. For example, in the district of Berkofça (Berkovitsa, Bulgaria) close to the Serbian and Romanian borders,

Community	Agricultural tax, in kuruş	Property tax, in kuruş	Property value, in kuruş
German	108	11	2,681
Bulgarian	101	10	2,585
Moldavian	86	7	1,874
Turkish	64	9	2,322
Crimean Tatar	63	8	2,082
Lipovan (Russian)	47	5	1,222
Circassian	36	3	823
All communities	70	8	2,079

Table 2. **Taxes in Babadağ District (now in Romania), 1873–77.**

The estimates are for average tax payments and property value per adult male in thirty-three monoethnic villages of Babadağ District. Mixed villages are not included here because tax registers do not provide a breakdown of tax payments by residents' religion or language. The estimate for all communities is for the district's fifty-six villages, both monoethnic and mixed.

Sources: NBKM Badagağ 9/12 (1877); 170/292 (c. 1876); Todorov-Khindalov, *Godishnik.*

Neighborhood	Property tax, in kuruş	Property value, in kuruş
Turkish	16	3,880
Jewish	12	2,950
Bulgarian	11	2,658
Armenian	6	1,378
Crimean Tatar	2	484
Circassian	1	331
All neighborhoods	8	1,961

Table 3. **Property in the town of Babadağ, 1877.**

The estimates are for average tax payments and property value per adult male in all neighborhoods of the town of Babadağ, except the Muslim Roma one because of the lack of population data.

Sources: NBKM Badagağ 9/12 (1877); 170A/243 (c. 1876).

by the 1870s almost two-thirds of Circassian households did not produce enough crops to feed a four-member household.[76] In almost every category— the amount of land, the price of land per dönüm, the cost of houses, and the size of harvest—Circassian muhajirs lagged behind their Bulgarian and Turkish neighbors (see table 4).[77]

Community	Land, in dönüm	Price of land, in kuruş per dönüm	Price of house, in kuruş	Harvested wheat, in sheaves	Harvested corn, in okka
Bulgarian	88	92	3,732	467	1,486
Turkish	56	87	2,300	272	1,060
Circassian	44	60	641	205	1,083
All communities	82	90	3,385	446	1,447

Table 4. **Household economy in Berkofça District (now in Bulgaria), 1873.**
Source: Draganova, *Berkovskoto selo,* 26–27, 38–39, 46.

The economic disparity between established populations and new refugee communities is not surprising in itself. One might expect that refugees who had arrived with nothing would trail their neighbors in the accumulation of wealth. Yet the refugees' poverty and economic inequality are an important and overlooked context for what happened next—the unraveling of the Balkans in 1876–78.

UNRAVELING THE BALKANS
The decline of refugee economies accelerated the militarization of refugee communities. While some turned to banditry, others joined the Ottoman gendarmerie (*zaptiye*). Those often were the only salaried positions available to muhajirs in the countryside. For example, in 1874, Abkhazian muhajirs from the village of Rakil, in Maçin District, sent to local authorities a petition in which they explained that they did not receive land or anything else from the government and, for that reason, were destitute. Men in the village

expressed their communal aspiration to join the *zaptiye* to escape poverty.[78] Military service was another way to gain a living, but muhajirs were temporarily exempt from conscription and were not actively recruited into the regular Ottoman army. They could join only irregular troops (*başıbozuk*). In the late 1870s, many muhajir men joined the notoriously ill-disciplined *başıbozuk*, whom the Ottomans had hired to maintain rural security but paid so poorly that many troops devolved into marauding gangs.[79]

In the 1860s and 1870s, many Bulgarians pushed for greater autonomy in their ecclesiastical and political governance. In 1870, they succeeded in having the Ottoman government restore the Bulgarian patriarchate, to the vociferous protests of the Greek-dominated patriarchate of Constantinople. In 1876, Bulgarian secret revolutionary committees launched the April Uprising against Ottoman rule. The Ottomans relied on local *başıbozuk* to suppress the uprising. By then, the *başıbozuk* had irregulars from different Muslim communities, including a large Circassian contingent. The militias destroyed entire villages and massacred thousands of Bulgarian civilians.[80] The atrocities committed by Ottoman irregular forces, especially the massacre of Bulgarians by the Pomak *başıbozuk* in the village of Batak, were widely reported in the international press as "Bulgarian horrors" and turned public opinion in Europe and the United States against the Ottoman government.

The April Uprising of 1876 was part of a series of conflicts in the Balkans in 1875–78, which ended with the Russo-Ottoman War of 1877–78. Russia and Austria-Hungary long wished to redraw the balance of power in the region in their favor. That opportunity came with the Herzegovina uprising against Ottoman rule in 1875–77, leading to the Ottoman wars with Serbia and Montenegro in 1876–78. The Great Powers convened the Constantinople Conference in late 1876 to agree on a demand for political reforms in Ottoman Bosnia and Bulgaria, without inviting the Ottoman delegation to the conference. The Porte refused the proposed reforms, which Russia then used as justification to declare war under the pretext of protecting Ottoman Christians in the Balkans.[81] In April 1877, Russian troops marched into Romania, upon Bucharest's invitation. In June, the Russian forces crossed the Danube into the Ottoman territory. The tsarist army, reinforced by Romanian troops and Bulgarian volunteers, defeated Ottoman forces in Danube Province and, in January 1878, reached Edirne, from where it threatened the Ottoman capital, less than 150 miles away.

The conflicts of 1876–78 turned explicitly sectarian in the northern Balkans, pitting Muslims, including muhajirs, against Christians. Before 1876, Christians were not the only victims of muhajir crimes; Turkish and Crimean Tatar communities also complained about Circassian banditry.[82] In contrast, in 1876, the *başıbozuk* directed their violence specifically against civilian Christian populations.[83] For example, in July an armed militia that counted in its ranks Circassian and Crimean Tatar muhajirs besieged the coastal town of Kavarna, near Varna, and demanded a hefty fee of 100,000 kuruş from townsfolk for their "protection." The predominantly Greek town was unable to raise the money, and failed negotiations escalated to the gang's massacring some of the residents, looting the town, and then setting it on fire.[84] The Bulgarians' resentment against Circassians grew amid the violence of 1876. An observing ethnographer captured the general feeling as follows: "When, in 1877, the tsar's army appeared on the Danube they were enthusiastically accepted by the Bulgarians, who thought they were being saved from their Circassian oppressors."[85] The intercommunal violence only escalated during the war. By then, even neighbors in mixed villages had turned on each other. In the village of Cafarka, for example, where Circassians had been living alongside their Christian neighbors, Circassian bandits looted a local Orthodox church and Christians' houses.[86] Meanwhile, the advancing Russian troops and their supporters among Balkan Christians, as Muslims had feared, exacted revenge against not only the *başıbozuk* but also Turkish, Circassian, and Crimean Tatar civilians.[87]

The economic decline of refugee economies paved the way to refugee banditry and militarization, but intercommunal tensions did not start with an uptick in Circassian robberies in the 1870s. The seeds of discord were sown during the refugees' arrival in the 1860s. Local communities, primarily Bulgarians but also Greeks, Serbs, and Muslims, were aggrieved over the loss of their land to muhajirs. The Ottoman government may well have regarded the *miri* land as state property, but muhajirs' neighbors disagreed. Throughout the 1860s, farmers from throughout the Balkans sent petitions to regional and imperial authorities to complain about their dispossession in favor of refugees. To add insult to injury, the Ottoman authorities typically required local peasants to host refugees, build houses for them, sow their first harvest, and provide provision for their first year. Bulgarian peasants often pushed back, like they did in a marvelously concise petition from Tırnova (Veliko Tarnovo) in 1864:

> The government ordered us to provide millet for Circassian muhajirs. In our area of the Balkan Mountains, it is difficult and even impossible for the following reasons. First, our people do not sow millet; it does not grow here. Second, we do not have available fields for millet because all fields are sown with other cereals. Third, we do not have enough oxen [to prepare millet fields]. Fourth, our men are scattered around Bulgaria looking for work.[88]

The Bulgarian peasants' final point hints at how one migration fueled another. The state's demands from local communities for the benefit of incoming refugees forced many Bulgarians to leave. After the Ottomans allotted some of their land to Circassians, many Bulgarians moved abroad—to Serbia, Romania, and Bessarabia—in search of land and a better life.[89]

The Russo-Ottoman War of 1877–78 was a turning point in the relationship between North Caucasian muhajirs and the Ottoman state. The Ottoman government had previously been reluctant to allow muhajirs to join the regular army but was now actively recruiting North Caucasians, many of whom excelled in horsemanship and had experience in fighting the Russians.[90] On the Balkan front, about 16,050 Circassian horsemen formed the bulk of the Ottoman cavalry.[91] The Ottomans also assembled four North Caucasian cavalry units, each 1,000 men strong, primarily from muhajirs living around Aziziye, Sivas, and Canik.[92] These units, later reorganized into three divisions, fought on the Caucasus front. Their division commanders were some of the most prominent Ottoman muhajir leaders: Musa Paşa, or Musa Kundukhov, a former tsarist general from Ossetia, who organized the Chechen emigration of 1865, and Ghazi Muhammad Paşa, the eldest surviving son of Imam Shamil.[93] Several thousand North Caucasian muhajirs helped the Ottoman navy to recapture Sukhum on Russia's Abkhazian coast.[94]

In the final Ottoman decades, the popular perception of who a Circassian was would undergo another transformation: from a refugee bandit whom the empire could not control to an imperial soldier. After the war of 1877–

78, North Caucasian muhajirs became a fixture in the Ottoman army. The North Caucasian cavalry of Musa Paşa participated in the suppression of the Kurdish revolt of Shaykh Ubeydullah in 1880–81.[95] North Caucasian officers in the Ottoman service were also involved in the creation of the infamous Hamidiye Light Cavalry Regiments in 1890, which were modeled after the Cossack troops that had proved effective in Russia's conquest of the Caucasus.[96] Military service lifted many North Caucasians out of poverty and bound them closer to the Ottoman state. It became a career choice for several generations of muhajirs, and hundreds of North Caucasians reached high ranks in the military and security apparatus in post-Ottoman Turkey, Jordan, and Syria.

The war of 1877–78 shaped the modern political map of the Balkans. The Ottoman Empire had lost the war to Russia and its Romanian, Serbian, Montenegrin, and Bulgarian allies. In the Treaty of San Stefano in March 1878, Russia carved out a massive Bulgarian state, which included much of Macedonia and even a sliver of the Aegean coast. Four months later, Britain, France, and Austria-Hungary forced Russia to revise the postwar settlement in the Treaty of Berlin. The new treaty recognized the independence of Romania, Serbia, and Montenegro. The Ottoman Empire ceded the subprovince of Tulça, within Danube Province, to Romania and the subprovince of Niş, within Kosovo Province by 1877, to Serbia. The rest of Danube Province became an autonomous principality of Bulgaria, under nominal Ottoman sovereignty but de facto independent. The European Powers fashioned the new Ottoman province of Eastern Rumelia out of the Edirne subprovinces of Filibe (Plovdiv) and İslimye (Sliven). Bulgaria would annex Eastern Rumelia in 1885, and their unification would be recognized internationally in 1908, when Bulgaria proclaimed its independence.

By 1878, virtually all North Caucasians fled Danube Province for the safety of Ottoman Anatolia or Syria, alongside the retreating Ottoman army and thousands of fellow Muslim and Jewish refugees.[97] In 1878, Russian troops remained in Bulgaria, and tsarist authorities took the lead in setting up the administration of the new Bulgarian state. The first head of the Russian provisional administration in Bulgaria was Vladimir Cherkassky, an avowed Pan-Slavist. In a twist of historical irony, he came from a princely Circassian family that had converted to Christianity and joined Russian service in the sixteenth century. In August 1878, Prince Aleksandr Dondukov-Korsakov, the new head of the Russian provisional administration, issued an order allowing Bulgaria's Muslims who had fled their homes to return, with the sole exception being the Circassians. He justified the ban on Circassian return by claiming that Circassians had committed crimes during the war and that Bulgaria's Christian population was likely to exact revenge should Circassians return.[98] Romania and Serbia also enacted policies that limited the return of Muslim refugees.[99] North Caucasians were not welcome back.

The lands vacated by North Caucasian muhajirs became a prized commodity in Bulgaria, Romania, and Serbia. After 1878, the three national governments passed legislation to ensure state ownership over those lands so that they could use them for internal colonization. In 1880, the Bulgarian government issued the Law on Circassian and Tatar Lands. While the law allowed the possibility of muhajirs' lands to be returned to private or communal use, the government claimed much of the land as state property.[100] Muhajirs, who were no longer physically present in Bulgaria, had no legal recourse to reclaim their former land, which was in contravention of the Treaty of Berlin's stipulation that Muslim landowners outside of Bulgaria could retain their land.[101] The Bulgarian government's appropriation of abandoned Circassian and Tatar lands proved controversial and generated numerous complaints from Bulgarian peasants who claimed that the Ottoman government had taken those fields and pastures from them by force and demanded that the new government in Sofia return their property.[102] In southern Dobruja alone, after a survey of abandoned Circassian and Tatar lands in 1886, the state took control of more than 157,147 dönüm of land, over 96 percent of which were agricultural fields.[103] The government distributed the lion's share of the land to new Bulgarian immigrants, or *preselnitsi*, who were returning to their "liberated" homeland from different parts of the Ottoman, Romanov, and Habsburg domains.[104] The Bulgarian population in southern Dobruja rose from 25 percent in 1874 to 33 percent in 1878 to 48 percent in 1910.[105] Romania, which had assumed control over northern Dobruja after 1878, also earmarked the land left behind by Circassians and Abkhazians for new immigrants, regulated by the Law Concerning Immovable Property in Dobruja of 1882.[106] In 1883, the Romanian government conducted a comprehensive cadastral survey to reapportion the land.[107] It allotted 104,550 hectares (258,349 acres) of land, once tilled by muhajirs, to Romanian immigrants who arrived from Wallachia, Moldavia, Transylvania, Bessarabia, and Banat.[108] The Romanian population of northern Dobruja grew from 21 percent in 1878 to 57 percent in 1912.[109] Serbia passed the Law on the Regulation of Agrarian Relations in the Newly Liberated Areas of 1880, which enabled the reassignment of the lands of Circassian muhajirs and Albanians who had fled the subprovince of Niş.[110] In the following years, Montenegrin and Serbian immigrants from the Ottoman and Habsburg empires moved to the new territories. The Serbian population in the area increased from 71 percent in 1873 to a staggering 97 percent in 1884.[111]

By 1878, an entire generation of North Caucasians had grown up in Ottoman Europe. They never got to return to the Balkans but did not forget their old homes and pastures. We know that if only because, twenty-five years since their expulsion from the Balkans, some of them had an opportunity to write one last batch of petitions about their land. In the early 1900s, a mixed Ottoman-Romanian Refugee Commission (Romanya Muhacirin Komisyonu) was established under the auspices of the Ottoman Foreign Ministry to collect information about Muslims' abandoned agricultural estates in northern Dobruja for compensation from the Romanian government.[112] The commission invited Ottoman subjects to send their old title deeds, and several thousand refugees, including North Caucasians, responded. For example, thirteen households who had once lived in the village of Balabanca, twenty-one in Tsiganka, and thirty-seven in Cafarka within Maçin District asked for compensation for their land. Likewise, fifteen households from the Circassian village of Vefikiye within Babadağ District requested compensation.[113] In their statements, muhajirs gave specific information about the size and location of their lost fields and pastures and attached title deeds, which they had carefully kept all of those years. Those petitions testify, perhaps, to the North Caucasians' emotional attachment to their former homes but also that they had learned important lessons from their experience in the Balkans. The land had legal, economic, and social value, and muhajirs' future in the Ottoman Empire depended on their ability to claim and secure the land.

Muslim refugee resettlement accelerated the collapse of Ottoman rule in the Balkans. In the age of the Bulgarians' national struggle, many Orthodox

Slavs understood the settlement of thousands of foreign Muslims as a hostile act by Istanbul. For them, Muslim refugees were part of a nefarious plan to reinforce Ottoman control over the Balkans. Not only were the political circumstances of refugee resettlement troubling, its logistics floundered at an early stage. The Ottoman government failed to deliver its key promises, including a sufficient amount of fertile agricultural land and subsidies in cattle, grain, and agricultural tools, for refugee economies to take off. As the state scaled down its support amid an economic downturn, hundreds of refugee villages were in distress. Poverty pushed many muhajirs to commit economic crimes against their neighbors and to join gendarmerie or irregular troops. Circassian banditry threw many Danubian areas into disarray, further inflaming social relations in the region. Finally, the violent suppression of the April Uprising of 1876 by refugee militias gave Russia the pretext it needed to redraw the map of the Balkans. By 1878, the Ottoman Empire lost Danube Province and, with it, some of the empire's oldest territories. It was also abundantly clear to everyone that the Ottoman Empire was on borrowed time in its remaining European territories in the central Balkans.

The short-lived settlement of North Caucasian muhajirs in the Balkans had far-reaching consequences. For the Balkan nation-states, the expulsion of nonnative North Caucasian Muslims foreshadowed a series of policies that diminished their once prominent native Muslim populations to small minorities over the course of the twentieth century.[114] The Ottoman government also drew conclusions from its troubled resettlement of refugees in the Balkans. It learned the demographic value of settling Muslims in frontier territories and the military use of a poor and loyal refugee population. It also recognized the risk that a lack of support for refugees posed to the social order. After 1878, the Ottomans paid closer attention to matters of land allotment and infrastructural support for muhajirs. The next chapter shows how those lessons were put to work. It follows some of the expelled refugees from the Balkans to the Levant and examines a different kind of resettlement, one that many would find a remarkable success.

FOUR

REAL ESTATE AND
NOMADIC FRONTIER
IN THE LEVANT

IN THE LATE 1890S, a young Circassian woman, Sayetkhan bint Qurash bin Qoghuluq, arrived in the Circassian village of Amman. She was a second-generation refugee, born to a family in the Golan Heights that had been expelled from the Caucasus in the 1860s and from the Ottoman Balkans in 1878. She married a fellow Kabardian muhajir and followed him to Transjordan, where Circassians set up the southernmost refugee villages in the Ottoman Empire. Sayetkhan's new family worked in agriculture and had a penchant for entrepreneurship. It invested profits from grain sale into moneylending and real estate, purchasing more land and building shops, which it sold to Arab merchants who arrived in Amman to trade with refugees and bedouin. Within a decade, Sayetkhan and her underage daughter Gül'azar were among the wealthiest muhajirs in Transjordan. Meanwhile, Amman turned from a refugee village into a boomtown on the Levant's nomadic frontier.

This chapter examines the settlement of North Caucasian refugees in the Ottoman Levant between 1878 and the outbreak of World War I. It focuses on the region of the Balqa' in central Transjordan. Three of the four largest cities in the Hashemite Kingdom of Jordan—Amman, Zarqa', and Rusayfa—were

founded by Circassian and Chechen refugees.¹ Today, Amman is the capital of Jordan and, with a population of over four million people, recently
overtook Tel Aviv, Damascus, Beirut, and Aleppo as the largest city in the
Levant. Established as a Circassian muhajir village in 1878, Amman became
a quintessential refugee city, expanding through the arrival of refugees from
elsewhere: Circassians until 1912, Armenians in 1915–22, Palestinians in 1948
and 1967, Iraqis after 2003, and Syrians after 2011.² By drawing on Islamic
court records and Ottoman land registers, this chapter tells the Circassian
origin story of Amman.³ Circassian refugees in Transjordan took full advantage of Ottoman land legislation and new infrastructure to facilitate the
expansion of the Ottoman state and new forms of market relations into the
interior Levant.

North Caucasian villages in Transjordan became thriving economic outposts on the nomadic frontier thanks to the convergence of refugee labor, Levantine mercantile capital, and access to the bedouin economy. This happened
gradually: first, by the 1890s North Caucasian muhajirs started registering
their land in the Ottoman land registry, in accordance with the Ottoman
Land Code of 1858, entrenching a new Ottoman land regime premised on
consistent cultivation and taxation on the land. Second, the opening of the
Damascus-Amman section of the Hejaz Railway in 1903 brought Transjordanian, Syrian, and Palestinian merchants to Amman, prompting a real estate
boom. Finally, the prosperity of Amman and other refugee villages, such as
Wadi al-Sir and Naʿur, depended on muhajir military alliances and trade with
surrounding bedouin communities. North Caucasian refugees boosted the
economy and improved travel security, which helped to strengthen Ottoman
rule in Transjordan.

SECOND CIRCASSIAN REFUGEE CRISIS, 1878–80

The flight of at least 300,000 muhajirs from the Ottoman Balkans during
the Russo-Ottoman War of 1877–78 turned into the second Circassian refugee crisis, in 1878–80. If the first Circassian refugee crisis, in 1863–65, had
unfolded on the shores of the Black Sea, the second one engulfed the Aegean
and Eastern Mediterranean coastlines. Circassian refugees spent months in
the ports of Varna, Istanbul, Salonica, and Kavala, waiting for ships that
would take them to safety farther east. Most North Caucasian refugees,

alongside Turkish-speaking refugees from the Balkans, were sent to Anatolia, especially the provinces of Kastamonu, Aydın, Hüdavendigar (Bursa), and Ankara.[4] The Ottoman government sent the rest to the Levantine provinces of Damascus and Aleppo, which had been spared the earlier refugee crisis because the authorities found it too expensive to send refugees there in the 1860s. In 1878, as the Ottoman government scrambled to find enough space for incoming refugees, it designated all ports between Alexandretta (now Iskenderun, Turkey) and Haifa as recipients of North Caucasian muhajirs. In February 1878, the first 1,000 Circassian refugees disembarked in Beirut, 1,500 in Acre, and 2,000 in Tripoli. The following month, 8,000 refugees arrived in Tripoli alone.[5] By September 1878, over 45,000 muhajirs, most of them Circassians, were present on the Levantine coast; 25,000 of them would be resettled in Damascus Province and 20,000 in Aleppo Province.[6]

The arrival of thousands of refugees spelled a humanitarian catastrophe in Levantine port cities. Accommodation was scarce, and thousands of refugees slept in mosques, tekkes (Sufi lodges), and army barracks. As those filled up, refugees were forced into bazaars and streets.[7] Refugees who had already experienced the horrors of displacement in 1863–65 had to live through a new one. The refugee crisis contributed to food shortages and rising inflation throughout the Levant. By March 1878, the price of an okka of bread in Tripoli reached 175 para, whereas the regular price was 60 para before the war. Meanwhile, Ottoman funding for resettlement did not rise alongside inflation. The available funds for refugees were so few that, by early 1880, the village councils of Jableh and ʿArab al-Mulk (now in Syria), which hosted over 2,000 refugees who disembarked in Tripoli and Latakia, could provide food to only 10 percent of their refugee population.[8] Typhus and smallpox broke out and decimated starving refugee communities. By December 1878, sixty muhajirs had been dying daily in Tripoli.[9]

While many local residents provided humanitarian aid to alleviate refugee suffering, some turned against refugees, blaming Circassians for high inflation, outbreak of disease, and a purported rise in crime in port cities. On separate occasions in 1878, port authorities in Beirut and Acre refused new ships with refugees in their ports.[10] Fear of refugees, perhaps owing to muhajir involvement in the "Bulgarian horrors" of 1876, spread widely. A British consul reported a local rumor that, upon leaving Bulgaria, Circassian refugees had abducted Christian girls and sought to sell them into slavery in Syria. The Beirut authorities investigated and found only one Christian woman living among muhajirs. She claimed to have voluntarily followed a young Circassian man by the name of Isma'il and wanted to marry him and convert to Islam. The governor put her under house arrest, and the Greek Orthodox clergy tried to change her mind, to no avail.[11] The Tripoli Christians also complained to local consuls that the Circassians had assaulted and robbed a Christian merchant. The ensuing investigation found that the aforementioned merchant was drunk at the time of the incident and harassed a Circassian woman, incurring the wrath of her compatriots.[12]

The second Circassian refugee crisis, while breeding misery for many, provided financial opportunities for a select few. The Refugee Commission largely footed the bill for muhajir expenses, which meant that municipal authorities could claim reimbursement for their incurred expenses. City councils contracted with private vendors to provide services for refugees. Bakers supplied tons of bread, pharmacists prescribed medications, and boaters and drovers transported refugee families. For example, in 1878, a Tripoli bread merchant, Mustafa Aga al-Shermene, received 309,851 kuruş for two and a half months' worth of bread and dry biscuits for refugees.[13] Contemporary observers noted nepotism and embezzlement of funds earmarked for refugees, as municipalities awarded generous contracts to local businesses on the Istanbul money.[14]

Municipal officials sought to move refugees out of port cities to interior locations as soon as possible to open space for new refugees and to prevent the further spread of the epidemics. The government would dispatch refugees from Beirut to Damascus, from Acre and Haifa to Nablus, from Tripoli and Latakia to Homs and Hama, and from Alexandretta to Aleppo. From those cities, North Caucasians were sent to surrounding Palestinian and Syrian villages, where they waited for several months for the government to find inland areas for their permanent settlement.

REFUGEE RESETTLEMENT IN THE LEVANT

Several North Caucasian refugee communities settled in the Levant before 1878. The first Circassians arrived in Syria by sea as early as 1859. They were few, and their agricultural villages around Quneitra, Nablus, and Aleppo likely failed.[15] By 1868, 13,648 Chechens settled in Ra's al-'Ayn in northeast-ern Syria. They were part of the Russo-Ottoman population transfer of 1865, which followed the uprising of 1864 in Chechnya, and came overland via Vladikavkaz, Kars, and Muş.[16] Around 1872, about 1,000 Circassians and 400 Dagestanis settled around Homs and Hama and in the Golan Heights.[17] Epidemics and conflicts with nomads took a toll on these early muhajir com-munities. By the late 1870s, only 5,000 Chechens remained in Ra's al-'Ayn, the rest having perished or moved to Iraq. Only 300–400 people lived in Quneitra, and refugee villages around Hama and Nablus lay abandoned.[18]

The second Circassian refugee crisis, in 1878–80, coincided with a change in provincial leadership in Syria. Midhat Pasha, who had served as governor of Danube Province between 1864 and 1868 and grand vizier during the First Constitutional Era in 1876–77, after a brief exile in Europe was appointed governor of Damascus Province in 1878. In his career, Midhat Pasha oversaw two Ottoman provinces, designated as major resettlement regions, during the two Circassian refugee crises. His vision for what muhajirs could do for the province remained the same. Midhat Pasha planned to double the revenues of Damascus Province by boosting agricultural production on the fertile but uncultivated *miri* lands, especially in southern Syria, and the new refugee population, whom he had previously settled as farmers in the Balkans, per-fectly fit his agenda.[19] The resettlement procedure was different the second time around. Midhat Pasha must have reflected on what happened in the Balkans, and his administration did not settle Muslim refugees into villages with other populations, especially Christians, but rather allowed them to choose where to settle. North Caucasians either joined their kin in the ref-ugee villages established before 1878 or founded new villages near rare wells and creeks on the outskirts of the Syrian Desert.

The Ottoman government pursued a more intentional refugee resettle-ment strategy after the Treaty of Berlin of 1878. With massive territorial losses in the Balkans and Russia's looming threat in the east, the Ottomans sought to fortify their rule in the Arab provinces. The government used the second Circassian refugee crisis to place refugees where it wanted them to be. The resettlement policy was both religiously conscious, especially in Christian-heavy regions of Anatolia, and ethnically conscious in Muslim-majority parts of the Levant. North Caucasians, as outsiders with no local allegiances, were expected to help Istanbul to strengthen its authority and even reclaim more territory for the state.

North Caucasian refugees settled in five clusters in the Ottoman Levant: Circassian and Chechen villages around Amman in Transjordan; Circassian, Chechen, and Ossetian villages around Quneitra in the Golan Heights; Circassian, Balkar, and Karachay villages around Marj al-Sultan in the Damascus area; Dagestani and Circassian villages between Homs and Hama; and Chechen villages around Ra's al-'Ayn in the Jazira region (see map 3). Circassians also revived the ancient town of Jerash in Transjordan and established the villages of Manbij and Khanasir in northern Syria and of Kafr Kama and Rehaniye in Palestine.[20] Furthermore, a mixed Circassian, Chechen, and Ossetian population settled in northern Syria in Raqqa, a city that would be catapulted to global prominence in 2014 as the capital of the self-proclaimed Islamic State. Between 1866 and 1908, up to 70,0000 North Caucasians arrived in the Levant.[21]

The North Caucasian resettlement proceeded along the Ottoman nomadic frontier in the Levant. Although refugee villages were located at a great distance from each other, one could draw a line going through most of them. This imaginary line was not random: it went along the western edge of the Syrian Desert and separated sedentary Levantine communities from nomadic ones. This line at times overlapped with the old pilgrimage caravan route connecting Aleppo with Damascus and Medina. The Ottomans pursued several interrelated goals in settling muhajirs there: to expand agricultural production eastward, to assert state control over nomads' land, to increase travel security in those areas, and—ultimately—to enforce taxation on both nomadic communities and nearby fellahin (peasants or villagers) who had shirked their responsibilities.

North Caucasian refugee resettlement in Transjordan was part of the Ottoman strategy to integrate the Levant's nomadic frontier into the empire by encouraging permanent settlement and cultivation of land. The Ottomans had claimed sovereignty over this arid region to the east of the Jordan River since 1516 but established minimal administrative and military presence there. For centuries, shaykhs of powerful bedouin communities exercised real authority across vast territories to the east of Nablus and to the south of Damascus. The nomadic frontier went through the region of the Balqa' in central

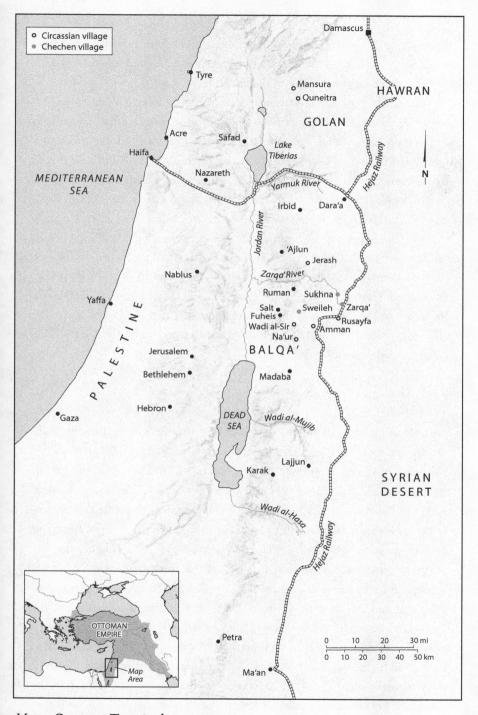

Map 5. **Ottoman Transjordan, 1914.**

Transjordan, where Arabic-speaking bedouin and fellahin communities long lived side by side. The urban population there was limited to the town of Salt, beyond which lay the domain of the bedouin.[22]

The settlement in late Ottoman Transjordan accelerated in the 1860s, when Transjordanian Christian communities started setting up new villages in the Balqa' because of overpopulation or strife in their old towns. Orthodox Arabs from Salt founded Fuheis and Rumaymin, and Catholic Arabs from Karak settled in the ruins of the ancient city of Madaba.[23] Bedouin communities also established dozens of agricultural estates and villages in an attempt to solidify their claims to their ancestral land and to stake out their share in agricultural production and trade. Between 1878 and 1914, Muslim refugee communities established their own villages, all to the east of Salt (see map 5). Turkmens settled in Ruman (1884) and Lajjun (1905).[24] Circassians established Amman (1878), Wadi al-Sir (1880), Jerash (1884), Na'ur (1901), and Rusayfa (1904). Chechens founded Zarqa' (1902), Sukhna (1905), and Sweileh (1906).[25] By the end of Ottoman rule, between 5,000 and 6,500 North Caucasian muhajirs lived in Transjordan.[26]

THE MAKING OF AMMAN

The foundation of Amman by Circassians in 1878 has multiple origin stories. Although Amman had an illustrious history in antiquity, thriving under the Babylonians, Romans, Byzantines, and Umayyads, it laid in ruins by the onset of Ottoman rule. It remains unclear how Circassian refugees in Amman ended up so far south. Laurence Oliphant, a Victorian traveler who surveyed Palestine in order to promote Jewish settlement, visited the Balqa' in 1878 and came upon destitute Circassian refugees in the ruins of Amman's Roman theater mere months after their arrival.[27] He believed that the Ottoman government had sent them there. Indeed, at that time the Ottomans prioritized agricultural development of the Balqa' and even considered creating the province of Amman, with the hope that the ruins of the ancient city would be settled again.[28] Amman's Circassian community preserves an alternative origins narrative, namely that Circassians scouted out the area and chose it themselves, after which Ottoman provincial officials approved the settlement site.[29] This type of refugee-led settlement was common in the Ottoman Levant and is how Chechen muhajirs established their villages in Transjordan.[30] Amman's prime attractions were two precious sources of water—Sayl ʿAmman, a stream running through the valley, and the Amman springs. The Circassian village grew on the banks of the stream, which dried up during the summer. By 1880, only 150 refugees remained of the original group of 500 refugees, but the settlement in Amman survived, thanks to successive arrivals of new refugees.[31]

The village of Amman had an almost exclusively Circassian population but remained far from culturally and economically homogeneous, divided into four distinct neighborhoods—Shapsugh, Qabartay, Abzakh, and Muhajirin. The first settlers were western Circassians of the Shapsugh community who had been expelled from Bulgaria in 1877–78. Some refugee founders were survivors of a shipwreck of the Austrian Lloyd's steamer Sphinx. The ship carried Circassian refugees from Kavala to Latakia and caught fire near Cyprus, claiming the lives of 500 Circassians.[32] The Shapsugh survivors made homes in the ruins of Amman's Roman theater (see figure 3) and the nearby caves. Their neighborhood stretched from the theater to the foothills of Jabal al-Qalʿa and Jabal al-Jofeh. The Shapsughs set up their gardens along Sayl ʿAmman into the valley and took up pastures to the south and east of the village. Kabardians (eastern Circassians) and Abzakhs (western Circassians) formed the second group of refugees. They arrived between 1880 and 1892 and came to be referred as "people of Amman" (ahl ʿAmman) to differentiate them, the core population of the village, from those who came before or after them.[33] Some of them had been expelled from the Balkans, others arrived from refugee villages in Anatolia, and later groups came directly from the Caucasus. The Qabartay quarter, named after Kabardians, was Amman's largest neighborhood, extending from the old ʿOmari mosque to the southern slopes of Jabal al-Qalʿa. The Abzakh quarter, the smallest in size, reached the slopes of Jabal Weibdeh and Wadi al-Haddadeh. By 1891, the Shapsugh quarter numbered about 120 households, the Qabartay quarter—139 households, and the Abzakh quarter—35 households.[34] The fourth and youngest Circassian neighborhood was founded by Kabardians who arrived from the Russian Empire in separate parties in 1902, 1904, and 1906–7. They settled at a distance from others, near the Amman springs, which gave the Arabic name to their quarter, Raʾs al-ʿAyn, although many locals called it Muhajirin.[35]

The architecture of early Amman was unlike anything else in the Levant.

Figure 3. **Ottoman Amman.**
Photograph by the American Colony in Jerusalem, between 1900 and 1920.
View from the Roman theater toward the Qabartay quarter. Library of
Congress, Prints and Photographs Division. LC-DIG-matpc-05751.

Circassians built their houses like they would in the Caucasus, while making
use of local materials. They took timber from the old oak forest, which once
grew to the west of Amman, to make long wooden beams that held up the
ceilings of their houses. Circassians used elaborate carpentry and woodcarv-
ing techniques. Their houses had a long outside porch that opened into different rooms in an elongated gallery-like floorplan. Many houses had chimneys,
which were common in the Caucasus but unusual in Transjordan. Circassians
learned to build house walls of mudbrick, like Transjordanian fellahin, and
lay roofs with tiles, instead of hay, as was typical back in the Caucasus.[36] In
1895, Frederick Jones Bliss, an American archaeologist and son of the founder
of the Syrian Protestant College (now the American University of Beirut),
complimented the orderly look of Amman: "The town has a neat, thrifty

appearance. Every room has a chimney; every house its porch or balcony. The yards are nicely swept."[37]

Muhajirs also transformed the landscape around Amman. When Circassians arrived, the stunning ruins of Rabbath Ammon, the capital of the Kingdom of Ammon, later known as Philadelphia under the Romans, were still visible above ground. The refugee village grew on top of the ruins, and Circassians used the old stones for construction. Within a generation, Rabbath Ammon faded away, although the great Roman theater, the Odeon (small theater), the Nymphaeum (public fountain), and the Citadel remained untouched. The Circassian village was surrounded by forests of pine, evergreen oak, and shrub, which provided refuge to leopards, wolves, and hyenas.[38] Circassians soon denuded forested hills and used the timber to build mills, granaries, and ox-drawn wheeled carts.[39] The latter were new to the region and gave Circassians an edge in agricultural logistics. They built roads connecting their villages with each other and the town of Salt and grew cereals. Amman and other villages were surrounded by fields of wheat and barley. The Circassians were turning the eastern Balqa' into bustling farming country.

The muhajirs' chief concern was securing their rights to the land. The Ottoman government guaranteed muhajirs the right to free land, but much of the land around Amman had already been claimed. Local bedouin communities regarded the eastern Balqa' as their territory, and in 1894 they attacked Circassians in Amman and Wadi al-Sir, destroying their crops and uprooting their trees.[40] Salti notables also laid claims to the land and, between 1889 and 1892, challenged the district government's award of 12,000 dönüm to recently arrived muhajirs. The Saltis involved officials in Damascus and Istanbul, who settled the case in their favor.[41] When the first land registry in the Balqa' opened in Salt in 1891, Circassians of Amman became some of its earliest clients, rushing to formalize and protect their right to the land.

The new Ottoman land regime, based on the Land Code of 1858, required Ottoman subjects to register land in new land registries that were set up throughout the empire. The new land regime accorded Ottoman subjects an individual title, not communal title, to the land, which accelerated the commodification of the land. The land registry recorded land in two types of registers: *yoklama* and *da'imi*. The *yoklama* (roll call) registers recorded the size of property and levied tax upon registration. Muhajirs did not pay tax during the registration because the land was given to them for free, in accordance with the Immigration Law of 1857. In contrast, settled Transjordanians and bedouin were required to pay taxes when registering land.[42] The *da'imi* registers recorded transactions on the land that had already been registered. In the Balqa', most agricultural land belonged in the *miri* category, whereas urban property, such as houses, gardens, stables, and caves, belonged in the *mülk* category. During the sale of *mülk* property, a seller transferred the right of ownership (Ott. Tur., *rakabe*; Ar., *raqāba*) to a buyer. During the sale of *miri* land, one transferred merely the usufruct to that land because the state remained the owner of the land; usufruct rights were indefinite and inheritable as long as the land was cultivated and the tithe was paid to the government. Muhajirs could sell only their usufruct after twenty years of tilling the land that they had received for free. They could, however, use their own funds to purchase usufruct rights to additional land, which they could then resell at any time.

Before the establishment of the land registry in Salt, property transactions were recorded in the town's shari'a court. Shari'a courts did not tax property transactions. Thereby, the land registry's assumption of the shari'a court's historical function of land registration expanded the state's control over land and tax revenue.[43] Yet even in the final Ottoman decades, residents of the Balqa', including muhajirs, regarded the court as a legitimate recordkeeper of their real estate history and often registered changes in the ownership and transfer of land in both the shari'a court and the land registry. Ottoman subjects also went to the shari'a court, or the new institution of the *nizamiye* court, to settle disputes over land.[44]

Land registers are a valuable source for tracing the transformation of property relations and capital in the late Ottoman Empire. Land registers were printed in Ottoman Turkish and filled out by a *tapu* (title deed) official. Each *da'imi* record included information on the land's category, location, size, seller and buyer names, transaction date, cadastral value at time of registration, and purchase price. Land registers remain authoritative records about land ownership and could be used in litigation, including in hypothetical compensation claims. This is why access to many late Ottoman registers has been limited, including at Turkey's General Directorate of Land Registry and Cadastre, which holds most Ottoman land records.[45] Ottoman land registers for Transjordan are preserved in the Department of Land and Survey in Amman. Thanks to an unexpected permission from Jordan's Interior Ministry, I received access to those records, which allowed me to compile a dataset of all property transactions by Circassian refugees in and around Amman between 1889 and 1913.[46] Ottoman land registers certainly have their limitations. A prerequisite for every transaction was the willingness of a buyer and a seller to place their business on record and pay tax. Land registers also could not account for the shadow real estate economy that was based on private agreements, especially within refugee and bedouin communities. And yet, this collection of Amman's real estate transactions allows extraordinary insight into the evolution of the new land regime in the Middle East.

The earliest *yoklama* registrations in Amman occurred in the 1880s, when *tapu* officials from other districts arrived to formally register the land that had been allotted to Shapsugh and Kabardian residents.[47] The opening of the land registry in Salt commenced mass land registration in the Shapsugh, Qabartay, and Abzakh quarters in 1893.[48] Circassian families also staked land outside of their villages, by the Amman springs, with fourteen households registering a total of 805 dönüm in 1893 and seventeen households registering 1,650 dönüm in 1897.[49] When new Kabardian muhajirs arrived and settled by the springs in 1902, little agricultural land was left for them. Tensions over land tenure ran high in Amman's Circassian community, and new immigrants traveled to the provincial capital of Damascus to complain about their mistreatment by fellow Circassians to the governor.[50] In 1906, another round of land registration took place. In the Qabartay quarter, 136 households each registered a house of 190 arşın (1,166 square feet), a garden of 400 arşın (2,454 square feet), and 70 dönüm of agricultural land.[51] By then, new Circassian immigrants were taking up land around Amman's hills, including in the area of 'Abdoun, which has some of Jordan's most expensive real estate today. The final round of Circassian registration of land in Amman occurred in 1912.[52]

The Circassian villages were soon integrated into the Levantine networks of capital. The chief commercial attraction of the Balqa' was cheap grain that had a ready market for consumption or resale in Damascus, Jerusalem, and Nablus. The main grain-producing area in the Levant was Hawran, now in southern Syria and northern Jordan. The cultivation of Hawrani wheat went up in the wake of increased European demand during the Crimean War of

1853–56 and poor harvests in Britain and France in the early 1860s. Syrian landowners and merchants then made a profit on the rising price of grain on global markets. The Long Depression crushed the prices and demand for Levantine grain, which contributed to social unrest in the Hawran between the 1860s and 1890s.[53] By the 1890s, the fortunes of Syrian grain producers and merchants rebounded thanks to the domestic market. The booming Levantine cities of Jaffa, Haifa, Beirut, Nablus, and Damascus drove the demand for Levantine grain. Yet the production of wheat in the fertile Hawran plain had long been dominated by Damascene landowning families. A fierce competition for slim profits in the 1870s and 1880s pushed grain merchants to develop new supply chains, including in the Balqaʾ. Urban merchants had previously been wary of investing in central Transjordan, with its small farming population and bedouin hold on the best land. The settlement of North Caucasian refugees and the establishment of private agricultural estates raised the investment potential of the Balqaʾ for Levantine merchants.[54]

The first Arab investment in Amman came from the nearby town of Salt. In the early 1890s, Raghib bin ʿAbd al-Qadir Shammut, a Salti merchant and moneylender, bought four shops in the Shapsugh quarter for 2,300 kuruş each.[55] Salti investors in Amman also came from al-Kurdi, Malhas, al-Mashini, al-Musharbash, al-Raghib, and al-Zaʿmat families.[56] Salti merchants lent money to fellahin and bedouin of the Balqaʾ, some of whom eventually defaulted on their obligations and handed over their land. Meanwhile, Saltis resold the Balqaʾ grain to their trade partners in Nablus and Jerusalem. The arrival of Salti business commenced the transformation of the village of Amman into a small town. Amman became the entrepôt of agricultural production in the eastern Balqaʾ, now linked via Salti merchants to networks of capital in eastern and northern Palestine.

The fortunes of Amman grew with the construction of the Hejaz Railway, which connected the town to Damascus in 1903 and Medina in 1908.[57] The railway followed the old pilgrimage caravan route. The Hejaz Railway, built as part of the Ottoman efforts to "modernize" the hajj, was the only railway ever funded solely by Ottoman capital.[58] A journey from Damascus to Amman, which previously took several days in a heavily armed caravan, could now be completed in thirteen hours, with Turkish coffee or Arabic tea served on demand.[59] The Hejaz Railway placed the southernmost refugee villages in the empire within the Levantine railway grid. The agricultural products of the Balqa' could now be delivered, through the railway extension in Dar'a, to Haifa and, via the French-built Syrian railway network, to Beirut, Homs, Tripoli, and Aleppo. The Hejaz Railway accelerated the economic transformation of central and northern Transjordan, laying the infrastructural foundation of the modern Jordanian state.

After the opening of the Hejaz Railway, Levantine investment in Amman's real estate increased dramatically. Previously, local Circassians and Salti merchants owned most shops in town. Between 1904 and 1909, Damascene merchants alone purchased thirteen shops, or 43 percent of all shops sold in this period (see table 5). In the Qabartay quarter, the average price of a shop rose from 543 kuruş in the 1890s to 1,580 kuruş in 1901–3, to 4,086 kuruş in 1904–9, and to 6,839 kuruş in 1910–12.[60] Damascene merchants brought the needed capital to facilitate the bulk purchase and export of the Balqa' grain out of Amman.

Many Syrian merchants who invested in shops in Amman operated from the Maydan district of Damascus, which specialized in southern Syrian markets, and came with a wealth of experience in buying grain in the Hawran and trading with Druze and bedouin communities.[61] Central Transjordan was a natural geographic extension of their already existing market of supply and demand. Many merchants invested in agricultural estates in the Balqa', purchasing land from bedouin shaykhs and employing local bedouin and fellahin as sharecroppers. Damascenes, Nabulsis, and Saltis often partnered with each other, when buying shops and stables from local Circassians. Damascene families that entered the Amman real estate market included al-Bostanji, al-Halawani, Hatahet, al-Khayr, al-Qassar, al-Qattan, al-Rabbat, al-Sa'di, al-Shami, and al-Smadi.[62] The arrival of Syrian capital signaled that the Balqa' was open for business on a new scale, further accelerating an influx of investment from elsewhere. Thus, the 'Asfur and Zaqdah from Nablus and al-Kiswani from around Jerusalem bought real estate in Amman in the 1900s.[63]

Arab merchants purchased not only shops but also houses, and many relocated to Amman (see table 6). The opening of the Hejaz Railway commenced a boom in residential property values. Before 1903, houses in Amman rarely sold for more than 2,000 kuruş. By the early 1910s, Damascene and

Buyers	1891–95	1896–99	1900–03	1904–09	1910–12
Circassians		6	2	9	4
Levantine merchants					
from Salt	4		5	3	6
from Damascus				13	7
from Nablus				1	2
from Jerusalem area				4	
Total	**4**	**6**	**7**	**30**	**19**

Table 5. **Shops purchased in Amman, 1891–1912.**
All sellers were Circassians.

Buyers	1889–95	1896–99	1900–03	1904–09	1910–12
Circassians			4	6	4
Transjordanian bedouin				4	1
Levantine merchants					
from Salt	2	2	3	2.5	1.5
from Damascus				9.5	8.5
from Nablus				1	3
Total	**2**	**2**	**7**	**23**	**18**

Table 6. **Houses purchased in Amman, 1889–1912.**
Most sellers were Circassians. Saltis started reselling houses in 1903, and Damascenes started in 1907. Several houses were purchased by partnerships of merchants from different cities.

Sources: DLS Defters 5/1/1, 7/1/1, 10/1/1, 18/1/1, 19/1/1, 30/1/2, 31/1/2, and 32/1/2; an expanded dataset from Hamed-Troyansky, "Making of Amman," 612.

Nabulsi families, such as Hatahet, Darwish, al-Smadi, al-Sukkar, and 'Asfur, paid 10,000 kuruş or more for their family residences in the Shapsugh and Abzakh quarters.[64] Bedouin shaykhs also purchased houses in Amman as an investment vehicle or as guest houses for their tribal members who visited the town for business. Thus, in 1912, Shaykh Idris, son of Shaykh Rajab, bought a property in the Abzakh quarter for 5,430 kuruş.[65]

The rise of Amman led to the emergence of wealthy Circassian landowners. Circassian muhajirs built their initial capital through the export of wheat. They used the profits from grain sale to purchase cattle from the bedouin, which helped them to expand their arable fields. Many families invested new profits into purchasing more land. By the 1900s, muhajirs would make a handsome profit by selling their land to Syrian and Palestinian merchants and further reinvesting into real estate. Circassian families, such as Khurma, Qursha, and Matkari, not only built and purchased shops, thereby establishing themselves in local trade, but also entered into partnerships with Arab merchants.[66] Entrepreneurial Circassian families usually belonged to the Shapsugh and Kabardian communities that arrived early and secured the best land in the area. Nevertheless, although still owning some of the best land in Amman, Circassian families could not compete with the Arab merchants' capital and access to the large markets of Damascus and Nablus.[67]

By the outbreak of World War I, Amman was a thriving Circassian town of 3,000–5,000 people.[68] It was a district center with its own government office, a postal and telegraph station, and a textile factory.[69] In March 1921, 'Abdullah bin al-Hussein, of the Hashemite family, which led the Arab Revolt against the Ottoman Empire, arrived in Amman. He would soon be proclaimed the ruler of the Emirate of Transjordan (1921–46) and then the Hashemite Kingdom of Transjordan (after 1946, and of Jordan since 1949). Amman was by no means the largest town in the country, but what served the Hashemites well was its strategic location on the Hejaz Railway, its access to Syrian and Palestinian merchant capital, its proximity to the Bani Sakhr who became Emir 'Abdullah's early allies, and its distance from other Transjordanian powerholders.[70] Amman was officially confirmed as Transjordan's capital city in 1928. A non-Arab refugee town, where people spoke Circassian on the streets well into the 1920s, became the capital of a new Arab state.[71] When the Hashemites first entered Amman, the first generation of Circassian refugees who had sheltered in the ruins of the Roman theater and in nearby caves in 1878 may have still been alive.

SAYETKHAN'S FAMILY HISTORY

This chapter's opening story about the Circassian woman Sayetkhan bint Qurash bin Qoghuluq gives us rare insight into the life of upper-status Circassians in Ottoman Amman. Sayetkhan was born in one of the villages founded by Circassian refugees in the Golan Heights after their expulsion from the Balkans.[72] Sometime in the mid-1890s, she married Hajj Hamid bin Hajj Islam, from a wealthy Kabardian family in Amman. It was common for Circassians in Jordan to seek a marital partner among Circassians in the Golan Heights well into the twentieth century.[73] They married in Quneitra (now in Syria) and then left for Amman. The couple had two children, daughter Gül'azar and son 'Azir. We do not have papers or photographs of this family, and even their family name seems lost to history. What remains is an extensive legal record that Sayetkhan and her loved ones left in Salt's shari'a court and land registry.

Sayetkhan's husband Hajj Hamid died in 1899, shortly after the birth of their son. Their two children inherited a large land portfolio, which included eleven plots of land around Amman totaling 1,258 dönüm at the cadastral price of 30,490 kuruş.[74] Hajj Hamid's family must have purchased much of this land from the bedouin with their profits from grain sale. The family also owned six shops in the Qabartay quarter. In 1901, Sayetkhan's father-in-law and the family's patriarch Hajj Islam passed as well. His death sparked a series of lawsuits that exposed tensions among grieving relatives and scandalized Amman's Circassian community.

Shortly after the patriarch's death, 'Amr Efendi, a relative acting on behalf of the family, filed a lawsuit against Sayetkhan. He accused the widow of concealing valuable items from the inventory of her late husband's property. She allegedly hid 20 French liras, 500 kile (28,285 pounds) of barley, two wool mattresses, two silk blankets, a copper dining table, a prayer rug, three carpets, a sewing machine, a harness, seven saddlebags, and a cow. The family accused her of intentionally lowering her own children's inheritance of Hajj Hamid's estate. The court stripped Sayetkhan of her guardianship rights over her five-year-old daughter and two-year-old son. Sayetkhan then hired a Circassian lawyer, Jawad Bey, as her defense attorney. Jawad Bey, born in Russia's Kuban region, was educated in Istanbul, briefly lived with the rest of his muhajir family in central Anatolia, and only recently arrived in Amman. His family members are the protagonists of the next chapter. Sayetkhan may have chosen him because, like her, he was an outsider in Amman's established Circassian community. Jawad Bey insisted in court that his client was innocent: Sayetkhan had put 'Amr Efendi in charge of conducting the inventory, and he must have omitted property, which remained in the house, on purpose. Moreover, Sayetkhan accused 'Amr Efendi of embezzling rent from her late husband's seven shops for the last two and a half years. The court, upon reviewing Sayetkhan's claims, kept its earlier verdict.[75]

'Amr Efendi then initiated a lawsuit against the Circassian imam of Amman's community, Hajj Sha'b Efendi bin Tahir bin Duruq. The late Hajj Islam had given the imam 60 Ottoman liras and 20 French liras as zakat to distribute to people in need. 'Amr Efendi claimed that the family patriarch had turned insane toward the end of his life and that therefore the transaction should be considered invalid and the money should be returned. The imam denied that the community's benefactor was mentally incapacitated and claimed that he had already distributed the money. 'Amr Efendi then summoned two witnesses to testify in court. Their job was to cast doubt on the sanity of the late Hajj Islam. They both recalled how "Hajj Islam entered the running stream, by his village, naked. People who were passing by, old and young, told him that it was shameful. He replied to them that it was not shameful." The Ottoman judge, upon hearing about skinny-dipping, asked two prominent members of Amman's Circassian community, a muhtar and another imam, to vouch for the trustworthiness of the two witnesses. They reported that the two witnesses should not be trusted. The judge then dismissed the unflattering testimonies and ruled that the plaintiff had no right to claim money from the defendant.[76] Accusing one's own deceased patriarch of insanity and reclaiming zakat from an imam, as well as inviting an Ottoman court to adjudicate this sensitive matter, certainly suggests a deep rift within the family and in its relationship with others.

The following day, the family was back in court. The judge read Hajj Islam's will to the family in the presence of two men: Jawad Bey, Sayetkhan's attorney, and Muhammad Agha, a cousin of Hajj Hamid who arrived in

Amman from Anatolia to take care of family business. The patriarch's underage daughter, Khadija, and two grandchildren, Gül'azar and 'Azir, inherited
all his property. All household items, farm animals, recent harvest, and un-
collected debts were painstakingly detailed in an inventory (see table 7).

The family that Sayetkhan had married into was among the wealthiest in
Amman. Notably, like most muhajirs, this family derived much of its income
from agriculture. About 58 percent of the inheritance was in harvested wheat,
barley, bulgur, and fennel, likely slated for export. The listing of "Tyghene(f),"
daughter of 'Abdullah, as a female slave in the inventory (table 7) with her declared value of 180 kuruş, less than half of a sewing machine, is jarring. Amid
a dozen court records involving the family of her mistresses and masters, her
name appears only once, in this inventory of property. We can only guess
what her fate was in Sayetkhan's or Khadija's households.

The following year, Sayetkhan married Muhammad Agha, her late husband's cousin from Anatolia. She might have been married off by her in-laws
who wished to rein her in, or she might have married him to find a new footing in her late husband's family. Shortly thereafter, she regained legal guardianship over her two children, which she shared with her new husband, but it
was Muhammad Agha whom the judge had appointed as the sole custodian
of the children's wealth. Muhammad Agha swore to manage their wealth in
the best interests of his stepchildren, namely "to preserve what ought to be
preserved and to sell what it is feared might be damaged."[77]

Muhammad Agha used the children's inheritance for moneylending. He
lent 27,799 kuruş to two men: the aforementioned 'Amr Efendi and his business partner Sa'id bin Khayr bin Abu Qura, a Damascene merchant and one
of the largest moneylenders in Salt.[78] They obliged to repay the loan, with interest, within nine months. As the Balqa' real estate and trade were booming,
well-off Circassians could grow their capital by moneylending to moneylenders. Muhammad Agha also lent 9,425 kuruş to Sayetkhan's attorney Jawad
Bey, in cash and in residential property.[79]

Sayetkhan's second wedding bliss, if there had been one, was short-lived.
Several months later, Sayetkhan sued her new husband over her dower from
her first marriage. Sayetkhan's dower, promised by the late Hajj Hamid,
constituted 240 Ottoman liras, including an advance payment (Ar., *mahr
mu'ajjal* or *muqaddam*) and a deferred one (Ar., *mahr mu'ajjal* or *mu'akhkhar*),

Quantity	Property	Value, kuruş
Furniture and household items		
9	Carpets	1,573
5	Rugs	301
2	Silk blankets	74
1	Sewing machine	435
1	Dye	16
2	Carriage axletrees	120
1	Mirror	13
33	Pillows	
5	Mattresses	628
7	Blankets	
2	Carpets	
8	Teacups	250
6	Spoons	
1	Copper tray	
5	Copper dishes	90
7	Tin dishes	
2	Copper jugs	
1	Copper pitcher	
2	Bowls	50
6	Spoons	
1	Copper pitcher	
1	Tin pitcher	180
3	Copper cauldrons	
2	Dining tables	
2	Wooden chests	144
4	Saddlebags	
1	Copper tray	81
6	Curtains	95
2	Oil lamps	
1	Iron chain	15
23	Glass beads	
1	Hand plough	110
4	Chinese-style pots	
2	Copper pots	87
2	Frying pans	
1	Circassian harness with saddle	720
1	Silver dagger	720
1	Circassian belt	
1	Mechanical clock	500
2	Qaradagh roses (?)	
1	Birdcage chair	48
6	Saddlebags	290
Agricultural products and farm animals		
1,530 şāʿ	Wheat	7,650
1,581 şāʿ	Barley	5,102.5
250 şāʿ	Wheat	
84 şāʿ	Barley	1,018
25 şāʿ	Burghul	
500 şāʿ	Barley, fennel	1,000
	Wheat, barley	82
73 şāʿ	Cheese	292
1	Calf	106
2	Oxen	1,360
2	Cows	
2	Donkeys	192
1	Agricultural cart	
Cash and loans		
8	Ottoman liras	1,607.5
5	French liras, in cash	
	Loan due (wheat and barley)	357
	Loan due	96.5
Slave		
	Tyghene(f) bint ʿAbdullah	180
Total		**25,583 kuruş 20 para**

Table 7. **Inventory of Hajj Islam's inheritance, 1901.**

Source: CDM Defter Salt 6, f. 53 (3 şaban 1901, 15 November 1901).

typically paid upon a husband's death or upon divorce. In both shari'a law and Circassian customary law, the dower belonged exclusively to the wife. In practice, it was rarely separated from the household value. Sayetkhan resorted to a lawsuit to reclaim that value out of her late husband's estate, which her new husband now controlled.[80] The court placed the burden of proof on the claimant. Jawad Bey, as Sayetkhan's attorney, brought forward five witnesses who had been present at the signing of the marriage contract: two Circassians from Amman and three Circassians from the Golan Heights. The latter confirmed her late husband's pledge of 240 Ottoman liras. In the absence of evidence that Sayetkhan ever received that money, the court ordered Muhammad Agha to pay the old dower to his wife out of her first husband's estate.[81] Sayetkhan, who had initially been maligned in the Salt shari'a court, now used the court to get her due.

By the early twentieth century, North Caucasian muhajirs, including refugee women, commonly sought justice by going to court. Muhajir trust in this Ottoman institution built over time. Circassian names start appearing in the registers of the Salt shari'a court around 1890–91.[82] At first, muhajirs came to court to register their marriages or to contest property with a non-Circassian party, typically a Salti merchant. Within a decade, muhajirs actively went to court to legitimize their economic transactions, especially the transfer of usufruct rights to the land, or to solve economic disputes within the Circassian community. The court even employed a Circassian translator for those muhajirs who did not speak Arabic.[83] Between 1901 and 1903, 34 percent of all court cases in Circassian villages concerned inheritance, 25 percent—the repayment of loans, and 23 percent—the sale of or dispute over property.[84] Circassian women regularly brought their husbands, brothers, and uncles to court to reclaim a dower or to contest an unfair division of inheritance. By then, muhajirs began to appear as witnesses in lawsuits between their Arab neighbors, as the court helped them to solidify their position as a trustworthy partner and part of the socioeconomic fabric of the Balqa'.[85]

Shari'a court records, while providing a remarkable snapshot of refugees' lives, reveal as much in their silences. Circassians proved willing to expose their economic affairs to the court, but most aspects of their social life remained hidden from outsiders. For muhajirs, the Ottoman system of justice coexisted with customary law, or 'adat, which North Caucasians had been practicing for centuries. Muhajirs brought with them an extensive oral tradition of adjudicating all manners of family and criminal law. Muhajir elders, through the institution of village councils, took upon themselves to police social mores and to dispense justice as it used to be done in the Caucasus.[86] Shari'a courts logged few criminal incidents, such as theft, within muhajir communities because such transgressions would typically be handled in-house. Likewise, the Salt court adjudicated many conflicts over land between muhajirs and Levantine merchants but few between muhajirs and bedouin. Altercations between refugees and nomads had serious repercussions for the safety of both communities and were typically resolved through direct negotiation or mediation by local powerholders.

Sayetkhan's story, known to us through ledgers and court records, ends abruptly in the late 1900s. Her son, 'Azir, died, and she inherited his shares in the agricultural estate of 1,258 dönüm.[87] Sayetkhan died shortly thereafter. Everything that she owned was divided equally between Gül'azar, her oldest daughter, and Najiya, Sayetkhan's daughter with Muhammad Agha.[88] In 1909–10, the two heiresses re-registered all land in their names and had the Salt land registry reevaluate the cadastral value of their real estate. Much of their land was appraised at over 100 kuruş per dönüm, making it among the most expensive land around Amman.[89] Then, in 1912, Gül'azar came of age and inherited over two-thirds of the remaining estate of her late father. The remaining shares, which must have been reserved for Sayetkhan, were divided between her second daughter, her siblings, and her second husband's family.[90] Of the nine beneficiaries, seven were women. The estate included a sixteen-room residence, which was the largest house on record in Ottoman Amman and evaluated at 12,500 kuruş, and six shops, appraised at 3,000–5,000 kuruş each. The properties lay in the Qabartay quarter, adjacent to the main road connecting Damascus to Medina. By then, Sayetkhan's daughter Gül'azar was one of the richest women in the Balqa', and her agricultural and urban holdings were the largest, on record, of any resident in Amman.

Gül'azar and her family sold the properties to Yusuf al-Sukkar, a scion of al-Sukkar house, a Salti family that was well-established in Transjordanian commerce and politics. After the Young Turk Revolution of 1908, al-Sukkar was elected to the lower house of the Ottoman Assembly as a Greek Orthodox representative. Al-Sukkar offered Gül'azar and her relatives a sum that almost tripled the cadastral value of the property: 9,000–15,000 kuruş for each of the six shops and 32,340 kuruş for the sixteen-room house.[91] The sale of the property is the last Ottoman land record that involves this Circassian family. The family had no male heirs. Sayetkhan's daughters, Gül'azar and Najiya, likely married into Amman's other prominent families. Yet the legacy of this family lives on, linked to that of al-Sukkar, which epitomizes the Circassian-Levantine genealogy of Ottoman Amman. Today, most tourists to Amman are familiar with the Husseini Mosque, at the very heart of downtown. To the east of the mosque lies Suq al-Sukkar. This market, one of the oldest in the city, started with the shops that Sayetkhan's in-laws had built to serve Amman's Kabardian refugees and that Sayetkhan's daughter Gül'azar and her eight relatives had sold before World War I.

REFUGEES ON THE NOMADIC FRONTIER

The growth of Amman rested not only on the Hejaz Railway and Levantine merchant investment but also on relations that Amman's Circassians had forged with Transjordanian bedouin. The Ottoman government employed a range of policies toward the empire's nomadic populations. What remained consistent was the drive to make nomads more legible for Ottoman bureaucracy, including enumerating their property and turning them into taxpaying subjects.[92] In Transjordan, Muslim refugees helped to advance that strategy. The establishment of muhajir villages prompted the bedouin to preemptively register their land to ensure that the Ottomans not reassign it to refugees.

Amman lay in the territories of two rival bedouin communities: the 'Adwan, who led the Balqawiyya tribal confederation, and the Bani Sakhr.[93] In 1879, within a year of arrival of the first Circassian refugees, the 'Adwan, 'Abbad, 'Ajarma, and Da'ja bedouin registered about 56,780 dönüm in the vicinity of Amman.[94] In the following year, Midhat Pasha's government in Damascus issued a landmark decision against the Bani Sakhr in their dispute with the Christian community of Karak over the land that would become the village of Madaba in the southern Balqa'. The government reaffirmed that, in accordance with the Ottoman Land Code of 1858, nomads could preserve title to their land only if they registered it with the authorities and paid tax on it for the last three years.[95] The government had the right to recategorize the miri land as mahlul (escheated land) and reassign it to others if the land laid uncultivated for three years.[96] The provincial government's readiness to hand over nomadic territories to muhajirs forced bedouin to register their land and to set up agricultural estates. In the 1880s, Sattam al-Fayiz, leader of the most powerful clan of the Bani Sakhr, registered large tracts of fertile land in central Transjordan.[97] By the late nineteenth century, nomadic communities registered hundreds of thousands of dönüm around new muhajir villages. Eugene L. Rogan aptly described this process as bedouin's "defensive registration" of land, which helped them to preserve their claims to their historical territories and significantly expanded agricultural production on Syria's nomadic frontier.[98] The phenomenon was not limited to the Levant. Throughout the empire, the settlement of North Caucasian muhajirs prompted local communities to rush to register their usufruct rights to the land in new land registries, thereby assenting to state taxation and the new land regime based on the Land Code of 1858.[99]

The Bani Sakhr initially opposed the Circassian settlement but then made a deal with muhajirs against their bedouin rivals in the Balqawiyya tribal confederation.[100] In the late 1890s, the Bani Sakhr and the Circassians concluded a defensive alliance that required each party to support the other in case of attack by rival bedouin communities.[101] This alliance bolstered the security of travel and commerce in central Transjordan and is still commemorated by both communities; it was even symbolically renewed in 2013.[102]

The Circassians' alliance with the Bani Sakhr allowed Amman's marketplace to become an important regional trading hub, where Transjordanian bedouin brought their grain and cattle for sale. Muhajirs served as intermediaries who marketed bedouin products for export. An Anglican missionary wrote in 1893 that "most of the corn of the Belka [Balqa'] is brought here, and afterwards sent in charge of Circassians to Jerusalem."[103] Oral history confirms that local Circassians established connections with merchants in Jerusalem and traveled to Palestine to trade in wheat, barley, timber, and coal; those ties survived into the emirate era.[104] In the early twentieth century, Syrian and Palestinian merchants favored Amman as an investment destination partially because it provided access to the large pastoral economy of the Bani Sakhr.

The alliance with the Bani Sakhr helped Circassians to weather their conflict with the Balqawiyya tribal confederation, locally known as the Balqawiyya war, in 1910. The conflict erupted, reportedly, when bedouin attacked a local Circassian landowner and kidnapped his children. With communal honor at stake, Amman's Circassian men mobilized for an assault on the Balqawiyya bedouin. The roots of the conflict lay in the contestation of land ownership and access to water in the eastern Balqa'. By the 1900s, Amman's Circassians had been taking up land far outside of their village, which many Balqawiyya bedouin saw as provocation. The Bani Sakhr mediated the conflict, which ended in a peace agreement between the two parties.[105]

The conflict between the Circassians and the Balqawiyya tribal confederation was one among many on the Levant's nomadic frontier. For nomadic and seminomadic communities, muhajirs were settlers whom the Ottoman government sent to occupy their lands. In the provinces of Damascus and Aleppo, bedouin lost hundreds of thousands of dönüm to muhajirs because the former did not have *tapu* papers or could not pay back taxes to retain their title to the land. Correspondingly, muhajirs and bedouin clashed over land throughout the Levant. Near Ra's al-'Ayn in northeastern Syria, Chechens and Karabulaks fought with two tribal confederations, the Shammar and the 'Anaza.[106] In the Aleppo region, Circassians of Manbij clashed with the Abu Sultan and Bani Sa'id bedouin, and Circassians of Khanasir feuded with the 'Anaza bedouin.[107] Near Homs and Hama, Circassians fought with the Fawa'ira bedouin, prompting the Ottomans to intervene and mediate a peace settlement.[108]

The North Caucasians' most serious conflict occurred with the Druze in the Golan Heights in southwestern Syria. Circassians settled the village of Quneitra in 1873, and after 1878 they established twelve villages between the Druze-dominated Mount Hermon and Jabal al-Duruz. In later years, muhajirs from Kabarda, Ossetia, and Chechnya founded new villages in the Golan Heights.[109] The arrival of refugees launched a conflict over usufruct and grazing rights to the land, ever so precious in the volcanic topography of the Golan Heights. Skirmishes between muhajirs and the Druze started in 1881 when about 600 Druze carried out the first raid against the Circassian village of Mansura.[110] In 1894, several Druze men attacked and looted a Circassian caravan, killing a Circassian woman. This incident escalated to new clashes, culminating in the Druze siege of Mansura. Hüsrev Pasha, the Circassian head of gendarmerie of Damascus Province, brought his regiment and, on behalf of the Ottoman government, forced the two parties into negotiations and eventually into a truce. The Ottomans compelled Druze elders to issue an apology and pay restitution of 1,000 Ottoman liras to the Circassians.[111] The coerced truce did not last long. In 1895, a 3,000-strong Druze force attacked the village of Mansura for the third time. For the Druze, a clash with Circassians was part of their larger conflict with the Ottoman government. In the same year, the Druze of Hawran had declared a rebellion against Ottoman authority, in part resisting the reintroduction of conscription, and had raided several Muslim and Christian villages in the area.[112] The Druze perceived the settlement of Circassians in the Golan Heights as a new Ottoman ploy to police, dispossess, and (over)tax them. The Druze of the Golan Heights received reinforcements from fellow Druze militias in Mount Lebanon and Jabal al-Duruz in southern Syria. The Circassians fought alongside al-Fadl bedouin, with whom they previously clashed over pasture rights but with whom they concluded a defensive alliance fifteen years earlier. Their joint forces numbered 2,000 men. The Circassian-bedouin alliance nearly lost the battle, but the tide turned in their favor when Ottoman reinforcements arrived from Damascus, this time headed by another Circassian, Mirza Wasfi, with additional troops from Beirut. The Ottoman forces pursued the Druze across the Golan Heights and burned down Majdal Shams and other Druze villages.[113] By intervening militarily on the side of muhajirs, the Ottoman government sent a clear signal throughout the region that, if needed, it would protect the muhajirs' right to the land because that also meant defending the state's authority to allot *miri* land to whomever it saw fit. Circassian skirmishes with Druze and bedouin over land in the Golan Heights continued into the early twentieth century.[114]

Mirza Wasfi, whose Circassian gendarmerie from Damascus helped Circassians to win a war against the Druze, would later become a military leader of Amman's Circassian community. His career underscores the importance of North Caucasian transregional connections and muhajirs' militarization. Mirza Wasfi was born in Russia and grew up as a muhajir in Ottoman Bulgaria. He joined the Ottoman military in 1873 and fought in the Serbian-Ottoman wars of 1876–78 and the Russo-Ottoman War of 1877–78. Following the Ottoman loss of the northern Balkans, he was reassigned to the Arab provinces. He participated in the suppression of the 'Urabi Revolt of 1879–82 in Egypt and was then posted to Damascus, where he recruited a Circassian militia. He briefly served as the head of gendarmerie in Beirut, Hawran, Mecca, and Yemen. Finally, he moved to Transjordan, where he again put together a Circassian militia, which enhanced the security of Ottoman Amman.[115] Seasoned in fighting the bedouin, Amman's Circassians emerged as one of the most effective troops in the southern Levant and one explicitly in the service of the Ottoman state as *zaptiye*. The Circassian *zaptiye* protected the Hejaz Railway, enforced taxation in the area, and assisted the Ottomans in suppressing the Karak Revolt of 1910.[116]

Muhajirs and their neighbors contested not only the right to use the land and resources but also the meanings of property ownership and the state's role in regulating land tenure. The Ottomans certainly favored muhajirs, whom they saw as a more taxable and reliable community when compared to bedouin and Druze, with their history of tax avoidance and resistance to Ottoman rule. Yet the role of the state should not be exaggerated. The government intervened militarily to support muhajirs only when their conflicts with local populations threatened regional stability, like the one in the Golan Heights, or risked wiping out the refugee population. Usually, refugees were on their own. The survival and prosperity of their villages depended on how skillfully they could navigate the fraught political terrain and coexist with their neighbors.

NORTH CAUCASIAN VILLAGES AROUND AMMAN

Circassian and Chechen muhajirs established most of their villages in Transjordan in the vicinity of Amman (see map 5). The economies of these villages mirrored that of Amman in many respects: refugees received free land from the state, registered it with the land registry, and used it to grow cereals for export. The notable difference was that the Hejaz Railway did not bring the comparable volume of Syrian capital to those villages. They depended to a greater extent on their relations with the surrounding bedouin communities: Wadi al-Sir with the 'Abbad and the Bani Sakhr, Na'ur with the Bani Sakhr and the 'Ajarma, Sweileh with the 'Adwan and the 'Abbad, Zarqa' and Sukhna with the Bani Hasan, and Rusayfa with the Da'ja and the Bani Hasan.[117] The Circassian villages of Wadi al-Sir and Na'ur provide good examples of how the settlement of muhajirs promoted economic development and facilitated trade on the Ottoman nomadic frontier.

Wadi al-Sir was the second oldest Circassian village in the area. Bzhedugh Circassians, who had arrived as refugees from the Balkans, founded the village in 1880 in a forested area to the west of Amman. Wadi al-Sir was divided into two quarters, each named after a Circassian subgroup: Bzhedugh and Abzakh. Each quarter had its own mosque with their Bzhedugh and Abzakh imams. The surviving records demonstrate fairly large allotments of land, even at the later rounds of *yoklama* registration. Thus, in 1909–10, fifty-four new households registered 88 dönüm on average.[118] Many land plots assigned to Circassians lay in the area of Bayader ("threshing floor") outside Wadi al-Sir. Circassian families of Wadi al-Sir, similar to those of Amman, invested their profits from grain export into purchasing more land and opening businesses in the village. For example, seven sons and a daughter of Shurukh Kokh registered 1,013 dönüm of free land and privately purchased 103 dönüm between 1909 and 1912. The siblings set up four shops and a bakery in Wadi al-Sir.[119]

Outside of Wadi al-Sir, much of the land belonged to the bedouin, who had preemptively registered their land. In 1881, following the Circassians' arrival in Wadi al-Sir, the 'Abbad, 'Adwan, and 'Ajarma bedouin registered 5,150 dönüm around the new village.[120] In 1897, sons of Sattam al-Fayiz of the Bani Sakhr registered 12,420 dönüm of land near Wadi al-Sir.[121] Defensive registration lessened the risk of intercommunal conflict by giving the bedouin an opportunity to sell their property to newcomers. For example, in 1897, the 'Abbad sold two mills to Circassians of Wadi al-Sir for 5,068 kuruş and 10,132 kuruş.[122]

The export of wheat and barley, bolstered by muhajir partnership with the Bani Sakhr, increased the prosperity of Wadi al-Sir. Already in 1891, a Russian expedition of the Imperial Orthodox Palestine Society found that Wadi al-Sir's "broad plateau, from one end to another, as far as our eyes could see, was sown with wheat that Circassians cultivated."[123] Circassians actively traded with the bedouin, buying wheat from the Balqawiyya "tent dwellers" near Salt and cattle from the Bani Sakhr, and the Bani Sakhr stored their grain in Wadi al-Sir.[124] Local Circassians also facilitated the sale of the bedouin's grain via their contacts in Amman on the larger Levantine markets.[125]

Wadi al-Sir, which was close to Fuheis and Salt, was integrated into Transjordanian networks of capital from the beginning. Thus, a year before the foundation of the Circassian village, Shukri bin Ibrahim Qaʿwar, of a prominent Christian family from the Hawran, registered 160 dönüm of land in the valley (*wadi*), which he later resold to a Circassian family for a staggering 18,000 kuruş.[126] In the late 1900s, several Muslim and Greek Orthodox Saltis purchased agricultural land and gardens in Wadi al-Sir.[127] Nevertheless, unlike in Amman, Damascene merchants did not arrive to buy shops in Wadi al-Sir, and Saltis did not come to dominate its trade. By the 1920s, Wadi al-Sir was still comparable in size to Amman.[128] It remained a largely Circassian town well into the twentieth century.

Naʿur, to the southwest of Amman, also benefited from cooperation between Circassian muhajirs, Salti merchants, and local bedouin communities. It was founded in 1900 by Circassians of Abzakh and Bzhedugh communities who set off from Russia's Kuban Province in 1898. They traveled to Istanbul by sea and from there across much of Anatolia and Syria by land to Salt, where they waited for nine months before finding an agreeable location for their village. Their representatives likely vetted the area of Naʿur and then, joined by a few Kabardian and Shapsugh families, negotiated it for their settlement with the Ottoman district authorities. Circassians chose a location by the Naʿur springs, which shaped the geography of the village. Muhajirs built a stone pool around the springs to use for drinking; a stream from the pool fed into a larger watering hole for animals; and the rest of the water radiated from the springs into canals that irrigated muhajirs' fruit gardens.[129] The land allotment was fairly generous and, at least on paper, equitable. In the first *yoklama* survey in 1902, sixty Circassian households registered a house and three plots of land, with each family receiving either 70, 100, or 130 dönüm, to the average of 106 dönüm.[130] The second *yoklama* survey in 1909 added nineteen new Circassian families, which received three plots of 70 dönüm total per household.[131]

The Circassian community in Naʿur cultivated transregional connections with its co-ethnic communities in the Middle East. The first imam in Naʿur was Shaykh Barakat Bazadogh, a Crimean-educated Circassian. According to communal memories, Shaykh Barakat was an ardent proponent of Muslim emigration from Russia and led his community into hijra.[132] After his party had settled in Naʿur, the Ottoman aid for the refugee village proved insufficient, and Shaykh Barakat sought funding elsewhere.[133] The Circassian elders' council of Naʿur, which generously met with me, shared the communal memory that Shaykh Barakat had traveled to Palestine and Egypt to solicit donations for the construction of the first mosque in Naʿur, built between 1904 and 1908. In Egypt, he reportedly found sponsors among the Turko-Circassian elites, a remnant of the Mamluk era, who served as benefactors of their ethnic brethren in Transjordan.[134] Shaykh Barakat sent his sons to study religion in Cairo's famed al-Azhar University and in Istanbul, as did many upper-status Circassian muhajirs in Transjordan.[135] Today, Naʿur prides itself as the best-preserved Circassian village in Jordan. Its downtown hosts an annual Circassian fair and retains traces of its early twentieth-century landscape, including the old mosque, fruit gardens, stone wells, and drinking fountains built by its first Circassian residents.

The land of Naʿur lay in the historical territory of the ʿAfashat branch of the ʿAjarma tribe. Land transactions between Circassians and the ʿAfashat bedouin began immediately after the establishment of the village. The ʿAfashat took an early initiative to register agricultural land around Naʿur in 1901, before the Circassians could obtain legal title to the land.[136] The ʿAfashat even staked out real estate within the young Circassian village, registering several houses as *mülk* property. After 1901, the ʿAfashat routinely sold their land to Naʿur's Circassians, usually for its cadastral price or higher.[137] Over the course of the twentieth century, many ʿAfashat families settled down in Naʿur, having founded their own neighborhood.

Naʿur also attracted Christian merchants from nearby Salt. Already in 1902, two Greek Orthodox Saltis, Faraj al-Ishaq and Najib al-Ibrahim, purchased usufruct rights to the plots previously registered by Circassians. Faraj al-Ishaq moved to the village and, in later years, bought two houses from the ʿAfashat bedouin, built new houses, and purchased land from the Circassian imam Shaykh Barakat.[138] Likewise, between 1910 and 1912, Greek Orthodox Salti merchants of al-Muʿasher and al-Mousa families registered houses and land that they bought from the ʿAfashat or other Saltis.[139] These merchants lay the foundation of Naʿur's Christian neighborhood. Prominent Muslim merchants, like Sulayman Tuqan from Nablus, also purchased land, houses, and stables from Circassians.[140]

The early sale of land by Naʿur's Circassians demonstrates that muhajirs did not always comply with the restriction on immediate sale of their usufruct rights to the land given to them for free. The Ottoman land registry exercised discretion in approving those transactions. The objective of the Ottoman administration was to entrench a new land regime in the Balqa', which is why land registration officials may have allowed those land sales between muhajirs and merchants, as long as the land remained in cultivation and all parties paid their respective taxes. Correspondingly, the village of Na'ur grew rapidly thanks to the mutually beneficial economic relationship between its Circassian residents, Salti merchants, and 'Afashat bedouin and its convenient location in the middle of Amman, Salt, and Madaba.

Prices of land grew steadily in muhajir villages throughout the Balqa' (see table 8). For example, only ten years after the establishment of Na'ur, the cadastral price of its agricultural land increased threefold.[141] Market prices did not, however, catch up with the government-estimated values, which the land registry artificially inflated to levy higher taxes on the registration of land. In the early 1910s, sale prices lagged behind cadastral prices by 52 percent in Amman's Shapsugh quarter, 40 percent in Na'ur, 33 percent in Amman's Qabartay quarter and Wadi al-Sir's Abzakh quarter, and 13 percent in Wadi al-Sir's Bzhedugh quarter. For regional standards, the prices of land in Circassian villages remained low. The best agricultural land around Amman that belonged to the first Shapsugh Circassian residents was still, on average, almost ten times cheaper than the price of land in neighboring Palestine.[142] The low prices kept the Balqa' an attractive investment destination for Levantine merchants.

After Amman became the administrative seat (in 1921) and capital city (in 1928) of Transjordan, its land continued to increase in value. Circassian muhajirs were chief beneficiaries of the rapid urbanization of the Balqa'. Several muhajir families succeeded in amassing impressive real estate portfolios and harnessing their power as landowners into careers in government and the military. North Caucasians are allocated three seats in Jordan's House of Representatives, and almost every Jordanian government has had a minister of Circassian or Chechen origin. The story of North Caucasian muhajirs in Jordan may appear as one of good fortune, but it also hides vast inequalities within the community. Many muhajirs sold their land to Arab newcomers during the late Ottoman or emirate era. The Circassian Charity Association, established in Amman in 1932, has its origins in supporting destitute

| Village | Yoklama | | | | Da'imi |
	1890s	1900–03	1904–09	1910–12	1910–12
Amman, Shapsugh quarter	72	53	174	281	134
Amman, Qabartay quarter	60	42	64	84	56
Wadi al-Sir, Bzhedugh quarter	40*	51	56	61	53
Wadi al-Sir, Abzakh quarter	67	49	63	72	48
Naʿur	—	34	53	101*	61

Table 8. **Land prices in Circassian villages in Transjordan, 1891–1912.**
Average price of agricultural land, in kuruş per dönüm. The *yoklama* prices are
government-estimated prices at the time of the initial registration of land. The
dāʾimi prices were dictated by the market and represent monetary transactions.

*The number of transactions on record is too low to serve as a reliable estimate.

Sources: DLS Defters 5/1/1, 7/1/1, 10/1/1, 18/1/1, 19/1/1, 30/1/2, 31/1/2, and 32/1/2.

Circassians, who ended up landless.[143] Since the interwar era, the early sale
of land and the erosion of economic power remained a grievance for many
Circassians in Amman. Perhaps unexpectedly, recent beneficiaries of Amman's booming real estate market are descendants of muhajirs in the farthest
villages from Amman, those of Wadi al-Sir and Naʿur. Their land held little
value throughout the twentieth century, which prevented many muhajir families from selling it. In the last decades, Amman expanded rapidly toward the
two villages. The area of Bayader, which the Ottomans apportioned to Circassians of Wadi al-Sir, has become one of Amman's popular shopping areas,
turning its landowners into millionaires.[144]

In the final decades of Ottoman rule, North Caucasian muhajirs facilitated
the expansion of Ottoman networks of capital to the nomadic frontier of
Transjordan. Their settlement prompted the defensive registration of land by
bedouin communities and attracted Transjordanian, Palestinian, and Syrian
merchants, who invested their capital in muhajir villages, especially Amman,
and set up agricultural estates in the eastern Balqaʾ. Muhajirs eagerly used the
new land registry and the old shariʿa court in Salt to record their transactions,

accelerating the commodification of land and the entrenchment of a new Ottoman land regime. The Ottoman presence in Transjordan was minimal, but the state remained critical to refugees' success because the Ottoman government created the legal framework and infrastructure for refugees to thrive. The construction of the Hejaz Railway, the single most important footprint of the Ottoman state in Transjordan, bolstered security on the nomadic frontier, brought Levantine investment, and facilitated the export of Circassian grain. Here, in the empire's southernmost area of refugee resettlement, muhajirs were able to tap into the needs of the expanding Levantine market and trade with local bedouin. The following chapter examines the North Caucasian settlement in Anatolia and follows a muhajir family that searched far and wide for a perfect location to call home.

FIVE

BUILDING
THE CAUCASUS
IN ANATOLIA

IN 1890, TWO HALF BROTHERS, Fuat and Cevat Khutat, eagerly expected the arrival of their mother, Hanife Hanım, from Russia. Fuat and Cevat had left their native Circassia ten years earlier and now lived in Istanbul. They long urged their mother to join them in the Ottoman Empire.[1] Fuat (Tasultan) bin Muhammad Shah, in his thirties, was in the graduating class of the Ottoman Military Academy, an elite institution that trained officers for the imperial army. His twenty-five-year-old half brother, Cevat (Anzor) bin Isma'il, studied law but left the university without finishing his degree.[2] The two ambitious young men aspired to careers in the Ottoman military and administration. They had come a long way from the mountainous village of Benoqa (now Benokovo, Krasnodar Krai, Russia), where their family had lived through Russia's expulsions of Circassians and colonization of their lands.

Their mother, Hanife Hanım, safely arrived and registered with the Refugee Commission as a muhajir. Despite the two brothers' pleas to let their mother move to Istanbul, the Refugee Commission sent her and the rest of her emigrant group to a refugee village near Adana in southern Anatolia. The Khutat family found itself dispersed in the Ottoman Empire. Fuat sat through his final military examinations in Istanbul; Cevat left the capital city and joined his mother and sister Şerife in southern Anatolia; Hanife Hanım's brother-in-law Selim Girey shortly thereafter returned to the Caucasus; and her sister-in-law Gulumkhan, who had emigrated earlier, lived with her family in a refugee village in Konya.[3] The Khutats would spend the next decade searching for a place where their family and friends could reunite and rebuild their piece of the Caucasus within the Ottoman Empire.

This chapter examines the North Caucasian resettlement in Ottoman Anatolia, particularly the mountain valley of Uzunyayla in Sivas Province on which the Khutats pinned their hopes. While North Caucasian muhajirs settled in mixed villages in the northern Balkans and monoethnic but scattered villages throughout the Levant, they established large clusters of villages in central Anatolia. Uzunyayla, with over seventy Circassian, Abazin, Chechen, Ossetian, and Karachay villages, was one of the most compact areas of refugee resettlement in the Ottoman Empire.[4] Uzunyayla, despite lying roughly in the geographic center of the Ottoman Empire, was isolated, hiding in between mountains. That remoteness allowed refugees to reconstruct many of their social institutions and to turn the mountain valley into a Little Caucasus, but it also hindered Ottoman investment and economic development. Uzunyayla was one of the earliest destinations for Circassian muhajirs, and in many ways it exemplified the Ottoman resettlement project. What happened to refugees there reverberated throughout the empire. Notably, North Caucasian muhajirs were rebuilding their community in the sheltered mountain valley, as the worlds of others—nomadic Muslims and settled Christians—were crumbling around them.

This chapter unfolds through the history of the Khutat family, which had emigrated to the Ottoman Empire in the 1880s and 1890s and was, at various times, scattered in western, central, southern, and eastern Anatolia, as well as the Levant and the Caucasus. I reconstruct the Khutat family history through fifty-eight letters that Fuat wrote, in Ottoman Turkish, to his family members between 1890 and 1905. Fuat's letters survive because his brother Cevat carefully copied them into his notebook. Cevat's descendants preserved these letters and photographs of Fuat and his siblings for over a century and, upon hearing that a clueless foreign researcher was looking for Ottoman-era letters, generously shared them with me.[5] At the turn of the century, the Khutats, an upper-status but refugee family nevertheless, skill-fully used their social capital and kinship networks to find a footing in their new empire. They lobbied Ottoman officials, gathered their old relations, and reached out to fellow Circassian notables in the search for a new home.

REFUGEE RESETTLEMENT IN ANATOLIA

Ottoman Anatolia was the ultimate destination for most North Caucasian refu-gees. During the first Circassian refugee crisis, in 1863–65, about half of incom-ing refugees from the Northwest Caucasus, or 250,000–400,000 people, settled in Anatolia. During the second Circassian refugee crisis, in 1878–80, about 300,000 Circassian refugees fled the Balkans, most of them to Anatolia. During both refugee crises, the coastal provinces of Hüdavendigar (Bursa), Aydın, and Kastamonu received particularly large shares of refugees, owing to the expedi-ence of moving Circassian muhajirs from ports to the surrounding countryside. To relieve the pressure on coastal regions, the Ottoman government directed as many refugees as possible for permanent settlement in the interior provinces of Ankara, Konya, and Sivas.[6] Most Chechen, Abkhazian, Ossetian, and other muhajirs, who arrived from the Caucasus by land, also settled in Anatolia. The particularly heavy areas of North Caucasian settlement were around Bandırma, Düzce, Eskişehir, Sinop, Samsun, and Çorum, and throughout the Sivas sub-provinces of Sivas, Amasya, and Tokat. Isolated clusters of North Caucasian villages were also found around Aydın, Yalova, Göksun, Muş, Sarıkamış, to the north of Konya, and to the east of Adana (see map 3).[7]

Muslim refugee resettlement resulted in nothing short of a demographic and economic transformation of Anatolia. The government used muhajirs as a counterweight to nomads, with an expectation that North Caucasians would settle the land and prompt others to take up farming. After 1878, the Hamidian government strategically placed many, although by no means all, Muslim refugees in districts with large Christian populations to alter demo-graphic ratios. The settlement of refugees had a profound impact on land usage throughout Anatolia. By the 1890s, 90 percent of all litigation over land in Sivas Province was related to the settlement of muhajirs.[8] In today's interior Anatolia, at least two-thirds of villages have been settled and nine-tenths of the cultivated land started being farmed only after 1860, largely because of refugee resettlement and sedentarization of nomads.[9]

Sivas Province became the largest recipient of North Caucasian refugees in Anatolia. This massive landlocked province shared borders with seven other provinces and was central to Ottoman control over Anatolia. It was home to Muslim (Turkish-, Turkmen-, and Kurdish-speaking), Armenian, and Greek communities. North Caucasians formed 10–15 percent of the total population of the province after 1880.[10] Muhajirs settled throughout Sivas Province: Circassians and Abkhazians in the subprovince of Amasya in the northwest; Circassians and Dagestanis in the subprovince of Tokat in the north; a cluster of Ossetian, Dagestani, Chechen, and Circassian villages to the west of the city of Sivas and Dagestani villages to its south; and the North Caucasian refugee valley of Uzunyayla in the south of the province. Both geographically and demographically, the North Caucasian diasporic world of the Middle East centered on Sivas Province, which, with its several hundred refugee villages, offered an ethnolinguistic snapshot of the Caucasus.

KHUTAT FAMILY: FROM THE CAUCASUS TO ANATOLIA

The Khutats were Kabardian notables who became refugees twice in the nineteenth century. Following Russia's conquest of Kabarda in the North-central Caucasus, they, with other *khadzhrety*, or "free" Kabardians, moved to western Circassia in the late 1810s. They settled in the village of Benoqa, which fell to the Russians in the final stage of the Caucasus War. In 1868, Benoqa and its neighboring villages rebelled against Russia's land reforms and abolition of Circassian slavery.[11] Later, many Benoqa families sought to join Circassian muhajirs, who had been expelled in 1862–64, and repeatedly petitioned the Russian government for permission to emigrate to the Ottoman Empire. In 1889, tsarist authorities allowed them to leave.[12] Isma'il Khutat, father of Cevat, led the emigrating party of 333 Circassian families.[13] He died before reaching the Ottoman Empire. In 1895, the village of Benoqa was repopulated with families of retired Russian soldiers who had taken part in the conquest of the Northwest Caucasus.[14]

By 1891, the recently widowed Hanife Hanım and two of her children, Cevat and Şerife (see figure 4), were near Adana, alongside their fellow Kabardian muhajirs. The Refugee Commission had planned to settle them in Kastamonu Province in northern Anatolia, but the plan fell through, and refugees were sent instead to the region of Çukurova (Cilicia) in southern

Figure 4. Şerife, Hanife, and Cevat Khutat.
Photograph taken in the 1890s. *Courtesy*: Khutat Family Collection.

Anatolia.[15] The Ottomans heavily invested in Çukurova's agriculture and, beginning in the mid-nineteenth century, settled muhajirs to work on its cotton plantations and in wheat fields.[16] The Khutats did not consider Çukurova to be a desirable location for a permanent settlement. Çukurova's marshes were a breeding ground for mosquitoes, and muhajirs in the region often contracted malaria and died in the thousands.[17] The Khutats sought to escape Çukurova for a safer area and repeatedly petitioned the Refugee Commission about their community "suffering from population loss due to its incompatibility with [local] water and air."[18] The Khutats' dream was to find a place with plenty of land where they could establish a Kabardian village for themselves and families that came with them from the Caucasus. Fuat, writing from Istanbul (see figure 5), urged Cevat, "Go to the people in [our] village and recruit those who have an affection for us and who want to escape from there."[19]

Figure 5. **Fuat Khutat.**
Photograph taken in the 1890s.
Courtesy: Khutat Family Collection.

In the autumn of 1892, Hanife Hanım received permission from the Ottoman government to move to Aziziye (now Pınarbaşı), a small Circassian refugee town in Sivas Province, to the north of Adana. Eventually, most of the family reunited in Aziziye, including Gulumkhan, who moved her family from Konya, and Selim Girey, who reemigrated from the Caucasus. Fuat stayed in Istanbul, pursuing a military career and, as the eldest son, assumed financial responsibility for his refugee family.[20] The Khutats sold their properties in western Circassia before emigrating. In the first years after everyone's arrival in Aziziye, Fuat followed closely the fluctuating exchange rate between the Russian ruble and the Ottoman lira on the markets of Istanbul, Trabzon, and Erzurum, waiting for an opportune moment to exchange the Russian currency that the family had brought from the Caucasus.[21] Fuat wrote tens of letters to his family members, instructing them on practical matters and learning their concerns, which he then tried to solve by lobbying various officials in Istanbul. In his correspondence with the government, Fuat used the name Khutatzade: he likely added the Persian suffix "zade" to denote his family's high social status and to Ottomanize its Circassian name.

Meanwhile, Cevat and the rest of the Khutats were making home in Aziziye. Cevat hoped to secure an administrative position in Aziziye or Sivas, but nothing came of those plans, and he turned his thoughts to entrepreneurship. He reasoned that his Circassian ancestry could help him in cross-border trade. He excitedly shared with his brother that he was considering traveling to the Caucasus to purchase commercial goods, likely textiles, which he would then smuggle into eastern Anatolia to circumvent the Russian customs and to maximize his profits. Fuat, upon hearing this, pointed out the glaring flaws in Cevat's project: he had no business experience in either country and would likely be swindled by everyone; as a Circassian muhajir, he was unlikely to receive tsarist permission to enter the Caucasus; and overall he faced high odds of bankruptcy or, worse, going to prison in either Russia or the Ottoman Empire. "On receiving a letter that spouts such nonsense, I could not keep myself from being greatly sorry. If these ideas are your own, my sorrow is double," said Fuat.[22] To soften the blow, in subsequent letters, Fuat made sure to compliment his brother's budding interest in business. "Really, trade is the sole means for leading a good life," he wrote.[23] Fuat urged his brother to set up a legal and respectable business in Aziziye, preferably with a Christian partner who would have experience and mercantile connections throughout the empire.[24] Fuat referred to the Armenian community, which formed a quarter of Aziziye's population.[25] The Khutats also hoped to settle in the countryside and planned to purchase land in Uzunyayla, a large plateau to the north and east of Aziziye.

UZUNYAYLA, THE LITTLE CAUCASUS

The mountain valley of Uzunyayla was a bustling North Caucasian countryside in the middle of Anatolia (see map 6). By the mid-1860s, its population reached 40,000 people, all of them refugees.[26] Uzunyayla, which means "long plateau" in Turkish, has a remarkable geography: it lies at 1,550–1,630 meters (5,085–5,348 feet) above sea level and, on all four sides, is surrounded by mountains—the Tahtalı Mountains of the great Taurus mountain chain and the foothills of the Tecer and Yama Mountains—reaching 1,800–2,700 meters (5,906–8,858 feet).[27] The mountains turn Uzunyayla into a narrow basin, about 30 miles wide. The only opening is to the west, where the Zamantı River, now Turkey's premier river for rafting, escapes the mountain valley before snaking its way south toward the fertile plain of Çukurova and the Mediterranean Sea. The town of Aziziye lay by that opening, near the springs (Tur., Pınarbaşı) in the foothills of the Şirvan Mountain. Uzunyayla lacked a settled population because of its unforgiving climate. Summers in Uzunyayla are cool, but winters are severe, with subzero temperatures holding for several months. In winter, heavy snowfall cuts off villages from each other, both in the Ottoman era and today. The climate of Uzunyayla resembles that of Kabarda, in the middle of the Caucasus Mountains, which made Kabardians particularly well-equipped to survive that environment.

In the early 1860s, Uzunyayla became a primary destination for North Caucasians in the Ottoman Empire. The mass arrival of Circassians started around 1859.[28] Rumors of a hidden plateau in central Anatolia, with abundant land and a familiar climate, traveled far and wide among muhajirs. Many refugees who had already been settled elsewhere in the Ottoman Empire were asking for their relocation to Uzunyayla. Between 1860 and 1862, several thousand Circassians moved to Uzunyayla, with or without permission, from their original settlements in the provinces of Silistre, Trabzon, Hüdavendigar (Bursa), Adana, Kastamonu, Aydın, and Ankara.[29] Muhajirs in Uzunyayla represented a wide social spectrum: Circassian princely families and notables, free landowning and landless peasants, serfs, and enslaved people.

The newly formed Refugee Commission in Istanbul absorbed some re-settlement costs, but the government also delegated to local populations the responsibility to help refugees, similar to what was done in the Ottoman Balkans. Between 1860 and 1864, residents of at least nineteen Sivas districts gave a total of 425,715 kuruş to aid refugees.[30] Many Anatolian residents, Muslim and Christian alike, helped to move muhajirs from the coast to the Anatolian interior, while others temporarily housed muhajirs during their transit, and those closest to Uzunyayla built houses, mosques, and schools for them.[31] Thus, in 1860, the Gedikçik district governor submitted a petition, cosigned by 100 villagers, asking for reimbursement for building thirty-two houses for Circassian muhajirs in eighteen villages in Uzunyayla.[32] The neighbors' contributions ranged from acts of charity to commissioned public works to coerced uncompensated labor.

Uzunyayla, the Little Caucasus, was soon divided into distinct regions, each with its own ethnic and subethnic characteristics. Once on the plateau, muhajirs had the freedom to choose where to settle and selected places for their new villages in relation to natural landmarks, such as rivers and springs, and to other North Caucasian villages. The core of Uzunyayla was Circassian, with refugees from both the Black Sea coast of western Circassia and the highlands of eastern Circassia (see map 6). Kabardians dominated Uzunyayla proper, around the village of Örenşehir. Many of their villages were set up in clusters to rebuild, or transplant, communities from the old country. For example, muhajirs from Kundet-ey, a region in Greater Kabarda, established seven villages in central Uzunyayla, which everyone knew as "Kundet-ey Seven Villages."[33] North Caucasian communities often named their new villages after their old villages, like the Kabardians' Anzorey (now Kaftangiyen) and the Hatuqwais' Pedisey (now Akören).[34] Kabardians and Abazins settled together in the area of Boğurbaşı, known today as "potato villages" for their signature crop. In the Çörümşek valley, on the southern slope of the Hınzır Mountain, lay villages of Abzakh and Hatuqwai Circassians. Abazins established a cluster of villages in the north of Uzunyayla.[35] Meanwhile, Ossetian, Chechen, and Karachay muhajirs founded villages on the margins of Uzunyayla.

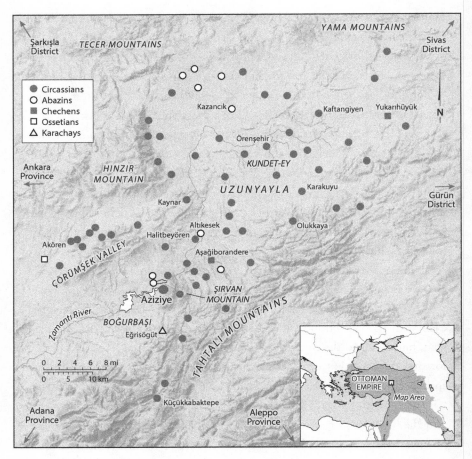

Map 6. Ottoman Uzunyayla, 1914.

   In 1861, the Sivas authorities approved the establishment of a new town
to accommodate new refugees and to guard the entrance into Uzunyayla
(see figure 6).[36] The new town was named Aziziye, in honor of Sultan Abdülaziz (r. 1861–76), who ascended to the throne a few months earlier and
during whose reign most North Caucasians would arrive in the Ottoman
Empire. It was the first place in the empire to bear the new sultan's name.[37]
The name of Aziziye later became a popular choice for muhajir settlements,
rivaled perhaps only by the name of Hamidiye, given to many villages established during the reign of Sultan Abdülhamid II (r. 1876–1909). Eight

chiefs of Hatuqwai and Kabardian Circassians wrote to the government, af-
firming the economic potential of their chosen area, lying by the springs
on the Zamantı River, as it had "vast grassy and watery lands" to facilitate
muhajir agriculture.[38] Even more importantly, sitting in the foothills of the
Şirvan Mountain, it was close to a forest. Uzunyayla was devoid of trees, and
muhajirs needed access to precious timber for their houses. The new refugee
town would also serve as a regional marketplace, where Uzunyayla's North
Caucasian farmers and nearby Turkic pastoralists would come to trade with
each other.[39] The town's first residents were 536 Kabardian and Hatuqwai
Circassian, Chechen, and Kumyk households.[40] For comparison, it would
take the refugee village of Amman, founded in 1878, several decades to reach
the inaugural size of Aziziye. Since 1861, Aziziye had been the center of the
eponymous administrative district, which included all of Uzunyayla. In 1865,
about 200 Armenian households from Haçin (now Saimbeyli) in the Taurus
Mountains petitioned authorities to allow their relocation to Aziziye, where
they would establish their own neighborhood.[41] The Aziziye district, in the
southwestern corner of Sivas Province, bordered the provinces of Ankara,
Adana, and Aleppo, which placed it on the crossroads of central Anatolia,
coastal Çukurova, and northern Syria. Yet, nestled in the mountains and
away from major roads, it felt isolated.

The remoteness of Uzunyayla and its almost exclusively North Caucasian
demographics allowed its communities to preserve much oral heritage that
faded elsewhere in exile, and in the twentieth century in the Soviet Caucasus,
too. The muhajirs carried with them the Nart sagas, or tales about the ancient
race of giants that had once lived in the Caucasus. These pre-Islamic tales
constitute the mythology of Circassians, Abazins, Abkhazians, Ossetians,
Karachays, Balkars, and to some extent Chechens, Ingush, Dagestanis, and
Georgians.[42] The Nart sagas rely on oral transmission, and muhajirs continued reciting stories of their mythical forebears, such as Sosruko, a mighty hero
born of stone and sometimes a trickster; Setenay, the immortal matriarch and
protector of the Narts; and Tlepsh, the Narts' blacksmith who forged their
weapons. Over the decades, Uzunyayla became a prominent center of Circassian cultural production in its own right. Muhajirs brought with them many
creatures of their lower mythology, with whom they populated Uzunyayla to
make sense of its unfamiliar landscapes. For example, *q'olbastä* (къолбастэ)

Figure 6. **Ottoman Aziziye.**
Hugo Grothe, *Geographische Charakterbilder aus der
Asiatischen Türkei* (Leipzig, 1909), xv.

is a female entity, similar to a mermaid, that lives in rivers and climbs out
on trees. In Uzunyayla, it turned into a dangerous creature that sets fires to
homes, but Uzunyaylans knew to use the Qur'an as a protection against it.
Other feared creatures were *blaghuä* (*благъуэ*), a red dragon guarding the
water, which in Uzunyayla was described as a massive python that had swallowed a young woman; *zhästeuä* (*жэщтеуэ*), a night demon that targets children when they are asleep, which in Uzunyayla manifested as a black turkey;
wd (*уд*), witches who terrorized Uzunyayla as eagles; and jinns, shapeshifting
spirits of Islamic mythology, who in Uzunyayla typically appeared as foxes.[43]
The North Caucasians helped their guardians and demons to adapt to the
Uzunyayla landscape and created new storylines for them within the post-
1864 historical timeline. For example, *ḥäṣḥävylhä* (*хъэщхъэвылъэ*) is a chi-
meric monster with a dog's head and bull's legs. In Uzunyayla, this mythical
creature became part of muhajirs' commemoration of World War I. In a pop-

ular local narrative, a Circassian soldier from Uzunyayla is taken captive by the Russians during the Ottoman defeat at the Battle of Sarıkamış of 1914–15. He ends up in Siberia in the captivity of the *ḥäšḥävylhä*, who keep him well fed so they could devour him later. The hero escapes, finds his way to the sea, and eventually returns to Uzunyayla.[44]

Muhajirs composed new folktales that reflected their journey from the Caucasus to Anatolia and their experiences in Uzunyayla. Muhajir folk singer-storytellers (*dzheguako*) wrote songs of lament (*ghybzä/гъыбзэ*) about those who had fallen in war or flight and songs about notable people of the Uzunyayla community, including prominent elders, healers, blacksmiths, singers, accordion players, and women hosts of bride rooms.[45] The *dzheguako* also cultivated an entire folklore genre of playful tales about cultural differences among Circassians. Many Circassian communities who had previously been separated by rivers and mountain ranges in the Caucasus now lived on the same plateau and learned a great deal about each other. New tales and sayings played on the stereotypes of each community: for example, Uzunyaylans would say, "a Shapsugh is made for war, a Bzhedugh is for labor, and a Kabardian is for chitchat." They would perceive Kabardians as slow, arrogant, and sticklers for etiquette; Hatuqwai as agreeable, sometimes naive, and liberal in following Circassian customs; and Abazins as quick of temper and ready to fight.[46] Over the years, Uzunyayla became a diasporic cultural marker, with Uzunyayla-style weddings, small talk (*wärshär/уэршэр*), stories (*xybar/хъыбар*), and types of folk dances (*śeśen/щещен, q'afä qw'anshä/къафэ къуаншэ*) admired among Turkey's Circassians.[47] In the Kabardian language in the diaspora, Uzunyayla is often called a "little motherland" or "Little Circassia" (*Khäkw Ts'ykw'/Хэку ЦӀыкӀу*).[48] Today, scholars from the Circassian republics in Russia visit Uzunyayla to study Circassian dialects and oral heritage that had been preserved in this refugee mountain valley.

Uzunyayla occupied a special place in the geography of North Caucasian resettlement. One may think of it as the buckle on a belt of refugee villages tied around the waist of the Ottoman Empire.[49] Uzunyayla lay roughly in the middle of several hundred muhajir villages running from the Black Sea coast through Anatolia and deep into the Syrian desert (see map 3). Within the Levant, as the previous chapter showed, this refugee belt lay upon the nomadic frontier in the provinces of Damascus and Aleppo. The nomadic frontier also extended into Anatolia, going through the provinces of Adana and Sivas. In Anatolia, as in the Levant, the Ottoman government expected muhajirs to settle the land that was claimed by nomads and brought no income to the state. The government categorized much of Uzunyayla's land as *vakıf*, part of the Atik Valide Sultan religious endowment, and *miri*, assigning both to muhajirs.[50] The Ottomans hoped that North Caucasians would turn Uzunyayla into a thriving region of settled taxpayers, while pushing out the nomads into lower-lying regions.

The Uzunyayla plateau had long been the land of the Afshars, a Turkic-speaking pastoral community that migrated within southern and central Anatolia. Many Afshars would spend winters tending to their numerous herds of horses and flocks of sheep in the foothills of Çukurova and, in summer, would move to the cooler climes of Uzunyayla.[51] From the 1830s, the Ottomans tried to sedentarize Anatolia's nomadic communities to increase their tax base, promote agricultural production, bolster military recruitment, and "pacify" far-flung regions of the empire.[52] The Afshars, who controlled a strategic region connecting Anatolia to the Levant, were an early target of a government bent on centralization. In the 1840s and 1850s, Ottoman authorities forcibly settled several Afshar clans in villages and mixed them with other tribes.[53] By the time muhajirs arrived in Uzunyayla, the Afshar world had been shrinking for several decades. The Afshars, similar to many bedouin and Druze of the Levant, viewed the settlement of muhajirs as another hostile act by the Ottoman state.

Clashes between the Afshars and muhajirs commenced shortly after the first Circassians stepped foot on the plateau. Already in 1860, Circassians in Uzunyayla complained to the government about the nomads' hostility.[54] The following year, more refugees moved to Uzunyayla and settled around the springs and by the Zamantı River, where the Afshars typically set up their camps. When the Afshars returned to Uzunyayla for the summer, they found several thousand refugees and their horses on the Afshars' historical pastures. Provincial authorities attempted an early intervention by asking the Afshars to leave their tents to Circassians in exchange for the government's forgiveness of their unpaid taxes.[55] In June, the Afshars raided a muhajir village, which led to the Circassians' pursuit of Afshar horsemen and escalated to a series of revenge attacks throughout the plateau. While the total losses on either side are unknown, the muhajirs' dead and wounded included members of Hatuqwai, Kabardian, Besleney, Ubykh, and Abazin (Altıkesek) communities, which suggests a joint North Caucasian effort to fight the Afshars.[56] These early clashes must have forged a sense of unity among Uzunyayla's various North Caucasian communities, as they banded together to survive.

By late 1861, the two communities were headed for an all-out war. The Afshars, in alliance with other nomadic communities, planned to assemble a force of about 5,000 men to fight the North Caucasians.[57] Muhajirs also gathered their forces and requested the government's military support. The Ottomans backed the refugees. The decision was easy. The government had spent millions of kuruş on transporting refugees to Uzunyayla and setting up their first villages. The conflict with the Afshars jeopardized that investment, as some North Caucasians already started fleeing Uzunyayla in fear of living near the nomads.[58] Moreover, muhajirs throughout the empire watched closely how the government would respond and whether it would defend their rights to the land that it had promised them. The Ottoman government also long wanted to rein in the Afshars. The North Caucasian villages disrupted the nomads' migration routes, giving the state further leverage over them. Muslim refugee resettlement in Uzunyayla and elsewhere in Sivas Province helped the Ottoman government to solidify its control over the more remote parts of central Anatolia.

In 1862, the Ottomans pulled troops from neighboring provinces into Uzunyayla. The governor of Sivas Province then personally arrived in the valley and forced the two sides to make peace.[59] The government, which was hardly impartial, pressured the Afshars to cede their claims to Uzunyayla and to pledge peaceful relations with muhajirs and tax compliance to the state.[60] In the following years, the government forcibly relocated several Afshar communities to the provinces of Kastamonu, Harput, and Diyarbakır and settled the rest in the Sarız valley and along the Zamantı River, respectively to the south and west of Aziziye.[61] The government created a separate administrative unit for the Afshars to ensure that their affairs were administered separately from the "Circassian" Aziziye District. The Afshars' loss of Uzunyayla, which was critical to their pastoral economy, had transregional repercussions. Thus, in 1864, Muslim and Armenian communities of the Kozan Mountains sent joint petitions, complaining about Afshar bandits who were coming

to Çukurova from Sivas Province, invading their mountains, killing their
people, and seizing their possessions.[62] To prevent the Afshars' attacks and
their return to Uzunyayla, the Ottomans maintained auxiliary troops in the
surrounding districts throughout the 1860s.

The muhajirs' conflict with the Afshars was formative for the muhajirs'
claim to Uzunyayla as their Little Caucasus. The echoes of that early contestation survive in various forms. One oral history, narrated by Uzunyaylan
Circassians to the anthropologist Eiji Miyazawa, relays a more peaceful rendering of what transpired in the 1860s:

> During the early period after Circassians were sent to Central Anatolia to
> settle, an Avşar bey fell in love with a Circassian girl. He asked her father,
> a Circassian bey, for the girl. The father demanded Uzunyayla in exchange
> for the girl. The Avşar bey accepted the proposal, and Circassians settled
> in Uzunyayla. The girl died young. The large plain was left for Circassians.
> Avşars were driven to tiny villages in the mountains. Avşars still resent the
> loss of Uzunyayla.[63]

This fanciful and gendered origin story of Circassian Uzunyayla captures two
important elements. It elevates the agency of "beys," or muhajir and nomadic
chiefs. Kabardian beys were typically of aristocratic descent and led their
communities into hijra in the Ottoman Empire. At the early stages of North
Caucasian migration, the Ottomans recorded groups of incoming muhajirs
by the names of their chiefs. These men made major decisions of where to
set up villages and when to wage war. This oral history also suggests that
muhajirs had directly negotiated the terms of their settlement with the Afshars, which was possible and would not feature in Ottoman records, as those
positioned the government as the ultimate arbiter of all resettlement matters.
In subsequent decades, some Afshars returned and settled on the margins of
Uzunyayla. The two communities occasionally clashed over cattle raids and
land seizures, but their beys and the Ottoman authorities resolved those individual transgressions before they could escalate the conflict.[64]

The North Caucasian economy of Uzunyayla was largely pastoral. The
harsh climate limited what could grow on the plateau, and agricultural
products could not be exported without good roads out of the mountains.
Reportedly, even the grain that local muhajirs paid in *öşür* tax rotted away

in Uzunyayla granaries because it could not be efficiently transported else-where.[65] The main staple of the Uzunyayla economy was horse breeding. In the 1860s, Kabardians, who had arrived from the Northcentral Caucasus by land, brought with them horses of the Kabarda breed. Those are hardy and strong horses, noted for their endurance and bred for stony and mountainous terrains. Much of the wealth of the Kabardian community was locked in their herds. The horses could not survive Uzunyayla winters, and the Kab-ardians quickly adopted the seasonal pastoral routes of the Afshars. In winter months, Circassians moved their herds—about 3,000 horses—to Çukurova in the south.[66] Transhumance, or seasonal movement of livestock, was not new to Kabardians, as many had practiced it back in the Caucasus.

In 1878, the Circassians of Uzunyayla nearly lost their precious horses. The Kozanoğlu rebellion had broken out in the Adana hinterland in response to the Ottoman government's heavy-handed measures against nomadic com-munities. The authorities suppressed the rebellion and issued a directive to curtail regional migrations, prohibiting, among other things, the Afshars and the Circassians from "com[ing] down to Çukurova during the winter under the pretext of wintering or grazing their animals."[67] The Uzunyayla muhajirs immediately sent representatives to Sivas, where they lobbied the provincial governor and the British vice-consul to intercede with the government on their behalf. The British sent the following telegram to their embassy in Istanbul:

> The [Uzunyayla] plateau . . . is entirely destitute of trees, and the winter is one of great severity. There is little or no material for building, and, even if there were, sheds could not be erected in time to save the horses. Snow has already fallen in the Yailas, and . . . winter sets in on these plateaus with slight warning; if the horses are caught by deep snow they will all perish.[68]

The Sivas governor also sent four telegrams to the Porte, likely fearing that if the Circassians lose their herds, they would turn to plundering neighbor-ing populations. Meanwhile, the Uzunyayla Circassians, preparing for their worst-case scenario, stood ready to lead their herds eastward across snowy mountains to Aleppo Province to sell any horses that would survive the trek.[69] The mobilization of support in Sivas paid off, and in November the Ottoman government issued permission for Circassians to take their herds south to Çukurova.[70] The tragedy was averted.

In the following decades, the Ottoman army became the largest buyer of Uzunyayla horses. The military representative of the Fourth Army would visit Aziziye in late May, around the time when Circassian herds were returning from Çukurova, to select and buy horses.[71] The military's reliance on Uzunyayla horses provided muhajirs with some leverage in their relationship with the government. For example, in 1903, the Ottoman government introduced a new tax on the ownership of horses, donkeys, and oxen. The Circassians of Aziziye telegraphed the Porte their request for an exemption from the tax and, in case of refusal, asked for permission to return to Russia. Not only had they threatened to empty out Uzunyayla but also to deprive the military of its supply of horses. That same year, the Ottoman army had purchased 500 Kabarda horses from Aziziye District, putting the muhajirs in a particularly advantageous position to ask for a tax exemption.[72] At the same time, the Russian army also came to depend on Kabarda horses for its cavalry. Kabardians in the Caucasus annually sold about 1,297 horses to the Russian military.[73] In the republican period, the Kabarda horses became known as Turkey's "Uzunyayla breed."

KHUTAT FAMILY: BECOMING OTTOMAN IN ANATOLIA

In 1893, Fuat had graduated from the Military Academy in Istanbul and was commissioned to the Ottoman Fourth Army.[74] The army headquarters in Erzincan was strategically located near the Russian and Iranian borders and in the heart of the Ottoman Empire's "six Armenian provinces." It was also relatively close to Aziziye, where Fuat visited his mother and the rest of the family. After two years of service, Fuat received an assignment to patrol the Russian border.[75] His military command likely considered Fuat's familiarity with the Caucasus and fluency in Circassian, and perhaps also Russian, to be an asset.

Meanwhile, while making their new home in Aziziye, the Khutats turned their attention to the education of their children. Fuat, a disciplined older brother, relentlessly reminded the younger and more carefree Cevat that his primary duty was to educate his children, nieces, and nephews. Fuat urged his brother to rent a house with a large salon that could be used as a school for the Khutat children. He instructed him to purchase desks and a blackboard and spent weeks devising an elaborate homeschooling curriculum. According to Fuat's schedule, each class would take two hours, divided between a lecture and pupils' recitations. The children would study five subjects: Ottoman Turkish grammar, Ottoman history, arithmetic, geography, and calligraphy. Fuat noted that in geography lessons, "the whole world, that is the five continents, should be discussed equally."[76] Fuat insisted that his nephew Ghazi master horsemanship and swordsmanship, as befitting a young Circassian man. He berated Cevat for neglecting the boy's schooling in mathematics, history, and geography, noting that Ghazi had only learned to recite the Qur'an.[77] As for the Khutat girls, Fuat held it essential to train them in "one or two of the fine arts."[78] Above all else, Fuat emphasized the importance of learning Ottoman Turkish. He sent his nephew and nieces books as gifts and instructed his brother to deliver to him monthly the children's writing samples so that he could assess their handwriting and progress in Ottoman Turkish.[79] The ultimate goal of rigorous homeschooling was for the Khutat children to gain admission to a prestigious secondary school in a big city.[80]

Access to education was a major concern for muhajirs, and Circassians of Aziziye were no exception. In 1903, Circassian notables from Aziziye District sent a collective petition on behalf of their communities to the office of the grand vizier in Istanbul. They coauthored their petition with Afshar notables, their old rivals, which further stressed the importance of their shared cause. They wrote:

> People in our district consist of Circassian and Afshar tribes living in poverty and want. We join our efforts to request funding from the Treasury to provide education to the sons of the homeland [Ott. Tur., *evlad-ı vatan*]. Previously, we attempted to enroll our children in high schools, to no avail. Every year, five to ten students graduate from our district's middle school, but they have no opportunities to excel here. The sons of the homeland from our district cannot escape ignorance and remain deprived of education. . . . We rely on your mercy and ask how many children of both our tribes could be admitted to Aşiret Mektebi [the imperial school for tribes].[81]

Aşiret Mektebi, established in Istanbul in 1892, was a five-year boarding school for children of tribal notables. The Ottomans founded the institution to integrate Kurdish and Arab nomadic elites into Ottoman governance, setting quotas for different "tribes." The government had not identified Turkic-

speaking Afshars or North Caucasian muhajirs as eligible for admission.[82]
Circassians and Afshars challenged that omission, reasoning that graduation
from Aşiret Mektebi would improve their children's chances in life and would
help their communities to build up networks of patronage in the imperial capital. To demonstrate their loyalty to the state, the two communities employed
the relatively new term *vatan* (homeland) to refer to the Ottoman Empire
and *evlad-ı vatan* (sons of the homeland) to their children.[83] Moreover, in
an attempt to claim eligibility for admission, Circassians self-designated as
an *aşiret* (tribe), which usually applied only to nomadic communities and,
for many Ottoman elites, carried negative cultural associations.[84] This petition was meant to signal to Istanbul that the lack of investment in Aziziye
left muhajirs with few opportunities and culturally disadvantaged, much
like nomads.[85] Ironically, Aşiret Mektebi was unpopular with many nomadic
communities that had been eligible for admission because they saw it as a top-
down compulsory initiative by the state. In 1907, the government closed the
school shortly after a student rebellion broke out over bad food.[86]

The dearth of educational opportunities in refugee villages further elevated the appeal of the military. It was no coincidence that, by the early
twentieth century, North Caucasians in the Middle East were associated with
the military and security apparatus rather than civil administration, arts, or
commerce. In the late Ottoman era, military service was the primary vehicle
of social mobility for muhajirs.[87] During the Russo-Ottoman War of 1877–
78, many North Caucasians joined the Ottoman military and then climbed
the ranks, which improved the lives of their families and inspired new generations of muhajirs to pursue military service. Fuat was one such example.
He benefited from his connections to higher-ranked Circassian officers in the
army, while encouraging young men in his own family to study hard, practice
martial skills, and enroll in military service.

THE SLAVE VALLEY

Migrations from the Caucasus turned Uzunyayla not only into a refugee
valley but also a slave valley. The remoteness and exclusively North Caucasian makeup of the valley sustained Circassian agricultural slavery for several
generations. In the early 1910s, local Circassians believed it to be a region with
the largest number of slaves in the Ottoman Empire.[88]

More than half of North Caucasian villages in Uzunyayla were Kabardian. By the mid-nineteenth century, the Kabardians maintained a rigid social
hierarchy, especially noted for slaveholding. As part of Russia's abolition reforms in the North Caucasus in the 1860s, the Russian government incen-
tivized slaveholders to manumit their slaves voluntarily, in exchange for state
compensation. In 1872, the Ottoman embassy in Saint Petersburg relayed a
petition, in French, to the Russian authorities. The petition came from thirteen Kabardian families who had left Russia and now resided in Ottoman
Uzunyayla. The families, represented by Arslan Bey of the Anzurzade (An-
zorov) family, collectively claimed to have left 103 male and female slaves in
the Caucasus and asked the Russian government for 16,867 rubles to "recover
the debts that they had left in Russia."[89] The families manumitted their slaves
before emigrating and now asked for compensation from the state. Whether
the Russian government issued a payment to the Uzunyayla beys remains
unknown. What matters is that these notables believed that they had legal
ground for compensation and, to that effect, sent a bill, with a detailed breakdown of prices for human beings they had once owned. They also had enough
political capital to ensure that the Sivas provincial authorities would sign off
on their petition and that the Ottoman Foreign Ministry would formally
transmit the demand on its letterhead. They were not the only emigrants
expecting to be reimbursed for manumission. In 1874, a group of Circassian
notables in Maraş Province requested an even greater sum of 53,720 rubles as
compensation for their former slaves who had remained in the Caucasus.[90]

Meanwhile, the Ottoman government was prompted to revisit its stance
on Circassian agricultural slavery because of the events in Sivas Province. In
1882, the Sivas authorities had attempted to draft local Circassians upon the
expiration of their military service exemption, but many muhajirs turned out
to be enslaved, and their masters vehemently opposed their draft. The case
was referred to the Ottoman Council of Ministers, which deliberated and
issued a decision. The government continued honoring hereditary agricultural slavery among Circassians but also insisted that, after the expiration of
twenty-five-year exemptions, slaves must serve in the Ottoman military. By
then, they had to be liberated through *mükatebe* (contract of manumission),
which they could pay to their masters by giving them their allotted land as
payment. If that land was not enough, they could service the debt to their

master later, upon returning from their military service.[91] The continued Circassian enslavement, with little prospect of liberation, provoked occasional slave rebellions in Uzunyayla. Already in 1880, 26 slaves fought their masters for their freedom in Aziziye. One slave and one slaveholder were killed, six slaves were recaptured, two slaves disappeared, and seventeen slaves reached Sivas, where they were arrested on the orders of the provincial governor.[92] Another revolt took place in 1911, when six slaves and five beys were killed in the village of Kazancık in Uzunyayla.[93]

A rare testimony of an unfree person from Uzunyayla illustrates the impunity of local slaveholders. In April 1899, a man knocked on the door of the British vice-consulate in Sivas. The man had traveled to the provincial capital from Uzunyayla and made the following statement:

> My name is Taka Oghlou Daoud, and I am a Chechen. I was as a child taken into the service of a Circassian of the village of Chamourli [Çamurlu] in the Kaza of Azizie and, on the death of my master, became the servant of his son Medjid but have never been a slave. I married and had two daughters, who were sold as slaves by Medjid for £135. I cried and protested in vain, and was hung up for three days with my toes just touching the ground. Later I had five more children, four sons and a daughter. A short time ago, my master said he intended to sell them also. I then went to Azizie and lodged a complaint in court against Medjid.[94]

The Ottoman judge in Aziziye was reportedly "terrorized by Circassians" and had ruled against Taka, who then appealed to the office of the grand mufti in Istanbul, which vacated the order from Aziziye and sent the case to the provincial court in Sivas. Taka thought that the presiding judge in Sivas would not dare issue a decision unfavorable to Uzunyayla's powerful slaveholders and asked the provincial governor to intervene in his case, although he feared that the provincial governor might also be bought off by Taka's wealthy master. He finally sought intercession of a foreign consul. Taka complained that the judicial system was stacked against people like him:

> I wish to employ an advocate but am not allowed to do so. I do not understand Turkish well and wish to have an interpreter of my own tribe but am not allowed to do so. I want to hand in a written statement of my case, but the Cadi's [judge's] clerk will not accept it. The Clerk wrote out a statement

of my case, and made me sign it, but I do not know what he has written
down. . . . I hear the Mufti intends to decide against me. I and my children
are living in a khan [inn], poor and hungry, and are not allowed to ask for
alms.[95]

We do not know how the Sivas provincial judge ruled and whether Taka kept
his children. Taka's case is unusual because he succeeded in taking his grievances outside of Uzunyayla. Most unfree people, toiling in various forms of
agricultural servitude, could not leave their well-hidden plateau where the old
Circassian customs were shielded from outside judgment.

Uzunyayla, as a diasporic extension of the "old Kabarda," had reproduced
and fortified social hierarchies, where one's aristocratic, plebeian, or slave
origins remain a marker of difference to this day. During my fieldwork, a
muhtar of one Uzunyayla village, which he asked not to name, showed me
an Ottoman population register from the late nineteenth century. Muhtars
had been using it to record births, deaths, and marriages in that village until
recently. The earliest entries were for Circassian muhajirs who had declared
the Caucasus as their birthplace. The register was physically organized by
social relations: the first entry for each household listed its patriarch, and
all subsequent family members were described below in relation to him: for
example, Ahmed's wife, Ahmed's son, Ahmed's daughter-in-law. Under that
man's household were often listed the households of his slaves. For example, a
new household would start with Ilyas, described as Ahmed's slave (*Ahmed'in
kölesi*). One of the previous muhtars, whose job was to update the register,
came from a family that used to be enslaved in that village. When he got
hold of the register, he whited out all references to his family having been
slaves and changed his ancestor's descriptor to Ahmed's son (*Ahmed'in oğlu*),
although the back side of the page, when read under the light, betrayed the
legacy of slavery in that village. So did the setup of the register, where families
that had once been enslaved were listed underneath the families that used to
own their bodies and labor. The last children recorded in this register were
born in the 1980s.[96]

Slavery, or more generally, bondage of some Circassian families to others
who denied them full autonomy over their lives, lingered in Uzunyayla and
the rest of Anatolia into the twentieth century. While the enslavement of

entire households ended in the early Turkish republican era, the sale of rural Circassian women into forced marriage to strangers continued into the 1970s.[97]

KHUTAT FAMILY: FROM ANATOLIA TO TRANSJORDAN

The Khutat family, who had arrived in Aziziye in the early 1890s, ultimately decided against staying for good. They had several reasons. Cevat tried to secure agricultural land near Aziziye but ran into problems. Local officials refused to issue the land for free because the permit for the Khutats to move to Uzunyayla never arrived from Istanbul.[98] The family considered purchasing land, but Fuat consulted with fellow officers with knowledge of Uzunyayla, who warned him that the government would not build roads to their chosen area because it was not worth the effort.[99] Moreover, the economy of Uzunyayla, in the absence of external investment and export routes, was on shaky foundations. Few refugee villages in Sivas Province prospered, and many muhajirs turned to banditry or the production and smuggling of drugs, particularly hemp and opium.[100] Already fifteen years earlier, the British vice-consul in Sivas called Aziziye the "chief resort of the robbers and murderers in this part of Anatolia."[101] The consul's ungenerous remark captures the sentiments of many, including well-off Circassians, about the refugee valley. Fuat wrote bluntly to Cevat in one of the letters, "We have been feigning ignorance, but we should own up to the truth that there is nothing desirable about living among people who used to be Circassians but lost their ways, are insufficiently civilized, and are seditious and rebellious in the highest degree."[102] The Khutats abandoned the idea of creating a new village in Uzunyayla and renewed their search for the ideal settlement location.

Fuat had long been writing to his friends, from other upper-status muhajir families, for information on which areas were best for settlement, specifically having cheap land, peaceful neighbors, and minimal bureaucratic red tape. Based on their advice, the Khutats discussed the possibility of relocating to Konya Province in central Anatolia and to the subprovince of Gümüşhane in northeastern Anatolia.[103] Fuat also corresponded directly with Ottoman officials in different provinces. Thus, the authorities of the subprovince of Malatya in eastern Anatolia encouraged the Khutats to relocate to their region and take up farming.[104] Fuat briefly considered purchasing land near

Istanbul in eastern Thrace.[105] At some point, the Khutats heard that plenty of fertile land was available on the Euphrates River between Gaziantep, Aleppo, and Birecik and wanted to send Selim Girey to vet the area.[106]

The Khutats' search ended with an unexpected invitation. Cevat received a letter from the Habjokas, an aristocratic Kabardian family to whom they were related. The Habjokas had recently settled in the small Circassian village of Amman and invited the Khutats to travel to Jerusalem and, from there, explore what the interior of the Levant had to offer new immigrants.[107] Fuat was not keen on the idea of his family relocating to the edge of the Syrian desert, but Cevat insisted on giving Amman a chance and departed for Transjordan in early 1895.[108] His trip proved more than an exploratory visit. Cevat was so impressed with Amman that he telegraphed his relatives in Aziziye and his brother in Erzincan for an express money order of 50 Ottoman liras so that he could immediately invest in local real estate.[109] Within weeks, he purchased land, tying the Khutats to their new property in Amman.[110]

The rest of the family moved from Aziziye to Amman in 1896. Some of them took the sea route via Beirut, and others traveled by land via Aleppo and Damascus.[111] The Khutats settled in Amman's Qabartay quarter, among fellow Kabardians. After much correspondence, the Refugee Commission finally signed off on the Khutats' final settlement location. Cevat, as the head of a muhajir household, received usufruct rights to 120 dönüm of land for free from the government.[112] Meanwhile, Fuat, who had remained in Erzincan, petitioned the military high command to transfer him to the Fifth Army, headquartered in Damascus, to be closer to family. His requests were repeatedly denied.[113] Fuat eventually became an ardent supporter of his family's settlement in Transjordan after his Circassian friends in the military persuaded him that the area would likely thrive when the government completed the Hejaz Railway.[114] In anticipation of an economic boom, Fuat enthusiastically pushed for the family's investment in a diverse land portfolio in Amman: "However much you can save, put it back into the soil immediately. That is, turn it into real estate. Do not think that owning land sufficient for your own farming is enough. Buy more land, do not sow it, let it stay empty for a while. When there is an opportunity, try to add more land to your estate and to purchase the adjoining land."[115] Fuat later followed up, "There is nothing more valuable than land to get by in this world."[116]

Cevat, who had initially hoped to find a position in the Ottoman administration in Salt, eagerly embraced his new role as a farmer and real estate
entrepreneur. Cevat's business strategy was simple: he would grow wheat,
sell grain to Salti merchants, and reinvest capital into more real estate. The
early years of farming were difficult for the Khutats: locust destroyed their
first harvest; they lacked proper agricultural tools to till all of their land;
and their oxen were stolen by a neighbor, as was investigated by the Salt
shari'a court.[117] By the late 1890s, the family farm turned a profit on grain
export. Cevat planned to import a stallion from Uzunyayla to breed Kabarda
horses in Transjordan and purchased two more pairs of oxen to plough more
land.[118] He asked his brother where he could get a rifle, likely for protection, as Circassians of Amman were heading into a conflict with bedouin
over surrounding pastures.[119] Fuat, who may have grown disillusioned with
public service, supported his brother's unforeseen entrepreneurial acumen,
"A single kuruş that you earn through your own effort and endeavor is more
blessed and beneficial than a thousand kuruş earned from the government's
treasury by holding a bureaucratic position."[120] Cevat eventually purchased
four shops in the Qabartay quarter of Amman for 563 kuruş each, as attested
by Ottoman land records, which was a sagacious investment because shops
in the neighborhood would sell for up to 7,000 kuruş by the early 1910s.[121]
He also found a way to put his Ottoman legal education to practice. After
improving his Arabic, he worked as an attorney for Amman's Circassians
in the Salt court. His most notable client was Sayetkhan bint Qurash bin
Qoghuluq, the protagonist of chapter 4. In Transjordan, Cevat had become
Jawad Bey.

The Khutats relied on kinship ties in their resettlement. When Cevat
moved to Amman, Fuat urged him to persuade families that were related to
them by blood or marital ties to follow the Khutats to Transjordan:

> My brother, are there any of our old in-laws who wish to go there with you?
> If such friends are available, accept them nicely and ease their business. Do
> not hesitate to make sacrifices in this matter. Do not forget that, however
> much you trust in friendship, no [new] friends would measure up to the old
> in-laws. It has been proven. It is not possible to find people like them again
> in distant places.[122]

Throughout their journey, from the Caucasus to Adana, to Aziziye, and to Amman, the Khutats had been accompanied by six families, whom the Refugee Commission called the "Khutat party."[123] Circassian muhajir notables often lived surrounded by families that had emigrated with them; some of them were of equal social status, whereas others used to rely on their patronage back in the Caucasus. Resettling together was not only a matter of emotional support, which by no means should be underestimated, but also a social and economic investment. For example, the Qul family, which moved to Amman with the Khutats, continued a close association and did business with them, having sold 20 dönüm of land to Cevat and his nephew Ghazi in 1910.[124] Kinship networks also raised muhajirs' political capital, especially when negotiating with third parties.

The Khutats, skilled letter-writers (see map 7), carefully cultivated rela-

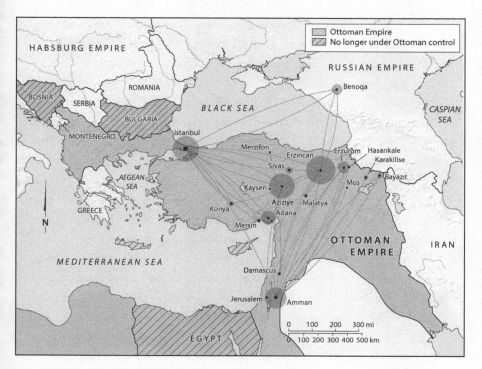

Map 7. **Khutats' correspondence, 1890–1905.**

Cevat preserved the contents of Fuat's 58 letters, which in turn referenced 122 other letters among the Khutats and with their friends and Ottoman officials.

tions with Ottoman imperial and regional powerholders. By corresponding
with the Refugee Commission and municipal authorities in Adana, Aziziye,
and Amman, the Khutats negotiated permissions and privileges for themselves and their client families. Muhajirs needed permission from the Refugee
Commission to leave their original settlement and relocate elsewhere, while
keeping the benefits that the muhajir status entailed. The Khutats spent the
better part of the 1890s petitioning the Commission to formalize their right
of settlement, to obtain permissions to leave, and to release their immigrant
subsidies. Dozens of family letters reveal the Khutats' frustration with the
slow pace of Ottoman bureaucracy and their reliance on patrons for support.
The family obtained the needed papers from the Commission through the
intercession of Fuat's military superiors in Istanbul and after involving local
officeholders, such as the Aziziye district governor and the Amman township
head.[125]

The Khutats stayed in Transjordan, while keeping their many transregional connections. Şerife (see figure 7), the sister of Fuat and Cevat, married
artillery captain Azmi Bey, who served with Fuat. His notable Circassian
family, the Haghandoqas, was scattered between Anatolia, Transjordan, and
Egypt. When Azmi Bey asked Fuat for her hand in marriage, Fuat wrote to
Cevat that the family should consider the proposal, but the decision must
be "basically, Şerife's view on the matter."[126] Şerife accepted Azmi Bey's proposal.[127] Meanwhile, Cevat (see figure 8) married his cousin Muzayan, the
daughter of Gulumkhan, and they had five daughters together.[128] Hanife
Hanım, the mother of Fuat, Cevat, and Şerife, remained in Amman as a matriarch of a growing family. In almost every letter, Fuat first inquired about
his mother's health and well-being. Latife, Cevat's cousin, married Isma'il
Babuq, the first mayor of Amman.[129] Ghazi, Selim Girey's son, after helping
Cevat to set up the family business in Amman, left to receive an education
in Istanbul, following in the footsteps of his two uncles. He then found work
in Egypt, where he managed the estate of a sister of Sultan Hussein Kamel
(r. 1914–17) and Sultan/King Fuad I (r. 1917–36) in Banha District in the
Nile Delta. Upon his death in 1927, his family moved back to Amman.[130]
Ghazi's son Jalal Ghazi pursued a career in financial administration and was
in charge of the finances of the Jordanian Armed Forces between 1965 and
1999.[131] The Khutats' friends, the Habjokas, who had invited them to move

to Transjordan, also did exceptionally well. Their scion Saʿid al-Mufti rose
to become a leader of the Circassian community and served as a three-term
prime minister of Jordan in the 1950s.

Fuat, whose detailed correspondence animated this family history, remained in Erzincan. In 1898, he received the Order of the Mecidiye of the
third class for his service on the Iranian border.[132] He was then reassigned
to a military desk job in Erzurum but was soon back to patrolling the Russian border.[133] His letters to Amman would arrive from different towns along
the border: Karakilise (Ağrı), Bayazıt (Doğubayazıt), Hasankale (Pasinler),
and Muş. Fuat was later handpicked for the Ottoman border commission
and traveled to the Caucasus to work with his tsarist counterparts on what

Figure 7. Şerife, Fuat, and Şefika Khutat.
Photograph taken circa 1906. *Courtesy*: Khutat Family Collection.

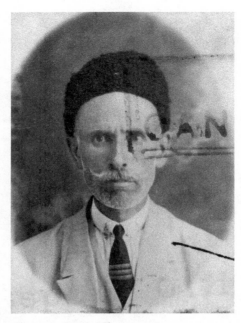

Figure 8. **Cevat Khutat.**
Photograph taken circa 1926.
Courtesy: Khutat Family Collection.

he referred to as "border-related problems," which could have been related
to contraband traffic or activities of Armenian revolutionaries.[134] Likely as
a result of that mission, he received a promotion from the rank of *kolağası*
(senior captain) to *binbaşı* (major) in 1900.[135] Based on the family's recollections, around the same time he married Şefika, an Armenian woman from
Erzincan (see figure 7).[136]

Fuat, who had left Circassia as a young boy, developed a keen interest
in tracing his family's ancestry. He wrote to his brother and older relatives
to help him to reconstruct their genealogical list and family tree.[137] "Our
family was known and esteemed in Circassia [Ott. Tur., *Çerkezistan*] and
distinguished in prestige," he wrote.[138] He traveled to Kabarda, which his
family had left for western Circassia three generations prior, to learn about his
ancestors. He excitedly related to Cevat what he had discovered: their family
was one of three branches of a larger kin, and one of their forefathers owned a
"famous grey horse," still fondly remembered in Kabarda.[139] A century later,

after the fall of communism, the Khutats would use the family tree that Fuat had drawn up to find their long-lost relatives in Russia.[140]

Fuat's surviving letters end abruptly in 1905, although he almost certainly continued corresponding with his family in Amman. But he left us another written artifact. The archaeological museum in Erzurum preserves a detailed map of the city drawn in 1904 by one "Kafkasyalı Kur. Yb. Fuat Bey." By that time, Fuat was promoted to *yarbay* (lieutenant colonel). While stationed in Erzurum, which was the Ottomans' eastern outpost near the Russian border, Fuat mapped the city's topography. On the map, he listed, with military precision, the names of the main mosques, churches, baths, markets, and schools and painstakingly counted Erzurum shops (2,735), textile manufacturers (243), tanners (106), jewelers (45), and others.[141]

Fuat eventually returned to Istanbul, a city that he loved, where he found himself in the thick of a rapidly changing empire. Sometime after the Young Turk Revolution of 1908, Fuat became superintendent in the Ottoman Military Academy (Mekteb-i Ulum-i Harbiye).[142] He trained a new generation of staff officers whose duty was to defend the empire and its reinstated constitution. In January 1913, the CUP carried out a coup d'état against grand vizier Kamil Paşa's liberal government and installed Mahmut Şevket Paşa as the grand vizier. In June, the new grand vizier was assassinated, which the CUP used as a pretext to unleash a purge of the liberal opposition, primarily supporters of the dissolved Freedom and Accord Party.[143] During the purge, Fuat was arrested and, shortly thereafter, executed. According to family memories, all charges against him were false and politically motivated.[144]

After Fuat's death, his widow and three children joined the rest of the Khutat family in Amman but then returned to Istanbul. Fuat and Şefika's children grew up in Istanbul, through the Allied occupation and early republican rule, as members of the first generation of the new Turkey. They all received a good education. Fuat and Şefika's daughter Şaziment graduated from the American College for Girls (now Robert College); son Suat became a lawyer, like his Transjordanian uncle Cevat; and son Reşat became an army officer, like his late father.[145]

By the early twentieth century, Uzunyayla was home to one of the largest and most ethnically diverse North Caucasian populations in the empire. The

town of Aziziye was one of the rare Ottoman refugee towns. The North Caucasians' resettlement in central Anatolia progressed differently than that in
the Balkans and Transjordan. In the Balkans, muhajirs struggled because of
insufficient Ottoman financial support, which led to banditry and sectarian
violence before muhajirs were expelled. In Uzunyayla, state funding for refugees was also inadequate, and contemporaries likewise lamented muhajir
poverty and banditry. The difference was that, in remote Uzunyayla, muhajirs did not clash with settled Christian populations and were not dragged
into a brewing war of national liberation. But Uzunyayla Circassians did not
thrive either, compared to their kin in Transjordan. The fortunes of Aziziye
and Amman, two Circassian refugee towns, could not be more different.
Amman, with four million residents, is now a global city, whereas Pınarbaşı,
as Aziziye has been known since 1926, had a population of 8,803 in 2019.

Uzunyayla's economic and demographic stagnation began already in the
Ottoman era. After all, the Khutats left Aziziye for Amman precisely because
the latter held better economic prospects. The North Caucasian experience
in Uzunyayla was a quintessential Ottoman story of refugee resettlement:
the Ottoman government had settled muhajirs in that region and provided
military support in the 1860s, when nomads had challenged muhajirs' rights
to the land, but afterward the state slowly retreated, leaving refugees to their
own devices. The government committed minimal resources to building up
refugee villages and, critically, did not invest in the logistical infrastructure of
the wider region. The massive Sivas Province, at the very center of Anatolia,
did not have a single railway, despite multiple attempts to build them. The
Ottomans sold early concessions to British entrepreneurs to build railways to
Sivas from Samsun in 1857 and Üsküdar in 1862, both of which were soon
abandoned.[146] In 1890, the Belgian Cockerill Company purchased a conces-
sion to build a railway between Samsun and Sivas, but its construction stalled
because of diplomatic opposition from Germany, whose Deutsche Bank had
funded the Anatolian Railway, established in 1888, and considered its own
prospective extension toward Sivas.[147] Meanwhile, the German-funded Baghdad Railway, designed to connect Baghdad to Istanbul and Berlin, could have
gone through central Anatolia, particularly Ankara, Sivas, and Diyarbakır,
as the Ottoman government pushed for that route.[148] It never came to pass
because, in 1900, Russia negotiated the Black Sea Agreement, which stipu-

lated that only the Ottoman government or Russia itself could build a railway anywhere between Ankara and the Russian border. The tsarist government sought to prevent the construction of any railway that could deliver Ottoman soldiers to the Russian border and knew that the Ottomans lacked funds to build such a railway on their own.[149] The first railway in central Anatolia connected Kayseri to Ankara only in 1927; it was extended to Sivas in 1930. No railway extension was ever built to Aziziye/Pınarbaşı. In the absence of a railway, it was nearly impossible to attract external capital to this little town and its mountain valley.

The economy and demographics of Uzunyayla took several hits in the twentieth century. During the Armenian genocide, Aziziye's Armenian population was deported and slaughtered.[150] Many Armenians of Aziziye were artisans and merchants, whose trades connected Uzunyayla to the outside world. Aziziye emerged from the war as an ethnically cleansed and economically devastated town, like so many in Anatolia. Furthermore, the muhajir pastoral economy declined. The Uzunyayla North Caucasians' most profitable trade was selling horses to the Ottoman military. As Turkey's military required progressively fewer animals, the export of horses dwindled and came to an end in the 1950s.[151] Today, driving through the plateau, one would see many cows but not the Uzunyayla horses, which almost disappeared as a breed. North Caucasians had to reorient their economy from horse breeding to agriculture and husbandry, but the lack of a nearby railway or trans-Anatolian highways meant that Uzunyaylans could not easily export their agricultural and pastoral production. Finally, it was modern Turkey's urbanization that hit Uzunyayla the hardest. Younger generations have been leaving Uzunyayla for bigger cities, especially Kayseri and Ankara, and for Germany as Turkish guest workers.[152] The population of Aziziye/Pınarbaşı District fell from 50,784 in 1907 to 31,695 in 1935; it recovered in the postwar years and then has been plummeting since the 1980s.[153] In 2022, its population stood at 21,240.[154]

The geographic isolation of Uzunyayla has sustained its North Caucasian cultural heritage. Uzunyayla is no longer exclusively North Caucasian: Afshars, Kurds, and Turkish muhajirs from Bulgaria established their own villages there. The population of Pınarbaşı, which was founded as a Circassian refugee town and a buffer against the Afshars, is primarily local Turks, whose Afshar ancestors had been expelled from Uzunyayla. And yet, about 10,000

North Caucasians remain in over sixty villages on the plateau.[155] Uzunyayla is one of the few places in the Middle East, where younger generations of North Caucasians still speak Circassian. In 2017, the Hatuqwai (western Circassian) village of Kaynar in Uzunyayla hosted the International Circassian Cultural Festival. This annual "Circassian Woodstock" attracts musicians, singers, storytellers, and dancers from Turkey, Jordan, and Russia. That year, the festival was sponsored by Turkey's Ministry of Culture and Tourism and almost all North Caucasian diasporic organizations, and it was attended by 15,000 people, most of whom chartered buses from Kayseri, Ankara, and Istanbul and even flew from Berlin. On two cool summer days, a small village on a high plateau came alive through the sounds of Circassian, Abazin, Chechen, and other languages. Anatolia's Little Caucasus created its own cultural legacy, and it remains a second homeland for many North Caucasians in the Middle East. The next chapter explores how North Caucasian refugees learned to think of themselves as one community, while dispersed throughout the empire.

Part III
DIASPORA AND RETURN

SIX

MAKING THE NORTH CAUCASIAN DIASPORA

IN THE EARLY TWENTIETH CENTURY, North Caucasian activists in the Ottoman Empire worked together to mold their disparate refugee groups into one community. The empire's many peoples—Greeks, Armenians, Jews, Bulgarians, Albanians, and others—increasingly couched their communal aspirations in ethnoreligious and ethnonational terms. Muhajir activists followed suit but faced many hurdles in articulating their collective identity. North Caucasian refugees belonged to different ethnic groups who spoke mutually unintelligible languages within four language families— Northwest Caucasian, Northeast Caucasian, Indo-European, and Turkic. What were they to call themselves collectively? Others typically referred to them as Circassians, but could Chechens, Ossetians, and Dagestanis be included in the collective designation as Circassians? Furthermore, North Caucasian refugees arrived with no written culture in their native languages. To foster a sense of community, they needed to learn how to read their languages and to agree on how to write them. Adyghe (Circassian) was the native language of most refugees, but what were its boundaries, and whose dialect would be favored in written Circassian? What script would refugees choose? The Latin script provided a better platform for the exceptionally rich range of consonants in Northwest Caucasian languages (Ubykh had eighty-four phonemic consonants). The Arabic script, however, was more familiar to Ottoman-educated muhajirs and was the preferred script of the empire's Muslim communities.[1] The questions of identity and self-representation guided debates among North Caucasian activists.

This chapter examines the evolution of the North Caucasian diaspora in the late Ottoman era. How muhajirs organized themselves sheds light on the political implications of their refugeedom for the Ottoman Empire and Russia. By the 1860s, North Caucasian muhajirs already held the main components of a diasporic community, as theorized by scholars of diasporas: ethnocommunal consciousness, dispersal from their homeland, collective memory of it, commitment to it, and—to some extent—desire to return and alienation from host societies.[2] It took several decades for North Caucasian intellectuals to publicly articulate that their refugee communities formed a whole: rooted in the Caucasus, distinct from the surrounding host communities, yet part of the Ottoman nation. The formation of the North Caucasian diaspora in the Ottoman Empire is extraordinary because it preceded the nation-building process in the homeland. The emergence of diasporas in global history is typically contingent on a strong sense of preexisting identity, fortified by a literary tradition. The North Caucasians did not have that. While making sense of their displacement from Russia and scattered resettlement in the Ottoman Empire, these communities wrote their histories and dictionaries. Not only did North Caucasians have to develop a written culture in exile, they did so with self-awareness as a multiethnic and multilingual diaspora.

This chapter moves through the vast world of Caucasus Muslims, which, by the late nineteenth century, spanned the Caspian and the Aegean coasts. It starts with refugee villages in the Ottoman Empire, exploring social structures and traditions that helped muhajirs to preserve their cultures. Refugee village networks facilitated the exchange of information within the North Caucasian diaspora and helped muhajirs to form a coherent social bloc within the empire. The story continues in Istanbul after the Young Turk Revolution of 1908. North Caucasian elites established the Circassian Union and Support Association (1908–23), which crafted the muhajirs' diasporic identity around the "Circassianness" of the dominant refugee group. It further promoted its vision of the North Caucasian place within the broader Ottoman nation and global Muslim community, or the *umma*.[3] Finally, this chapter focuses on the transimperial debate about *hijra*, or Muslim emigration, which greatly animated North Caucasians on both sides of the Russo-Ottoman border. While many muhajirs urged their families in the Caucasus to join them in the Ottoman Empire, others opposed any further emigration from Russia. North Caucasian intellectuals in the Ottoman and Russian empires used the nascent Muslim print media, in Ottoman Turkish, Arabic, Russian, and— for the first time—Circassian, to dissuade Caucasus Muslims from becoming muhajirs. This chapter, by following muhajirs' writings about education, abolition, and emigration, tells the origin story of North Caucasian diasporic politics in the Middle East.

NORTH CAUCASIAN VILLAGES

Following their displacement, hundreds of thousands of North Caucasians found themselves scattered across the rural vastness of the Ottoman Empire. They had no formal institutions to represent them and were separated from much of their traditional leadership, who perished during the Caucasus War, remained in Russia, or moved to Ottoman cities. North Caucasians were also torn away from their homeland; from their sacred mountains, forests, shrines, and cemeteries of their ancestors; and from their communal histories, as told through songs, legends, and lineages, because many of their elders died in war or in flight. What helped refugees to survive and, in a broader sense, to remain Circassian or Chechen was staying together in muhajir villages. The formation of the North Caucasian diaspora occurred in the Ottoman countryside through indigenous social institutions and refugee village networks.

North Caucasian refugees brought with them the elaborate social structures of their old societies, which were unlike those of their new neighbors in the Middle East and also differed significantly among North Caucasian communities. Several Circassian communities, such as Kabardians, Besleneys, and Bzhedughs, had a rigid social order, dominated by hereditary aristocracy. The society in Kabarda was divided into *pshi* (princely families); *werq* (notables), including upper-rank *tlekotlesh* and *dizhenugo* and lower-rank *beslan-werq*, *werq-shaotlugus*, and *pshikeu*, serving as troops for princes and upper-rank notables; and free peasants, including *azat* (freedmen), who formed the majority of Kabarda's population by the mid-nineteenth century.[4] The rest were in various categories of bondage: *og* (in land corvée), *lagunapyt* (in land and household corvée), and *unaut* (enslaved).[5] Other Circassian communities, including Shapsughs, Abzakhs, and Natukhais, had a smaller nobility stratum and elected their leadership in people's assemblies. The Soviet historiography referred to the former as "aristocratic" Circassians and the latter as "democratic" Circassians, which was an oversimplification and distortion of complex political dynamics in pre-conquest Circassia.[6] By the mid-nineteenth century, many Circassian communities had been reforming their old social order and moving toward more inclusive forms of governance.[7] This political transformation was interrupted by the Caucasus War and mass expulsions from the Circassian coast.

Chechen society was structured differently, around kins and historical alliances. Every Chechen household belonged to a *taip*, or clan, which descended from the same ancestor. The largest social unit was a *tukkhum*, or a union of multiple *taip* that had banded together for economic or defensive purposes. By the mid-nineteenth century, the Chechens were split into 135 *taip*, of which three-quarters formed the nine *tukkhum*: Aekkkhii, Chaberloi, Chanti, Orstkhoi (Karabulak), Malkhi, Nokhchmekhkakhoi, Sharoi, Shatoi, and T'erloi.[8] The Chechen society was less hierarchical than the Circassian one, with few notables and, by the mid-nineteenth century, fewer slaves than in neighboring North Caucasian communities.[9] Chechen villages were governed by elected councils, and in exceptional circumstances many *taip* came together to convene the elders' council to rule on matters of war and peace.

Every North Caucasian ethnic group had its own social hierarchy, on which muhajirs relied to organize their communities in exile, from the physical setup of their villages to the distribution of land and labor. These structures, under tremendous strain after displacement, inevitably evolved in diaspora. The North Caucasians in the Ottoman Empire were an extension of their societies in the Caucasus, but they also formed radically new communities because, amid the hardships of resettlement, different subethnic groups and social strata mixed like they never did before. Muhajirs developed their own criteria for inclusion and exclusion. For example, in many areas, marriages between North Caucasians from different ethnic groups or between notables and freemen, which would have been frowned upon in the Caucasus, were gradually accepted. At the same time, many muhajirs refused to marry non–North Caucasians or muhajirs of slave descent.[10]

North Caucasians arrived with distinct sets of social and legal practices that governed their communities. They were specific to each ethnic group but had broad similarities throughout the Caucasus. The first one was customary law, or 'adat, which regulated various aspects of North Caucasian lives, including marriage, inheritance, trade, and punishment.[11] For example, in Dagestan, customary law bound together groups of villages into free confederacies and set their mutual obligations in defense and communal farming and shepherding.[12] In the Caucasus, customary law had long coexisted with Islamic law, but their differences were politicized in the nineteenth century. In the Caucasus Imamate under the leadership of Imam Shamil, shari'a replaced 'adat in many matters, whereas the Russian administration in the Caucasus often elevated customary law over Islamic law in the administration of mountaineer affairs.[13] In the Ottoman Empire, muhajirs often followed their customary law, for example, in setting dowers for the bride, which some shari'a courts recognized.[14]

The second set of uniquely North Caucasian practices was an unwritten moral code: Adyghe Khabze for Circassians, Apsuara for Abkhazians, Tau Adet for Karachays and Balkars, Nokhchalla for Chechens, Ezdel for Ingush, and Aghdau for Ossetians. Each community's moral code incorporated its mythologies and prehistories and prescribed certain gender and class hierarchies, wedding etiquette, and other behavioral norms. For example, Circassian fathers could not call their children by their names in public. Likewise, a husband and wife considered it taboo to call each other by their given names, instead using pet names.[15] For Circassians, Adyghe Khabze informed Adygaghe, the ethics of being a Circassian, or "Circassianness."[16]

In addition to North Caucasian customary law and moral codes, several social institutions helped North Caucasians to preserve connections among their scattered communities in exile. One was the atalık custom, a type of fosterage practiced by Circassians, Abkhazians, Ossetians, and Turkic people in the North Caucasus. Children were often sent away to be raised by a foster father (atalık) and would return to their birth parents only upon reaching marriageable age. For example, the Gerays, the Chinggisid ruling family of Crimea that in terms of the prestige of lineage was regarded second only to the Ottoman dynasty in the Ottoman world, traditionally sent their boys to Circassian notables for upbringing.[17] Some of their Circassianized offspring also became muhajirs in the Ottoman Empire.[18] In the past, the *atalık* tradition helped to solidify alliances between upper-status families. By the nineteenth century, it was more commonly practiced as an unequal relationship, wherein lower-status families were expected to raise children of their social superiors. Thus, Kabardian princes would send their children to notables, and notables would send theirs to free peasants; Abkhazian semidependent (*ankhaiu*) peasants could pass their children onto dependent (*akhuiu*) peasants.[19] In various forms, this custom continued in the North Caucasian diaspora, binding many refugee families together.

Another social institution was *khachesh*, a traditional guest house that upper-status Circassian families used to have. Travelers passing through a Circassian village could stay in a *khachesh* for free, availing themselves of the expected hospitality of their hosts. In diaspora, *khachesh* was a site of communal transmission of knowledge, to which notables invited folk singer-storytellers (*dzheguako*), thereby enabling greater mobility and communication within the muhajir world. For example, in Uzunyayla, several prominent families maintained well-known *khachesh* into the 1970s.[20] A *khachesh* also served as a place where the elders' council deliberated village affairs and adjudicated disagreements by customary law.[21]

North Caucasian muhajirs stayed in touch with each other through village networks. These networks connected clusters of monoethnic villages, at a great distance from each other, tied primarily through kinship. The networks were informal, fluid, and served different purposes. Muhajirs commonly visited their extended families and searched for a prospective spouse in other villages. They bartered agricultural produce and moved around for services of blacksmiths, cart makers, and healers who spoke their language. North Caucasians reportedly established routes of horse and cattle trade between the tsarist Caucasus and Ottoman Kars, Sivas, and Damascus, which lay through North Caucasian refugee villages.[22] Muhajirs rallied other villages for shared defense, or assault, when in conflict with nomadic populations, as happened in Uzunyayla, Transjordan, and the Golan Heights. Some village networks were more extensive and tight-knit than others, depending on the geography of resettlement. For most refugees, these connections provided a lifeline to preserving their languages, economies, and ways of life as North Caucasians. Not all muhajirs were mobile; most were firmly tied down by their allotted land and farming schedule and never left their districts, but they were also part of village networks, as news of what was happening to muhajirs elsewhere traveled from village to village, holding together the scattered refugee realm.

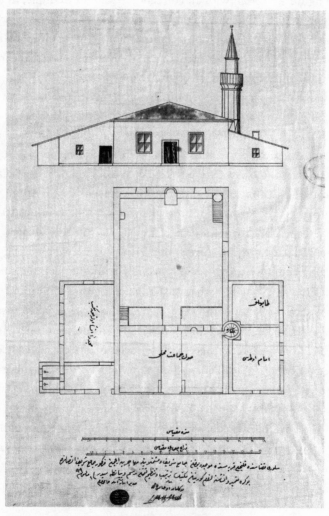

Figure 9. **Blueprint of a mosque for refugees.**
BOA PLK.p 187 (Silivri District, 6 *recep* 1300, 13 May 1883).

Village mosques and schools sustained the circulation of knowledge in the North Caucasian community. Refugee villages formed a job market for the diaspora's most educated members. Many muhajirs arrived with their own 'ulama, educated in madrasas of Dagestan, Crimea, Kazan, Egypt, and the Ottoman Empire. In the early 1860s, the Ottoman government envisioned every refugee village to have a mosque—a small *mescit* or a larger *cami* (see figure 9)—often with an adjacent school. For example, in 1861, the government funded the construction of seven mosques in Uzunyayla.[23] In later years, the scope of migration from the Caucasus had overwhelmed the Ottoman treasury, drastically reducing state investment into the refugees' religious and educational infrastructure. Nevertheless, in 1870, the government mandated that every new muhajir village have a mosque and a primary school.[24] It fell upon the muhajirs themselves to pay for, or negotiate the government's cosponsorship of, mosques and schools in their villages. In some villages, muhajirs established charitable endowments that supported the maintenance of mosques and payment of salaries to imams and teachers.[25] The educated muhajirs commonly traveled from village to village for new appointments. At the early stage of resettlement, Ottoman authorities favored the North Caucasian 'ulama for appointments in muhajir villages, as they needed to cultivate a loyal refugee elite.[26] The 'ulama were among the few refugees who could write and speak in Arabic and often became communal representatives and mediators between their refugee communities and the government. In the Hamidian era, the government preferred to instead appoint non-muhajir imams in refugee villages to ensure the proper "Islamization" of North Caucasian refugees whose social practices, such as collective mixed-gender dancing, bewildered their Ottoman Muslim neighbors.[27]

In the first generation after displacement, muhajirs relied on centuries-old social institutions and new village networks to sustain their communities in the vast Ottoman countryside. Meanwhile, many muhajir elites found themselves in Ottoman cities, where they helped to formulate what it meant to be Circassian and North Caucasian as Ottoman subjects.

NORTH CAUCASIAN DIASPORIC ORGANIZATIONS

By the late nineteenth century, Ottoman communities espoused new forms of affiliation. Ethnic nationalism transformed how many Ottoman subjects perceived their place in history and their relationship with the Ottoman state. Ethnic and religious identities were often fused, especially for the empire's Christian subjects. Private institutions of Ottoman Christians—schools, printing presses, and charitable associations—increasingly emphasized language and shared history, in addition to faith, as binding their members together. Many of the empire's Muslim communities, from Albania to Kurdistan, also pressed for acknowledgment of their ethnic and linguistic differences through new cultural associations, educational initiatives, and literary works. The Hamidian authorities were paranoid about any forms of dissent and widely employed secret police to crack down on any activities that might suggest political opposition. The government was anxious about ethnic politics, especially by the empire's Muslim subjects, as the Treaty of Berlin of 1878 all but confirmed ethnicity as key to sovereignty and border delineation.

The first North Caucasian association was the Society for Circassian Unity (Ott. Tur., Cemiyet-i İttihadiye-i Çerakise), founded in Cairo in 1899. Turn-of-the-century Egypt, under British occupation, served as a haven, alongside Paris and Geneva, for Ottoman intellectuals facing censorship by the Hamidian regime.[28] The founder of the society was Mehmed Emin Bey (Loh), a Caucasus-born Abazin notable who had earlier been exiled to Tripolitania for his ties to the Young Turks. The establishment of the society was announced in the inaugural issue of its newspaper, *İttihad Gazetesi* (1899), in Ottoman Turkish. In what would be its only issue, the newspaper criticized the Ottoman government for its inadequate handling of the first Circassian refugee crisis, in 1863–65. The editorial emphasized that muhajirs moved to the Ottoman caliphate to preserve their Muslim faith but did not receive a warm welcome by the Ottoman government.[29] The harsh criticism was likely the reason for the Porte swiftly banning the Cairene newspaper from entering the Ottoman domains.[30] The Circassian newspaper, however, also urged muhajirs to be loyal to their "common Ottoman homeland" and advocated a "strong alliance" between "the noble Ottomans" and "their Circassian brothers." Likewise, the statute of the Society for Circassian Unity committed to working for the benefit of the "whole Ottoman and Muslim nation" (*millet*), while protecting the "nationality (*kavmiyet*) of the Circassians."[31] The organization withered away soon after its establishment. Its founder returned to the Ottoman Empire after being pardoned by Sultan Abdülhamid II, who appointed him as inspector for the settlement of muhajirs in Eskişehir.[32]

The Young Turk Revolution of 1908 transformed the Ottoman political environment. A group of revolutionaries, led by the CUP, forced Sultan Abdülhamid II to restore the Ottoman constitution and the Ottoman parliament, the hallmarks of the First Constitutional Era in 1876–78. The revolution promised legal equality, political representation, and the government's accountability to the empire's many subjects. The revolution ended the Hamidian-era censorship of political associations and allowed Ottoman subjects to assemble openly. The freedoms, which jubilant crowds celebrated on the streets of Ottoman cities in 1908, started shrinking soon after the revolution and were diminished after the CUP coup of 1913, but for a while they generated a political and cultural awakening for many communities, including the North Caucasians.[33]

The second North Caucasian diasporic organization was the Circassian Union and Support Association (Çerkes İttihad ve Teavün Cemiyeti; hereafter, the Association). Established in Istanbul after the Young Turk Revolution, it was the largest and dominant North Caucasian organization in the Ottoman Empire between 1908 and 1923. Under the leadership of Ahmed Cavid Paşa (1840–1916), a Caucasus-born Ottoman-Ubykh civil administrator, the Association claimed to represent all North Caucasian communities in the empire. Its primary goals included funding North Caucasian cultural and educational initiatives and lobbying the Ottoman government on issues most relevant to muhajirs, such as access to education and abolition of slavery.

The Association became an umbrella group for North Caucasian elites from different ethnic and social groups: some were the old Ottoman-Circassian elites, who had descended from palace slaves and janissaries; others were scions of aristocratic families or Imam Shamil's generals, who had left the Caucasus for Ottoman cities; and many were army officers and civil administrators, who may have been of humble refugee origins but rose through the Ottoman ranks. The Association's prominent members included Deli Fuat Paşa (1835–1931), a member of the Ottoman Senate in 1908; Hüseyin Tosun Bey (1875–1930), Hüseyin Kadri Bey (1870–1934), İsmail Canbulat Bey

(1880–1926), and Tahir Hayrettin Bey (1875–1937), members of the Chamber of Deputies in 1908–14; Mehmet Şemsettin Paşa (1855–1917), minister for *vakıf* in 1908–9 and, at various times, ambassador in Bucharest and Tehran and the Sultan's regent to Tripoli and Benghazi; Mehmet Reşit Bey (1873–1919), one of the four founders of the CUP in 1889, governor of Diyarbakır in 1915, and one of the chief perpetrators of the Armenian genocide; and Musa Kundukhov's son Bekir Sami Bey (1867–1933), governor of Van, Trabzon, Bursa, Beirut, and Aleppo, and later minister of foreign affairs in Mustafa Kemal's first cabinet in 1920–21. Several Circassian ministers and generals, if not formal members of the Association, had ties to it: Salih Hulusi Paşa (1864–1939), minister of war in 1909, minister of navy in 1910–11, minister of public works in 1912, and grand vizier in 1920; Hurşid Paşa (1854–1934), minister of navy in 1911–12; and Hüseyin Nazım Paşa (1848–1913), minister of war in 1912–13.[34] Many Association members were actively involved with the CUP; some joined the Freedom and Accord Party and smaller constitutionalist parties, and others held loyalty to the Hamidian regime and retained close ties to the palace.

The Association laid out its vision for the North Caucasian diasporic identity in its inaugural proclamation in 1908. The founders addressed North Caucasians as "fellow countrymen" (*yurttaşlar*) and referred to the Caucasus as their "true country" (*gerçek yurdumuz*).[35] Yet the Association stressed, similar to its Cairene predecessor, that the Ottoman Empire was the North Caucasians' new homeland, where muhajirs could freely profess their faith, preserve their culture, and now enjoy civic freedoms. The Association also attributed a much greater role to religion in narrating the muhajirs' displacement than would become customary for the North Caucasian diaspora over the course of the twentieth century: "May God Almighty preserve our sublime state as the Islamic caliphate and the Ottoman sultanate. Had a strong Muslim government, such as the Ottoman Empire, not provided refuge to us, or rather had this sacred caliphate, this glorious government, and this holy land not accepted and protected us, we would have lost our religion. . . . Had we lost our religion, we would have definitely lost our freedom too."[36] The Association, which sought to reach rural refugee populations, was fusing the rhetoric of Islamic refuge and the Ottoman caliphate, ubiquitous in the Hamidian age, with that of freedom, emblematic of the post-1908 years.

The Association promoted three overlapping affiliations for muhajirs: with the Circassian community, the Ottoman nation, and the *umma*. First, the Association pressed that, to preserve their identity in exile, Circassians needed to educate their children in the Circassian language and culture. It appealed to its members: "We, the Circassians, are the most backward people among all Ottoman communities in terms of education. Today, we cannot write in Circassian, and, with time, the number of Circassian speakers will only diminish."[37] Second, the Association declared that every muhajir's duty was to "serve the Ottoman constitutional government, which ensures protection of our community (*milliyetimiz*), justice, and prosperity."[38] The Association worked on the doctrine of Circassianism (*Çerkesçilik*), or a commitment to the Circassian nation as a constituent element of the Ottoman nation, but it was never fully conceptualized in its publications.[39] Finally, the Association emphasized that muhajirs should strive to be good Muslims by nurturing their "moral beauty" in the "pure and righteous way of [the Prophet] Muhammad," as well as be studious and hardworking.[40] Muhajir education and labor would further contribute to the glory of the Circassian community and the Ottoman nation.

North Caucasian activists never denied an Ottoman identity. On the contrary, the Association embraced the notion of Ottomanism (*Osmanlılık*), which encompassed loyalty to the state, equality of Ottoman citizens, and belonging to the Ottoman nation. It first emerged as an imperial project in the nineteenth century. As Michelle Campos demonstrated, after decades of Hamidian rule, the grassroots movement of "civic Ottomanism" was the guiding principle of the Young Turk Revolution.[41] Ottoman subjects—urban, rural, Muslim, Jewish, and Christian—celebrated the restored Constitution and their equality as Ottoman subjects. Many longed for a future when one could proudly be Ottoman *and* Armenian, Greek, or Jewish, while having the exact same rights. The Association's proclamation captured those very sentiments. The Ottoman identity was not imagined as second to the refugees' ethnic identity. They reinforced each other: by educating themselves about their Circassianness, muhajirs were better Ottoman citizens, and, by serving the Ottoman nation and state loyally, they could thrive as Circassians. The muhajir identity of North Caucasians further reinforced their allegiance to Ottomanism: the sultan-caliph offered them refuge, and they relied on the

Ottoman refugee regime. North Caucasians were loyal Ottomans because they were refugees.

The Association encouraged the North Caucasian diaspora to cultivate a distinct economic profile. It advocated the creation of North Caucasian monopolies within the Ottoman economy. The Association recognized that most muhajirs toiled in agriculture and urged them to supplement their unsteady farming income by taking up traditional North Caucasian trades as blacksmiths, weavers, skinners, and furriers. It also favored the development of a parallel muhajir economy that would produce new jobs while sustaining North Caucasian cultures. For example, the Association called on muhajirs to don their distinctive fur hats: "Absolutely refuse to wear a *fez* [red Ottoman headdress] . . . and opt for wearing a *kalpak* [high fur hat]. Because a *kalpak* is our sole national headdress. Make *kalpaks* yourselves! Furthermore, every village could establish local monopolies in the production of *yamçı* [woolen coats] and saddles and trade them on the market."[42]

The Association urged North Caucasian notables to invest in horse breeding. By the 1900s, Kabarda horses were easily the most profitable articles of North Caucasian trade in the empire, as the Ottoman army required ever more horses to deliver soldiers and ammunition to its many frontlines. The Association reasoned that the Circassians, who already made a name for themselves as excellent cavalry, had a rare opportunity to monopolize this lucrative market. It urged Circassian notables to send young specialists to Russia and Hungary to "study their methods of horse care and breeding and how they operate their stud farms, so that they could acquire necessary knowledge and apply it in our country"; to import thoroughbred stallions and mares from overseas to improve the Kabarda breed; and to establish Ottoman stud farms and trading companies. It warned Circassian notables to "not let this extraordinary trade slip out of your hands because of your quarrels and disagreements with each other."[43] The Association, a proud product of the Young Turk Revolution, presented horse breeding not only as a financial opportunity but also as a patriotic act and North Caucasian contribution to the Ottoman economy and military success. Several Circassian entrepreneurs established large stud farms in the provinces of Sivas and Konya, which supplied riding and pack horses to the Ottoman army beginning with the Balkan Wars of 1912–13.[44]

The Association published its own newspaper, *Ğuaze* (Circassian for "guide"), in 1911–14. The Young Turk Revolution restored the freedom of the press, opening space for new periodicals, of various political persuasions, in Ottoman Turkish, Greek, Armenian, Ladino, Bulgarian, Arabic, and other languages of the empire. In Istanbul alone, over 200 new publications appeared in the year after the revolution.[45] *Ğuaze* was a bilingual publication in Ottoman Turkish and Circassian and the first Circassian-language newspaper in history. Its task was arguably more difficult than that of other Ottoman newspapers because, in order to publish in Circassian, its editors first needed to decide how to write in Circassian.

Attempts to create an alphabet for the Circassian language started in the early nineteenth century. Circassian and Russian scholars proposed several alphabets, using Cyrillic, Latin, and Arabic letters and even special marks for distinct Circassian sounds. In 1840, the Kabardian philologist Shora Nogmov used Cyrillic and Latin letters and diacritics for his alphabet, and then in 1843, under pressure from the Circassian ʿulama, he relaid the alphabet on the Arabic script. Yet few works were produced in Circassian by the time of the mass displacement of Circassians from the Caucasus. In diaspora, Ottoman-Circassian intellectuals devised new alphabets. In 1897, Ahmed Cavid Paşa, who would become the first chairman of the Association, developed an Arabic script–based alphabet for the Circassian language. The Syria-born Circassian physician Mehmet Ali Pçehatluk (1882–1935) created another Arabic script–based alphabet in 1902 and a Latin script–based one in 1904. The educators Nuri Tsagov (1883–1936) and Yusuf Suad Neğuç (1877–1930), both of whom would later return to and teach in the Caucasus, proposed their own Arabic script–based alphabet in 1909; and Muhamed Kemal Huaj proposed yet another one in a Cairo-printed primer in 1910.[46] Those alphabets were largely confined to single publications.

In 1911, the Association convened a special alphabet commission to select an alphabet for its future publications. The commission unveiled its new alphabet, prepared by Yusuf İzzet Paşa (1876–1922), on the pages of *Ğuaze*: the alphabet was based on the Arabic script and had 55 letters for 57 sounds. Curiously, its letters were fixed to the initial position and did not change depending on their position within a word, as familiar to Arabic and Ottoman Turkish readers.[47] Shortly afterward, the newspaper published responses from readers that were critical of the chosen alphabet's script or the excessive number of letters. Mehmet Ali Pçehatluk then proposed an alternative Latin script–based alphabet in *Ğuaze* in 1912. After that, the newspaper alternated between the two alphabets when printing articles and poems.[48] The alphabet issue was far from settled. Between 1915 and 1921, Ottoman muhajir educators published at least four other alphabets for Circassian in alphabet primers.[49] While North Caucasian intellectuals favored the Arabic script before World War I, the Latin script gained an upper hand after the war.[50]

The alphabet remains a contentious issue within the North Caucasian diaspora in the Middle East to this day. In the Soviet Caucasus, the Bolsheviks endorsed the Latin alphabet for North Caucasian languages between 1923 and 1928, as part of their drive to Latinize all Soviet languages.[51] The Soviet government replaced Latin with Cyrillic for Kabardino-Cherkess, or eastern Circassian, in 1936 and for all other North Caucasian languages in 1938.[52] Since World War II, the literary output in North Caucasian languages has been almost exclusively in the Cyrillic script.[53] In 2015, the Turkish government endorsed the teaching of the Circassian language, recently available in several Turkish universities, in the Latin script. In response, the Federation of Caucasian Associations in Turkey (KAFFED), an umbrella group of several dozen North Caucasian organizations, protested the government's decision.[54] Many Circassian activists in Turkey now favor the Cyrillic alphabet, fearing that multiple scripts would undermine diasporic unity and Turkish Circassians' access to Circassian literature and media in the Caucasus.[55]

In the early 1910s, the Association faced another challenge in deciding what the preferred version of the Circassian language was. Without a written culture, Circassians did not have a literary version of Circassian. The very questions of who spoke Circassian and where the linguistic boundaries of the language lay were not easy to answer. Notably, the Ubykh and Abazin communities had lived on the lands between historical Circassia and Abkhazia and spoke languages that shared similarities with both the Circassian and Abkhazian languages. Ubykh (extinct since 1992) and Abazin are recognized as separate languages today, but their status was less clear in the 1900s. By alphabetizing the language and preparing the first Ottoman Turkish-Circassian dictionary, published by Ahmed Cavid Paşa and Mehmet Ali Pçehatluk in *Ğuaze* in 1912, muhajir intellectuals were elevating to preferred literary norms the vocabularies of select Circassian communities, especially Shapsughs, Abzakhs, and Kabardians, who were well-represented in diaspora.[56] This process was not systematic but rather dependent on the vocabularies of individual writers.

The Association's emphasis on the Circassian language, and not on others, exemplifies its major dilemma: how to create a united diasporic identity while acknowledging the ethnic diversity of the North Caucasian community. Diasporic intellectuals were well aware of cultural distinctions among their people, but to amplify muhajir voices they chose to downplay their differences and forge one communal identity as *Circassian* (Çerkes). The choice of the term *Circassian* was easy: western and eastern Circassians formed the majority of the North Caucasian diaspora, and the Ottomans already called most muhajirs from the Caucasus *Circassians*. The Association applied this term in inclusive and exclusive ways, depending on its audience. Externally, *Circassian* was an all-encompassing term for North Caucasians. Many muhajir elites came from Ossetian, Abkhazian, and Dagestani families but acquiesced to the identification as Circassian when that served their community goals.[57] Internally, on the pages of *Ğuaze, Circassian* denoted an ethnic group, but that identity was not unambiguous. The Association, through its publications about the culture and history of Circassia, aimed to develop the collective consciousness of Bzhedugh, Natukhai, Kabardian, and other Adyghe-speaking refugees as Circassians.[58] Meanwhile, Abkhazians, Chechens, Ossetians, and Avars, who did not have their own ethnic organizations, were part of the Association's larger ideological project but were not prioritized in its literary output. The printed production in their languages remained limited in the late Ottoman era.

The Association's next task was to create a unified diasporic narrative that explained why muhajirs had left the Caucasus for the Middle East. Ottoman-Circassian intellectuals made previous attempts to document their communities' history. In 1882, Circassian notables in Istanbul established a commission to write a comprehensive "History of Circassia," based on Ottoman and European sources and oral testimonies of muhajir elders. Ahmet Mithat Efendi (1844–1912), an Istanbul-born Shapsugh best known as the founder of the Ottoman novel, headed the commission. Hayreddin Paşa (1820–90), a Caucasus-born Abkhazian grand vizier of Tunis in 1873–77 and of the Ottoman Empire in 1878–79, served as the commission's treasurer. The ambitious work was never completed. Sultan Abdülhamid II grew suspicious of the North Caucasian elites. In the same year, Imam Shamil's second son, Ghazi Muhammad Paşa (1833–1902), his Avar brother-in-law Dağıstanlı Mehmet Fazıl (1853–1916), and Cairo-born marshal Deli Fuat Paşa (1835–1931) were accused of plotting to overthrow the sultan; the former two were exiled to, respectively, Medina and Baghdad. Then, in 1884, the commission's editor Ahmet Mithat Efendi's play *Çerkes Özdenleri* (Circassian notables) came under the attention of Ottoman authorities as allegedly encouraging the "Circassian question."[59] The authorities shut it down and razed the theater that had staged the play. Shortly thereafter, the palace ordered the commission to disband and exiled some of its members, which marked the end of their scholarly enterprise.[60]

In the 1910s, the Association crafted the North Caucasian diaspora's historical narrative. On the pages of *Ğuaze*, muhajir intellectuals weaved together threads to which North Caucasians of different ethnic groups could relate: their shared origin in the Caucasus, refuge in the sultan-caliph's domains, hardship of Ottoman resettlement, and membership in the Ottoman nation. Their account centered the sacrifices of muhajirs, their love for the Caucasus, and commitment to the Ottoman Empire but was thin on the details of displacement itself. Notably, *Ğuaze* did not stress the violence that western Circassians had endured, perhaps because many mountaineers held public acknowledgment of trauma to be taboo. Neither *Ğuaze* nor the earlier *İttihad Gazetesi* was particularly critical of the Russian government in the 1860s, focusing instead on the Ottoman authorities' shortcomings since then. Today's narrative about the diaspora's origins has shifted significantly. The ethnic cleansing of western Circassians has become the formative event for the Circassian and North Caucasian diaspora at large, but its public commemoration began only in the late 1980s, with new historical scholarship in the diaspora and the Caucasus and the rise of the Circassian national movement.[61]

As diasporic activists set out to improve the North Caucasian condition in the Ottoman Empire, no issue was more inculpatory than slavery. The first newspaper, *İttihad Gazetesi*, set the tone by identifying slavery as the main injustice against refugees. It blamed Ottoman officials, who had allegedly turned a blind eye to the continuing Circassian enslavement and illegal slave

trade. The editors wrote, "The evil fortune has brought many miserable muhajirs, who lamented their fate in swamplands of Anatolia, into the hands of
coldhearted slave traders who dispatched them from marshy swamps to hell-
ishly hot deserts. They were sold, as if they were prisoners of war, to faraway
lands such as Bornu, Wadai,[62] Cape of Good Hope, Zanzibar, Java, Sumatra,
etc. . . . These ruthless [Ottoman] officials, through cunning and deception,
misled desperate muhajirs and destroyed many notable families. They trafficked captured children not only here [to Egypt] but also to such distant
countries as India, China, America, and Britain."[63] The *İttihad Gazetesi* editors, from their vantage point in Cairo, must have been well-informed about
the illegal Circassian slave trade in North Africa and Hejaz. The editorial still
suggests a much broader geography of Circassian slavery than conventionally
assumed.[64]

The abolitionist cause united progressive North Caucasian educators who
had witnessed agricultural slavery in muhajir villages and the old Ottoman-
Circassian elites who were intimately familiar with the realities of their kin's
enslavement in harems. The Association acted behind the scenes to secure
the release of concubines, most of whom were Circassians, from the imperial
harem after Sultan Abdülhamid II was deposed and exiled to Salonica in
1909. In 1910, the Association submitted petitions to the grand vizier, the
Interior Ministry, and the Ottoman Assembly in support of abolition, stress-
ing that Circassian slavery went against both Islamic law and the Ottoman
constitution's principles of freedom and equality for all. The Association's
activists then published several pro-abolition articles in the leading Ottoman
newspapers to drum up public support for their cause.[65]

The newspaper *Ğuaze*, likewise, came out as abolitionist in its very first
issue in 1911. Throughout its run, the newspaper published a series of editorials under the unambiguous title "Against Slavery." The editors presented
abolition as consistent with the ideals of the new Ottoman nation, of which
North Caucasians were an integral part.[66] The editors subversively noted that
even Russia banned slavery among Caucasus Muslims, which should serve as
an example for the Ottoman Empire.[67] When several slave revolts broke out
in Uzunyayla, the newspaper supported mounting voices in the Ottoman
Assembly to abolish slavery for good.[68] One of the strongest cases for abolition came from Hayriye Melek Hunç, a leading Circassian woman activist.

She condemned slavery in national terms, arguing that, because the Circassian nation (*millet*) was split between masters and slaves, only abolition could achieve the Circassians' unity, which was a prerequisite for their cultural advancement. She proclaimed, "I am a daughter of a bey. If there is some right that was handed down to me from my ancestors, I am ready to share it with all members of my nation, without exception; and if my right impedes those of others, I am ready to sacrifice that right, and of that I am proud. To save the nation from the brink of extinction, one must rise above . . . and Circassianness (*Çerkeslik*) today expects it from all of its people."[69]

The Association invested in the educational infrastructure for North Caucasian refugees. In its bylaws of 1908, it set an ambitious goal to have a primary school in every muhajir village. As a self-appointed representative of North Caucasian muhajirs, it lobbied the Ottoman government for funding to establish new schools and appoint schoolteachers. In areas of compact North Caucasian settlement, the Association planned to open vocational schools and, in Istanbul, a high school to prepare North Caucasian students for higher education, even aspiring to send its best graduates to foreign universities.[70] In 1910, the Association founded the first Circassian private school for boys in Istanbul, which offered instruction in speaking and reading Circassian, in addition to core subjects.[71] The Istanbul Society for the Diffusion of Knowledge Among Caucasians (İstanbul'da Kafkasyalılar Arasında Neşr-i Maarif Cemiyeti) was established in 1914 to facilitate the education of muhajirs' children. Muhajir activists also emphasized physical education, a marker of modernity and national pride, as attested by new sports clubs affiliated with Istanbul's ethnoreligious communities.[72] Ottoman-Circassian sports enthusiasts founded the Bereket[iko] Gymnastics Club in Istanbul's Beşiktaş district in 1903. The club was renamed Beşiktaş in 1908 and soon thereafter lost its Circassian character.[73] Today, it is one of Istanbul's "Big Three" (with Galatasaray and Fenerbahçe) and Turkey's top sports clubs, internationally renowned for its soccer team.

The Association's members maintained a transimperial dimension to their cultural work. While their target audience was North Caucasians in the Ottoman Empire, they also engaged with communities in the Caucasus. *Ğuaze* had subscribers in the Caucasus and sometimes printed direct appeals to Muslims in Russia. The Association's educational work extended to the

Caucasus through its members' teaching missions. In 1909, the Ottoman-Circassian educator İbrahim Hızetl founded schools in six villages in Russia's Kuban Province. These schools employed muhajir teachers from the Ottoman Empire and used the Circassian-language curriculum, which was entirely new in historical Circassia. Through *Ğuaze*, the North Caucasian diaspora had been collecting money for the upkeep of those schools. The schools did not have an official permit, and, in 1913, the local administration closed the schools and deported their teachers.[74] In the same year, Nuri Tsagov, the Golan Heights–born editor of *Ğuaze*, emigrated—or returned—to his family's old village in Kabarda. He opened his own school, popularly known as Tsagov University, which educated teachers for Kabarda's village schools. He used Circassian-language textbooks that he had published in Istanbul to provide instruction in the Circassian language. He also cofounded the first Circassian printing house and used his editorial experience at *Ğuaze* to establish the first Circassian-language newspaper in Russia, *Adige Maq* (Circ. for "Adyghe Voice") (1918–19). Tsagov became one of the founders of the Baksan cultural movement, formative for modern Kabardian literature and education.[75]

The outbreak of World War I opened a new chapter in the political history of North Caucasians in the Middle East. During the war, the Association ceased its cultural activities, including the publication of *Ğuaze*. The war allowed North Caucasian elites to contemplate previously unimaginable scenarios in the Caucasus, and many Association members shifted their focus on political advocacy. Members of the Association established the Society for the Caucasus Unity (Kafkasya İttihad Cemiyeti, 1915) and the Committee for the Caucasus Independence (Kafkasya İstiklal Komitesi, 1915), both of which advocated the independence of the entire Caucasus, including Georgian, Armenian, and Azerbaijani territories, from Russia. These organizations, while advancing many North Caucasians' political ideals, also aligned with the CUP's foreign policy goals and enjoyed full support and funding from the Ottoman government. The Committee for the Caucasus Independence later became the Committee of Turkey's North Caucasian Political Emigrants (Türkiye'deki Kuzey Kafkasya Siyasi Göçmenleri Komitesi, 1916–19), which pressed for the autonomy or independence of the North Caucasus. In this era, muhajir elites stressed their identity as *North Caucasian* (*Şimali* or *Kuzey*

Kafkasyalı) over *Circassian*, just as they now used *Turkey* instead of *Ottoman Empire* and the Turkish neologism *göçmen* over *muhacir*.[76]

Following the Bolshevik Revolution of 1917, several Committee members traveled to the North Caucasus to fight for its independence. Ottoman muhajir elites then established the North Caucasus Society (Şimali Kafkas Cemiyeti, 1918), which actively lobbied the Ottoman government on behalf of the North Caucasus–based national movements. The diaspora's political efforts helped to legitimize and secure Ottoman recognition of the short-lived Mountain Republic of the North Caucasus (1918–20).[77] After the Bolsheviks annexed the Republic, its leadership fled into exile in Istanbul and European capitals.[78] In its place, the Bolsheviks established the Mountain Autonomous Soviet Socialist Republic (1921–24), later to be reorganized into autonomous national units within Soviet Russia.[79]

The Association resumed its activities between 1918 and 1923. Its headquarters remained in Istanbul, which was under the Allied occupation. Some of its leadership perished during the war, and it had to navigate—with the rest of the North Caucasian diaspora—the fraught politics of the Turkish War of Independence. In that environment, the Association eschewed its members' transnational politics of the 1914–18 era in favor of cultural activism, characteristic of the 1908–13 era. After the war, North Caucasian women played a more prominent role in diasporic activism, thanks to the Circassian Women's Support Association (Çerkes Kadınları Teavün Cemiyeti, 1918–23), led by Hayriye Melek Hunç. In 1919, the Circassian Women's Support Association founded its own journal, *Diyane* (Circassian for "Our Mother"), published in Ottoman Turkish and Latin-scripted Circassian. The women's organization revived the Association's educational work and established a new private school in Beşiktaş. This six-year school enrolled 150–180 boys and girls and, reportedly, was the first coeducational institution for Muslim children in the empire. The school taught, in addition to regular arts and sciences, the history and geography of the Caucasus and Circassian language and folklore. It remained open until 1923 and was the last school in Turkey to offer the Circassian curriculum in the twentieth century.[80]

DEBATE OVER HIJRA

The North Caucasian diaspora actively participated in the transimperial debate over the necessity of *hijra*, or Muslim emigration. Ever since the Russian conquest, many Muslim communities in the Caucasus questioned whether remaining under Christian rule was permissible. Could they preserve their Muslim faith while living in the tsardom, which many held to be *dār al-ḥarb* (the "domain of war")? Did they have a religious obligation to emigrate to *dār al-islām* (the "domain of Islam")? Generations of Muslims had been grappling with the same questions over the centuries, as their territories came under non-Muslim rule.[81] In the Caucasus, the Muslim religious establishment was split on the issue. Some 'ulama advocated emigration and led parties of muhajirs into the Ottoman Empire, whereas others argued that Russia, whose tsar claimed to be a patron of the Muslim community, was part of *dār al-islām* and urged their followers to stay put in the Caucasus.[82] The debate over hijra was prominent in the Northcentral and Northeast Caucasus after 1864. It was less significant in the Northwest Caucasus, from where most western Circassians had been expelled by 1864. However, many Circassians in the Ottoman Empire joined the debate, as they shared with prospective muhajirs their own experiences in exile. The debate over hijra helped to bind together the world of Caucasus Muslims, now straddling the Russian and Ottoman empires.

The Russian government's stringent policy on Muslim emigration prompted many North Caucasian Muslims to ask for Ottoman intercession in their hijra. The Russian government discouraged the emigration of western Circassians from Kuban Province after late 1864 and of Muslims from the rest of the North Caucasus after 1867. In 1866, Circassian Abzakh leaders from Russia sent an open letter to the Ottoman newspaper *Tasvir-i Efkar*. In it, they lamented oppression by the Russians and urged the Ottoman government to support their emigration.[83] One family in Kizilyurt, Dagestan, preserved copies of letters that its village had sent to the Ottoman sultan. In one letter, residents complain that the Russian authorities would not let them leave for the Ottoman Empire.[84] The same family also keeps a letter that its ancestors had reportedly received from Ghazi Muhammad in Istanbul. The letter urged Caucasus Muslims to emigrate to the Ottoman Empire because it was both permissible, as the Russians and the Ottomans had allegedly signed a treaty to that effect, and necessary, because religious authorities in Mecca endorsed it.[85] Whether Ghazi Muhammad was the author of this letter or not, many Dagestanis believed that such letters were authentic and that Imam Shamil's son urged them to conduct hijra.[86]

Many muhajirs encouraged emigration from the Caucasus. In 1867, Gushasukh, a Kabardian woman of the Atazhukin princely family, wrote a letter to be smuggled into Terek Province berating her relatives in the Caucasus for not having joined her in the Ottoman Empire: "When a person comes into need in *dār al-ḥarb*, their duty is to leave for *dār al-islām* to alleviate their sufferings. How are you God's creatures if you do not move to *dār al-bayḍā'* [Ar. for "white house," here likely the Ottoman Empire] to claim your rights and settle your affairs?"[87] Gushasukh, as many others, considered it her duty as a good Muslim to have moved to the Ottoman Empire. Most private letters that survive in state archives in the Caucasus strongly advocated emigration. While they certainly represent what many muhajirs were saying, we should be conscious of the imperial archive's selection bias. The letters, like the one by Gushasukh, survive because the Russian government intercepted them on the border, translated them, and preserved the most pro-hijra ones as evidence of the diaspora's purported pro-Ottoman propaganda among Russia's Muslim subjects.[88]

Many religious figures from the Northeast Caucasus supported emigration. 'Abd al-Rahman al-Thughuri (Sogratlinskii), a Naqshbandi shaykh and student of Imam Shamil's adviser, Jamal al-Din al-Ghazi-Ghumuqi, wrote an Arabic-language treatise on hijra in the late 1870s. He urged North Caucasian Muslims to emigrate because it was their religious duty to leave *dār al-ḥarb* when no hope remained to regain their lands for Islam through *jihād* (holy war).[89] Another Naqshbandi shaykh, Muhammad al-Kikuni, based in the Ottoman refugee village of Reşadiye, or "Little Dagestan," also called on his followers in the Caucasus to emigrate to the Ottoman Empire. Remarkably, his call for hijra was published, in its original Arabic and Arabic-scripted Avar translation, in Petrovsk (now Makhachkala), Dagestan.[90] It must have slipped through the Russian censorship of pro-emigration writings.

In the early twentieth century, Ottoman-Circassian intellectuals in Istanbul voiced strong opposition to emigration from the Caucasus. The flagship diasporic newspaper *Ğuaze* vocally opposed hijra. In 1911, the newspaper published a series of anonymous articles, amounting to editorials, on the question of emigration. The title of the first article in the series asked whether emigration (*hicret*) was a debacle (*hezimet*). The author's answer was affirmative, criticizing the Ottomān government for not investing enough in housing for refugees and subjecting them to gradual extinction.[91] The following article both discouraged emigration from the Caucasus and approved of muhajirs' return migration. It declared that the purest form of Islam, out of all Muslim countries, was found in Circassia, that life in Circassia was more prosperous than in the Ottoman Empire, and that, after the Russian Revolution of 1905, Russia's Circassians were enjoying ever more freedoms. The article ended with a damning statement for an Ottoman newspaper, "In conclusion, no reason remains to prefer Turkey [sic] to the Caucasus."[92] *Ğuaze* also directly addressed its readers in the Caucasus, warning them not to listen to their Muslim notables who agitated in favor of emigration and accusing the notables of acting in self-interest after the Ottomans had allegedly promised them houses and privileges in the Ottoman Empire.[93] The final article in the series came out against the often cited religious justification for hijra, namely that the Caucasus had become *dār al-ḥarb* after the Russian conquest, which Muslims were required to leave. The author argued that the Caucasus remained part of *dār al-islām* because Russia and the Ottoman Empire had diplomatic relations and the Ottoman ambassador and consuls could not possibly reside within the "domain of war." They concluded that, under current conditions, Muslim emigration from the Caucasus could not be considered hijra and had harmed the Muslim community in the Caucasus.[94]

The Russian-language journal *Musul'manin* (Rus. for "Muslim") (1908–11), published in Paris, also resolutely opposed hijra. Its enigmatic editor, Magomet-bek Hadzhetlashe, who claimed to be a Circassian notable from the Ottoman Empire, published a series of articles about resettlement in the Ottoman Empire.[95] The journal criticized the Young Turks' regime for failing to provide for new immigrants from the Caucasus.[96]

Russia's Muslim intellectuals published in local newspapers to dissuade Muslims from leaving. Arabophone intellectuals of the Northeast Caucasus used *Jarīdat Dāghistān* (Ar. for "newspaper of Dagestan") (1913–18), a Jadidist newspaper published in Temir-Khan-Shura (now Buynaksk). Following *Ğuaze*'s lead, *Jarīdat Dāghistān* criticized hijra on religious grounds. In 1913, its al-Azhar-educated Lak editor, Ali Kaiaev, argued that it was a duty of Muslims to remain in their country as long as they were free to profess Islam, which had been the case under Russian rule.[97] Likewise, Crimean Tatar intellectual and editor Ismail Gasprinskii (Gaspıralı) agitated against emigration. In 1902, he published four articles in *Tercüman* (Ott. Tur. / Tatar for "the interpreter") (1883–1918), a leading newspaper for Russia's Turkic-speaking populations, urging its readers to ignore the pro-hijra propaganda and remain in Russia.[98]

In the Kuban and Terek provinces, many Muslim educators opposed emigration, blaming it for decimating their communities and paving the way for Russian colonization. The Kabardian intellectuals, such as Bekmurza Pachev, Dmitrii Kodzokov, and Kazi Atazhukin, decried social inequality in their communities, which often made the emigration of thousands a decision made by a few notables. They wrote poems against emigration and toured the countryside, urging the peasantry to stay put in the Caucasus.[99] The intellectuals' anti-emigration efforts were often countered by local figures. For example, the Kumyk poet Irchi Kazak wrote poems in support of hijra. While praising the schools and railroads that the Russians had built in the region, he lamented tsarist officials' corruption. He encouraged his compatriots to emigrate: "Muslims, let us gather our families and leave for the Ottoman state. The sultan is our pillar. . . . Whoever will leave will find a paradise."[100]

As the debate over hijra divided the Muslim public in the Caucasus, the decision whether to stay or leave became not only about individual choice but also about the preservation of one's identity. Folk songs lamented what had become of muhajirs in the Ottoman Empire. One remarkably scathing Kabardian song, collected by ethnographers in the Caucasus, shamed muhajirs for the sorry state of their villages and alleged loss of Circassian traditions in exile:

> *Your toilet is in the river,*
> *Your mosque is abandoned.*
> *You have to dig wells for water.*
> *You ride donkeys. . . .*
> *You have one gun for five households,*
> *And one haystack for six households. . . .*
> *Your plough is two pieces of wood,*

And your bull's hooves plow the field. . . .
Look at you, a pig village!

You have no Khabze or order,
You fight often.
Your honesty is gone. . . .
Your bellies are filled with cabbage,
And cabbage grows in your garden.
You are glad to sow millet,
And you nibble grass like geese. . . .
You wear fez and Turkish garb.
You carry tobacco pouches,
And you all smoke cigarettes.
Look at you, a pig village!

You dry meat on the roof,
Thresh wheat with stones,
Sell watermelon by weight.
An okka of melons costs ten kopeks. . . .
Your markets are noisy,
Instead of money, you have paper.
You have no corn.
Oh, you are the land of misfortune!

You are eating chicken yourselves,
And would not offer rooster to a guest.
Look where the Russians have driven you![101]

The harsh mockery of muhajir life in the Ottoman Empire meant to discourage those who considered leaving the Caucasus. The song impressed on its listeners that hijra inevitably led to the abandonment of the cultural norms that made one a Circassian.

The debate over hijra continued through the remainder of tsarist rule. The notion of hijra as a religious obligation appealed to many Muslims, and so did the promise of family reunification and escape from tsarist governance. But ever since the formation of diasporic organizations, the anti-hijra voices grew louder. North Caucasian intellectuals in the Ottoman and Russian empires utilized print media to dissuade Caucasus Muslims from leaving Russia. The debate, at the heart of which lay loss and separation, traversed the imperial borders and generated new connections between the North Caucasian diaspora and its homeland.

———

After the Young Turk Revolution of 1908, muhajir activists in Istanbul achieved a series of firsts—the first newspaper in Circassian, the first dictionary, and the first schools—and, via the Circassian Union and Support Association, they created a new narrative of what it meant to be Circassian in the Ottoman Empire. As Ottoman rule came to an end, so did the freedoms to be Circassian and North Caucasian. The new Turkish nationalist regime in Ankara did not envision for Ottoman Muslims to become anything but Turks. The republican government mandated North Caucasians to be "Caucasian Turks," similar to how Kurds became "mountain Turks." In 1923, all North Caucasian organizations were closed, and their publications ceased. Muhajirs could no longer safely speak their native languages in public, as the campaign "Citizen, speak Turkish!" swept across Turkey's cities.

Yet the Association's legacy lived on in the diaspora and its homeland. The Association's emphases on a separate cultural identity within the host nation and on solidarity among different groups from the Caucasus survived in the Anatolian countryside, where Circassian, Abkhazian, and other muhajir villages were under lesser surveillance from Ankara. The old village networks helped many North Caucasians to preserve their languages, stay close to each other, and weather the excesses of Kemalism. Turkey's first North Caucasian organizations appeared in the 1950s, and their publications substantially drew on the research conducted by the *Ğuaze* generation.[102] The Association's ideas also had a second breath of life in the Caucasus. Many projects that had started in Istanbul, from alphabetization to native-language curricula, were picked up by the Bolsheviks, who used them in their nation-building projects in the new Soviet autonomous units in the North Caucasus. The *Ğuaze* editor Nuri Tsagov and his students, educated on Istanbul-published Circassian textbooks, helped to build up Soviet Kabarda's educational system in the 1920s and 1930s.

The Association laid the institutional and intellectual foundations for the North Caucasian diaspora in the Middle East. Since World War I, North Caucasian diasporic communities have had to navigate different political landscapes, defined by Turkish republicanism, British and French occupation, Arab nationalism, Ba'athism, Islamism, and Zionism. Yet the fundamentals of the diaspora's communal identification—as a constituent element of the host nation (Ottoman, Turkish, Syrian, Jordanian, Israeli), of the Circassian or North Caucasian community, and of the *umma*—had been articulated in the late Ottoman era.[103] Today's major diasporic associations, including KAFFED in Turkey, the Circassian Charity Associations in Jordan and in Syria, and the Charitable Solidarity Association of Chechens, Dagestanis, and Circassians of Iraq, are ideological heirs to the Ottoman-era Association. The contemporary diasporic associations grapple with similar challenges that the Association had faced: how to advocate on behalf of different ethnic groups yet to speak in one voice and how to preserve North Caucasian identities without jeopardizing their places within their new nations. The final chapter examines the muhajir alternative to remaining in diaspora—return to their homeland.

SEVEN

RETURN MIGRATION
TO RUSSIA

IN JANUARY 1907, three brothers, Nagoi, Talib, and Hajibekir, and their sister Khazizet arrived in the Kabardian village of Babyguei (Babukovo) in the Northcentral Caucasus. The oldest was twenty-three, and the youngest, Khazizet, was only twelve. Their family had emigrated from that village to the Ottoman Empire a few years earlier, but, shortly after having settled in Syria, their parents died. The siblings found themselves orphaned in a foreign country and decided to return to the Caucasus. Amid a harsh winter, they rode and walked for weeks across Syria and Kurdistan, into Georgia, and through the Caucasus Mountains to their home village in Kabarda. Village elders agreed to formally readmit the orphans into their community, and the government then allowed them to stay in the village.[1] The siblings were among thousands of North Caucasian Muslims who returned to Russia from the Ottoman Empire. The stories of those returnees are largely forgotten, in both the Middle East and the Caucasus, but they reveal much about migration in the late imperial era.[2]

This chapter examines return migration of North Caucasians to Russia and the evolution of tsarist reimmigration policies in the Caucasus. In 1861, Russia instituted a formal ban on the return of North Caucasian Muslims. The authorities justified this ban on fiscal and ideological grounds, painting returnees as wasteful vagabonds or dangerous fanatics. Yet tsarist authorities in the Caucasus developed a mechanism to readmit some muhajirs in the aftermath of the Chechen "returnee refugee crisis" of 1865 and the Abkhazian one in 1880. Based on archival work in Tbilisi, Vladikavkaz, Nalchik, and Makhachkala, I reconstruct Russia's unwritten reimmigration policy between 1867 and World War I, under which many North Caucasians had been readmitted to their homeland and into Russian subjecthood. This policy was held secret from the Ottoman government and North Caucasian muhajirs so as not to encourage mass return. The official ban on repatriation survived Russian imperial rule and, under various guises, persisted into the Soviet era (1922–91) and Russian Federation era (1991–).[3]

North Caucasian muhajirs employed different strategies to return to the Caucasus. Some petitioned Russian consuls, and others surrendered at the Russo-Ottoman border, but most crossed the border in secret. Unsanctioned return was by far the most dangerous and ultimately successful strategy. I estimate that, against all odds, between 1860 and World War I, about 40,000 muhajirs, primarily Abkhazians, Chechens, Kabardians, Ossetians, and Nogai Tatars, returned to the Caucasus. Muhajirs had been readmitted throughout the region (see map 8), including in the North Caucasus provinces of Kuban, Terek, and Dagestan and governorate of Stavropol, and the South Caucasus department (since 1883, district) of Sukhum.

It should not be surprising that North Caucasian refugees attempted to return. Return migration is an essential part of any mass migration, voluntary or forced. In the words of an early theorist of migration, "each main current of migration produces a compensating counter-current."[4] Yet return migration often gets overlooked. Returnees slip through the cracks, as officials do not know of their return, or migrants would not speak of their experiences because of shame, fear, or stigma.[5] Furthermore, national and nationalist historiographies prefer to focus on people who arrived and stayed rather than those who left. For example, migration to the United States, which is commonly imagined as a one-way journey, was followed by return migration of a quarter to a third of all immigrants, reaching as high as 89 percent for Bulgarians and Serbs and 60 percent for southern Italians in 1908–23.[6] Even in the history of Russo-Ottoman migrations, marked by tremendous violence in the borderlands, return migration was common. North Caucasian returnees were not alone in trying to retrace their journey back. In a reverse

Map 8. **Caucasus Viceroyalty, 1878.**

process, thousands of Bulgarian refugees who had left the Ottoman Balkans for tsarist Bessarabia and Crimea, and thousands of Greeks and Armenians who had left Anatolia for the Caucasus, returned to their Ottoman homeland in the second half of the nineteenth century.[7]

The North Caucasians' return brings into focus how Russia constructed its migration policy toward Muslims and how muhajirs challenged imperial restrictions on their mobility. Three types of return migration are common in modern history: repatriation, usually spearheaded by a nation-state or an international agency; refoulement, or forcible repatriation; and self-initiated return. All three are contingent on the country of origin being willing to accept its returnees. In these cases, returnees are typically an ethnic or religious majority of the country to which they return, or, at the very least, their cultural identity was not a reason for their displacement.[8] The return migration of North Caucasians to Russia was different—a self-initiated return that was perceived as "illegal" by the Russian government. A self-initiated but unsanctioned return migration typically occurs when the country of origin is occupied or when the ruling regime considers returnees, who are not part of the favored ethnoreligious group, undesirable for its purposes of state building. The Ottoman government did not endorse the return to Russia either, and it rarely granted muhajirs permission to leave. The North Caucasians' return journey had to be a clandestine one.

REASONS FOR RETURN MIGRATION

Return migration from the Ottoman Empire started already in the late 1850s and lasted until the end of imperial rule. Similar to emigrants, returnees came from every ethnolinguistic community and different social groups in the Caucasus. Sometimes entire families traveled back to Russia together, but men often undertook the arduous journey alone, hoping that, should they be successful, they would bring their families later. Two patterns in muhajir return migration stand out. First, North Caucasians were likely to return within the first few years after their departure. Their return journey often followed a difficult winter when refugees starved in their temporary or permanent settlements in the Ottoman Empire. Second, refugees who had been forcibly expelled were less likely to return than those who had emigrated of their own volition or at least had some choice in the matter. After 1864, western Circassians rarely attempted to cross the border into Russia; their ancestral villages had been depopulated, and few of their kin remained in the Northwest Caucasus. Kabardians, Chechens, and Ossetians were more frequent returnees, despite their lands lying farther away from the Ottoman border, because their extended families still lived in the Northcentral Caucasus.

The vast majority of returnees crossed the Ottoman-Russian border into the Caucasus without authorization from the tsarist government. Returnees often traveled in small groups, through forested and mountainous areas, and avoided roads and towns. Many of them were apprehended by border patrol or local police on their way to their home villages or voluntarily reported to the authorities in the hope to regain a residence permit and legal status. Upon detention, returnees were required to make an oral statement, translated and recorded in Russian by a state-provided interpreter. These testimonies provide a rare insight into the motivations of returnees, albeit carefully filtered by interviewees and curated by tsarist interrogators. The stories of three returnees—a Chechen free peasant, a Kabardian enslaved man, and a divorced Dagestani woman—testify to why many Muslims sought to return to the Caucasus under Russian rule.

Nur Dadaev, a Chechen peasant, emigrated in 1865. The Ottoman Refugee Commission had temporarily housed him near Erzurum, while looking for a final place of settlement. The following year, tsarist authorities detained him within Russian borders. Dadaev provided the following explanation for his return: "I feared that the Turkish government would send me and my family to Arabistan [sic], where it had already settled many Chechens. To avoid being settled in a distant and unknown country, I, along with thirteen other people, decided to return to our former place of residence, Chechnya. . . . Trying to avoid running into Turkish troops, we reached the [Russian] border at night. Then, unnoticed by anyone, we crossed the border within two verst [1.3 miles] of Aleksandropol."[9]

The major reason for return migration throughout the late imperial era was the North Caucasians' disappointment with the conditions of their resettlement, namely the designated locations of their new villages and lack of Ottoman support. Many returnees complained about small land allotments or settlement on infertile land, which all but condemned them to famine. Some Chechens, like Dadaev, noted their unwillingness to move to Syria as their reason for returning to Russia.[10] Others returned after having lost family members to epidemics in an unfamiliar climate or clashes with local communities. Based on returnee testimonies, many muhajirs considered return migration to the Caucasus a measure of last resort that they took to survive.[11]

Many returnees craved delivery not only from hunger and want but also from enslavement. Ogurli, a Kabardian man, arrived at the office of the Kabarda district governor in 1862 and testified as follows:

> In 1861, I followed my owner, uzden [notable] Nasran Kozhev, by consent [Rus., *po dobrovol'nomu soglasiiu*], to a permanent settlement in Turkey. After a short while, my owner kept my wife and children but sold me to some Arab [man] whose name I do not know. Considering myself to having

been improperly sold and not knowing the language of my new owner, I
decided to escape to my homeland. I never committed a crime anywhere. I
arrived in Nalchik, not having been stopped by anyone on my way here and
without documents."[12]

Many returnees from Kabarda were, like Ogurli, enslaved people or landless
peasants who had left the Caucasus in large groups, led by notables, and
were often mistreated and cheated out of their freedom or land allotments,
often by the same notables, in the Ottoman Empire. In Kabarda, Ogurli had
likely been an unfree peasant in land corvée. Upon arriving in the Ottoman
Empire, his legal status became that of *köle*, which allowed his owner to break
up Ogurli's family and sell him separately. Ogurli showed tremendous resolve
to better his fate by escaping slavery, becoming a fugitive in the Ottoman
Empire, and then retracing his journey to the Caucasus. Ogurli asked tsarist
authorities not only for permission to settle back in Kabarda but also for
his freedom because, for many muhajirs like him, return migration held the
promise of manumission. Ogurli was readmitted to Kabarda as a free man.[13]

Women's voices are rare among returnee testimonies. Few women returned on their own, and those who traveled in groups were usually claimed
as spoken for by their husbands or brothers. All the more remarkable is the
story of Suydukh Vali Kızı, who returned with two children to the village of
Erpeli in central Dagestan in 1870. She had been married to a man who had
previously emigrated to the Ottoman Empire on his own. He then returned,
without tsarist authorization, to Dagestan, where he was arrested and exiled
to Siberia for permanent settlement. He fled his internment in Siberia, some-
how made it across the vastness of Russia back to Dagestan, and tracked
down his wife. Suydukh Vali Kızı testified about what happened next:

> My husband ordered me to get on the horse. Our children were put by my
> side and tied up to the saddle. Then, we headed to Talgam [on the Caspian
> Sea] and from there down the coast. We did not stop in villages, rode at night,
> and in the daytime waited in forests and steppes, away from the road. . . . We
> passed Derbent, Quba, Shemakha [Şamahı], and Aleksandropol [Gyumri].
> We crossed the border by wading across the Arpachay River and arrived in
> Kars. There . . . my husband joined the Turkish infantry, and I worked as a
> servant in the governor's family. Longing for my homeland, I asked my hus-

band to grant me a divorce, so that I could return to Dagestan. . . . Finally, he agreed, and, together with pilgrims returning from Mecca, I left from Kars for Tiflis. . . . I now arrived in Temir-Khan-Shura and wish to live in the village of Erpeli as before.[14]

Suydukh Vali Kızı claimed that her longing for Dagestan was her main motivation for the return, strong enough for her to end her marriage. The pain of separation from homeland prompted thousands of muhajirs to attempt a dangerous trek to the Caucasus, as many explained to the Russian authorities. Many returned because they missed their loved ones. Few muhajirs were able to stay in touch with their families in the Caucasus. After the mid-1860s, the Russian government surveilled postal mail from muhajirs in the Ottoman Empire to their families in the Caucasus and searched for and confiscated letters smuggled across the Russo-Ottoman border.[15] Return meant being able to see one's relatives again and was a powerful motivation for several generations of muhajirs. Finally, return often followed the breakdown of a family unit, whether through spousal separation, or death of a breadwinner, or the loss of parents, as in the case of the four orphans in the beginning of this chapter. In all these cases, returnees hoped to reclaim their community and the homeland they had lost.

BAN ON RETURN TO RUSSIA

Amid the war for the control of the North Caucasus, Russia was averse to readmitting Muslim returnees from the Ottoman Empire. In the early years of North Caucasian return, the Russian government decided whom to let through based on where they had left from. The government was more likely to readmit Kabardians, Ossetians, and Chechens who came from territories that had been under tsarist control by 1859. Meanwhile, western Circassian returnees who were apprehended by the tsarist military faced two outcomes: to be deported to the interior of Russia for permanent settlement, if their communities had already surrendered to Russia; or to be held hostage and exchanged for Russian prisoners of war captured by Circassians, if their communities still resisted Russian advances.[16]

In June 1861, the Caucasus Army issued a ban on the return of North Caucasian Muslims. From then on, Russian border officials would only readmit North Caucasians who had an unexpired Russian passport that authorized their temporary travel to the Ottoman Empire.[17] All other returnees were denied entry and effectively denaturalized as Russian subjects. The tsarist government denaturalized muhajirs in large part because it wished to prevent their return migration. The ban on return of Muslims, enacted by the Russian military, was upheld by the civil authorities after the Caucasus War.[18]

Over the following decades, the Russian authorities articulated three justifications for their stringent no-return policy for North Caucasian Muslims. First, the government refused to accept returnees because of an alleged lack of available land. In the 1860s, the Russians had passed a comprehensive land reform, mandating new forms of land ownership in the North Caucasus. Those who had emigrated before the reform would have their properties swallowed up and reallocated within their village or to different villages. Mass return from the Ottoman Empire would have required the government to redraw village land grants. Furthermore, many Circassian, Abazin, and Chechen lands had been redistributed to Slavic immigrants, and the return of native Muslim communities would generate vociferous opposition from Cossacks and other settlers.[19]

Second, the authorities cited the high costs of reimmigration to public order and the treasury. During the war, the commander-in-chief of the Caucasus Army described returnees as "homeless vagabonds" (Rus., *bezdomnye brodiagi*) whose return would increase robberies and unrest in the Caucasus.[20] A generation later, the Terek provincial governor called returnees "parasites and adventure seekers" (Rus., *tuneiadtsy i iskateli prikliuchenii*) whose readmittance, he predicted, would lead to high crime.[21] To turn returnees into productive residents would require the state to pay for their housing, transportation, and financial aid. The administration of the Caucasus Viceroyalty argued that even massive expenditure might not be sufficient because returnees "do not burden themselves with becoming settled and instead develop a habit of vagrancy, which leads to the kind of penury in which they return [to the Caucasus]."[22] Drawing on negative stereotypes about returnees and North Caucasians at large, the government's fiscal logic behind the ban was that the open-door policy on return would lessen Russian Muslims' commitment to staying in the Caucasus and would promote emigration, which would in turn increase the numbers of returnees and the costs of their resettlement. Ultimately, the government justified its ban on the return of North Caucasians as a public good, for it preserved the social order and saved money.

The government's third objection to return migration was on ideological grounds. It was the most serious and enduring one, permeating internal correspondence of the Caucasus Viceroyalty throughout the late imperial rule. The previous two reasons were often excuses given to deny entry, whereas the true opposition lay in the government's paranoia about who returnees might be and what they might do. After the war, the Russian government sought to control the flow of information and to suppress ideas that could undermine tsarist authority in its newest Muslim-majority region near the Ottoman and Iranian borders. In the 1860s, the government cast returnees as likely pro-Ottoman emissaries whom the sultan's government had clandestinely sent back to agitate for Caucasus Muslim emigration to the Ottoman Empire or uprisings against Russian rule.[23] By the mid-1870s, tsarist authorities grew paranoid about Pan-Islamism, or political advocacy for the unity of the *umma*, and suspected North Caucasian muhajirs of spreading Pan-Islamic ideas to Caucasus Muslims.[24] During the Russo-Ottoman War of 1877–78, pro-Ottoman uprisings broke out in Abkhazia, Chechnya, and Dagestan, allegedly inspired by letters from Imam Shamil's son Ghazi Muhammad, which were smuggled into the Caucasus by returnees. It fueled tsarist anxieties about returnee impact on Russia's Muslim subjects.[25] Finally, a new line of accusations emerged after 1908, when local authorities considered North Caucasian returnees suspect for having lived through the Young Turk Revolution and thereby potentially carrying constitutionalist ideals into the tsar's autocratic domains.[26]

Russia was not alone at the time in opposing return migration because of the ideas that purportedly posed a danger to imperial stability. For example, conservative parties in nineteenth-century Europe cast returnees from the United States as too progressive. The Hungarian leadership considered blocking the return of Slovaks who could disrupt a political balance within the unstable Dual Monarchy; the Austrians and the Russians were wary of Polish returnees who may have been "radicalized" by Polish nationalist ideas in Chicago and New York; and the Protestant unionist leadership of Ireland feared a mass return of Irish Catholics from a country that had successfully defied British rule.[27] For a multiethnic empire, return migration risked the proliferation of new narratives undermining imperial rule, especially when returnees belonged to a minority or a subjugated population.

The Ottoman government did not look favorably at muhajir return migration either. The Ottomans had spent millions of kuruş on the resettlement of North Caucasians. Losing this population to Russia would be the loss of investment and, critically, an ideological defeat, should it become widely known that the newest Ottoman Muslim subjects preferred a Christian sovereign's rule to the caliph's authority. To limit muhajir mobility, the Ottoman government confiscated muhajirs' Russian passports upon arrival and tied their subsidies and exemptions to their staying on their allotted land, in accordance with the Immigration Law of 1857. The Ottoman Passport Law (Pasaport Odası Nizamnamesi) of 1867 required Ottoman subjects to obtain prior permission from the government to travel outside the empire.[28]

Many muhajirs made it clear to the Ottoman authorities that they were dissatisfied with their lot and wished to return to Russia. For example, in 1863, a Shapsugh muhajir, Muhammed Sheretlukov, initiated a mass campaign for return migration. He toured refugee villages in northern Bulgaria, collecting signatures of Circassians and Crimean and Nogai Tatars for a petition to return to Russia. Sheretlukov planned to travel to Istanbul and present the petition to the Ottoman government and the Russian ambassador. Unfortunately for him, his campaign attracted the attention of local authorities, and the Varna district governor had him arrested.[29] The authorities then summoned many local Circassians and Tatars who had signed the petition, demanding an explanation, and, to their displeasure, all signatories affirmed their wish for an immediate return to Russia.[30]

When North Caucasian muhajirs requested to leave, the Ottoman authorities attempted to dissuade them by negotiating with their leadership. If needed, they took more forceful measures. In 1867, 400 Circassian families abandoned their settlements in Kosovo and headed toward the Danube River, intending to cross into Russia and then make their way through Bessarabia, Ukraine, and southern Russia into the Caucasus. They reached as far as the districts of Niş (now in Serbia) and Tatar Pazarcık (now Pazardzhik, Bulgaria) before local authorities ordered the cavalry to prevent their further travel, and then the muhajirs had to return to Kosovo.[31] In other cases, Ottoman authorities acquiesced to letting muhajirs leave, if only out of fear that

they might otherwise turn to violence and crime. The Ottomans required de-
parting muhajirs to return all land and cattle that they had received for free.[32]

North Caucasian Muslims created a network of hideout locations and
safe houses to facilitate passage across the Ottoman-Russian border. Away
from the view of imperial officials, only rarely did this secretive world reveal
itself in state records. Returnees typically moved to Ottoman frontier provinces and waited for an opportune moment to cross into the Russian domains. Thus, in 1865, the Russian consul in Trabzon reported that up to
2,500 Circassians gathered in Trabzon Province with the hope of returning
home.[33] North Caucasian returnees stayed in villages of their ethnic kin,
which turned into a kind of clearing houses for successive groups of migrants.
In 1880, Abkhazians from Sivas moved to Trabzon Province and stayed in
Abkhazian muhajir villages, waiting to hire boats to sail home.[34] Likewise,
Chechens, Lezgins, and Ossetians had been arriving from throughout Anatolia to their fellow muhajirs' villages near Kars before starting a dangerous trek
across the border.[35] Staying in frontier provinces allowed returnees to gather
information on where border security was the weakest.[36]

North Caucasian returnees relied on an elaborate infrastructure of clandestine border crossings in the Russo-Ottoman borderlands. Local Greeks,
Armenians, and Turkish- and Laz-speaking Muslims had developed their
own smuggling routes across the border. Russian and Ottoman subjects
who did not have the right documents to enter another empire likely used
those routes. The Russian authorities suspected as much and complained that
North Caucasians were helped by villagers on both sides of the border and
occasionally returned with the migrating Kurdish and Turkoman nomads
or returning Muslim pilgrims.[37] Some muhajirs became guides themselves,
retracing their own journey with returnees into Russia, or new muhajirs out
of Russia, or families from the Caucasus who wished to visit their loved ones
in the Ottoman Empire.[38] By the early twentieth century, the Ottomans grew
increasingly paranoid about unauthorized border crossings and feared that
North Caucasian muhajirs, who knew the borderland terrain well, might
serve as guides for Armenian revolutionaries who clandestinely crossed the
Russo-Ottoman border.[39]

CHECHEN RETURNEE CRISIS OF 1865

The Chechen returnee crisis of 1865 tested Russia's ban on North Caucasian return. The crisis followed the mass emigration of Muslims out of Terek
Province earlier that year, which was a jointly coordinated Russo-Ottoman
population transfer. Some 4,990 families, or 23,057 people—mostly Chechens and some Ingush, Karabulaks, Ossetians, and Kabardians—had left for
the Ottoman Empire. Many of the muhajirs participated in, or sympathized
with, the failed uprising in Chechnya in 1864. Over the summer of 1865,
the Russian military escorted 28 emigrating parties from Vladikavkaz to
the Aleksandropol-Kars border post, where they were entrusted to Ottoman
authorities. The emigrating families took with them 4,531 horses and 11,420
heads of cattle.[40] The Ottoman government agreed to accept muhajirs and
resettle them far from the Russian border, which had been the Russians' consistent demand from the Porte since at least 1861.[41]

When in eastern Anatolia, muhajirs learned that the Ottoman government planned to break them up and resettle them separately, which Chechen
elders refused to accept. The early emigrating parties were then temporarily
housed in villages around Muş and Erzurum. The new incoming parties,
upon hearing where their kinsfolk were, categorically refused to go anywhere
but Muş and Erzurum. The Ottoman authorities had limited infrastructure
and minimal support for refugees at these transit locations. Some refugees
turned to looting. In the subprovince of Muş, which hosted 18,000–20,000
Chechen muhajirs, refugees raided local villages. One gang pillaged an Armenian monastery and killed a bishop at Madnavank.[42] Reportedly 5,000–
6,000 Chechen muhajirs attempted to besiege the town of Muş itself.[43] The
situation was not much better around Erzurum, where Chechen muhajirs
became involved in a conflict with local Kurdish populations after the murder
of two Kurdish chiefs.[44] As the temporary settlement of Chechens risked unraveling the region, mutual accusations abounded. Muhajir leaders blamed
the Ottoman authorities for abandoning them and not providing a viable settlement option for their people. The British, who sympathized with local aggrieved Christians, accused the organizer of the emigration, Ossetian notable
Musa Kundukhov, of fomenting muhajir separatism, calling him "possessed
with the chimera of establishing an independent Circassian nation in Turkey
subject to the payment of a yearly tribute to the Porte but independent of it in

227 RETURN MIGRATION TO RUSSIA

all matters relative to their internal policy as a distinct national body."[45] The Russians blamed Chechen muhajirs for their looting spree and the Ottomans for breaking their side of the agreement by settling Chechen refugees near the Russian border.[46] Meanwhile, some Ottoman officials were convinced that the Russians had instigated muhajir insubordination as a way to sow chaos in the Ottoman eastern provinces, for which they had their own designs.[47]

As winter approached and the Ottoman authorities and Chechen elders had not agreed on the final place of settlement, refugees started moving back to the border with an intention to return to the Caucasus. By October 1865, 2,680 muhajirs, mostly Chechens and some Ingush and Karabulaks, amassed at the Arpachay River (Tur., Arpaçay; Arm., Akhuryan), which served as a natural frontier between the Russian and Ottoman empires and serves today as a border between Armenia and Turkey. The Russians mobilized their Cossack border patrol to guard the riverbank. Every other night, a number of Chechens attempted to wade across the river, only to be pushed back by the Russian troops. Eventually, the Russian authorities allowed muhajir deputies to present their requests.[48]

The ensuing exchange between the two parties reveals how much Chechen muhajirs were willing to concede to return home. The Russian government justified its refusal to readmit Chechens by stating that they had left the empire voluntarily, thereby losing all rights as Russian subjects. As Ottoman subjects, they needed proper documentation to enter Russia. Chechen deputies argued that, while they had left of their own will, they never stopped considering themselves Russian subjects. Tsarist authorities countered that the Chechens' former lands had already been redistributed and they had no homes to return to. In response, Chechen deputies expressed willingness to resettle in any Russian province that the authorities would choose for them. They further stated that, if needed, all refugees would convert from Islam to Orthodox Christianity right there, on the border. This statement testifies to not only the Chechen refugees' desperation but also their perception of a constitutive relationship between one's subjecthood and faith, or an expectation of the Russian government's bias against their faith. They figured that the Russians were more likely to admit new Christian subjects than old Muslim ones.[49] The Chechen deputies complained that Ottoman authorities had cheated them by giving them subpar land, with stony soil, and that their people would rather die on the Arpachay River than go back to the Ottoman Empire. The Russian authorities refused to readmit any Chechen returnees.[50]

The Chechens remained in a makeshift camp on the Ottoman side of the Arpachay River, pleading for their readmittance to Russia. In mid-November 1865, Ottoman troops arrived at the scene. They cut off muhajir access to the riverbank and placed several cannons between the river and the refugee camp. The Ottoman military, after having failed to persuade the Chechens to leave the border, fired the weapons at the camp. Refugees started fleeing, and, by the next day, the Ottoman military escorted all Chechens away from the border.[51] The Ottoman authorities then broke up the muhajirs into groups and settled them at a considerable distance from each other. By 1868, the Ottoman government moved 13,648 muhajirs of 1865 to Ra's al-ʿAyn, in northeastern Syria; 7,196 to the subprovince of Sivas, in central Anatolia; 621 to the subprovince of Biga, in northwestern Anatolia; and 300 to the subprovince of Maraş, in southeastern Anatolia. Only 155 remained around Kars in eastern Anatolia.[52] The two imperial governments came to regard the population transfer of 1865 as a success and an example of mutually beneficial cooperation. The Ottoman government bestowed its Mecidi Orders to eight Russian officials in charge of emigration, while the Russians awarded their Orders of St. Anna and St. Stanislaus to eleven Ottoman officials, including officers responsible for dispersing the Arpachay camp with cannon fire.[53]

What the Chechen refugees did not know and likely never found out was that the Russians did not trust the Ottoman troops to arrive in time and were prepared to readmit the Chechens if Russian border troops could not hold the refugees back any longer. The Caucasus authorities had found land for returnees in Stavropol Governorate and Lesser Kabarda.[54] Resettling returnees there would have been Russia's solution of last resort. As the Ottoman troops cleared the makeshift refugee camp, the Russian resettlement plan for Chechens was shelved, never to be implemented.

RUSSIA'S REIMMIGRATION POLICY AFTER 1867

The Chechen returnee crisis of 1865 foreshadowed prolonged unauthorized return migration of Chechen refugees. Many of them refused to stay in their new Ottoman settlements. In the following years, Russian authorities apprehended thousands of Chechen returnees who had crossed the border into the

RETURN MIGRATION TO RUSSIA   229

Caucasus in small groups. The news of detentions of returnees throughout the South Caucasus prompted the Caucasus authorities in Tiflis to review their no-return policy.

After 1867, the Caucasus authorities followed a new, unwritten reimmigration policy, which preserved the official ban while allowing provincial authorities to readmit returnees on a case-by-case basis. The authorities' decision on readmittance depended on how far into the Russian territory the returnees had advanced. Those intercepted near the border in Aleksandropol District (now in Armenia) or Akhalkalaki District (now in Georgia) were deported on the spot. Those who reached interior districts of the South Caucasus or who were apprehended on the Georgian Military Road leading into the North Caucasus were sent to Tiflis to be reviewed for readmittance.[55] The rationale for the new policy was the cost of deportation: returnees refused to voluntarily self-deport to the Ottoman Empire, which meant that the Russian military had to escort them to the border, at a considerable expense to the Caucasus Viceroyalty's treasury. The liberalization of the policy of no return rested not on humanitarian reasons but on fiscal ones.

During the first round of review in Tiflis, returnees who had a prior criminal record in Russia, carried weapons, or had enough money for a journey back to the Ottoman Empire were deported. The returnees could bolster their case for readmittance if they had submitted to the Russian police voluntarily, showed evidence that their families would take care of them and they would not be a drain on the treasury, or were willing to resettle in whichever province the state would assign them.[56] All those who passed the first round were issued temporary travel documents to Vladikavkaz, the capital of Terek Province. During the second round of review, the Terek authorities sought communal statements from returnees' villages, whereby a village council agreed to readmit them and provide them with a plot of land out of the communal land grant that the village had received.[57] Village communities almost always agreed to accept their returning residents, owing to deeply-rooted kinship loyalty.

The policy was likely a compromise between different stakeholders in the Caucasus. The Caucasus Army, credited with conquering the region and tasked with guarding the border, adamantly opposed any readmittances. Civil authorities were more open-minded. For example, Baron Nikolai, chief

of the civil administration in the Caucasus, wrote that many Circassians and
Chechens were so impoverished that they were returning "almost naked" and
should be welcomed back, "if only because [our] sense of humanity did not
allow to send them back."[58] The compromise meant that, while provincial
governors were free to readmit returnees into their jurisdictions, the government redoubled its efforts to enhance security on the Russo-Ottoman border.
Already in 1865, the Caucasus Army dispatched additional Cossack troops
to patrol the Black Sea coast, ready to do so even at night, to prevent unauthorized Circassian return migration by sea.[59] In 1871, to stem the return
of Chechens, the tsarist government increased Cossack policing of the land
border and asked Ottoman authorities to prohibit muhajirs from entering any
Ottoman frontier districts.[60]

The new reimmigration policy never became official law so as not to cir-
cumscribe the autonomy of local administrations to assess individual cases
and deport as they please. The policy extended to Kabardians, Chechens,
Ingush, and Ossetians of Terek Province, but not to Karabulaks, whom the
Russian government considered particularly rebellious and troublesome and
refused to readmit under any circumstances.[61] A similar policy, namely that a
provincial governor would have the discretion to readmit those apprehended
deep within the Russian territory, also applied in the provinces of Kuban and
Dagestan.[62] The Russian government kept the unwritten policy secret lest it
leak to muhajirs in the Ottoman Empire. Between 1867 and 1871, the authorities recorded the unauthorized return of at least 5,453 Chechens and readmitted 64 percent of those returnees (see table 9). In 1872 and 1873, 834 and 276
more Chechens passed the review in Tiflis and journeyed to Vladikavkaz.[63]
Tsarist reports suggest the readmittance of 20 to 25 percent of the Chechen
muhajirs of 1865 and an even higher attempted return rate.[64]

Russia's formal ban on return remained in place. In 1872, the Russian
ambassador in Istanbul received a petition on behalf of 8,500 Circassian families, most of whom were enslaved, who wished to return to Russia. They
complained of having been duped into emigration by their notables, who
preserved their lifestyle and were accorded privileges by the Ottomans while
ordinary muhajirs suffered from poverty and famine.[65] This communal petition and others, received by Russian diplomats in the Ottoman Empire in
subsequent decades, were rejected (see table 10).

Year	Apprehended	Admitted		Deported	
1867	162	121	75%	41	25%
1868	664	422	64%	242	36%
1869	369	203	55%	166	45%
1870	1,282	453	35%	829	65%
1871	2,976	2,311	78%	665	22%
Total	**5,453**	**3,510**	**64%**	**1,943**	**36%**

Table 9. Chechen returnees to Russia, 1867–71.

Source: SSSA f. 545, op. 1, d. 2852, ll. 79–83 (1867–71). Individual cases are recorded in SSSA f. 545, op. 1, d. 250 (1867–70).

Year	Petitioners	Specifics	Outcome
1860	Ubykhs and Abkhazians	Signed by 26 notables	Rejected
1863	Circassians, Crimean and Nogai Tatars	From Danube Province	Likely never submitted
1865	2,000 Circassians	From Trabzon Province	Rejected
1872	8,500 Circassian families	Many families enslaved	Rejected
1879	Abkhazians	Signed by 300 deputies; claimed to be Christians	Rejected
1880	1,200 Abkhazians	Claimed to be Christians	Rejected, later admitted
1896	Abazins	From Konya Province	Rejected

Table 10. North Caucasian petitions to return to Russia.

Sources, in order: RGVIA f. 38, op. 7, d. 384, ll. 4–7; MnV f. 5, op. 2, d. 24, ll. 147–50; SSSA f. 416, op. 3, d. 1124; SSSA f. 5, op. 1, d. 3011, ll. 3–5; *Tiflisskii Vestnik*, no. 98; SSSA f. 545, op. 1, d. 2069, l. 86; BOA HR.SFR.1 116/35.

Muslim communities in the Caucasus actively facilitated the return of muhajirs. Since the Caucasus War, village councils throughout the region sent communal petitions to the Russian government asking for readmittance of muhajirs. For example, in 1870, Ingush communities petitioned the authorities to allow the reimmigration of seventy-six Ingush families into twelve villages in Nazran District. The petition, in Russian, was signed by fourteen Ingush officers in the Russian army, whose endorsement must have carried significant weight with the government. The Ingush pledged to take care of all expenses related to reimmigration and to provide returnees with their own land.[66]

The unwritten liberalization of Russia's no-return policy was an outcome of internal conversations within the tsarist administration about Muslim migration. By the late 1860s, the authorities contemplated whether Muslim return migration, when vetted and authorized by the state, might advance tsarist goals in the Caucasus. While some officials feared that returnees could spread pro-Ottoman propaganda, others argued that returnees, disillusioned with resettlement in the Ottoman Empire, might dissuade people from emigrating. The authorities even orchestrated some returnees' engagement with communities that wished to emigrate. In 1868, the government readmitted several groups of Chechens and sent them to Chechnya via a detour in Zaqatala District (now in Azerbaijan) and Dagestan so that they could share their experiences with local Muslims and dispel popular misconceptions about life in the sultan's domains. Reportedly, Zaqatalan and Dagestani residents dismissed those Chechens as the Russian government's stooges and ignored their message.[67]

The Russian authorities also considered readmitting, and even asking to return, Muslim notables in an attempt to stem mass emigration. In 1870, the Russian ambassador in Istanbul petitioned the Porte to allow Pshemakho Dzhambotov, a Kabardian prince, to return to Russia. He claimed that the prince himself asked for Russia's intercession. The Ottoman government agreed, provided that the prince return all land and money that he had received from the state. It later transpired that the prince never asked to return but rather that his family and other Kabardian aristocrats had lobbied the Terek provincial governor to secure Dzhambotov's return. The Terek provincial governor then initiated the diplomatic request on the belief that "the return to Kabarda of a person like Prince Dzhambotov would, without doubt, affect the entire population of Kabarda and destroy the [local Muslim] desire of moving to Turkey." The prince chose to remain in the Ottoman Empire.[68]

The readmittance of returnees on the government's terms led to some officials suggesting that returnees be used in social experiments. The administration of the Caucasus Viceroyalty considered making reimmigration conditional on the returnees forever losing the right to own and carry weapons. Carrying sabers and daggers was a social norm and customary right in many mountaineer communities. The Viceroyalty's internal report plainly stated that the abrogation of that right for returnees would constitute "an important step to the total disarmament of all Chechens, which is what the administration pursues."[69]

The Russian government also considered using returnees to further its economic objectives, specifically to colonize sparsely populated uncultivated areas. It discussed settling North Caucasian returnees in the governorates of Orenburg and Stavropol and Kuban Province in the 1860s. Ultimately, the government abandoned these plans because of the high cost of such resettlement, and returnees were allowed to settle among their ethnic kin.[70] In 1871, the Terek provincial governor lobbied the Caucasus Viceroyalty administration to allot free land in Kizlyar District to 2,200 Chechen returnees. The earmarked land lay in a dry riverbed in a drought-stricken region. Through irrigation works, returnees were expected to open up this near-Caspian region to cultivation and reinvigorate the economy of Kizlyar, once the largest city in the North Caucasus but now in steep decline. In 1872, the government authorized land surveys to determine the feasibility of resettlement in Kizlyar. Two years later, a staggering price tag to build returnees' villages and a decreasing number of Chechen returnees prompted the authorities to shelve the project.[71] The Russian plans to use North Caucasian returnees to redeem the land were similar to the Ottoman ones for North Caucasian refugees. For example, in 1912, the Ottoman subprovincial governor of Deir az-Zor proposed to use muhajir labor to dig irrigation canals between the Euphrates, Tigris, and Khabur rivers to transform the Mesopotamian desert into agricultural land. The ambitious Ottoman project, like the Russian one in Dagestan, did not come to pass.[72]

North Caucasian returnees who were officially readmitted to Russia often asked the government to help them to bring their families from the Ottoman Empire. The official process, when the Russian authorities took up the case, was to deliver a petition from Tiflis, via the Russian ambassador in Istanbul, to the Ottoman authorities, asking them to facilitate the return of specific individuals. This formal procedure took years and rarely ended in repatriation. Ottoman provincial officials either were reluctant to let muhajirs go or could not locate requested individuals. In 1867, the Terek authorities boldly advised Chechen petitioners that their best chance of retrieving their families was to send someone from Chechnya to smuggle their relatives out of the Ottoman Empire, in contravention of Ottoman laws.[73] In another instance, the Terek provincial governor asked the Caucasus Viceroyalty administration to allow a readmitted Kabardian returnee, who had been formerly enslaved, to go back to Sivas to buy his mother, brother, wife, and four children out of slavery and to bring them back.[74] While such cases of imperial benevolence toward returnees were rare, they demonstrate that provincial administrations had an evolving discussion about the merits of reimmigration and that the tsarist state could, under exceptional circumstances, serve as a patron of Muslim repatriation. Not supporting repatriation for all was a deliberate choice.

ABKHAZIAN RETURNEE CRISIS OF 1880

The Abkhazian returnee crisis of 1880 was the second major Russo-Ottoman border crisis involving returnees, after the Chechen one of 1865. During the Russo-Ottoman War of 1877–78, several uprisings against Russian rule broke out throughout the Caucasus, including in Abkhazia. The Ottomans briefly occupied the port city of Sukhum, with support from local Muslim communities. By the end of the war, 40,000–50,000 Abkhazians, up to 60 percent of Abkhazia's population, followed the retreating Ottoman troops into Anatolia.[75]

The Abkhazians started returning to the Caucasus shortly afterward. They would hire boats in Samsun and Trabzon and sail to Batum (now Batumi, Georgia), the Ottoman port annexed by Russia in 1878, or directly to Sukhum. During the war, the Russian government deported all returnees, in case they were Ottoman spies.[76] Abkhazian refugees also formally petitioned the Caucasus authorities through Russian consulates in the Ottoman Empire. Most applicants claimed that they had been captured by Ottoman forces and taken to the Ottoman Empire against their will. Many claimed to be Abkhazian Christians.[77] In May 1879, the Russian embassy in Istanbul notified its consuls that the Abkhazians' return was undesirable.[78] Most petitions were denied. However, tsarist authorities selectively readmitted some Abkhazians, especially Christian notables who had powerful protectors in Abkhazia vouching for them.[79] Those singular cases of readmittance, conveyed through the Ottoman Foreign Ministry, may have encouraged the mass return of Abkhazians from the Ottoman Empire.

In August 1880, *Aghios Petros*, a vessel under the British flag with a Greek crew, sailed into the Batum harbor. The ship carried 1,200 Abkhazians who requested to return to Abkhazia. The administration of the Caucasus Viceroyalty ordered an immediate deportation of those returnees back to the Ottoman Empire, regarding them as Ottoman subjects without Russian authorization to enter. The Ottoman authorities refused to accept Abkhazians aboard the ship. The Porte, which suffered a major defeat during the previous war and faced bankruptcy, had little interest in resettling the Abkhazians who did not want to be the sultan's subjects. The Ottoman consul in Batum had previously stated his government's position in unambiguous terms: the Abkhazian returnees did not hold Ottoman passports and were never Ottoman subjects; they held Russian subjecthood, were within the Russian territory, and remained the responsibility of the Russian government.[80] This stance marked a rare occasion of the Ottoman government disavowing migrants from the Caucasus, although it was done precisely because the migrants in question refused to consider themselves muhajirs. Provincial officials vowed to uphold their governments' positions. The Ottoman governor of the frontier province of Trabzon gave orders to the Ottoman coastal guard to prevent, by force if needed, Abkhazian refugees from disembarking on Ottoman shores.[81] Meanwhile, the newly installed tsarist administration of Batum prohibited the crew of *Aghios Petros*, docked in the Batum harbor, to disembark refugees.[82]

Forcibly keeping 1,200 refugees on a ship meant for 200 passengers was a humanitarian disaster in the making. Epidemics soon broke out among Abkhazians, who had been starving, had little water, and reportedly had among them the corpses of four refugees who had died during the journey. Five days in, the old vessel developed a leak, and the ship started sinking. Only then did the Batum authorities allow refugees to disembark. While the ship's holes were being patched up, the refugees stayed in a makeshift camp, with old sails turned into tents.[83] Up to 200 Abkhazian men escaped the campsite into the city before the ship was repaired. The remaining refugees were escorted back to the vessel. The Abkhazians then sent a communal petition, by telegram, to the Caucasus Viceroy in Tiflis. It read, "The Batum governor forces us to return to Turkey. We beg Your Excellency to take pity on us, Christians, . . . as your coreligionists. . . . Have mercy on our children, who account for more than half of us and who are innocent! There is nothing for us in Turkey but starvation and persecution from the merciless Turkish government. We beg you to send us to Sukhum Department. . . . Your refusal would condemn us to perishing at sea."[84] The self-declared Christian identity of the petitioners did not sway the Caucasus authorities, unwilling to set a precedent by publicly allowing a large number of refugees to return to Russia. Several weeks later, about 400 women on the ship sent another petition to the Caucasus authorities, pleading for their and their children's lives, also to no avail.[85]

The Russian military ordered the ship captain to leave Russian waters and to disembark refugees in Trabzon, despite Ottoman protests. The Greek crew refused to follow the order and did not raise the mainsail. By the end of the fourth week, the ship was towed out of the Batum harbor under the convoy of a Russian military schooner. When the ship approached the Ottoman shore, the Ottomans opened gunfire, which made the Russian convoy retreat. The ship with Abkhazian refugees was then lingering in Ottoman waters, unable to dock in any Ottoman port. The following night, the ship's captain clandestinely sailed back into Russian waters and unloaded all refugees on a beach, to the west of Batum. The beach was surrounded by cliffs on all sides and had no escape path onto the land. The captain left the refugees there, returned to Batum, and falsely reported that his crew had disembarked the refugees on the Ottoman coast. News of what had transpired, however, spread quickly, and the Batum police arrested the offending captain and navigating officer before they could return to the Ottoman Empire.[86] The Russian authorities sent a rescue party to retrieve the refugees from the beach. The survivors arrived in Batum and shortly afterward were given permission to return to Abkhazia. This returnee crisis lasted thirty-seven days and claimed the lives of at least 178 refugees aboard *Aghios Petros*.[87]

The Abkhazian returnee crisis of 1880 prompted the Russian government to adopt the same unwritten reimmigration policy for Sukhum Department that had been in place in the North Caucasus. All Abkhazian refugees who managed to reach the Abkhazian shore were to be accepted and resettled. They would be treated not as returnees (Rus., *vozvrashchaiushchiesia*) but rather as immigrants (*prishel'tsy*, or *pereselentsy*), similar to Greek, Georgian, and Estonian colonists in Abkhazia. To ensure public order during reimmigration, the Russian police in Abkhazia were to be reinforced by Cossack troops. The new policy was not communicated to the Ottoman government to keep it hidden from Abkhazian muhajirs.[88] Nevertheless, the scope of return migration in Abkhazia was immense. By June 1881, the district of Gudauta had at least 1,487 returnee families, 47 percent of all households. By 1881, about a third of the Abkhazian refugees of 1877–78, or 21 percent of the entire population of Abkhazia, returned home, and small groups of people continued returning for years after that.[89]

MAKING THE CAUCASUS HOME AGAIN

Between 1860 and World War I, approximately 40,000 Muslims returned to the Caucasus (see table 11).[90] The numbers of returnees were particularly high after the Chechen emigration of 1865 and the Abkhazian emigration of 1878. An imperial archive has blind spots on return migration similar to those on emigration. The government documented only what it knew or what it wanted preserved, while many returnees made it their goal to avoid being recorded at any cost. The scope of return migration from the Ottoman Empire exceeded that of formal readmittance: many muhajirs returned and were never apprehended; others were deported on the border and not recorded; many more attempted to return but turned back or died on their perilous journeys. Thousands of muhajirs submitted verbal or written petitions to Russian consuls and never heard back. Dreaming of, planning, executing, or deciding against the return to the Caucasus were an integral part of the experience of being a North Caucasian muhajir in the Ottoman Empire.

A small group of North Caucasian muhajirs did not need to cross the Russo-Ottoman border because the border had crossed them. In the 1860s, the Ottoman government had settled some Circassians and Chechens in the region of Kars, which Russia annexed in 1878. Many muhajirs then fled

Years	Destination & Ethnic Groups	Estimates
1860–63	Stavropol Governorate *Nogai Tatars*	1,293
1861–65	Kuban and Terek Provinces *western Circassians, Kabardians, Ossetians,* *Chechens, Ingush, Kumyks, Nogai Tatars*	9,000
1866–78	Grozny District *Chechens*	5,857
1866–68	Sukhum Department *Abkhazians*	2,100
1878–81	Sukhum Department *Abkhazians*	13,258–15,000
1881–1914	All regions of the North Caucasus and Abkhazia	7,000
Total		**38,508–40,250**

Table 11. **Returnees to the Caucasus, 1860–1914.**
The estimates are for Muslim muhajirs who returned to the Caucasus from
the Ottoman Empire and were readmitted by the Russian government.

Russian occupation for the safety of Anatolia, alongside other Muslims of
Kars, Ardahan, and Batum. Other muhajirs stayed put and petitioned tsarist
authorities to allow them to cross the mountains and return to the North
Caucasus.[91]

We know little of how returnees fared after reimmigration. The government did not follow up on the progress of readmitted muhajirs. What remains
clear is that reimmigration came with high social costs, as returnees usually
came back penniless and had to rely on their broader community for support.
In a rare autobiographical story about the return, Inal Kanukov (1850/51–99),
an Ossetian writer and ethnographer, recalls how his family had emigrated to
the Ottoman Empire in 1860, when he was a child, and returned with ninety
other families soon afterward. The Kanukovs, who were notables, found their
old village abandoned and themselves homeless. A family of their former serfs

generously hosted them in a neighboring village. Kanukov describes their first days back in Ossetia as follows: "Although everyone came out to greet us and welcomed us back with genuine happiness, we entered the village not as equal members but as foreign strangers, who had been excluded from the family and were accepted back as a favor." Kanukov notes that what prevented many muhajirs from returning to the Caucasus was the fear of being perceived as a failure. When Kanukov's father had surveyed the poor soil of their new lands near Kars and decided to return to Ossetia, other Ossetian elders tried to dissuade him, "Do not shame us all! What will people in our homeland think when they see that you, one of the best muhajirs, returned?"[92] The shame of returning kept many muhajirs from becoming returnees.

Returnees usually found a very different homeland back in the Caucasus. Many muhajirs were not allowed to return to the same village and were resettled elsewhere. Many who returned to the same village lived under new laws and borders and had a diminished support network because their friends and neighbors had emigrated. It was not uncommon for returnees to change their minds and leave Russia for good for the second time. Return migration to the Caucasus sometimes provoked tensions between returnees and local populations. Mass return to Abkhazia led to returnees trying to reclaim their houses and fruit gardens that had been seized by others or redistributed to new immigrants. Meanwhile, many Abkhazians protested the returnees' squatting on their land and the government's confiscation of their land in favor of returnees.[93] Likewise, in Chechnya some villagers were displeased with having to carve out land for returnees from the state-allotted village land grant.[94] Return migration inevitably led to the readjustment of power dynamics, land usage, and distribution of resources and labor. Return migration, similar to emigration, affected not only migrants themselves but also communities around them.

Returnees left their mark on the economy of the Caucasus. The North Caucasian migration dispersed crop cultures, livestock, and agricultural and artisanal expertise between the Caucasus and the Middle East. Thus, Circassians brought their distinctive oxen-drawn carts to Transjordan and Kabarda horses to Uzunyayla. Likewise, returnees carried a piece of the Ottoman Empire to the Caucasus. Many Chechens learned to grow tobacco in their villages in central Anatolia and found their skills in demand when they returned to Chechnya. In the second half of the nineteenth century, the Caucasus became Russia's premier region for tobacco cultivation. Between 1865 and 1878, the area of tobacco plantations in the North Caucasus increased over thirty-fold to 11,808 acres. The number of tobacco factories in the North Caucasus grew from two in 1865 to eighteen, including six in Terek Province, in 1869. Local tobacco factories also purchased the highly priced Ottoman tobacco seeds that Chechen returnees had smuggled with them into Russia.[95]

The North Caucasian return migration from the Ottoman Empire to the Caucasus continued through the remainder of the late imperial era. Some North Caucasians returned to Russia as Ottoman subjects. While the Russian government had banned the return of North Caucasians as denaturalized Russian subjects, it issued visas to Ottoman subjects. Many muhajirs had understood this loophole and lawfully reentered the Caucasus with Ottoman passports. Some of them visited their families and left, but many settled down and blended in with local populations. In the 1870s and 1880s, the Kuban and Terek authorities made attempts to restrict access to their provinces to Ottoman-subject North Caucasians.[96] Those policies were difficult to enforce because neither Russian consular officials nor border guards could easily tell people's ancestry from their Ottoman documents. Ottoman passports recorded a personal name and a *nasab*, or patronymic—for example, Isma'il bin Musa—but rarely Kabardian or Chechen family names, which was a blessing in disguise for many North Caucasian returnees. Beginning in the 1880s, the Russian government conducted regular checks on Ottoman subjects residing in the Caucasus and deported those who had overstayed their visas.[97] In response, local communities routinely petitioned the authorities to pardon them. For example, a Kabardian muhajir, Muhammad (Magomet) Ghassan, returned to the Caucasus with an Ottoman passport. He fell in love with a local woman and married her. Her village had registered him as a local resident, and he lived there for ten years before the government found and arrested him. His father-in-law wrote an exasperated petition begging to release the man, to whom "he would have never given his only daughter had he known that Muhammad Ghassan would not gain legal status in Russia."[98]

In the final decades of imperial rule, a new type of returnees appeared in the Caucasus—young muhajir men who grew up in the Ottoman Empire but felt that the Caucasus was their true homeland. Their return was an act of defiance against the two empires, which created roadblocks for their migration, and against their parents, of whose emigration they strongly disapproved. One petition to the Russian government stated that a young Avar returnee, Abdurakhman Kurakhma oğlu, had "lost Russian subjecthood not because of his own fault but because of his parents' fault."[99] His fellow Dagestani, a Lezgin man, Shamsuddin Murtuzali oğlu, had moved to the Ottoman Empire as a child with his father in 1899. He returned to Dagestan, was deported to the Ottoman Empire in 1908, and since then kept coming back, getting deported, and reappearing in the Caucasus again. He insisted that he never considered himself an Ottoman subject.[100] These strong-willed members of the younger generation of North Caucasian muhajirs rejected the legal status imposed on them and, through their return migration, aspired to reverse the previous generations' displacement.

The North Caucasian return migration testifies to the will of refugees to return to their homeland. Thousands risked their lives to undertake a return journey, and many succeeded in reimmigrating. How the tsarist government handled return migration provides a new perspective on Russian governance in the Caucasus. First, while the Caucasus authorities upheld the Russian military's wartime ban of 1861 on the return of North Caucasian Muslims, they instituted an unwritten reimmigration policy that gave provincial officials leeway to readmit returnees after 1867. Decisions to readmit were based on how expensive it would be to deport returnees and whether returnees could be used to advance the government's goals. Both the ban and its backdoor served to ensure the government's control over demographics in the Caucasus, while minimizing its expenses on resettlement or deportations. Second, the Russian government used Muslims' return to consolidate its control over the Caucasus. The Caucasus authorities presented unauthorized breaches of the Russian border as a threat to the region's security and public order, which enabled the government to increase its policing of Caucasus Muslims. Tsarist officials instituted stricter requirements for Muslim subjects to leave and return to Russia, and they required village councils to sign off on all emigration and reimmigration requests. The Russian government extended its reach deep into frontier districts of the South Caucasus and mountain areas of Kabarda, Chechnya, and Dagestan through its search for undocumented returnees, while also militarizing the Russo-Ottoman border through increased Cossack patrols. Russia used migration policies to prop up its authority in the Caucasus.

The return of Muslims from the Middle East to the Caucasus was a challenge to the Ottoman and Russian empires. It undermined the Ottoman claim of being a refuge to foreign Muslims. Many Muslim refugees, it turns out, would risk everything to leave the caliphate for a life in the tsardom. It also countered Russia's attempts to seal the porous Russo-Ottoman border and control Muslim mobility in the Caucasus. Many North Caucasians refused to recognize arbitrary decisions that barred them from their homeland and pressed on in their return journeys. Returnees, each in their own way, challenged what the two imperial governments expected of them.

CONCLUSION

THE MODERN HISTORY OF REFUGEE RESETTLEMENT in the Middle East and the Balkans begins with the Ottoman refugee regime. The late Ottoman state maintained an open-door policy for Muslim refugees. It promised resettlement, free land, exemptions from taxation and military service, agricultural subsidies, and financial aid to incoming Muslims. All muhajirs had an open path to Ottoman naturalization. The Ottoman refugee regime provided protections to about a million North Caucasian Muslims and several million Muslims from Crimea, the Balkans, the South Caucasus, and Crete. It inaugurated expectations of what kind of aid must be provided to refugees and what the state's obligations were in an age before international protections for refugees were codified. Muhajirs were accepted into the Ottoman body politic with almost no reservations because one's status as a refugee was tied to their Muslim identity, favored by the Ottoman government. In the twentieth century, ethnicity and nationality would become key categories in constructing refugee identities. In the Middle East alone, that left millions of Armenian, Assyrian, Kurdish, Palestinian, Jewish, Iraqi, Syrian, Sudanese, South Sudanese, and other refugees excluded and marginalized after World War I.

While the Ottoman government welcomed refugees, its funding rarely matched its ambitions. The Ottoman authorities spent an enormous amount of money on settling refugees but could not invest much beyond the resettlement stage. This meant that refugees were largely left to fend for themselves, and their well-being depended on whether they could tap into local economies. In the Balkans, refugee villages were in economic distress, which led to banditry and paramilitarism that drowned the region in sectarian violence between 1876 and 1878. In central Anatolia, refugee villages stagnated in their splendid isolation, hidden among the mountains with no export routes. In Transjordan, Circassian villages thrived because the Hejaz Railway transformed the economy of the region. Muhajirs took advantage of new opportunities by marketing bedouin products, exporting their own, and selling real estate to Levantine merchants. Local circumstances mattered a great deal in refugee resettlement.

The Ottoman and Russian policies on Muslim migration were intentional and served to strengthen the state. The Ottoman government saw foreign Muslim refugees as a solution to the besieged empire's many problems. The Ottomans used refugees to expand agriculture and to tighten the empire's hold on nomadic and Christian-majority frontier regions. Muslim refugee settlement, indeed, fortified Ottoman authority in central Anatolia and Transjordan. The Russian government initially adopted an exclusionary policy, expelling western Circassians in the early 1860s to finalize its conquest of the Caucasus and control of the northern coast of the Black Sea. After 1867, it formally discouraged North Caucasian emigration lest it depopulate the Caucasus but allowed those bent on emigrating to leave. By redrawing demographics in the Caucasus, Russia solidified its hold on its newest Muslim-majority region. Neither empire was keen on having a fluid transimperial population: the Russian government banned the return of North Caucasians and increased policing on the Russo-Ottoman border, while the Ottoman authorities confiscated muhajirs' Russian documents upon arrival and made their exemptions contingent on them staying in their villages. The Ottoman and Russian policies had room for negotiation with different groups, especially upper-status North Caucasians, but overall they were remarkably consistent throughout the late imperial era.

North Caucasian refugees were not mere spectators of their displacement. They were key actors in reshaping the Ottoman state. By World War I, North Caucasians lived in almost every Ottoman province and made up to 5 percent of the empire's population.[1] Most were farmers and helped to entrench the new Ottoman land regime, which reaffirmed the state's ownership of agricultural land, promoted consistent cultivation, and enforced taxation. As the empire's newest and some of its most vulnerable subjects, muhajirs were eager to follow the Ottoman Refugee Commission's regulations to secure their permanent usufruct rights to the land. By registering, tilling, improving, and reselling the land, they prompted their many neighbors to also formalize their rights to the land. Contestation of land led to muhajirs' many conflicts throughout the empire. Muhajirs defended their right to the land promised to them by the Ottoman government, while seizing the land claimed by Balkan Christians, Armenians, Druze, and Turkic, Kurdish, and Arab nomads. The Ottoman government aided the militarization of refugee communities by recruiting them into the army and coopting paramilitary organizations. Many muhajirs traded a plough for a rifle, becoming soldiers, gendarmes, guards, militia, or bandits.

The history of muhajirs challenges many artificial boundaries in traditional accounts of migration. It invites us to reexamine what made one a refugee in the age of European imperialism and in Islamic history. Muhajirs were refugees, immigrants, and emigrants. They fled ethnic cleansing and discrimination or left home for a better life, while some considered their journey a religious obligation. Many were double and triple refugees, having been displaced multiple times in the Caucasus and the Ottoman Empire. Some refugees became settlers and enforcers of the Ottoman state, and many were slaves or slaveholders.

By the end of the empire, North Caucasians precariously navigated the ethnonational aspirations of their neighbors. During World War I, many muhajirs fought for the Ottoman state, which gave them refuge and a sense of belonging as a Muslim community. In Transjordan, the Circassian Volunteer Cavalry served as the main line of defense against anti-Ottoman bedouin militias.[2] After the war, refugee communities aligned with different forces, depending on where they were. In Anatolia, many North Caucasians supported the Ottoman government in Istanbul, while those in the Marmara region briefly cooperated with Greek and British occupying forces.[3] An increasing number of muhajirs fought for the Turkish national movement in Ankara, but, following the so-called rebellions against Mustafa Kemal's authority by the prominent Circassian militia leaders Ahmet Anzavur in 1919–20 and

Çerkes Ethem in 1920–21, many North Caucasians were purged from positions of power in the Turkish national movement.[4] In subsequent decades, Circassians were painted as traitors to the national cause, an accusation that maligned Turkey's North Caucasian diaspora for generations.[5]

In the interwar Levant, North Caucasians generally forged good relations with the Hashemite dynasty and British and French mandatory officials. Those relations rested on the military expertise that North Caucasians were willing to offer the new governments. In Transjordan, Circassian notables, led by Mirza Wasfi, head of Amman's Circassian community and a former Ottoman loyalist, welcomed Emir ʿAbdullah to Amman in 1921 and offered him a private force, which has served Jordan's ruling family ever since as the Circassian Royal Guard.[6] The British mandatory authorities also heavily recruited Circassians into the Transjordanian Reserve Force, later reorganized as the Arab Legion, where Circassians represented 30 percent of troops by 1924.[7] In Syria, the French drafted North Caucasians, alongside Druze, Alawis, and Christians, into the Special Troops of the Levant and relied on Circassian and other minority auxiliaries to suppress the Great Syrian Revolt of 1925–27.[8] The military remained a career aspiration for many Circassians in independent Jordan and Syria.[9] The government of Israel, established in 1948, also courted the small Circassian community, treating it differently than the Palestinian Muslim population. Circassians became the second minority group, after the Druze, to be drafted into the Israel Defense Forces in 1958.[10]

Ottoman and tsarist migration policies had a lasting effect in the twentieth and twenty-first centuries. After World War I, new nation-states inherited the Ottoman legislation on immigration, refugee resettlement, and land ownership, which shaped how they managed their own population movements. The largest impact of North Caucasian, especially Circassian, displacement, however, was indirect. It demonstrated that a modern state could carry out near-complete relocation of a population from one region to another. A population exchange, as a type of forced migration, built on that experience. While neither the Russians nor the Ottomans affirmed North Caucasian resettlement as a population exchange, many contemporaries perceived it as such, and the two imperial governments cooperated in multiple ways, even implementing the jointly coordinated transfer of Chechens, Ingush, Karabulaks, Ossetians, and Kabardians in 1865. The Porte sanctioned its first formal population exchange in 1913, when the Ottoman Empire and Bulgaria exchanged Muslim and Christian villages along their border.[11] In 1919, Greece and Bulgaria agreed on their own population exchange, formalizing the flight of about 30,000 Greeks from southern Bulgaria and 150,000 Bulgarians from Macedonia and Thrace.[12] It paved the way for a far larger Greek-Turkish population exchange in 1923. Over 1.2 million Greek Orthodox in the Ottoman Empire and up to 400,000 Muslims in Greece crossed the Aegean into their new, unfamiliar "homeland."[13] That forced migration was endorsed by the League of Nations and served as a model for the Palestine partition plans in 1937 and 1947, neither of which came to be; the Potsdam Agreement of 1945 allowing for expulsions of Germans out of Central Europe; and population transfers of 1947–50 between India and Pakistan.[14]

The Ottoman refugee regime left a deep-rooted legacy in the Middle East and the Balkans and contributed to the interwar refugee regime implemented by the League of Nations and various colonial and national authorities. The agricultural resettlement of refugees, as practiced by the Ottoman government for decades, continued in the 1920s and 1930s. For example, Greece prioritized rural resettlement for Anatolian refugees of the Greek-Turkish population exchange.[15] The British authorities and the Iraqi government placed Assyrian refugees in agricultural settlements, dispersed among Kurdish villages; and the French authorities resettled many Armenian and Assyrian refugees in villages throughout northern Syria.[16] Furthermore, the Ottoman government's warm welcome of Muslim refugees exemplified the drive for ethnoreligious homogenization, which, by the interwar era, was on full display in Turkey, the Balkans, and the rest of Europe. The national governments' logic when choosing which refugees to accept was clear: an ideal immigrant needed to be similar—religiously or ethnically, or both—to the country's majority population. The Ottoman refugee regime and the interwar one both had religious dimensions. The Ottoman refugee regime benefited Muslims. Meanwhile, the League of Nations focused its efforts to aid Christian refugees from Europe and the Middle East, to a lesser extent Jewish refugees, and rarely Muslim refugees. That bias was consistent throughout the interwar era, reflecting whom the core national members of the League considered deserving of aid and desirable for resettlement.[17]

Tsarist migration policies transformed demographics in the Caucasus. The remaining western Circassian communities had been dramatically reduced in size, with their territories no longer contiguous. When the Soviet government pursued its own nation-building policies in the Caucasus, it preferred to keep the Circassians administratively apart and affirmed four distinct "nationalities" for Circassians: Adyghe, Kabardian, Cherkess, and Shapsugh.[18] They all received their own administrative units, of which three survive as autonomous republics within the Russian Federation: Adygea, with an ethnic Russian majority, and Kabardino-Balkaria and Karachay-Cherkessia, each shared with a Turkic-speaking "titular nation."[19] The Soviet government sanctioned the development of two literary Circassian languages: Adyghe, or western Circassian, and Kabardino-Cherkess, or eastern Circassian. For much of the twentieth century, Soviet North Caucasians and descendants of North Caucasian muhajirs in the Middle East could not freely communicate and visit each other, largely because of Soviet restrictions.

More recently, tsarist migration policies in the Caucasus kindled important discussions about the legacy of Russian imperialism. Since the 1990s, Circassian organizations in Russia and the Middle East diaspora called for the recognition of massacres and expulsions during the Caucasus War as a genocide. The parliaments of Russia's autonomous republics of Kabardino-Balkaria and Adygea recognized the Circassian genocide in, respectively, 1992 and 1996. In 2011, Georgia became the first sovereign state to recognize the genocide. In contrast, the Russian federal government denies that the events of 1863–64 constituted an ethnic cleansing, let alone a genocide, and rejects that the Russian Federation bears responsibility for tsarist-era displacements. In 2014, Russia hosted the Winter Olympic Games in Sochi, which coincided with the 150th anniversary of the Circassian expulsions from that very site. The event, absent a commemoration or acknowledgment of violence, prompted renewed calls by diasporic activists for genocide recognition.[20] Furthermore, return migration to the North Caucasus remains out of reach for many in the diaspora. The governments of the Soviet Union and the Russian Federation consistently rejected the right of return of the North Caucasian diaspora and denied communal requests for repatriation. Since the 1990s, the autonomous republics in the North Caucasus have welcomed their co-ethnic diasporas back, but North Caucasians can only immigrate as individuals, under regular Russian policies for all foreigners.[21] After the outbreak of the

Syrian civil war in 2011, about 5,000 Syrian Circassians traveled to the North Caucasus on tourist visas, and about 2,000 stayed, mostly as undocumented immigrants.[22] The issues of Circassian genocide recognition and North Caucasian repatriation strike at the heart of the ongoing, painful reevaluation of the Russian Federation's continuity with the Soviet Union and the Russian Empire.

This book explored how the Ottoman and Russian empires managed Muslim migration in their final decades. Their policies on immigration, emigration, and refugee resettlement transformed entire regions in the Middle East, the Balkans, and the Caucasus. It is also a story of how North Caucasian refugees fought for survival, navigating imperial policies, settling land, grappling with their identities, and making their own histories in the process. It exists thanks to refugees whose voices and names survive in the historical record, and it is a tribute to those who inspired this work: to Sayetkhan, who had troubles with her in-laws while managing real estate in Amman; to Kerim-Sultan, who sent letters to his family in Dagestan with Chechen pilgrims; to Fuat Khutat, an Ottoman officer who searched for a perfect settlement area for his refugee family; to four Kabardian orphans, who in the dead of winter returned from Syria to their remote village in the Caucasus; and to countless others. Muhajirs tied the histories of the Ottoman and Russian empires and also created a world of their own, the legacy of which lives on in the contemporary Middle East.

NOTES

Introduction

1. For contemporary accounts of the Circassian refugee crisis of 1863–65, see House of Commons, *Papers Respecting the Settlement of Circassian Emigrants in Turkey*; Dulaurier, "La Russie dans le Caucase"; Berzhe, "Vyselenie gortsev s Kavkaza."

2. Presidential State Archives of the Republic of Turkey, Ottoman Archives (T.C. Cumhurbaşkanlığı Devlet Arşivleri Başkanlığı, Osmanlı Arşivi, Istanbul, hereafter cited as BOA) MVL 1016/36 (2 *muharrem* 1282, 28 May 1865); TŞRBNM 19/13 (24 *zilkade* 1280, 1 May 1864); TŞRBNM 25/120 (15 *safer* 1281, 20 July 1864); İ.DH 953/75394 (27 *şaban* 1302, 11 June 1885).

3. Skran, *Refugees in Inter-War Europe*.

4. Robson, *States of Separation*; Watenpaugh, *Bread from Stones*; Watenpaugh, "League of Nations' Rescue"; White, "Refugees and the Definition of Syria."

5. Akin, *When the War Came Home*; Aksakal, *Ottoman Road to War*; Campos, *Ottoman Brothers*; Gingeras, *Sorrowful Shores*; Makdisi, *Culture of Sectarianism*; Reynolds, *Shattering Empires*.

6. Crews, *For Prophet and Tsar*; Campbell, *Muslim Question*; Kefeli, *Becoming Muslim*; Meyer, "Speaking Sharia to the State"; Ross, *Tatar Empire*; Tuna, *Imperial Russia's Muslims*.

7. On transimperial subjects, see Rothman, *Brokering Empire*; and on transimperial Muslims, see Meyer, *Turks across Empires*.

8. Besleney, *Circassian Diaspora*, 31–32; Jaimoukha, *Circassians*, 101–22; Katav and Duman, "Iraqi Circassians."

9. On the critique of the Eurocentric view of late imperial migrations, see McKeown, "Global Migration."

10. Amrith, *Crossing the Bay of Bengal*; Datta, *Fleeting Agencies*.

11. For the idea of the internal frontier, see Rogan, *Frontiers of the State*; for how the Ottomans' "civilizing attitude" led to refugee settlement on the internal frontier, see Adamiak, "To the Edge of the Desert," esp. 17–61.

12. Gatrell, *Making of the Modern Refugee*, 52–72; Ther, *Outsiders*, 388–98.

13. UN General Assembly, Convention Relating to the Status of Refugees, art. 1(A) (2) (28 July 1951).

14. Can, *Spiritual Subjects*; Kane, *Russian Hajj*.

15. Meyer, *Turks across Empires*; Khalid, *Politics of Muslim Cultural Reform*.

16. Smiley, *From Slaves to Prisoners of War*; Taki, *Tsar and Sultan*, 115–91.

17. Robarts, *Migration and Disease*; Balistreri, "Persistence of the Periphery."

18. Marrus, *Unwanted*, 41; see also Brubaker, "Aftermaths of Empire."

19. An important unpublished work on Russo-Ottoman migrations is Pinson, "Demographic Warfare."

20. On works conceptualizing Russo-Ottoman and adjacent borderlands, see Goff and Siegelbaum, *Empire and Belonging*; Frary and Kozelsky, *Russian-Ottoman Borderlands*; Bartov and Weitz, *Shatterzone of Empires*; and on comparative empires, see Barkey and Hagen, *After Empire*; Brisku, *Political Reform*.

21. Balloffet, *Argentina in the Global Middle East*; Fahrenthold, *Between the Ottomans and the Entente*; Mays, *Forging Ties*; Pastor, *Mexican Mahjar*.

22. Klier, *Russians, Jews, and the Pogroms*, 382; Fishman, *Jews and Palestinians*, 49.

23. Barker, *Most Precious Merchandise*; Peirce, *Imperial Harem*.

24. On Ottoman abolitionism, see Toledano, *Ottoman Slave Trade*; Erdem, *Slavery in the Ottoman Empire*, 94–151.

25. Karamürsel, "Transplanted Slavery."

26. Catford, "Mountain of Tongues."

27. The exact number of, and boundaries between, Circassian communities are contested both in the Caucasus and in diaspora. For example, the Ubykh are sometimes considered a separate people. For an overview of different Circassian communities, see Richmond, *Northwest Caucasus*, 20–25.

28. See Grant, *Captive and the Gift*, 19–42; Layton, *Russian Literature and Empire*, 89–109.

29. Karpat, *Ottoman Population*; see also Toumarkine, *Populations musulmanes balkaniques*.

30. For example, Jagodić, *Naseljavanje Kneževine Srbije*, 38–43; Muchinov, *Migratsionna politika na Osmanskata imperiia*, 171–88; İpek, *Türk Göçleri*; Şimşir, *Rumeli'den Türk Göçleri*.

31. McCarthy, *Death and Exile*.

32. Cuthell, "Muhacirin Komisyonu"; Fratantuono, "Migration Administration"; Blumi, *Ottoman Refugees*.

33. Kasaba, *Moveable Empire*.

34. Chatty, *Displacement and Dispossession*.

35. For early works by North Caucasian diasporic writers, see Berkok, *Tarihte Kafkasya*; Mufti, *Heroes and Emperors*.

36. Aydemir, *Göç*; Bice, *Kafkasya'dan Anadolu'ya Göçler*; Eren, *Türkiye'de Göç*; Erkan, *Kırım ve Kafkasya Göçleri*; Habiçoğlu, *Kafkasya'dan Anadolu'ya Göçler*; Orat, Arslan, and Tanrıverdi, *Kafkas Göçleri*; Saydam, *Kırım ve Kafkas Göçleri*.

37. Berzeg, *Türkiye Kurtuluş Savaşı'nda Çerkes Göçmenleri*; Ünal, *Kurtuluş Savaşı'nda Çerkeslerin Rolü*.

38. Haghandoqa, *Circassians*; Isma'il, *Dalil al-Ansab al-Sharkasiyya*. For later works, see Mamsir Batsaj, *al-Mawsu'a al-Tarikhiyya li-l-Umma al-Sharkasiyya*; Nashkhu, *Tarikh al-Sharkas (al-Adigha) wa-l-Shishan*.

39. On North Caucasian diasporic identities, see Besleney, *Circassian Diaspora*; Doğan, "Circassians in Turkey"; Kaya, *Türkiye'de Çerkesler*; Shami, "Prehistories of Globalization"; Shami, "Disjuncture in Ethnicity"; Yelbaşı, *Circassians of Turkey*. For recent works drawing on oral history, see Aksoy, *Benim Adım 1864*; Aksoy, *Beyaz Köleler*; Sunata, *Hafızam Çerkesçe*.

40. The early and groundbreaking work on displacement from the Caucasus is Dzidzariia, *Makhadzhirstvo*. On archival possibilities and limitations for scholars of the Caucasus and the Russo-Ottoman world, see Bobrovnikov, "Rossiiskie musul'mane posle arkhivnoi revoliutsii"; Meyer, "Guide to the Archives of Eurasia."

41. Ganich, *Cherkesy v Iordanii*; Kasumov and Kasumov, *Genotsid adygov*; Kudaeva, *Ognem i zhelezom*; Kushkhabiev, *Cherkesskaia diaspora*; Kushkhabiev, *Cherkesy v Sirii*; Kushkhabiev, *Ocherki istorii zarubezhnoi cherkesskoi diaspory*; Polovinkina, *Cherkesiia*.

42. Borlakova, "Karachaevo-balkarskaia emigratsiia"; Dumanov, *Adygskaia i karachaevo-balkarskaia zarubezhnaia diaspora*; Kipkeeva, *Karachaevo-balkarskaia diaspora*.

43. Badaev, *Chechenskaia diaspora*; Garsaev and Garsaev, *Chechenskie mukhadzhiry*; Ibragimova, *Emigratsiia chechentsev*.

44. Abdullaeva, *Vnutripoliticheskaia situatsiia v Dagestane*; Magomeddadaev, *Emigratsiia dagestantsev*; Magomedkhanov, *Dagestantsy v Turtsii*; Murtazaliev, *Literatura dagestanskoi diaspory Turtsii*.

45. Aliev, "Severokavkazskaia diaspora"; Baderkhan, *Severokavkazskaia diaspora*.

46. On refugeedom and approaches to refugee history, see Banko, Nowak, and Gatrell, "What Is Refugee History, Now?"; Gatrell, "What's Wrong with History?"; Tejel and Öztan, "Forced Migration and Refugeedom."

47. See Gatrell et al., "Reckoning with Refugeedom."

48. Hamed-Troyansky, "Letters from the Ottoman Empire."

49. For inspiring use of private letters and family histories, see Stein, *Family Papers*; Alff, "Business of Property"; Seikaly, "Matter of Time."

Chapter 1: Muslim Migrations from the North Caucasus

1. Letter A (1910), Ahmed bin Saltmurad to Kerim-Sultan, Sultan Private Collection. I thank Farid F. Sultan for providing access to the collection. The Dagestani village of Keshen-Evla, on the border with Chechnya, is now called Chapaevo. In 1944, its Chechen population was deported to Central Asia, and it was repopulated with Laks.

2. Interview with Sultan in Zarqa', Jordan (17 August 2014).

3. Letter B (c. 1910–12), Hajj Janʿaq to Kerim-Sultan, Sultan Private Collection.

4. Letter C (c. 1910–12), Kerim-Sultan to Hajj Janʿaq, Sultan Private Collection.

5. On migration in Russian history, see Hoerder, "Migrations in Slavic, Tsarist Russian and Soviet History"; Randolph and Avrutin, *Russia in Motion*; Siegelbaum and Moch, *Broad Is My Native Land*; and on emigration, see Hillis, *Utopia's Discontents*.

6. Crews; *For Prophet and Tsar*, esp. 39–60; Crews, "Empire and the Confessional State."

7. On recent reevaluation of the Eastern Question, see Rodogno, *Against Massacre*; Ozavcı, *Dangerous Gifts*.

8. On histories of the South Caucasus, see Suny, *Looking toward Ararat*; Suny, *Making of the Georgian Nation*; Swietochowski, *Russian Azerbaijan*.

9. On the North Caucasus as an imperial frontier, see Barrett, *At the Edge of the Empire*; Barrett, "Lines of Uncertainty"; Khodarkovsky, *Russia's Steppe Frontier*; Yaşar, *North Caucasus Borderland*.

10. For an overview of the history of the Caucasus, see King, *Ghost of Freedom*; on the tsarist North Caucasus, see Bobrovnikov and Babich, *Severnyi Kavkaz*; on displacement in the North Caucasus, see Perović, *From Conquest to Deportation*. For classic works on the Caucasus War, see Baddeley, *Russian Conquest of the Caucasus*; Allen and Muratoff, *Caucasian Battlefields*.

11. On the origins and impact of Sufi movements in the North Caucasus, see Kemper, "North Caucasian Khalidiyya"; Knysh, "Sufism"; Zelkina, *In Quest for God and Freedom*. On anticolonial Sufi movements, see Motadel, *Islam and the European Empires*, 13–20.

12. On the Caucasus Imamate, see Gammer, *Muslim Resistance to the Tsar*; Kemper, "Khalidiyya Networks." On distinctions between *ghaza* and *jihād*, see Kafadar, *Between Two Worlds*, 79–80.

13. Sharafutdinova, *Araboiazychnye dokumenty*, letters 49–50, 65.

14. On Chechen, Dagestani, and Georgian experiences of colonialism and colonial resistance, see Gould, *Writers and Rebels*.

15. King, "Imagining Circassia"; Manning, "Just Like England." David Urquhart encouraged a Scottish merchant, James Stanislaus Bell, and a *Times* journalist, J.A. Longworth, to travel to Circassia in the 1830s; their accounts remain important sources on the pre-1864 Circassian society; Bell, *Residence in Circassia*; Longworth, *Year among Circassians*. For other travelers' accounts, see Taitbout de Marigny, *Three Voyages*; DuBois de Montpéreux, *Voyage autour du Caucase*.

16. Muhammad Amin (1818–1901), or Magomet Amin, was the third deputy of Imam Shamil in Circassia. After his surrender in 1859, he emigrated to Istanbul, spent some time in Egypt, and then settled in Bursa. He was appointed an annual Russian pension of 3,000 rubles and became an informant of the Russian government on Circassian political activities in the Ottoman Empire; Russian State Military Historical Archive (Rossiiskii gosudarstvennyi voenno-istoricheskii arkhiv, Moscow, hereafter cited as RGVIA) f. 38 (*fond*, collection), op. 7 (*opis'*, inventory), d. 396 (*delo*, file) (1861–63), ll. 25–29, 47 (or l., *list*, page[s]); see also Magomeddadaev, *Mukhammad-Amin*.

17. Fadeev, "Ubykhi," 174–79; Berzhe, Kobiakov, and Veidenbaum, *Akty sobrannye Kavkazskoi arkheograficheskoi komissiei*, vol. 12, no. 796, 798.

18. A Circassian delegation arrived in Istanbul in summer 1862, and two deputies visited Britain in October 1862; Brock, "Fall of Circassia," 412–14.

19. RGVIA f. 38, op. 7, d. 410, ll. 27–28ob (30 June 1862).

20. RGVIA f. 38, op. 7, d. 422, ll. 3–4 (11 January 1863), 5–50b (17 January 1863), as reported by Muhammad Amin. At the same time, a new Circassian delegation from the Caucasus arrived in Istanbul, where they declared Circassians to be subjects of the Ottoman sultan and asked the Porte to send them a governor; ibid., ll. 10–120b (sometime in 1862–63); Gugov, Kasumov, and Shabaev, *Tragicheskie posledstviia*, 56–72.

21. Brooks, "Conquest of the Caucasus."

22. *Akty sobrannye Kavkazskoi arkheograficheskoi komissiei*, vol. 12, no. 644 (Miliutin's note to the report on 29 November 1857); for Miliutin's proposal to resettle most Circassians on the Don River, see no. 642, 645 (1857).

23. Holquist, "To Count, to Extract, to Exterminate"; Sherry, "Social Alchemy."

24. The approved regulation was "Polozhenie o zaselenii predgorii zapadnoi chasti Kavkazskago khrebta Kubanskimi kazakami i drugimi pereselentsami iz Rossii" (10 May 1862); see also Miliutin, *Vospominaniia*, 474–76.

25. For other periodizations, see Bobrovnikov and Babich, *Severnyi Kavkaz*, 155–83; Habiçoğlu, *Kafkasya'dan Anadolu'ya Göçler*, 74–84.

26. Habiçoğlu, *Kafkasya'dan Anadolu'ya Göçler*, 75.

27. The Russian interpretation of the agreement was more liberal and assumed the Ottomans' continued responsibility for accepting North Caucasian Muslims; Karpat, "Status of the Muslim," 653n6; Bobrovnikov and Babich, *Severnyi Kavkaz*, 172.

28. The destruction of Circassian villages had proceeded already in 1857–59; *Akty sobrannye Kavkazskoi arkheograficheskoi komissiei*, 12:1283–86. On violence in the final years of the Caucasus War, see National Historical Archive of Georgia (Sakartvelos sakhelmtsipo saistorio arkivi, Tbilisi, hereafter cited as SSSA) f. 416, op. 3, d. 1148, ll. 40b–120b (1863); d. 1177, ll. 1–199 (1863); d. 1190, ll. 1–25 (1864).

29. Holquist, "To Count, to Extract, to Exterminate," 118.

30. Kumykov, *Vyselenie adygov v Turtsiiu*, 12–14, 47–87; *Akty sobrannye Kavkazskoi arkheograficheskoi komissiei*, vol. 12, no. 858, 889 (1862).

31. "O razreshenii tsaria vydelit' sredstva na raskhody po perevozke gortsev v Turtsiiu" (8 April 1864), in Gugov, Kasumov, and Shabaev, *Tragicheskie posledstviia*, 127.

32. For published Russian archival sources on Circassian displacement, see Gugov, Kasumov, and Shabaev, *Tragicheskie posledstviia*, 13–228; Kumykov, *Problemy Kavkazskoi voiny*; Dzamikhov, *Adygi*, 45–100.

33. Western Circassians in the Caucasus numbered around 571,000 in 1835, 52,100 in 1867, 45,100 in 1882, and 38,300 in 1897; Kabuzan, *Naselenie Severnogo Kavkaza*, 173, 198–99, 202–4.

34. The Turkish-Circassian newspaper *Jıneps* called for the adoption of the term *Tsitsekun* in 2014, during its commemoration of the 150th anniversary of Circassian displacement. "Tsitsekun," *Jıneps* (10 May 2014); etymology in Hans Vogt, *Dictionnaire de la langue oubykh* (Oslo: Universitetsforlaget, 1963), 99 (*c̣ac̣a*—people), 133 (*kʷ'*—to kill).

35. For an interpretation of the events of 1863–64 as a genocide, see Richmond, *Circassian Genocide*; Kasumov and Kasumov, *Genotsid adygov*.

36. SSSA f. 416, op. 3, d. 146 (1864); Kumykov, *Vyselenie adygov*, 21–47, 98–109; Kumykov, *Problemy Kavkazskoi voiny*, 2:142–67.

37. Fonvil', *Poslednii god voiny*, 45.

38. Kushkhabiev, *Cherkesy Sirii*, 27–28.

39. *Derby Mercury* (9 November 1864), 3; for another report, see Fratantuono, "Migration Administration," 164–65.

40. Karpat cites 500,000 dead, or a third of all Circassian muhajirs; "Status of the Muslim," 654. The British vice-consul in Trabzon reported the mortality of 50 percent in that port; The National Archives of the United Kingdom, Records of the Foreign Office (London, hereafter cited as TNA FO) 881/3065, Stevens to Bulwer, #20 (24 September 1864), f. 14.

41. I thank Peter Holquist for letting me consult his unpublished paper, "An 'Indispensable Precondition for the Region's Definitive Conquest': The Russian Expulsion of the Mountain Tribes from the Western Caucasus, 1859–1864." On the evolution of Russia's policy in the Northwest Caucasus in 1857–65, see Brooks, "Conquest of the Caucasus"; Holquist, "To Count, to Extract, to Exterminate," esp. 116–19; Kreiten, "Colonial Experiment in Cleansing"; Pinson, "Demographic Warfare," 85–124; Sherry, "Social Alchemy."

42. The Caucasus Viceroyalty existed in 1785–96, 1844–81, and 1905–17. Between 1881 and 1905, it was reorganized as the Caucasus Administration.

43. See Romaniello, *Elusive Empire*.

44. Fisher, "Emigration of Muslims," 356–57n3.

45. Pinson estimates 210,000–230,000 Crimean Tatar muhajirs; "Emigration of the Crimean Tatars," 109. Williams cites 200,000 muhajirs after 1856; "Hijra and Forced Migration," 79. Kozelsky estimates up to 200,000 muhajirs after the mid-1850s, peaking in 1860–63; "Crimean Tatars," 866. Kırımlı counts 20,000–25,000 muhajirs in 1855–1856/57; "Emigrations from the Crimea," 767.

46. Williams, *Crimean Tatars*, 184–89; see also Kırımlı, *Kırım Tatar ve Nogay Köy Yerleşimleri*.

47. See Özel, "Georgian Immigrants in Turkey."

48. Suny, "Eastern Armenians under Tsarist Rule," 112.

49. National Archives of Armenia (Hayastani Azgayin Arkhiv, Yerevan, hereafter cited as HAA) f. 1262, op. 1, d. 7II, l. 2160b (25 August 1880). For other estimates, see Badem, *Kars, Ardahan, Artvin*, 139–46.

50. Can, *Spiritual Subjects*, 149–74; Chokobaeva, Drieu, and Morrison, *Central Asian Revolt of 1916*, esp. 2, 179–80.

51. Robarts, *Migration and Disease*, 45; Meshcheriuk, *Pereselenie bolgar*, 94–96.

52. *Akty sobrannye Kavkazskoi arkheograficheskoi komissiei*, vol. 7, no. 830 (1831). Dana Sherry estimates that 130,000 Armenians and Greeks arrived in Russia from the Ottoman Empire and Iran in 1828–29; "Imperial Alchemy," 32.

53. HAA f. 94, op. 1, d. 207–8, 247, 500, 504 (1877–85); 976 (1885–94); Shavrov, *Novaia ugroza*, 63–64. On the Hamidian massacres, see Adjemian and Nichanian, "Massacres."

54. Shavrov, *Novaia ugroza*, 63.

55. Hacısalihoğlu, "Population Transfers," 33–41.

56. Pinson, "Demographic Warfare," 3, 146–48, 149; see also Bobrovnikov, "Mukhadzhirstvo v 'demograficheskikh voinakh.' "

57. The idea of a population exchange was widespread. The British consul in Trabzon referred to refugee migrations in 1864 as "the exchange which the Turkish Government is sanctioning between Greek and Circassian"; TNA FO 78/1832, Stevens to Russell, f. 101 (3 August 1864).

58. BOA A.MKT.UM 465/92 (5 şevval 1277, 16 April 1861).

59. BOA A.MKT.UM 459/3 (20 şevval 1277, 1 May 1861), in Gerov, *Dokumenti za Bŭlgarskata istoriia*, 404–5.

60. SSSA f. 11, d. 3239, l. 12 (1859); f. 545, op. 1, d. 2811, ll. 12–13 (1868).

61. See Blauvelt, "Military-Civil Administration."

62. Bobrovnikov and Babich, *Severnyi Kavkaz*, 204–9. On further comparison between Russian and British colonial rule, see Morrison, *Russian Rule in Samarkand*.

63. Bobrovnikov and Babich, *Severnyi Kavkaz*, 196–98, 200, 202–3.

64. Muslims' requests to emigrate from the Caucasus are preserved in BOA HR.SFR.1 129/53 (1902); SSSA f. 7, op. 1, d. 2694 (1872); f. 545, op. 1, d. 614–15 (1872); Central State Archive of the Republic of North Ossetia-Alania (Tsentral'nyi gosudarstvennyi arkhiv Respubliki Severnaia Osetiia-Alaniia, Vladikavkaz, hereafter cited as TsGA RSO-A) f. 12, op. 2, d. 963–65, 968–70, 1039, 1045–46, 1057–63 (1890s); Central State Archive of the Republic of Kabardino-Balkaria (Tsentral'nyi gosudarstvennyi arkhiv Kabardino-Balkarskoi Respubliki, Nalchik, hereafter cited as TsGA KBR) f. I-6, op. 1, d. 331 (1895); Central State Archive of the Republic of Dagestan (Tsentral'nyi gosudarstvennyi arkhiv Respubliki Dagestan, Makhachkala, hereafter cited as TsGA RD) f. 2, op. 2, d. 84–85 (1899–1901), d. 92 (1914); op. 6, d. 13 (1900–1910); f. 126, op. 4, d. 3–4 (1869–70).

65. National Archive of the Republic of Azerbaijan (Azərbaycan Respublikası Dövlət Tarix Arxivi, Baku, hereafter cited as ARDTA) f. 45, op. 2, d. 110 (1871), 114–15 (1871–74); f. 291, op. 1, d. 1642 (1894); HAA f. 1262, op. 1, d. 7i–ii (1878–81); op. 3, d. 130 (1906–7), 256 (1907); SSSA f. 5, op. 1, d. 622 (1868); f. 7, op. 1, d. 313 (1867–69), 718 (1868), 2695 (1872).

66. On Russian land reforms in Kuban Province, see SSSA f. 545, op. 1, d. 27 (1861); in Terek Province, SSSA f. 1087, op. 2, d. 201 (1869); TsGA KBR f. I-2, op. 1, d. 739 (1865–67); f. I-40, op. 1, d. 4 (1863–67); North Ossetian Institute for Research in Humanities and Social Sciences (Severo-Osetinskii institut gumanitarnykh i sotsial'nykh issledovanii, Vladikavkaz, hereafter cited as SOIGSI) f. 16, op. 1, d. 41 (1867–74); in Sukhum Department, SSSA f. 416, op. 3, d. 1021 (1870–72); throughout the region, Bobrovnikov and Babich, *Severnyi Kavkaz*, 211–28.

67. SSSA f. 416, op. 3, d. 118 (1865).

68. TsGA KBR f. I-40, op. 1, d. 7, ll. 69–71.

69. Kasaba, *Moveable Empire*, 103–22.

70. Gugov, Kasumov, and Shabaev, *Tragicheskie posledstviia*, 165.

71. Troinitskii et al., *Obshchii svod po Imperii*, vol. 2, table 13; Tsutsiev, *Atlas*, 39–44.

72. SSSA f. 545, op. 1, d. 16 (1861); f. 5, op. 1, d. 195 (1865); f. 12, op. 3, d. 147 (1904); RGVIA f. 38, op. 7, d. 398 (1861–62); Tsutsiev, *Atlas*, 45–47.

73. For Russian colonization in the North Caucasus, see Sherry, "Imperial Alchemy";

in the South Caucasus, see Breyfogle, *Heretics and Colonizers*; and empire-wide, see Etkind, *Internal Colonization*; Sunderland, *Taming the Wild Field*.

74. Werth, *Tsar's Foreign Faiths*, esp. 46–73. On the government's hierarchy of faiths in the Caucasus, see Hamed-Troyansky, "Becoming Armenian."

75. See Werth, *Tsar's Foreign Faiths*, 150–53; Breyfogle, *Heretics and Colonizers*, 4, 164–69.

76. "Po voprosu zaseleniia vostochnogo berega Chernogo moria" (3 November 1864), in Kumykov, *Problemy Kavkazskoi voiny*, 2:247–56, quote on 253.

77. Ibid., 254–55; Sherry, "Social Alchemy," 22–27, esp. 25.

78. HAA f. 1262, op. 1, d. 71, ll. 66–75 (6 February 1879), 76–790b (4 February 1879). On the complex relationship between the Russian government and Armenians, see Riegg, *Russia's Entangled Embrace*.

79. "O pereselenii gortsev v Turtsiiu" (16 April 1893), in Gugov, Kasumov, and Shabaev, *Tragicheskie posledstviia*, 320–22.

80. For example, in discussing Muslim emigration in 1903, the Caucasus authorities described Circassians, Dagestanis, Kurds, Azerbaijanis, and other Muslims leaving for the Ottoman Empire as *pereselenets* and *emigrant*, and Ottoman Armenians arriving in Russia as *bezhenets*; SSSA f. 12, op. 2, d. 469 (1903). The term *bezhenets* was in widespread use by World War I; see Gatrell, *Whole Empire Walking*, 12–13.

81. SSSA f. 416, op. 3, d. 315 (1866).

82. Black slaves were present in Abkhazia and Kabarda as late as the 1860s; TsGA KBR f. 2, op. 1, d. 665 (1862–63); f. 24, op. 1, d. 7 (1852–67); Blakely, *Russia and the Negro*, 5–12.

83. Dzidzariia, *Vosstanie 1866 goda*, 31–33.

84. Moon, "Reassessing Russian Serfdom."

85. On preparing abolitionist legislation for western Circassians, see SSSA f. 7, op. 8, d. 9; f. 416, op. 3, d. 307, 309, 312–15, 317–19; Terek Cossacks: d. 320; Kabardians: d. 122–23, 321–23; Ossetians: d. 324, 1054; Chechens: d. 325; Kumyks: d. 326; Abkhazians: d. 1019; and Dagestanis: d. 1034.

86. On Russia's abolitionism in the Caucasus, see Salushchev, "Reluctant Abolitionists"; Kumykov, *Sotsial'no-ekonomicheskie otnosheniia*; Kurtynova-D'Herlugnan, *Tsar's Abolitionists*; and in Central Asia, see Eden, *Slavery and Empire*.

87. SSSA f. 416, op. 3, d. 311 (1864); TsGA RSO-A f. 53, op. 1, d. 772, l. 97 (1867).

88. On agricultural Circassian slavery, see Toledano, *Slavery and Abolition*, 81–111, estimate on 84.

89. TNA FO 195/934, Blunt to Elliot, #12 (Edirne, 23 February 1871); FO 195/1405, Bennet to Dufferin, #12 (Kayseri, 17 July 1882).

90. Harris, *Last Slave Ships*.

91. National Archive of the Russian Federation (Gosudarstvennyi arkhiv Rossiiskoi Federatsii, Moscow, hereafter cited as GARF) f. 677, op. 1, d. 511, ll. 7–10; SSSA f. 416, op. 3, d. 1305, l. 13 (1876).

92. On the uprising of Kunta Hajji of 1864, see SSSA f. 416, op. 3, d. 617–19 (1864); TsGA RSO-A f. 12, op. 6, d. 1248–49 (1864–79); Bennigsen, "Qadiriyah (Kunta Hajji) Tariqah."

93. On the emigration of 1865, see Hamed-Troyansky, "Population Transfer." For published Russian archival sources on emigration from Terek Province in 1863–67, see Dzagurov, *Pereselenie gortsev v Turtsiiu*, 7–148.

94. Karabulaks, or Orstkhoy, are related to Ingush and Chechens. Most Karabulaks were pushed toward emigration to the Ottoman Empire, and their lands were distributed among Cossack troops. By 1865, 6,187 Karabulaks left for the Ottoman Empire; Badaev, *Chechenskaia diaspora*, 101. In the Soviet era, the remaining Karabulaks were claimed as a subgroup within both the Ingush and Chechen "nationalities."

95. Musa Kundukhov (1818–89), who received 10,000 rubles from the Russian government for organizing emigration, decided to stay in the Ottoman Empire and settled in Sivas Province. In 1867, the Ottomans appointed him a major general (*mirliva*), and, in the Russo-Ottoman War of 1877–78, he led a 4,000-strong Circassian cavalry unit against the Russian army on the Anatolian front, then briefly commanded the Anatolian army and took charge of Erzurum after the end of the Russian occupation of the city; see Kundukhov, "Memuary Generala Musa-Pashi Kundukhova"; Chochiev, "General Musa Kundukhov"; Perović, *From Conquest to Deportation*, 53–74. In his final years, while based in Erzurum, he agreed to become an informant to the British on developments in the Russian Caucasus; TNA FO 195/1652, Chermside to White, #21 (16 June 1889), ff. 166–69.

96. Dzidzariia, *Vosstanie 1866 goda*.

97. On the Abkhazian emigration of 1867, see Dzidzariia, *Makhadzhirstvo*, 278–95; SSSA f. 545, op. 1, d. 191 (1866–67).

98. On the Abkhazian emigration of 1877, see Dzidzariia, *Makhadzhirstvo*, 356–80. Bezhan Khorava estimates 31,964 emigrants from Abkhazia in 1877; *Mukhadzhirstvo abkhazov*, 78.

99. Bobrovnikov and Babich, *Severnyi Kavkaz*, 167.

100. For example, SSSA f. 416, op. 3, d. 1132, ll. 8–9 (9 March 1874); Abramov, "Kavkazskie gortsy." On Russian reforms in the North Caucasus, see Bobrovnikov and Babich, *Severnyi Kavkaz*, 184–210, 211–28; Richmond, *Northwest Caucasus*, 81–103; see also on the Southeast Caucasus: Mostashari, *On the Religious Frontier*.

101. SSSA f. 5, op. 1, d. 622, ll. 3–6 (14 December 1868); GARF f. 102, op. 52, d. 31, ch. 2, ll. 10b (20 January 1895); TsGA RD f. 2, op. 6, d. 13, ll. 2–3 (1 February 1900).

102. Mikhail S. Totoev, "Materialy po pereseleniiu gortsev v Turtsiiu (1941)," in SOIGSI f. 17, op. 1, d. 27, l. 38.

103. TsGA RD f. 2, op. 9, d. 16, ll. 96–990b (2 August 1912).

104. Totoev, "Materialy po pereseleniiu gortsev," in SOIGSI f. 17, op. 1, d. 28, l. 28.

105. Fahmy, *All the Pasha's Men*, 99–103, 260–63; Sharkey, *Muslims, Christians, and Jews*, 164.

106. "Ob uvedomlenii gortsev, chto pereseliat'sia v Turtsiiu massami okonchatel'no zapreshchaetsia" (15 October 1865), in Gugov, Kasumov, and Shabaev, *Tragicheskie posledstviia*, 214–15; "Ob otkaze sodeistvovat' Porte v dal'neishem pereselenii abkhaztsev i abadzekhov v Turtsiiu" (20 September 1867), in ibid., 228.

107. Meyer, "Russian Muslims in the Ottoman Empire," 19–20; Meyer, *Turks across Empires*, 25.

108. Gugov, Kasumov, and Shabaev, *Tragicheskie posledstviia*, 228.

109. Sherry, "Social Alchemy," 22–24, 27–29; see also Barrett, "Land Is Spoiled by Water."

110. For example, Gugov, Kasumov, and Shabaev, *Tragicheskie posledstviia*, 26–30 (1860), 221–22 (1865).

111. The *zagranichnyi pasport* was valid for one foreign trip and was used outside, not inside, Russia. In addition to, or in lieu of, a passport, Russian officials sometimes issued a ticket of leave (*otpusknoi* or *uvol'nitel'nyi bilet*), which allowed its carrier to travel away from their place of work or residence.

112. "O pravilakh vozvrashcheniia gortsev iz Turtsii" (19 May 1861), in Kumykov, *Problemy Kavkazskoi voiny*, 1:122–23.

113. On Russian debates about Muslim emigration in the 1870s, see Bobrovnikov and Babich, *Severnyi Kavkaz*, 173–75; and about the hajj, see Kane, *Russian Hajj*, 61–66; Brower, "Russian Roads to Mecca," 569–70.

114. SSSA f. 7, op. 1, d. 2694, l. 7 (2 September 1872).

115. On the emigration policies of 1872, see SSSA f. 7, op. 1, d. 2694, ll. 43–46 (27 December 1872). The authorities delayed publicizing the new regulations until the end of the harvest season in 1873, expecting that Muslim communities would abandon their fields and leave; d. 2694, l. 69 (15 August 1873).

116. "Proekt pravil o pereselenii gortsev v Turtsiiu" (1876), in Gugov, Kasumov, and Shabaev, *Tragicheskie posledstviia*, 235–37; "O pereselenii gortsev v Turtsiiu" (1893), in ibid., 320–22.

117. The pattern applied to others. By the late nineteenth century, between 50 and 90 percent of Russia's emigrants, most of whom were Jews and Germans, left without authorization; Lohr, *Russian Citizenship*, 95.

118. "Pravila otnositel'no vozvrashchaiushchikhsia iz Turtsii kavkazskikh pereselentsev" (June 1861), in Kumykov, *Problemy Kavkazskoi voiny*, 1:124–29.

119. Kumykov, *Problemy Kavkazskoi voiny*, 1:156–57 (20 April 1862).

120. "O pravilakh vozvrashcheniia gortsev iz Turtsii" (19 May 1861), in Kumykov, *Problemy Kavkazskoi voiny*, 1:122–23.

121. "Pravila otnositel'no vozvrashchaiushchikhsia iz Turtsii kavkazskikh pereselentsev" (June 1861); RGVIA f. 38, op. 7, d. 382, ll. 64–64ob (26 July 1861), 148–51 (29 May 1862).

122. "O poriadke emigratsii gortsev" (23 March 1861), in Kumykov, *Problemy Kavkazskoi voiny*, 1:118.

123. The administration of the Caucasus Viceroyalty reaffirmed the ban on the return of any North Caucasians, for example, in 1867; TsGA KBR f. I-2, op. 1, d. 964, l. 2 (13 January 1867).

124. Hamed-Troyansky, "Letters from the Ottoman Empire."

125. Gutman, *Armenian Migration*, 21–22, 34–42.

126. In the imperial context, I use *denaturalization* to encompass the modern meanings of both *denaturalization* (of naturalized citizens) and *denationalization* (of citizens by birth).

127. Lohr, *Russian Citizenship*, 100–114.

128. Tukholka, *Russkie poddannye v Turtsii*, 1–5.

129. Lohr, *Russian Citizenship*, 91, 113.

130. Instruction of Russia's Ministry of Foreign Affairs to Ambassador to the Porte Lobanov-Rostovskii (1861); RGVIA f. 38, op. 7, d. 382, ll. 15–18 (undated, summer 1861), in Gugov, Kasumov, and Shabaev, *Tragicheskie posledstviia*, 40–42.

131. Instructions of 1899 in TsGA KBR f. I-6, op. 1, d. 693, ll. 67–68 (8 March 1907), in Gugov, Kasumov, and Shabaev, *Tragicheskie posledstviia*, 415–16.

132. "Pravila otnositel'no vozvrashchaiushchikhsia iz Turtsii kavkazskikh pereselentsev" (June 1861).

133. Russia's Penal Code of 1845, art. 354; Penal Code of 1885, art. 325.

134. Meyer, *Turks across Empires*, 34–36; Meyer, "Russian Muslims in the Ottoman Empire," esp. 23–27; Can, "Protection Question."

135. Smiley, "Burdens of Subjecthood"; Can, *Spiritual Subjects*, 101, 107–11.

136. Kane, *Russian Hajj*, 62–64.

137. Here I disagree with Meyer's claim that "the Russian authorities continued to recognize as Russian subjects virtually all Muslims who left the country"; "Russian Muslims in the Ottoman Empire," 26.

138. Lohr, *Russian Citizenship*, 145–51.

139. Arendt, *Origins of Totalitarianism*, 269, 276–79.

140. Marrus, *Unwanted*, 96, 172–74, 178–79.

141. Several scholars cautioned against generalizing Russia's policies toward Muslims and noted the harshness of policies in the Caucasus, as shaped by the Caucasus War; Crews, *For Prophet and Tsar*, 12, 15; Meyer, *Turks across Empires*, 34, 51.

142. Among the emigrating parties after 1878 were (a) at least 5,000 Karachays and 2,000 Balkars in 1884–87; Kipkeeva, *Karachaevo-balkarskaia diaspora*, 29; (b) around 6,000 Kabardians by 1890; ibid., 29; (c) 16,573 western Circassians in 1888–95; Kasumov and Kasumov, *Genotsid adygov*, 189; including 9,100 in 1890; BOA DH.MKT 1749/28 (21 *zilhicce* 1307, 8 August 1890); (d) 16,000 Kabardians and about 1,500–2,000 Chechens in 1895; Badaev, *Chechenskaia diaspora*, 227; (e) up to 4,000 Chechens, Kabardians, and Balkars in 1900–1902; *Cherkesy v Sirii*, 31, 71; Badaev, *Chechenskaia diaspora*, 227; (f) over 1,000 Ingush in 1904; Badaev, *Chechenskaia diaspora*, 221; (g) 1,454 Kabardians and 600 Dagestanis, in 1905; Kushkhabiev, *Cherkesy v Sirii*, 72–73, 161; (h) about 5,000 Karachays and over 2,000 Balkars in 1905–6; Kipkeeva, *Karachaevo-balkarskaia diaspora*, 52; (i) 700 Chechen families in 1905–6; Ibragimova, *Chechenskii narod*, 393; and (j) about 2,000 Ingush and Chechens in 1912; Badaev, *Chechenskaia diaspora*, 227.

143. Berzhe "Vyselenie gortsev," 4.

144. Salaheddin Bey, *La Turquie*, 213, 216–17.

145. Dzidzariia, *Makhadzhirstvo*, 420.

146. For western Circassians, Berzhe cites that 470,753 muhajirs left from the Circassian coast in 1858–65, according to the Russian military data, which he acknowledged to be an incomplete number; of them, 436,103 were western Circassians; "Vyselenie gortsev," 7–9. After the war, at least 27,990 more left: 11,417 in 1871–83; 3,421 in 1888; 9,153 in 1890; and 3,999 in 1895; Dzidzariia, *Makhadzhirstvo*, 417; Kasumov and Kasumov, *Genotsid adygov*, 189. The minimum total for western Circassians is 464,093. For an upper estimate, I use Salaheddin Bey's Ottoman data that, in 1855–66, 1,008,000 "Tcherkesses," comprising Muslims from the Caucasus and Crimea, had entered the Ottoman Empire; *La Turquie*, 213, 216–17. From that number, I subtract 200,000 Crimean Tatars of 1856–62 and 23,057 Muslims of Terek Province of 1865, and I add 27,990 western Circassians that left between 1871 and 1895, for the total of 812,933. For eastern Circassians, Kumykov cites

60,000 Kabardians for the total period; *Vyselenie adygov*, 17. Berzhe cites 4,000 Besleneys in 1858–64; "Vyselenie gortsev," 7. For Abkhazians and Abazins, Habiçoğlu cites 50,000 muhajirs in 1858–79, which is an underestimate if only because he counts 8,000–10,000 refugees until 1864, whereas the Russian military data suggest 30,000 Abazins in 1858–64; *Kafkasya'dan Anadolu'ya Göçler*, 89; Berzhe, "Vyselenie gortsev," 7. Fisher cites 100,000 Abkhazian muhajirs in 1859–64 and 14,500 "Abaza" muhajirs in 1861–63; "Emigration of Muslims," 363. Dzidzariia estimates 135,000 Abkhazian and Abazin muhajirs in the 1860s and 1870s; *Makhadzhirstvo*, 373. Aydemir counts over 145,000 Abkhazian muhajirs in 1858–79; *Göç*, 113–14. For Nogai Tatars, Habiçoğlu cites 30,000 Kuban Nogai muhajirs in 1858–63, which is an undercount because Russian officials recorded 30,650 muhajirs in 1858–60 alone; *Kafkasya'dan Anadolu'ya Göçler*, 87; SSSA f. 416, op. 3, d. 146, l. 60b (1864). Karpat estimates that 46,000–50,000 Nogai Tatars emigrated in 1856–60; *Ottoman Population*, 66. Kipkeeva cites 70,000 Nogai muhajirs in 1858–66; *Severnyi Kavkaz*, 357. For Karachays and Balkars, Borlakova estimates 10,000 Karachay and Balkar muhajirs, including 3,000 Karachays and 1,000 Balkars in 1884–93 and 4,000 Karachays and 2,000 Balkars in 1901–7; "Karachaevo-balkarskaia emigratsiia," 16. Kipkeeva provides the total of 14,000 Karachay and Balkar muhajirs in the 1884–87 and 1905–6 periods; *Karachaevo-balkarskaia diaspora*, 29, 52. Laipanov cites 15,756 Karachay muhajirs overall, with migration peaks in 1887, 1894, and 1905–6; "K istorii pereseleniia gortsev," 114. For Chechens and Ingush, Bobrovnikov and Babich cite 40,000 Chechen and Ingush muhajirs; *Severnyi Kavkaz*, 179. Habiçoğlu estimates fewer than 45,000 Chechen and Ingush muhajirs between 1863 and 1901; *Kafkasya'dan Anadolu'ya Göçler*, 86. Ibragimova suggests 90,000 muhajirs for 1865 alone, while acknowledging that the available archival evidence does not support this number; *Emigratsiia chechentsev*, 43. For Ossetians, Chochiev cites 5,000 muhajirs; "Anatolian Ossetians," 105. Kushkhabiev estimates 10,000 Ossetian muhajirs; *Cherkesy v Sirii*, 31. For Dagestanis, Magomeddadaev estimates that 20,000–25,000 muhajirs emigrated between the 1820s and the 1920s; *Emigratsiia dagestantsev*, 2:85. Habiçoğlu cites 20,000 Dagestani muhajirs in 1847–1907; *Kafkasya'dan Anadolu'ya Göçler*, 85–86.

147. For comparison, Karpat estimates that between 1859 and 1879 up to two million people, mostly Circassians, left the Caucasus for the Ottoman Empire, but only 1.5 million survived and were resettled. In 1881–1914, 500,000 more Circassians and Crimean Tatars arrived; *Ottoman Population*, 69–70. McCarthy estimates that 1.2 million Muslims left the North Caucasus and 800,000 survived the journey, including 600,000 in 1856–64 and 200,000 after 1864; *Death and Exile*, 36, 53n45. Kushkhabiev holds the number of muhajirs from the North and West Caucasus to have been at least 1.5 million; *Cherkesy v Sirii*, 33. Habiçoğlu counts 600,000 North Caucasians who reached the Ottoman Empire between 1855 and 1907; *Kafkasya'dan Anadolu'ya Göçler*, 73. For other overviews of demographic estimates, see Fisher, "Emigration of Muslims," 362–64; Habiçoğlu, *Kafkasya'dan Anadolu'ya Göçler*, 70–73; Jersild, *Orientalism and Empire*, 25–27, 171–72n102; Kushkhabiev, *Cherkesy v Sirii*, 31–34.

148. Berzhe "Vyselenie gortsev," 6.

149. RGVIA f. 13453, op. 15, d. 343, ll. 112–13 (March 1860).

150. On rare works emphasizing hijra, see Karpat, "Hijra from Russia and the Balkans"; Williams, "Hijra and Forced Migration."

151. Khodarkovsky, *Bitter Choices*, 148.

152. Kemper, "Khalidiyya Networks," 50–51.

153. On the uprisings of 1877, see Aitberov, Dadaev, and Omarov, *Vosstaniia dagestantsev i chechentsev*.

154. Toumarkine, "Entre Empire ottoman et État-nation turc," 356–73.

155. GARF f. 102, op. 47, d. 314, ll. 232–47 (1896); Kane, *Russian Hajj*, 47–53, 82–84.

156. Russian officials insisted that the hajj stimulated North Caucasian Muslims' desire to emigrate to the Ottoman Empire and considered the hajj an impediment to the consolidation of Russian rule in the Caucasus; SSSA f. 416, op. 3, d. 672 (1872), f. 545, op. 1, d. 966 (1873).

157. Interview with Farid F. Sultan in Zarqa', Jordan (17 August 2014). On *mücavirin*, see Can, *Spiritual Subjects*, 161–72.

158. Tsarist and Soviet historiography regarded Ottoman emissaries as main instigators of Muslim emigration, as reflected in reports by the Caucasus authorities; SSSA f. 11, d. 3239, l. 12 (1859); f. 416, op. 3, d. 1115 (1864); GARF f. P5235, op. 4, d. 504 (1903–18). Meanwhile, the Ottomans and the British complained of "Russian emissaries" who propagandized emigration to Russia among Ottoman Greeks and Armenians; TNA FO 195/1315, Clayton to Layard, ff. 216–17 (Van, 22 November 1880), 252–53 (Van, 2 November 1880); FO 195/953, Palgrave to Villiers, ff. 27–28 (Trabzon, 4 February 1869).

159. Dzidzariia, *Makhadzhirstvo*, 373.

160. Cuthell, "Muhacirin Komisyonu," 134–37; for example, BOA A.MKT.MHM 239/39 (1862); MVL 646/69 (1863); İ.MVL 486/22044 (1863).

161. Gutov et al., *Adygskie pesni*, 606–8.

162. My translation of the Russian-language version. Excerpted from Gutov et al., *Adygskie pesni*, 601–5; see other Circassian songs of lament about leaving for the Ottoman Empire in ibid., 582–89, 598–610.

Chapter 2: Ottoman Refugee Regime

1. BOA A.MKT.MHM 520/8, in Gurulkan, *Osmanlı Belgelerinde Kafkas Göçleri*, 1:532, 534 (4 *ağustos* 1318, 17 August 1902).

2. Ibid., 1:532–33, 535 (8 *cemaziyelahir* 1320, 12 September 1902).

3. See Benbassa and Rodrigue, *Sephardi Jewry*.

4. Robarts, *Migration and Disease*, 14–18.

5. Eren, *Türkiye'de Göç*, 50–54.

6. The government enacted the Silistre Ordinance of 1856 to alleviate the refugee crisis in the Balkan ports; Saydam, *Kırım ve Kafkas Göçleri*, 82–85, 102–5; Eren, *Türkiye'de Göç*, 41–49.

7. For the text of the Ottoman Immigration Law of 1857, see "Conditions arrêtées par le Gouvernement Impérial au sujet de la colonisation en Turquie," in Aristarchi Bey, *Législation ottomane*, 1:16–19; BOA HR.İD 24/23, f. 3 (1 *recep* 1273, 25 February 1857).

8. BOA HR.İD 24/2–10 (1857–59); Karpat, *Ottoman Population*, 62–63.

9. Fratantuono, "Producing Ottomans," 1–2.

10. For the text of the Ottoman Land Code, see Fisher, *Ottoman Land Laws*; BOA TK.GM.d 2535 (7 *ramazan* 1274, 21 April 1858).

11. Kaufman, *Pereselenie i kolonizatsiia*, 24–30.

12. See White, *It's Your Misfortune*, 137–54.

13. For pathbreaking works on the Ottoman Refugee Commission, see Cuthell, "Muhacirin Komisyonu"; Fratantuono, "Migration Administration."

14. On the first Circassian refugee crisis, in 1863–65, see Cuthell, "Circassian Sürgün"; Çiçek, "Talihsiz Çerkesleri İngiliz Peksimeti"; Grassi, *Nuova patria*; Şaşmaz, "Immigration and Settlement of Circassians."

15. Archive of Foreign Policy of the Russian Empire (Arkhiv vneshnei politiki Rossiiskoi imperii, Moscow, hereafter cited as AVPRI) f. 180, op. 517/2, d. 2603, ll. 266–67 (Trabzon, 26 December 1863).

16. *Papers Respecting the Settlement of Circassian Emigrants in Turkey*, 11 (Trabzon, 19 May 1864).

17. AVPRI, f. 161, I-9, op. 8, d. 19, ll. 127–28 (Trabzon, 10 June 1864).

18. *The Times* (13 June 1864), 10, col. 4.

19. *Russkii invalid*, no. 129 (11 June 1864).

20. Kocacık, "Balkanlar'dan Anadolu'ya Yönelik Göçler," 168; Cuthell, "Circassian Sürgün," 163.

21. The Oriental Collection at the SS. Cyril and Methodius National Library (Natsionalna biblioteka "Sv. Sv. Kiril i Metodii," Sofia, hereafter cited as NBKM) 22/733 (3 *mayıs* 1286, 3 May 1870).

22. On origins of the modern refugee regime in the interwar Middle East, see Robson, *States of Separation*, 35–64; Watenpaugh, *Bread from Stones*, esp. 157–82.

23. On the interwar refugee regime, see Skran, *Refugees in Inter-War Europe*; Frank and Reinisch, "Refugees and the Nation-State."

24. The contemporary refugee regime does not offer equal protections to all in practice. On its Cold War–era iteration for citizens of the socialist bloc, see Keely, "International Refugee Regime(s)." On limited protections for Palestinian refugees, see Akram, "Palestinian Refugees."

25. Malkki, "Refugees and Exile."

26. On Muslim emigration from Russia, see chapter 1, esp. 48–49.

27. McCarthy, *Death and Exile*, 90, 113. The exact numbers are disputed: İpek estimates that, by 1879, the Ottoman Empire hosted 1.23 million Muslim refugees from the Balkans; *Türk Göçleri*, 41; Karpat cites 1.5 million refugees of the war of 1877–78; *Ottoman Population*, 75.

28. Karpat, *Ottoman Population*, 55.

29. Toumarkine, *Populations musulmanes balkaniques*, 33.

30. Ibid., 35–36; see also Peçe, "Island Unmixed."

31. al-Arnaut, "Islam and Muslims in Bosnia," 234n5.

32. İpek, *Türk Göçleri*, 154.

33. McCarthy counts almost 2.5 million Muslim refugees in 1856–1914 and 2.85 million Muslim refugees and internally displaced persons in 1914–22; *Death and Exile*, 339. Karpat cites five to seven million immigrants, mostly Muslims, in the Ottoman Empire between 1860 and 1914; "*Hijra* from Russia and the Balkans," 691. Quataert estimates five to seven million Muslim immigrants between 1783 and 1913; "Age of Reforms," 2:793.

For other works on Muslim refugees in the late Ottoman era, see Emgili, *Boşnakların Türkiye'ye Göçleri*; Erkan, *Kırım ve Kafkasya Göçleri*; İpek, *Türk Göçleri*; Halaçoğlu, *Türk Göçleri*; Saydam, *Kırım ve Kafkas Göçleri*; Şimşir, *Rumeli'den Türk Göçleri*; Toumarkine, *Populations musulmanes balkaniques*.

34. On Ottoman Christians' immigration in Russia, see chapter 1: 33–34.

35. Manasek, "Protection, Repatriation and Categorization."

36. Gutman, *Armenian Migration*, 4.

37. Fahrenthold, *Between the Ottomans and the Entente*, 6.

38. On the early modern Ottoman caliphate, see Casale, *Ottoman Age of Exploration*, 117–51; Yılmaz, *Caliphate Redefined*.

39. On the Hamidian caliphate, see Deringil, "Legitimacy Structures"; Özcan, *Pan-Islamism*.

40. See Aydın, *Idea of the Muslim World*; Hassan, *Longing for the Lost Caliphate*.

41. The exact date of the establishment of the Commission for Muslim Refugees is disputed. Its statute was adopted only in 1905; Erdem, *Muhacir Komisyonları ve Faaliyetleri*, 137–38. Karpat dates it to 1897; "Status of the Muslim," 663.

42. On the institutional history of the Commission, see Dündar, "How Migration Institutions 'Think' "; Erdem, *Muhacir Komisyonları ve Faaliyetleri*. For the Commission's statute of 1878, see BOA İ.MMS 59/2786 (2 *şubat* 1295, 1 August 1878), transliterated in Eren, *Türkiye'de Göç*, 96–116; of 1897, see İ.DH 1352/8 (3 *recep* 1315, 28 November 1897), summarized in Erdem, *Muhacir Komisyonları ve Faaliyetleri*, 132–34; of 1905, see summary in ibid., 139–40; and of 1913, see summary in ibid., 59–62.

43. The Commission for Tripoli Refugees (Trablusgarp Mülteci Komisyonu, 1911–13) and the Mixed Commission for Population Exchange (Muhtelit Mübadele Komisyonu, 1914).

44. Saydam, *Kırım ve Kafkas Göçleri*, 105–19.

45. On the Commission's ordinances and instructions, see BOA İ.MMS 22/961 (2 *zilkade* 1277, 12 May 1861), transliterated in Gurulkan, *Osmanlı Belgelerinde Kafkas Göçleri*, 1:58–63; İ.MVL 541/24269 (18 *cemaziyelevvel* 1282, 9 October 1865); Y.PRK.KOM 1/26 (30 *rebiülevvel* 1295, 3 April 1878); A.DVN.MKL 18/10 (29 *zilhicce* 1296, 14 December 1879).

46. BOA Y.PRK.DH 2/93 (29 *zilhicce* 1305, 6 September 1888), transliterated in Gurulkan, *Osmanlı Belgelerinde Kafkas Göçleri*, 1:148–70; see also Fratantuono, "State Fears," 107.

47. Tsarist officials reported that Muslims in the Northwest Caucasus knew of the Ottoman government's free land allotments as early as 1859; SSSA f. 11, op. 1, d. 3239, l. 12 (19 November 1859).

48. Hamed-Troyansky, "Letters from the Ottoman Empire."

49. See Ben-Bassat, *Petitioning the Sultan*.

50. For the term *Ottoman humanitarianism*, see Chatty, "Refugees, Exiles, and Other Forced Migrants," 42–44.

51. BOA A.MKT.UM 390/1 (c. 1860), in Kushkhabiev, *Istoriia adygov*, 78–79.

52. Kushkhabiev, *Cherkesy v Sirii*, 28.

53. *The Free Press: Journal of the Foreign Affairs Committees* 12, no. 8 (3 August 1864): 66, col. 2.

54. Rosser-Owen, "First 'Circassian Exodus,'" 47–49.

55. On late Ottoman charity and patriotism, see Özbek, "Philanthropic Activity." On the Hamidian ideology, see Deringil, *Well-Protected Domains*.

56. Erdem, *Muhacir Komisyonları ve Faaliyetleri*, 142–47. Donations for refugees were often publicized in Ottoman periodicals; see Dobreva, "Çerkes Tehcirinin Medyaya Yankısı."

57. İpek, *Türk Göçleri*, 74–77.

58. On Ottoman refugee charity organizations, see Fratantuono, "Migration Administration," 54–58.

59. On muhajir as an administrative status, see Fratantuono, "State Fears."

60. See Cuthell, "Muhacirin Komisyonu," 127–64.

61. BOA HR.İD 24/11–21 (1863–76).

62. Braude, "Foundation Myths of the Millet System."

63. Ottoman officials sometimes applied the term *muhacir* to non-Muslims, such as Russian Cossacks in Bulgaria or German farmers in Libya—BOA A.MKT.MHM 232/34 (1862); HR.TO 33/18 (1887)—but those were exceptions to regular usage.

64. For example, Kale, "Transforming an Empire," 253. Fratantuono proposes to view Ottoman policies toward different muhajirs as "tiered systems of rights and aid"; "State Fears," 101.

65. BOA HR.İD 24/13 (11 February 1864).

66. Norman, *Outstretched Arm*, 21, 54–68, 106–8.

67. For the text of the Law of Ottoman Nationality (19 January 1869), see Kern, *Imperial Citizen*, 157–58.

68. For rich scholarship on Ottoman citizenship, see Can and Low, "'Subjects' of Ottoman International Law"; Can et al., *Subjects of Ottoman International Law*; Hanley, "Ottoman Nationality"; on Russian citizenship: Burbank, "Imperial Rights Regime"; David-Fox, Holquist, and Martin, "Subjecthood and Citizenship"; Lohr, *Russian Citizenship*; and on comparative citizenship, see Akçasu, "Laws on Nationality"; Hanley, *Identifying with Nationality*, esp. 53–66; Rizk and Glebov, "Late Ottoman and Russian Empires."

69. For example, BOA Y.MTV 290/143 (1906), in Gurulkan, *Osmanlı Belgelerinde Kafkas Göçleri*, 2:375–77.

70. BOA MVL 103/27 (23 şaban 1319, 5 October 1901); A.MKT.MHM 524/29 (18 muharrem 1322, 4 April 1904).

71. For example, ARDTA f. 45, op. 1, d. 35, ll. 17–23 (1901–2).

72. On the unfulfilled Ottoman plan to settle Circassians in the province, and then subprovince, of Benghazi in the 1880s and 1890s, see Adamiak, "To the Edge of the Desert," 62–88.

73. BOA DH.MKT 8/44 (2 *nisan* 1301, 14 April 1885), in Kushkhabiev, *Istoriia adygov*, 128.

74. In 1860, the Ottoman government agreed not to settle muhajirs near the Russian border; Pinson, "Demographic Warfare," 121. In 1865, it reaffirmed its policy; SSSA f. 545, op. 1, d. 97, ll. 27–30, 184–89 (1865). On general resettlement policy in eastern Anatolia, see Chochiev and Koç, "Migrants from the North Caucasus in Eastern Anatolia."

75. I am particularly grateful to Murat Papşu, who shared with me his digital map of villages and a list of Sivas villages. For a list of villages in Turkey, see İbrahim Sediyani, "Türkiye'deki Çerkes Köyleri" (6 September 2008), www.circassiancenter.com/cc-tur kiye/arastirma/0500-cerkeskoyleri.htm. Chirikba identifies 228 Abkhazian and Abazin villages, some of which now have Circassian ethnic majorities; "Rasselenie abkhazov i abazin v Turtsii." For Ossetian villages, see Chochiev, "Anatolian Ossetians," 125.

76. BOA İ.DH 460/30579 (26 *muharrem* 1277, 14 August 1860); Karpat, "Ottoman Urbanism."

77. The Ottomans also used model settlements to sedentarize nomads. In the 1860s, its special fighting force Fırka-i İslahiye built four towns and thirty-five villages near the Gavur (Nur) Mountains in southern Anatolia; Kasaba, *Moveable Empire*, 101–2. In the mid-1860s, Ottoman authorities in Diyarbakır proposed to build an ambitious "string of settlements" for Chechen muhajirs between Ra's al-'Ayn and Deir az-Zor, across almost 2,000 square kilometers in northeastern Syria; Adamiak, "To the Edge of the Desert," 195–97. Ultimately, Chechens settled only in Ra's al-'Ayn; TNA FO 195/889, ff. 6–18r (Diyarbakır, 15 January 1867).

78. Mitchell, *Colonising Egypt*, 44–48, 92–93.

79. On Ottoman muhajir villages, see İpek, "Göçmen Köylerine Dair"; Dündar, *İskan Politikası*, 201–13.

80. On different types of settlement by the Commission, see Cuthell, "Muhacirin Komisyonu," 187–88.

81. On the economic objective in refugee resettlement, see Rogan, *Frontiers of the State*, 70–94; Karpat, *Ottoman Population*, 76–77; Lorenz, "Second Egypt."

82. Saydam, *Kırım ve Kafkas Göçleri*, 199–203.

83. Kocacık, "Balkanlar'dan Anadolu'ya Yönelik Göçler," 168.

84. Gutman, "Travel Documents."

85. On *mevat* lands, see Gratien, "Ottoman Quagmire."

86. Dobreva, "Circassian Colonization in the Danube Vilayet," 17.

87. Kocacık, "Balkanlar'dan Anadolu'ya Yönelik Göçler," 168, 178; Dündar, *İskan Politikası*, 193, 198; see also İpek, *Türk Göçleri*, 221–23.

88. See Adamiak, "To the Edge of the Desert," esp. 17–61; Rogan, *Frontiers of the State*, 21–43.

89. On the antinomadic objective in refugee resettlement, see Lewis, *Nomads and Settlers*, 100–101; Klein, *Margins of Empire*, 206n169; Haghandoqa, *Circassians*, 40–42; Dolbee, "Empire on the Edge," 141–43.

90. On "Ottoman settlerism" and refugees, see Lorenz, "Empire of Frontiers."

91. On territoriality in Middle Eastern history, see Schayegh, *Making of the Modern World*, esp. 340–41; Robson, *Politics of Mass Violence*, 6–7.

92. Karpat, "Status of the Muslim," 654; Baderkhan, *Severokavkazskaia diaspora*, 45–46.

93. Konstantin D. Petkovich, a Russian vice-consul in Beirut in 1869–96, believed that the Ottoman government sought to settle Circassians in Syria to "counter Arab Muslims, whom it did not trust, with new Muslim fanatics"; Kushkhabiev, *Cherkesy v Sirii*, 63–64. Henry D. Barnham, a British consul in Aleppo, thought that the Ottomans settled Circassian muhajirs around Manbij and in Raqqa to create "a force on whose

fidelity the Sultan can rely in the event of a serious rising of the Syrian Arabs against his authority"; TNA FO 195/2213, Barnham to O'Conor, #1 (Aleppo, 1 January 1906).

94. Makdisi, "Ottoman Orientalism"; Deringil, "They Live in a State of Nomadism."

95. Chochiev, "North Caucasian Diaspora in Turkey," 216.

96. Kasaba, *Moveable Empire*, 18–19.

97. İnalcık, "Policy of Mehmed II"; Barkan, "Sürgünler."

98. See Cuthell, "Circassian Sürgün"; Hacısalihoğlu, *1864 Kafkas Tehciri*. The Soviet deportation of Crimean Tatars in 1944 is known as *sürgün* in Turkish and *sürgünlik* in Crimean Tatar.

99. Kasaba, *Moveable Empire*, 71–72.

100. BOA A.MKT.MHM 302/3 (1864), 302/68 (1864).

101. Schweig, "Tracking Technology and Society," 154.

102. Haghandoqa, *Mirza Pasha Wasfi*, 31.

103. On the war of 1877–78, see Yavuz and Sluglett, *Russo-Turkish War of 1877–1878*.

104. On counting people in the late Ottoman Empire, see Dündar, *Crime of Numbers*; Hacısalihoğlu, "Borders, maps, and Censuses"; and in Russia, see Holquist, "To Count, to Extract, to Exterminate."

105. In 1858–62, the Ottoman government settled 30,000 Circassians around Zeitun, Maraş, and Haçin and allegedly instigated muhajir clashes with Armenians, in which it backed Muslim newcomers; Avakian, Cherkesskii faktor, 177; Astourian, "Silence of the Land," 72.

106. İpek, *Türk Göçleri*, 155–59, 176–79, 205–7; Terzibaşoğlu, "Land Disputes," 163.

107. Terzibaşoğlu, "Land Disputes," 170.

108. İpek, *Türk Göçleri*, 158; Karpat, *Ottoman Population*, 86.

109. See Greble, *Muslims and the Making of Modern Europe*, esp. 91–92, 119–22. The anti-Muslim refugee rhetoric persisted in diplomacy. Thus, in negotiations on the administration of the eastern provinces, into which Russia forced the Ottoman Empire in 1913–14, the Russians insisted on the exclusion of muhajirs from resettlement in *Vilayat-ı Sitte*. The Porte succeeded in removing this demand from the final draft; Reynolds, *Shattering Empires*, 73–77.

110. National Archives and Records Administration (College Park, Maryland, hereafter cited as NARA) RG 59, Notes from the Turkish Legation in the United States to the Department of State, 1867–1906, 188282009, T-815, roll 7, f. 639: "Violations of the Hatti Humayoun" (12 February 1895), f. 15; Despatches from U.S. consuls in Erzurum, 1895–1904, 196007085, T-568, roll 2, f. 212: Leo Bergholz to David J. Hill, no. 199 (8 August 1902); Despatches from U.S. consuls in Sivas, 1886–1906, 212451686, T-681, roll 2, f. 355: Milo A. Jewett to David J. Hill, no. 151 (2 August 1902); Klein, *Margins of Empire*, 149.

111. BOA Y.PRK.KOM 4/54 (15 *teşrin-i sani* 1300, 27 November 1884), translated and cited in Fratantuono, "Producing Ottomans," 13–14.

112. BOA.Y.A.HUS 198/69 (26 *rebiülahir* 1304, 22 January 1887), cited in Fratantuono, "Migration Administration," 206; also, Karpat, "Status of the Muslim," 661–63.

113. On the early objection to the immigration of foreign Jews, see Mandel, "Restrictions on Jewish Settlement," 312–13. Ottoman Jews, fleeing former Ottoman territories, were allowed to immigrate freely until 1899, when the Ottoman government restricted

settlement in Palestine to both non-Ottoman and Ottoman Jews; Karpat, "Jewish Population Movements," 152, 156.

114. Karpat, "Settlement in Palestine," 794–96.

115. In practice, the Ottoman government could not enforce its restrictions on Jewish immigration in Palestine; Mandel, "Jewish Settlement in Palestine." The arrival of new Jewish refugees came at a time when the Ottoman Jewish community prepared to celebrate the 400th anniversary of refuge in 1492; see Cohen, *Becoming Ottomans*, 48–62.

116. Mandel, "Restrictions on Jewish Settlement," 314–15.

117. Karpat, *Ottoman Population*, 160.

118. Karpat, *Ottoman Population*, 72, 188–89.

119. Klein, "Making Minorities."

120. Karpat, *Politicization of Islam*, 328–52.

121. On the Committee of Union and Progress, see Hanioğlu, *Preparation for a Revolution*; Ahmed, *Young Turks*.

122. Hanioğlu, *Young Turks in Opposition*, 71–72, 168–69.

123. On Pan-Islamism and Pan-Turkism, and their limits, in Ottoman foreign policy, see Can, *Spiritual Subjects*, 20–23, 178–80; Reynolds, *Shattering Empires*, 18, 122–23, 129–30; Reynolds, "Buffers, Not Brethren."

124. For example, Jews from the Russian Empire and Romania were occasionally called muhajirs (*Musevi* or *Yahudi muhacirler*); BOA İ.DH 1295 1/101862 (1880); BEO 2/113 (1892); BEO 3302/247585 (1908). By the late 1910s, Ottoman officials, failing to see the hypocrisy, sometimes used the term *muhacir*, which had originally denoted one's persecution and desire to preserve their faith, to describe Armenian and Greek deportees and survivors of the genocide; BOA DH.ŞFR 545/11 (1917); DH.ŞFR 601/81 (1918); DH.UMVM 159/65 (1919).

125. Saydam, "1849 Macar-Leh Mültecileri Meselesi."

126. *İskan-ı Muhacirin Nizamnamesi* (13 May 1913), art. 2–4.

127. Dündar, *İskan Politikası*, 227–44.

128. In 1909, the Ottoman government reaffirmed that North Caucasian muhajirs should have their Russian subjecthood revoked before arriving in the Ottoman Empire; BOA MV 126/51 (23 *rebiülevvel* 1327, 14 April 1909).

129. In the Balkan Wars of 1912–13, the Ottoman Empire lost 83 percent of its territory and 69 percent of its population in Europe. On the wars, see Öztan, "Point of No Return"; Yavuz and Blumi, *Balkan Wars*.

130. Terzibaşoğlu, "Land Disputes," 170.

131. On Ottoman demographic, or social, engineering, see Dündar, *Modern Türkiye'nin Şifresi*; Sigalas and Toumarkine, "Demographic Engineering"; Üngör, "Seeing Like a Nation-State." On the CUP designs for North Caucasians, see Dündar, *İskan Politikası*, 130–34.

132. Üngör, "Seeing Like a Nation-State," 22–23.

133. On *Teşkilat-ı Mahsusa*, see Safi, "History in the Trench"; Reynolds, *Shattering Empires*, 121. On Eşref Kuşçubaşı (1883–1964), a prominent Circassian member of the organization, see Fortna, *Circassian*.

134. For a foray into the rich scholarship on the Armenian genocide, see Akçam, *Young*

Turks' Crime against Humanity; Kévorkian, *Armenian Genocide*; Suny, Naimark, and Göçek, *Question of Genocide*.

135. Avakian, *Cherkesskii faktor*, 236–43; Bloxham, "Development of the Armenian Genocide," 271, 403n74; Kévorkian, *Armenian Genocide*, 435–49, 800–831; Mugerditchian, *Diyarbekir Massacres*, 23, 26–27, 45–49.

136. Dündar argues that "during the First World War, the aim of the Unionist demographic policy was to find land for homeless refugees from the Balkans [which] meant evacuating certain areas where 'troublesome' Armenians lived"; *Crime of Numbers*, 2. Klein also finds that the CUP did not want to restore lands usurped by local aghas to Kurdish and Armenian peasants because it intended to use these lands to settle Kurdish nomads and Circassian immigrants; *Margins of Empire*, 165–66. On connections between Muslim immigration and Christian displacement, see Ferrara and Pianciola, "Dark Side of Connectedness."

137. Morack, *Dowry of the State*, 44–48, 78–79, 83–104.

138. On dispossession of Ottoman Christians, see Kurt, *Armenians of Aintab*; Üngör and Polatel, *Confiscation and Destruction*.

139. See Karpat, *Ottoman Population*, 57; Cuthell, "Muhacirin Komisyonu," 16–17, 263–64.

Chapter 3: Inequality and Sectarian Violence in the Balkans

1. NBKM 169/1534 (11 *eylül* 1290, 23 September 1874).

2. On Europe's "questions," see Case, *Age of Questions*.

3. On economic origins of sectarian conflict, see Terzibaşoğlu, "Landlords, Nomads, and Refugees," 117–58; Blumi, *Ottoman Refugees*, 17–42.

4. Habiçoğlu, *Kafkasya'dan Anadolu'ya Göçler*, 159–62; İpek, *Türk Göçleri*, 174–80.

5. On North Caucasians in Danube Province, see Dobreva, "Circassian Colonization in the Danube Vilayet"; Dobreva, "Circassian Settlements in the Kaza of Lom and of Belogradçik"; Dobreva, "Çerkeslerin Nüfus Yapısı ve İktisadi Etkinlikleri"; Muchinov, "Circassian Refugees in the Danube Vilayet"; Balkanski, *Cherkezite v bŭlgarskite zemi*; Pinson, "Circassians in Rumili."

6. Muchinov, "Circassian Refugees in the Danube Vilayet," 85. Karpat estimates the Circassian population of Danube Province at a quarter million; *Ottoman Population*, 68.

7. On demography in Danube Province, see Angelova, *Demografsko razvitie na Bŭlgarskoto Chernomorsko kraibrezhie*; Koyuncu, "Tuna Vilayeti'nde Nüfus ve Demografi"; Todorov, *Balkan City*, 340–65.

8. Museum of the Bulgarian Renaissance (Muzeĭ na Vŭzrazhdaneto, Varna, hereafter cited as MnV) f. 5 (*fond*, collection), op. 2 (*opis*, inventory), a.e. 23 (*arkhivna edinitsa*, archival unit), no. 1619, #27 (24 August 1867), ll. 2036–38 (or l., *list*, page[s]).

9. Kanitz, "Die Tscherkessen Emigration," 240; also, Dobreva, "Circassian Settlements in the Kaza of Lom and Belogradçik," 106.

10. See Koç, "Tuna Vilayeti Göçmenleri"; Petrov, "Tanzimat for the Countryside."

11. Muchinov, "Circassian Refugees in the Danube Vilayet," 87.

12. NBKM 22/274a (1874).

13. The Ottoman government implemented the same policy for Crimean Tatar muhajirs in 1860; Saydam, *Kırım ve Kafkas Göçleri*, 128.

14. Karpat, "Ottoman Family"; Cherkasov et al., "Demographic Characteristics," 384.

15. Dobreva, "Çerkeslerin Nüfus Yapısı ve İktisadi Etkinlikleri," 54–55.

16. Çadırcı, "Muhtarlık Teşkilâtının Kurulması."

17. *Tuna*, no. 67 (24 April 1866); also, Dobreva, "Circassian Colonization in the Danube Vilayet," 18.

18. Ottoman Land Code of 1858, art. 131.

19. Terzibaşoğlu, "Landlords, Nomads, and Refugees," 129.

20. Tonev et al., *Izvori za istoriiata na Dobrudzha*, 4:44. On the history of Dobruja, see Dimitrov, Zhechev, and Tonev, *Istoriia na Dobrudzha*.

21. On Crimean Tatars in Dobruja, see Karpat, "Ottoman Urbanism," estimate on 212; Williams, *Crimean Tatars*, 196–226.

22. Karpat, "Ottoman Urbanism," 222.

23. For example, NBKM 169/1517 (26 *nisan* 1288, 8 May 1872).

24. NBKM 169/1511 (9 *kanun-ı evvel* 1281, 21 December 1865); 172/50–51 (31 *kanun-ı evvel* 1281, 12 January 1866); 172A/84 (1281).

25. NBKM Maçin (hereafter, a location after NBKM denotes "pre-collection" funds), 172/87, f. 72a, no. 25 (14 *muharrem* 1289, 24 March 1872).

26. NBKM 169/2955, f. 22b, no. 46 (12 *nisan* 1287, 24 April 1871).

27. Loupouleskou, "Russkie kolonii v Dobrudzhe," 149, 153.

28. NBKM 169/1511.

29. NBKM Tulça 55/20, f. 37b, no. 36 (11 *mart* 1289, 23 March 1873).

30. NBKM Maçin 172/87, f. 72a, no. 25.

31. NBKM Tulça 55/20, f. 37b, no. 36.

32. NBKM Maçin 172/87, f. 75b, no. 48 (22 *muharrem* 1289, 1 April 1872).

33. NBKM Tulça 57/1, ff. 1, 20 (15 *şevval* 1288, 28 December 1871), f. 22 (22 *şevval* 1288, 4 January 1872).

34. NBKM 169/1553 (5 *nisan* 1293, 17 April 1877).

35. Circassians even had a conflict with Greek monks of Mount Athos over land or, to be precise, Circassians' squatting on monastery-owned land; *Levant Herald* (11 December 1867), 341–42, in NARA RG 59/188270786, Notes from the Greek Legation in the United States to the Department of State.

36. For example, NBKM OAK Collection 172/86, p. 9a, no. 64 (1870); 170/321 (1873); 170A/238 (1873).

37. On *tapu*, see Minkov, "Ottoman *Tapu* Title Deeds."

38. Dobreva, "Çerkeslerin Nüfus Yapısı ve İktisadi Etkinlikleri," 70.

39. Peirce, *Imperial Harem*, 57–149, 229–65.

40. On racialized Ottoman slavery, see Troutt Powell, *Tell This in My Memory*; Walz and Cuno, *Race and Slavery in the Middle East*.

41. Frost, *Never One Nation*, 56–85.

42. Toledano, *Slavery and Abolition*, 112–34.

43. For example, TNA FO 195/901, Blunt to Elliot, #8 (Edirne, 25 January 1868), ff. 64–64r.

44. Toledano, *Slavery and Abolition*, 85–95; Cuthell, "Muhacirin Komisyonu," 240–46. Reportedly, the governor of Trabzon attempted to suppress slave trade in the Circassian refugee camp of Sarıdere near Trabzon but backed down when threatened with a rebellion; *Kavkaz* 53 (12 July 1864), 313.

45. MnV f. 5, op. 2, a.e. 23, no. 1621, #65 (26 August 1870), ll. 2258–60.

46. TNA FO 195/901, Blunt to Elliot, #8 (Edirne, 25 January 1868), f. 65r.

47. Dzidzariia, *Makhadzhirstvo*, 231.

48. On relations between the Ottoman government, Circassian slaveholders, and their slaves, see Toledano, *As If Silent and Absent*, 108–52; Karamürsel, "In the Age of Freedom."

49. Toledano, *As If Silent and Absent*, 95.

50. Ottoman land registers occasionally spelled out that those muhajirs who had not received land were enslaved; NBKM 170/81 (1874). See also TNA FO 195/934, Blunt to Elliot, #12 (Edirne, 23 February 1871), ff. 9641–42.

51. Smiley, "Burdens of Subjecthood."

52. NBKM Tulça 54/20 (8 *kanun-ı sani* 1292, 20 January 1877).

53. NBKM 169/1551 (9 *şubat* 1292, 21 February 1877).

54. TNA FO 195/937, Sankey to Dalyell, #13 (Köstence, 29 May 1871), f. 461.

55. *Pravo* 8, no. 21 (6 August 1873): appendix. Other recorded incidents include a Circassian slave riot in Mandira, Edirne, in 1866 and Circassian slaveholders' retaliation against their slaves' requests for freedom in Çorlu, Tekfurdağı, in 1874; Toledano, *Slavery and Abolition*, 95–96, 100.

56. NBKM 170A/221 (3 *kanun-ı sani* 1292, 15 January 1877); see also Karamürsel, "Transplanted Slavery," 706.

57. TNA FO 195/934, Blunt to Elliot, #18 (Edirne, 25 April 1870).

58. Iakimov, "Vŭzrozhdenskiiat pechat za cherkezite," 74.

59. See Gingeras, *Sorrowful Shores*, 29–30, 33–34; Saraçoğlu, *Governance in Ottoman Bulgaria*, 146–64; Yelbaşı and Akman, "Chechens in Mardin."

60. MnV f. 5, op. 2, a.e. 23, no. 1619, #87 (17 October 1869), ll. 2184–94.

61. Palairet, *Balkan Economies*, 62–63; see also Lampe and Jackson, *Balkan Economic History*, 138–39.

62. NBKM 169/1538 (9 *tişrin-i evvel* 1291, 21 March 1875).

63. Shaw and Shaw, *Ottoman Empire and Modern Turkey*, 2:156.

64. Quataert, "Age of Reforms," 2:773; see also Birdal, *Ottoman Public Debt*.

65. NBKM 175/46 (27 *ağustos* 1289, 8 September 1873), 22/293 (9 May 1874).

66. For example, NBKM Badagağ 9/12 (25 *mayıs* 1293, 6 June 1877).

67. NBKM 22/289 (8 *mart* 1288, 20 March 1872); 22A/333 (26 *nisan* 1286, 8 May 1870).

68. NBKM 170A/128 (20 *muharrem* 1283, 4 June 1866); 173/308 (17 *zilhicce* 1290, 5 February 1874).

69. Dobreva, "Circassian Colonization in the Danube Vilayet," 18.

70. NBKM 169/3010 (14 *ağustos* 1289, 26 August 1873).

71. The Ottoman Public Benefits Bank became the Agricultural Bank (*Ziraat Bankası*) in 1887. As of 2023, it remains state-owned and is Turkey's largest bank by total assets.

72. Dobreva, "Circassian Settlements in the Kaza of Lom and Belogradçik," 125.

73. Other taxes included a military tax for non-Muslims, an animal tax, a sales tax for agricultural produce, and a road construction tax.

74. NBKM 170A/169, no. 2, 4 (1 *mayıs* 1292, 13 May 1876).

75. NBKM 170A/169, no. 1, 3 (2 *mayıs* 1292, 14 May 1876).

76. Dobreva, "Circassian Colonization in the Danube Vilayet," 19–20.

77. For published data on other Danubian districts, see Draganova, *Materiali za Dunavskiia vilaet.*

78. NBKM 172A/127 (2 *mart* 1290, 14 March 1874).

79. The first state-sanctioned militias of Circassian and Crimean Tatar muhajirs had formed already during the tenure of Midhat Paşa (1864–68); Pletn'ov, *Midkhat Pasha,* 193–94.

80. Exact numbers of fatalities in 1876 are unknown and disputed. Eugene Schuyler, U.S. consul in Istanbul, who had visited the region after the atrocities, claimed that sixty-five Christian villages were destroyed and 15,000 people were killed; "Mr. Schuyler's Preliminary Report on the Moslem Atrocities" (10 August 1876), in MacGahan and Schuyler, *Turkish Atrocities in Bulgaria,* 89–94.

81. See Rodogno, *Against Massacre,* 141–69.

82. NBKM Babadağ 9/13 (1868); 20/823 (1871).

83. Şimşir, *Rumeli'den Türk Göçleri,* 1:122–23; Tonev et al., *Izvori za istoriiata na Dobrudzha,* 3:306–7; 4:210–12, 308–12, 343–49, 362–67, 371–73, 383–93.

84. Tonev et al., *Izvori za istoriiata na Dobrudzha,* 4:389–93, 398–405.

85. Kanitz in 1882, cited in Saraçoğlu, *Governance in Ottoman Bulgaria,* 153.

86. NBKM OAK 36/37 (11 *mayıs* 1293, 23 May 1877).

87. Şimşir, *Rumeli'den Türk Göçleri,* 1:130–31, 172–73, 178–81, 199–200, 350; NBKM Varna 24/22 (11 *haziran* 1294, 13 June 1878).

88. NBKM IIA.2892 (29 May 1864). I thank Gergana Georgieva for sharing this document with me.

89. Central State Archive of Bulgaria (Tsentralen dŭrzhaven arkhiv, Sofia, hereafter cited as TsDA) f. 159K, op. 1, a.e. 26, ll. 12–120b (17 May 1880).

90. General Staff Military History and Strategic Studies Archive (T.C. Genelkurmay Başkanlığı Askeri Tarih ve Stratejik Etüt Arşivi, Ankara, hereafter cited as ATASE) ORH (Osmanlı-Rus [1293] Harbi) 32/23 (13 March 1877); 42/160 (30 April 1877); see also Beşikçi, "Başıbozuk Savaşçıdan 'Makbul' Tebaaya."

91. ATASE ORH 3/162 (4 July 1877); 20/33 (1 September 1877); Hotko, "Russian-Turkish War," 224–25.

92. ATASE OSK (Osmanlı-Sırp-Karadağ Harbi) 17/151 (24 February 1877); ORH 1/12 (29 April 1877); see also Kushkhabiev, *Cherkesy v Sirii,* 36.

93. ATASE ORH 1/132 (29 April 1877); 1/188 (9 June 1877); 51/23 (30 May 1877); Koliubakin, *Russo-Turetskaia voina,* 1:67. Reportedly, Musa Paşa promised the Ottomans to recruit 15,000 Circassians; TNA FO 195/1140, Zohrab to Elliot, #54 (Erzurum, 1 May 1877) ff. 203–4; #58 (Erzurum, 4 May 1877), ff. 217–18.

94. ATASE ORH 2/3 (15 May 1877); 130/753 (23 May 1877); TNA FO 195/1140, Zohrab to Elliot, #67, f. 268 (Erzurum, 17 May 1877).

95. Chochiev, "General Musa Kundukhov," 73.

96. GARF f. 102, op. 242, d. 74, ch. 36, list B, l. 3 (1912); Avakian, *Cherkesskii faktor*, 167–68. On the Hamidiye regiments, renamed the Tribal Light Cavalry Regiments in 1909, see Klein, *Margins of Empire*.

97. Aydemir estimates that out of half a million displaced Muslims, 300,000 were Circassians; *Göç*, 141.

98. Ovsianyi, *Sbornik materialov*, 5:22–26.

99. For example, in 1880, Romania mandated that Muslim refugees could retain their property if they returned to northern Dobruja within three years, counted from 1878; in 1882, the same principle was reaffirmed with a one-year return window; Hunt, "Muslims of Dobruca," 151, 155. Likewise, in 1880, Serbia set the short deadline of one year for Muslim absentee landowners to reclaim their land; Radovanović, "Contested Legacy," 127–34, 167.

100. "Zakon za cherkezkite i tatarskite zemi" (14 December 1880) in TsDA f. 159K, op. 1, a.e. 5, ll. 29–32; revision (1 March 1883), in f. 159K, op. 1, d. 5; a.e. 66, ll. 16–19.

101. Treaty of Berlin (13 July 1878), art. 12.

102. On Bulgarian peasants' petitions for restitution of Circassian lands after 1878, see Hamed-Troyansky, "Imperial Refuge," 102–5.

103. TsDA f. 159K, op. 1, a.e. 107, ll. 73–84 (1886).

104. State Archive, Dobrich Branch (Dŭrzhaven arkhiv, Dobrich, Bulgaria) f. 181K, op. 1, a.e. 1, ll. 60–600b, 62–620b (November 1879); TsDA f. 159K, op. 1, a.e. 26, ll. 12–120b (1880).

105. Koyuncu, "Tuna Vilayeti'nde Nüfus ve Demografi," 717, 726; Genov, *Bulgaria and the Treaty of Neuilly*, 161.

106. "Lege pentru regularea proprietățeі imobilare in Dobrogea" (31 March 1882).

107. National Archive of Romania, Tulcea Branch (Direcția Județeană Tulcea a Arhivelor Naționale) 156/28: survey in the former subprovince of Tulça; 173/112: the villages of Balabanca (Balabancea) and Cafarka (Giaferca).

108. Todorov, *Iuzhna Dobrudzha*, 13.

109. Karpat, *Ottoman Population*, 199; Iordachi, *Making of Romanian Citizens*, 477–83.

110. "Zakon o uređenju agrarnih odnošaja u novo-oslobođenii predelima" (3 February 1880), in *Leskovački zbornik* 21 (1981): 9–13 of the appendix. On property in post-Ottoman Niš, see Radovanović, "Contested Legacy."

111. Jagodić, *Naseljavanje Kneževine Srbije*, 79–93; Jagodić, "Emigration of Muslims."

112. Hunt, "Muslims of Dobruca," 197–99.

113. Petitions are preserved in BOA HR.MHC.02 collection (c. 1903–7).

114. On Muslims in the Balkans after 1878, see Amzi-Erdoğdular, *Afterlife of Ottoman Europe*; Greble, *Muslims and the Making of Modern Europe*; Methodieva, *Between Empire and Nation*; Mirkova, *Muslim Land, Christian Labor*.

Chapter 4: Real Estate and Nomadic Frontier in the Levant

An earlier version of this chapter appeared as the article "Circassian Refugees and the Making of Amman, 1878–1914," *International Journal of Middle East Studies* 49, no. 4 (2017): 605–23. Reprinted with permission of Cambridge University Press.

1. On North Caucasians in Jordan, see Abujaber, *Pioneers over Jordan*, 197–216; Ganich, *Cherkesy v Iordanii*; Garsaev, *Chechenskie mukhadzhiry*; Lewis, *Nomads and Settlers*, 96–123. For Jordanian-Circassian accounts, see Batsaj, *al-Mawsuʿa al-Tarikhiyya li-l-Umma al-Sharkasiyya*, vol. 5; Haghandoqa, *Circassians*; Nashkhu, *Tarikh al-Sharkas (al-Adigha) wa-l-Shishan*. On Circassian identity in Jordan, see Shami, "Ethnicity and Leadership"; Shami, "Identity Formation."

2. On histories of Amman, see Hacker, *Modern ʿAmman*; Hanania, "From Colony to Capital" (2010); Hanania, "From Colony to Capital" (2019); al-Hmoud, *ʿAmman wa Jiwaruha*; al-Shaʿr and al-Hmoud, *ʿAmman fi al-ʿAhd al-Hashimi*.

3. Court records for Salt District are preserved at the Center of Documents and Manuscripts (Markaz al-Wathaʾiq wa-l-Makhṭūṭāt, University of Jordan, Amman, hereafter cited as CDM). For the catalogue of court records, see Muhammad ʿAdnan Bakhit, *Kashshaf Ihsaʾi Zamani li-Sijillat al-Mahakim al-Sharʿiyya wa-l-Awqaf al-Islamiyya fi Bilad al-Sham* (Amman: University of Jordan, 1984), and for published Amman court records, see Qazan, *ʿAmman fi Matlaʿ al-Qarn al-ʿAshrin*. Ottoman land registers for Salt District are kept at the Department of Land and Survey (Dairat al-Arāḍi wa al-Masāḥa, Amman, hereafter cited as DLS). For the catalogue of land registers, see Hind Abu al-Shaʿr, *Sijillat al-Aradi fi al-Urdun, 1876–1960* (Amman: al-Bayt University, 2002).

4. Habiçoğlu, *Kafkasya'dan Anadolu'ya Göçler*, 143–50.

5. For numbers of Circassian refugees in 1878–80, see Hamed-Troyansky, "Imperial Refuge," 115–16.

6. According to Russian consular data, by September 1878, 45,090 muhajirs were present on the Syrian coast, of them around 20,000 earmarked for Aleppo Province; Kushkhabiev, *Cherkesy v Sirii*, 159. According to Ottoman sources, by September 1879, 26,713 refugees from the Balkans, chiefly Circassians, had been sent to Damascus Province and 15,709 to Aleppo Province from Istanbul alone; BOA Y.A.HUS 162/43 (7 şevval 1296, 24 September 1879).

7. Şimşir, *Rumeli'den Türk Göçleri*, 1:357.

8. NBKM 282A/200 (27 teşrin-i sani 1294, 9 December 1878); NBKM 279A/2299 (21 kanun-ı sani 1295, 2 February 1880); 287Ar/11 (24 şubat 1295, 7 March 1880).

9. NBKM 286Ar/60 (1878–81).

10. Şimşir, *Rumeli'den Türk Göçleri*, 1:544; Kushkhabiev, *Cherkesy v Sirii*, 67–68.

11. Şimşir, *Rumeli'den Türk Göçleri*, 1:351–52.

12. Ibid., 542–44.

13. NBKM 279A/358 (28 eylül 1294, 10 October 1878).

14. Maksimov, *Dve voiny*, 574.

15. See, for Quneitra, BOA A.MKT.MHM 169/66 (10 rebiülahir 1276, 6 November 1859); for Aleppo villages, A.MKT.MHM 203/14 (5 cemaziyelahir 1277, 19 December 1860); for Nablus villages, A.MKT.NZD 336/57 (11 cemaziyelahir 1277, 25 December 1860).

16. On the Chechen settlement in Raʾs al-ʿAyn, see Hamed-Troyansky, "Population Transfer"; Adamiak, "To the Edge of the Desert," 177–223; Dolbee, *Locusts of Power*, 45–49.

17. Kushkhabiev, *Cherkesy v Sirii*, 65; Lewis, *Settlers and Nomads*, 117, 119. Several Dagestani villages were established near Hama as early as 1865; BOA İ.MMS 50/2155 (15 şaban 1291, 27 September 1874).

18. Kushkhabiev, *Cherkesy v Sirii*, 65; Lewis, *Nomads and Settlers*, 104–5.

19. Rogan, *Frontiers of the State*, 72; see also Saliba, "Achievements of Midhat Pasha."

20. Lewis, *Nomads and Settlers*, 115–23; Habiçoğlu, *Kafkasya'dan Anadolu'ya Göçler*, 172–73.

21. Chochiev, "Rasselenie severokavkazskikh immigrantov," 102–3; also, Aydemir, *Göç*, 171.

22. On the history of Salt, see Dawud, *al-Salt wa Jiwaruha*.

23. Khuraysat, *al-Salt, al-Fuhays, al-Rumaymin*.

24. Rogan, "Turkuman of al-Ruman"; Rogan, *Frontiers of the State*, 45–47.

25. I use dates from Lewis, *Nomads and Settlers*, 115–17; Abujaber, *Pioneers over Jordan*, 215. Hanania dates Sweileh and Sukhna to, respectively, 1907 and 1912; "From Colony to Capital" (2010), 69–70. Fischbach dates Jerash to 1878; *State, Society, and Land in Jordan*, 12. All villages were in Salt District, except Jerash in 'Ajlun District and Lajjun in Karak District. In 1932, Chechen muhajirs established a new settlement in the oasis of Azraq.

26. Rogan, *Frontiers of the State*, 76n26.

27. Oliphant, *Land of Gilead*, 251–57. In 1880, Oliphant lobbied the Ottoman government to allow Jewish settlement in the Balqa'. The Ottoman Council of Ministers rejected Oliphant's proposal; Buzpınar, "Ottoman Response." European and American travel accounts are invaluable in piecing together the early years of Amman. On travel accounts of Ottoman Amman, see Hamarneh, "Amman in British Travel Accounts"; Hanania, "From Colony to Capital" (2010), 56–70.

28. Sahillioğlu, "Amman *Vilayet*"; Hanania, "From Colony to Capital" (2019), 2–3.

29. According to one oral recollection, the first settlers were Shapsugh refugees from Ottoman Bulgaria, who, having arrived in Acre, were sent inland to Nablus and its environs for temporary settlement. A group of refugees then moved eastward and, after crossing the Jordan River, sent out scouting expeditions to locate an appropriate location for a permanent settlement. Two horsemen first arrived at the ruins of the Citadel at Jabal al-Qal'a. One of them heard the sound of running water down in the valley and, upon descending down the hill, found the stream, or Sayl 'Amman. The first Circassian village in Transjordan was founded on its banks; interview with 'O.Kh. in Amman (14 August 2014). Archival evidence confirms that, following muhajir flight from the Balkans and arrival in Haifa and Acre, some temporarily stayed in villages around Nablus, Safed, Tiberius, and Jenin in 1878–79; NBKM f. 279A, d. 359; f. 280Ar, d. 29, 34; f. 283Ar., d. 54, 55, 56.

30. Unpublished manuscripts by Hajj Muhammad Ja'far Janbi, 'Abdulghani Hasan, and Hajj Mirza bin Salmirza bin Shahmirza, Sultan Private Collection.

31. In 1880, a second group of twenty-five families arrived in Amman; Hacker, *Modern 'Amman*, 10.

32. Şimşir, *Rumeli'den Türk Göçleri*, 1:387–90; Abujaber, *Pioneers over Jordan*, 198–99.

33. Shami, "Circassians of Amman," 308.

34. al-Hmoud, " 'Amman fi Awakhir al-'Ahd al-'Uthmani," 77, 79, 82.

35. Lewis, *Nomads and Settlers*, 108; Shami, "Circassians of Amman," 308–9.

36. Khammash, *Village Architecture in Jordan*, 85–90.

37. Bliss, "Expedition to Moab and Gilead."

38. Hacker, *Modern 'Amman*, 12, 20.

39. Goodrich-Freer, *In a Syrian Saddle*, 101–2.

40. Rogan, *Frontiers of the State*, 75.

41. Barakat, "Regulating Land Rights," 116–18.

42. In the Balqa', the buyer paid a valuation tax (Ott. Tur., *harc-ı mutad*) in the amount of 3 percent of the purchase price of the property, alongside the cost of a title deed, which ranged from 4 to 7.5 kuruş, and an administrative fee (*katibiye*) of one kuruş. If property was not yet registered, the seller was required to obtain a title by registering it through *yoklama* and to pay relevant taxes and fees before selling it. In those cases, the land registry imposed a 1.5 percent tax each on a vendor and a buyer. *Harc-ı mutad* was also charged during registration when cultivators could prove that they had a right to usufruct (*hakk-ı karar*), based on long-standing tenure and payment of tax. Local cultivators who could not verify the record of cultivation in the last ten years paid a higher-rate *bedel-i misil*; Mundy and Smith, *Governing Property*, on *hakk-ı karar*, 28–29, 48–49; on *harc-ı mutad* and *bedel-i misil*, 68–73, 260n32.

43. Rogan, *Frontiers of the State*, 90–91.

44. Barakat, "Regulating Land Rights," 112–13.

45. Üngör and Polatel, *Confiscation and Destruction*, ix–x.

46. DLS Defters 1/1/1, 1/5/1, 5/1/1, 7/1/1, 9/1/1, 10/1/1, 18/1/1, 19/1/1, 30/1/2, 31/1/2, and 32/1/2. I am grateful to A.B., A.H., and I.B. of DLS for their hospitality, patience, and lessons about cadastral importance, as I copied late Ottoman land registers by hand in their office every day for three weeks.

47. Six land registers for Salt District (1879–86) that Eugene L. Rogan had access to in the 1980s were inaccessible at DLS by 2014; "Incorporating the Periphery," 314.

48. DLS Defters 30/1/2, 31/1/2, 32/1/2.

49. DLS Defter 18/1/1, ff. 123–30, #25–77 (1893); Defter 19/1/1, ff. 43–46, #28–44 (1896).

50. Shami, "Circassians of Amman," 310–11.

51. DLS Defter 7/1/1, ff. 1–92, #1–549 (1906).

52. Nine households registered 70 or 100 dönüm each in the Shapsugh quarter, and fifty-nine households registered 70, 100, or 130 dönüm each in the Qabartay quarter. DLS Defter 5/1/1, ff. 274–75, #134–42; f. 1, #1–12, 143–202 (1912).

53. See Schilcher, "Hauran Conflicts"; Schilcher, "Violence in Rural Syria."

54. Rogan, *Frontiers of the State*, 99–112.

55. DLS Defter 18/1/1, ff. 78–79, #13–16 (1891–95).

56. DLS Defter 30/1/2, ff. 274–75, #1–4 (1893–1903); Defter 31/1/2, ff. 7–8, #2 (1904), ff. 308–9, #1 (1895), ff. 375–76, #60–61 (1903–10).

57. TNA FO 195/2144, Richards to O'Conor, #91 (Damascus, 15 December 1903).

58. On the Hejaz Railway, see Ochsenwald, *Hijaz Railroad*; Özyüksel, *Hejaz Railway*.

59. Özyüksel, *Hejaz Railway*, 124.

60. Hamed-Troyansky, "Imperial Refuge," 156.

61. Khoury, *Urban Notables*, 21.

62. DLS Defter 10/1/1, f. 4, #35; Defter 31/1/2, ff. 81–82, #9, ff. 237–38, #29, ff. 283–84, #9–11, ff. 308–9, #1, ff. 332–33, #32–34; Defter 32/1/2, ff. 55–56, #28, ff. 57–58, #44–45, ff. 173–74, #36 (all transactions 1903–12).

63. DLS Defter 10/1/1, f. 40, #67; Defter 31/1/2, ff. 167–68, #34–37, ff. 341–42, #81, ff.

369–70, #27; Defter 32/1/2, ff. 15–16, #110, ff. 125–26, #28, ff. 153–54, #34 (all transactions 1903–12).

64. DLS Defter 31/1/2, ff. 283–84, #7 (1905); 32/1/2, ff. 129–30, #1 (1907), ff. 65–66, #43 (1910); 10/1/1, f. 40, #7–8, f. 47, #22 (1912), f. 40, #67 (1912).

65. DLS Defter 32/1/2, ff. 345–46, #91 (1912).

66. See for Khurma: DLS Defter 31/1/2, ff. 275–76, #40, ff. 341–44, #82, 95 (1903–10); Defter 32/1/2, ff. 55–56, #33 (1910–12); Qursha: Defter 32/1/2, ff. 127–28, #41–51 (*yoklama* 1893, *da'imi* 1910), ff. 271–74, #47–50 (1912); Matkari: Defter 31/1/2, ff. 95–98, #1–9 (1903–10); 32/1/2, ff. 119–20, #26–28 (1910), ff. 125–26, #28 (1910).

67. See Amawi, "Enterprising Merchants of Amman."

68. Hacker, *Modern 'Amman*, 59.

69. al-Hmoud, " 'Amman fi Awakhir al-'Ahd al-'Uthmani," 80–83.

70. Rogan, "Making of a Capital"; Alon, *Shaykh of Shaykhs*, 49–62. On the early Hashemite era, see Wilson, *Making of Jordan*; Tell, *Monarchy in Jordan*.

71. Interviews in Amman with N.S., T.T., and Y.A. (8 August 2014) and K.J. (10 August 2014).

72. Sayetkhan's Circassian family name was likely Къэгъэлокъуэ or Кагалоков.

73. Interview with 'O.Kh. in Amman (14 August 2014).

74. DLS Defter 31/1/2, ff. 353–56, #50–60 (*yoklama* 1893, *da'imi* 1897).

75. CDM Defter Salt 6, ff. 6–8 (26 *rebiülahir* 1319, 12 August 1901).

76. CDM Defter Salt 6, ff. 49–50 (2 *şaban* 1319, 14 November 1901).

77. CDM Defter Salt 7, #54 (28 *zilkade* 1319, 8 March 1902).

78. CDM Defter Salt 6, f. 70 (24 *şaban* 1319, 6 December 1901).

79. CDM Defter Salt 9, f. 159 (12 *zilkade* 1320, 10 February 1903); Salt 7, #237 (21 *zilkade* 1320, 19 February 1903).

80. CDM Defter Salt 7, #198 (10 *recep* 1320, 13 October 1902).

81. CDM Defter Salt 6, ff. 118–19 (10 *recep* 1320, 13 October 1902).

82. CDM Defter Salt 4, #11, 26, 36.

83. Ganich, *Cherkesy v Iordanii*, 70.

84. CDM Defters Salt 6 and 7 (August 1901–February 1903).

85. On the Circassians' use of shari'a court, see Dazey, "Trial and Error"; Hamed-Troyansky, "Imperial Refuge," 177–82.

86. For *'adat* law in the Caucasus, see Bobrovnikov, *Musul'mane Severnogo Kavkaza*.

87. DLS Defter 31/1/2, ff. 355–58, #61–71 (1909).

88. DLS Defter 31/1/2, ff. 357–60, #72–82 (1909).

89. DLS Defter 31/1/2, ff. 359–66, #83–120 (1909). The third owner of the shares was 'Amr Efendi.

90. Gül'azar owned 2,210 out of 3,240 shares; other heirs were her half sister Najiya; Sayetkhan's siblings 'Ali Mirza, Devlet Mirza, and Fatima; Muhammad Agha's second wife Amina; his other daughters, Kheyriya and Zakiya; and his sister Kushanay; DLS Defter 10/1/1, ff. 46–47, #15–21 (1912).

91. DLS Defter 10/1/1, f. 40, #7–20, f. 47, #22, 24–35 (1912).

92. See Barakat, *Bedouin Bureaucrats*.

93. The 'Adwan were dominant in the western Balqa' until the late 1860s but lost many lands because of the Ottoman land registration. The Balqawiyya tribal confederation included the 'Adwan, 'Ajarma, Balqawiyya, Bani Hasan, Bani Hamida, Da'ja, al-Hadid, Saltiyya, and other tribes and clans. The Bani Sakhr were a dominant tribe to the east of the pilgrimage route, or the Hejaz Railway; Alon, *Making of Jordan*, 29–30, 159–61; Abujaber, *Pioneers over Jordan*, 68, 184–85, 203–4.

94. Rogan, *Frontiers of the State*, 86n66.

95. Ibid., 79–82.

96. On *mahlul* lands, see Barakat, *Bedouin Bureaucrats*, 167–81; Morack, *Dowry of the State*, 46–48, 66–67.

97. On Sattam al-Fayiz, see Alon, *Shaykh of Shaykhs*, 7–22; Abujaber, *Pioneers over Jordan*, 177–96.

98. Rogan, *Frontiers of the State*, 85–92. On bedouin's registration of land, see also Barakat, *Bedouin Bureaucrats*, esp. 121–22, 140–46.

99. Terzibaşoğlu finds that, in western Anatolia, whenever villagers learned of a planned refugee settlement in the area, they acquired title deeds to the lands that they had claimed by properly registering the land and paying all required taxes; "Landlords, Nomads, and Refugees," 134–37.

100. Lewis, *Nomads and Settlers*, 107.

101. On the Circassian-Bani Sakhr alliance, see Haghandoqa, *Circassians*, 44–45; Mufti, *Heroes and Emperors*, 275–76. According to one retelling of the story, the alliance agreement was written in blood; interview with N.S., T.T., and Y.A. in Amman (8 August 2014). The alliance, perhaps, covered only some Bani Sakhr clans because, in 1904, Circassians fought the Khuraysha (Khurshan) clan of the Bani Sakhr over rights to pastures near Amman; Kushkhabiev, *Cherkesy v Sirii*, 84.

102. "B'ada qarn min al-zaman .. Bani Sakhr wa al-Sharkas yujaddidan al-wathiqa al-tarikhiyya," *Ammon News* (23 June 2013), www.ammonnews.net/article/157277.

103. The "corn" could refer to wheat or barley; Lees, "Across Southern Bashan": 4.

104. Interviews in Amman with 'O.Kh. (14 August 2014) and J.Sh. (17 August 2014); Mousa, "Jordan," 391.

105. On the Balqawiyya war, see Haghandoqa, *Circassians*, 44–46; Shami, "Circassians of Amman," 312–13. Mufti attributes the conflict to the kidnapping of a "Circassian maiden" by the Balqawiyya tribe and dates it to 1900; *Heroes and Emperors*, 275–76. Abujaber dates it to 1904; *Pioneers over Jordan*, 211. Lewis suggests that it took place after 1906; *Nomads and Settlers*, 108. On another conflict, between Chechens of Sweileh and the surrounding bedouin, in 1907, see Barakat, *Bedouin Bureaucrats*, 158–60.

106. TNA FO 195/1368, Stewart to Dufferin, #21 (Aleppo, 14 July 1881); Dolbee, *Locusts of Power*, 51–52.

107. Kushkhabiev, *Cherkesy v Sirii*, 83–84.

108. BOA DH.ŞFR 376/81 (15 şubat 1322, 28 February 1907); ŞD 2303/36 (27 şevval 1325, 3 December 1907).

109. North Caucasian villages in the Golan Heights included Mansura, 'Ayn Ziwan, Juwaiza, al-Burayka, Bi'r 'Ajam, Ruhina, Mumsiya, Surman, 'Ayn Surman, Khushniya,

al-Faham, Fazara, Hamidiye, Sindaniye, and Faraj; Lewis, *Nomads and Settlers*, 104–5, 117–18. Natho dates Quneitra to 1872; *Circassian History*, 507. See also Chatty, *Displacement and Dispossession*, 91–92, 112–15.

110. Kushkhabiev, *Cherkesy v Sirii*, 86–87; Firro, *History of the Druzes*, 230.

111. On the Druze-Circassian conflict of 1894, Ottoman, British, and Russian accounts are BOA Y.MTV 97/9 (2 *zilhicce* 1311, 6 June 1894); TNA FO 195/1839, Meshaka to Currie, #13 (Damascus, 11 June 1894); AVPRI f. 151, op. 482, d. 750, ll. 80–86, 89–91, 96–101 (1 July–18 August 1894).

112. TNA FO 195/1886, Drummond Hay to Herbert, #68 (Beirut, 10 November 1895).

113. See published accounts of the Druze-Circassian conflict, as based on Circassian oral history: Mufti, *Heroes and Emperors*, 276–77; from Druze perspective: Firro, *History of the Druzes*, 231–34; based on Russian sources: Kushkhabiev, *Cherkesy v Sirii*, 86–92; and on Ottoman and British sources: Adamiak, "To the Edge of the Desert," 150–76.

114. In 1909, Ottoman authorities reported another conflict between Circassians of Mansura and Druze of Majdal Shams; Y.EE 37/93 (6 *rebiülahir* 1327, 27 April 1909).

115. Rogan, *Frontiers of the State*, 67–68.

116. Ibid., 67; Haghandoqa, *Circassians*, 61–62.

117. Natho, *Circassian History*, 479–80; Haghandoqa, *Circassians*, 40–41. On tribes in the Balqaʾ, see Barakat, *Bedouin Bureaucrats*, 139.

118. DLS Defter 31/1/2, ff. 85–88, #8–20, ff. 324–25, #14–18 (1909); 32/1/2, ff. 105–371 (1909–10); Defter 9/1/1, ff. 138–383 (1910).

119. DLS Defter 32/1/2 and 9/1/1, esp. ff. 240–41, #1406–15; ff. 246–49, #1452–56; ff. 360–63, #533–44, 545–53 (1910).

120. Rogan, *Frontiers of the State*, 86n67.

121. The cadastral value of the plot was 621,000 kuruş; DLS Defter 32/1/2, ff. 348–49, #13 (1897).

122. DLS Defter 19/1/1, ff. 5–6, #1–4 (1897).

123. Kondakov, *Arkheologicheskoe puteshestvie po Sirii i Palestine*, 124.

124. CDM Salt 7/53 (24 *recep* 1321, 16 October 1903); Janib, *Muwatin Sharkasi*, 9.

125. Interview with M.A.J. in Wadi al-Sir (11 August 2014).

126. DLS Defter 30/1/2, ff. 45–46, #6 (1879).

127. DLS Defter 32/1/2, ff. 33–34, #219–20, ff. 85–86, #19, ff. 147–48, #57–58, ff. 165–66, #4 (1909–11).

128. Wilson lists the population of Wadi al-Sir at 3,200 as larger than that of Amman at 2,400 in 1922; *Making of Jordan*, 56.

129. Interview with the Circassian elders' council in Naʿur (31 August 2014).

130. DLS Defter 30/1/1, ff. 126–65, #42–271 (1900–1902).

131. DLS Defter 1/5/1, ff. 1–2, #1–73 (1909).

132. Interview with the Circassian elders' council in Naʿur (31 August 2014).

133. BOA DH.TMIK.S 36/48 (11 *zilkade* 1319, 19 February 1902); DH.MHC 59/15, f. 15 (24 *safer* 1320, 2 June 1902).

134. Interview with the Circassian elders' council in Naʿur (31 August 2014).

135. Interview with N.S., T.T., and Y.A. in Amman (8 August 2014).

136. DLS Defter 30/1/1, ff. 310–11, #2–3 (1901).

137. DLS Defter 30/1/2, ff. 174–75, #3, 5–6, ff. 194–95, #5, 11–12, ff. 310–11, #2–3 (1902–9); Defter 32/1/2, ff. 173–74, #45–46 (1910–12), ff. 392–93, #169 (1913); CDM Defter Salt 8, f. 18 (24 şevval 1330, 6 October 1912).

138. DLS Defter 30/1/2, ff. 118–19, #1 (1902); Defter 32/1/2, ff. 161–62, #26, ff. 267–268, #6 (yoklama 1902, da'imi 1910–12); CDM Defter Salt 10, f. 302 (29 şevval 1329, 23 October 1911).

139. DLS Defter 32/1/2, ff. 185–86, #39–44, ff. 392–93, #170 (1910–12); Defter 10/1/1, f. 18, #39–44 (1910–12).

140. CDM Defter Salt 8, f. 35 (29 şevval 1331, 1 October 1913).

141. DLS Defter 30/1/2, 1/5/1, 10/1/1, and 32/1/2.

142. Shortly before World War I, the average cost of agricultural land in Palestine was 300 francs (1,320 kuruş) per dönüm; Kark, "Jerusalem and Jaffa," 49.

143. Interview with J.B.Sh. in Amman (9 September 2014).

144. Interviews with M.A.J. in Wadi al-Sir (11 August 2014) and A.J. in Amman (21 August 2014).

Chapter 5: Building the Caucasus in Anatolia

1. Khutat Family Collection, letter 1, Fuat to Hanife (4 February 1891).

2. According to family history, Cevat studied law; interview with Salim Khutat (10 January 2017). Ottoman records place him as a student of the military school Soğukçeşme Askeri Rüştiyesi; BOA DH.MKT 1814/95 (21 recep 1308, 2 March 1891).

3. Khutat Family Collection, letter 1, Fuat to Hanife (4 February 1891); letter 4, Fuat to Cevat (30 September 1892); letter 7, Fuat to Cevat (1 January 1893).

4. On North Caucasians in Uzunyayla, see Karataş, "Çerkeslerin Sivas-Uzunyayla'ya İskanları"; Miyazawa, "Memory Politics"; Şahin, Uzunyayla Çerkesleri; Yel and Gündüz, "Uzunyayla'ya Yerleştirilmeleri." For the list of Uzunyayla villages, see Hamed-Troyansky, "Imperial Refuge," 512–15.

5. I thank Salim Khutat for access to his family collection and for entertaining my questions about Fuat and Cevat over the years.

6. Habiçoğlu, Kafkasya'dan Anadolu'ya Göçler, 153–58, 163–66.

7. Aydemir, Göç, 111–16; İpek, Türk Göçleri, 180–208.

8. Karaca, Anadolu İslahatı, 110.

9. Hütteroth, "Settlement in Inner Anatolia," 21.

10. The Sivas population was estimated at 708,550 to 895,682 in 1881; Karpat, Ottoman Population, 34. I estimate that after the second Circassian refugee crisis, in 1878–80, the North Caucasian population in Sivas Province reached at least 100,000.

11. On the Khodz' insurrection of 1868, see Salushchev, "Reluctant Abolitionists," 326–30.

12. Gugov, Kasumov, and Shabaev, Tragicheskie posledstviia, 282–83.

13. Isma'il (bin) Khutat (Houtat) and Bekmirza bin Qardan were leaders of Benoqa muhajirs. The emigrating party of 982 families also included 354 families from the village of Foz, 214 from Bougouch, and 81 from Bzedoug; BOA HR.TH 88/14, f. 2 (26 March

1889). The 982 families were part of about 9,100 Muslims from Russia's Kuban Province who were sent to the Kastamonu, Ankara, Konya, Mamuret-ül-Aziz, Sivas, and Adana provinces in 1890; DH.MKT 1749/28 (21 *zilhicce* 1307, 8 August 1890).

14. Mikhailov, *Spravochnik po Stavropol'skoi eparkhii*, 648–49.

15. BOA HR.TH 88/25 (2 April 1889); 88/66 (18 April 1889).

16. Toksöz, *Nomads, Migrants and Cotton*, 65–81. In the 1890s, the German-Levantine Cotton Society brought 50,000 Circassian and "Danubian" peasants to work on its cotton fields; Penslar, *Zionism and Technocracy*, 63.

17. On Circassians suffering from malaria in Çukurova, see Gratien, *Unsettled Plain*, 70–71, 83–84. Most of the 30,000 Nogai Tatars who had settled in Çukurova after 1856 died of malaria; Quataert, "Age of Reforms," 2:794. On unhealthy environments for refugee resettlement, see Fratantuono, "Migration Administration," 128–66.

18. Khutat Family Collection, letter 3, Fuat to Cevat (4 July 1892).

19. Khutat Family Collection, letter 4, Fuat to Cevat (30 September 1892).

20. Khutat Family Collection, letter 14, Fuat to Cevat (27 November 1893); letter 16, Fuat to Cevat (25 February 1894).

21. Khutat Family Collection, letter 19, Fuat to Cevat (24 May 1894); letter 21, Fuat to Cevat (12 July 1894).

22. Khutat Family Collection, letter 15, Fuat to Cevat (14 February 1894).

23. Khutat Family Collection, letter 18, Fuat to Cevat (6 April 1894).

24. Khutat Family Collection, letter 18, Fuat to Cevat (6 April 1894).

25. The population of Aziziye in 1897–98 was 1,600, of whom 400 were non-Muslims; Güler, *Osmanlı Devletinde Azınlıklar*, 53.

26. Yel and Gündüz estimate that 40,200 North Caucasians moved to Uzunyayla in 1860–65; "Uzunyayla'ya Yerleştirilmeleri," 965.

27. Miyazawa, "Memory Politics," 16–17; İzbırak, "Uzunyayla'da Coğrafya Araştırmaları."

28. Habiçoğlu, *Kafkasya'dan Anadolu'ya Göçler*, 167.

29. Hamed-Troyansky, "Imperial Refuge," 209–10; Karataş, "Çerkeslerin Sivas-Uzunyayla'ya İskanları," 53–57.

30. Karataş, "Çerkeslerin Sivas-Uzunyayla'ya İskanları," 99–102.

31. BOA A.MKT.MHM 202/24 (27 *cemaziyelevvel* 1277, 11 December 1860); 215/88 (12 *şevval* 1277, 23 April 1861).

32. BOA A.MKT.UM 430/11 (27 *safer* 1277, 14 September 1860).

33. Miyazawa, "Memory Politics," 20–21, 130–31.

34. Çatalkılıç, "Kafkasya'dan Uzunyayla'ya Taşınan Hafıza Mekanları."

35. Miyazawa, "Memory Politics," 76–77.

36. BOA A.MKT.MHM 233/23 (21 *safer* 1278, 28 August 1861).

37. Murphey, *Exploring Ottoman Sovereignty*, 12, 282n27.

38. BOA A.MKT.UM 491/43, f. 1 (7 *safer* 1278, 14 August 1861).

39. Karataş, "Çerkeslerin Sivas-Uzunyayla'ya İskanları," 107–9.

40. BOA A.MKT.UM 491/43, f. 2 (15 *muharrem* 1278, 23 July 1861).

41. BOA A.MKT.MHM 348/18 (8 *şaban* 1282, 27 December 1865).

42. Colarusso, *Nart Sagas.*

43. Pashtova, "Fol'klor cherkesskoi diaspory," 101–18.

44. Ibid., 75.

45. Ibid., 47–62, 221–46.

46. Ibid., 201–20.

47. Ibid., 51, 76–79, 273–77.

48. Ibid., 73.

49. I borrow this metaphor from Miyazawa, "Memory Politics," 17.

50. BOA İ.MVL 452/20210, f. 3 (15 *safer* 1278, 22 August 1861); Karataş, "Çerkeslerin Sivas-Uzunyayla'ya İskanları," 19–23.

51. Gratien, *Unsettled Plain*, 27–28.

52. Kasaba, *Moveable Empire*, 99–108.

53. Ibid., 100, 105.

54. BOA A.MKT.UM 403/86 (12 *şevval* 1276, 3 May 1860).

55. Karataş, "Çerkeslerin Sivas-Uzunyayla'ya İskanları," 20.

56. Ibid., 211–18.

57. BOA A.MKT.UM 483/67 (5 *muharrem* 1278, 13 July 1861); Karataş, "Çerkeslerin Sivas-Uzunyayla'ya İskanları," 213, 218.

58. BOA MVL 416/88 (12 *şaban* 1279, 2 February 1863).

59. BOA MVL 636/67 (13 *rebiülevvel* 1279, 8 September 1862), 638/3 (20 *rebiülevvel* 1279, 15 September 1862).

60. On the Circassian-Afshar conflict, see Gratien, *Unsettled Plain*, 62–63; Karataş, "Çerkeslerin Sivas-Uzunyayla'ya İskanları," 202–51.

61. BOA MVL 670/38 (19 *şevval* 1280, 28 March 1864), 675/82 (9 *muharrem* 1281, 14 June 1864), 712/104 (11 *rebiülahir* 1282, 3 September 1865).

62. BOA MVL 694/66, ff. 1–2 (*cemaziyelahir* 1281, November 1864).

63. Miyazawa, "Memory Politics," 47.

64. BOA MVL 736/77 (19 *rebiülevvel* 1284, 21 July 1867); HR.SYS 2941/87 (23 September 1878).

65. TNA FO 424/122, Richards to Wilson, enclosure 1 in #130 (Sivas, 8 March 1881).

66. TNA FO 424/91, Wilson to Layard, enclosure 4 in #99 (Sivas, 28 October 1879).

67. Gratien, "Mountains Are Ours," 211–14.

68. TNA FO 424/91, Wilson to Layard, enclosure 4 in #99 (Sivas, 28 October 1879).

69. TNA FO 424/91, Wilson to Layard, enclosure 1 in #100 (Sivas, 3 November 1879).

70. TNA FO 424/106, Wilson to Layard, enclosure 6 in #2 (Sivas, 21 November 1879).

71. TNA FO 195/2025, Maunsell to O'Conor, #42 (Sivas, 15 June 1898), ff. 278r–279.

72. TNA FO 195/2136, Anderson to O'Conor, #9 (Sivas, 7 October 1903).

73. Ibragimova, *Chechenskaia istoriia*, 291–92.

74. Khutat Family Collection, letter 8, Fuat to Cevat (13 March 1893).

75. Khutat Family Collection, letter 34, Fuat to Cevat (25 August 1895).

76. Khutat Family Collection, letter 11, Fuat to Cevat (16 August 1893).

77. Khutat Family Collection, letter 46, Fuat to Cevat (17 June 1899).

78. Khutat Family Collection, letter 51, Fuat to Cevat (10 July 1900).

79. Khutat Family Collection, letter 19, Fuat to Cevat (24 May 1894).

80. Khutat Family Collection, letter 16, Fuat to Cevat (25 February 1894); letter 35, Fuat to Cevat (6 February 1896).

81. BOA BEO 2241/168041, f. 4 (16 *teşrin-i evvel* 1319, 29 October 1903).

82. Rogan, "Aşiret Mektebi," esp. 88–90.

83. The term *vatan* started gaining prominence in Ottoman literature in the 1870s; Karpat, "Nation and Nationalism," 548.

84. Deringil, "They Live in a State of Nomadism."

85. North Caucasians briefly adopted self-designation as a tribe in Jordan after the government formalized the institution of tribal councils for bedouin, establishing the Circassian Tribal Council in 1969 and the Circassian-Chechen Tribal Council in 1979; Massad, *Colonial Effects*, 67.

86. Rogan, "Aşiret Mektebi," 100.

87. On Ottoman military education, see Provence, *Last Ottoman Generation*, 18–28.

88. "Kölelik Aleyhinde," *Ğuaze* 2 (10 April 1911), 6. Local informants reported 1,407 slaves held in 388 households in 1911; "Köleliğe Karşı," *Ğuaze* 6 (18 May 1911), 2. The British reported 2,000 slaves in Aziziye District in 1880; Stewart to Goschen, enclosure in #7 (Kayseri, 30 June 1880), in House of Commons, *Parliamentary Papers*, Turkey, no. 6 (1881), 5.

89. BOA HR.SFR.1 32/38 (18 March 1872).

90. BOA HR.SFR.1 53/44 (10 December 1874).

91. Toledano, *Slavery and Abolition*, 102–4.

92. G. Rolin-Jacquemyns, "Armenia, the Armenians and Treaties, Part III," *Armenian Herald* 1, no. 7 (1918): 381n47.

93. "Kölelik Hakkında," *Ğuaze* 9 (1 June 1911), 4.

94. TNA FO 195/2059, Anderson to O'Conor, #1 (Sivas, 4 May 1899), ff. 195–95r.

95. Ibid., 195r–96.

96. Fieldwork notes, Uzunyayla (25–26 July 2017). On modern-day discrimination against descendants of slaves in Uzunyayla, see Miyazawa, "Memory Politics," 127–210.

97. The Circassian *vase* (bride price) tradition was used as a justification for the sale of Circassian women into marriage to men from outside their community. According to one recollection, Turkish men annually visited Circassian villages around Maraş (now Kahramanmaraş) to buy women for marriage. One such sale took place in 1957–58, when twenty-three Circassian women were sold; Aksoy, *Beyaz Köleler*, 290–92, based on our interview in Istanbul with R.T., from a Circassian village near Maraş, who bore witness to the sale (1 November 2014).

98. Khutat Family Collection, letter 23, Fuat to Cevat (30 September 1894).

99. Khutat Family Collection, letter 24, Fuat to Cevat (19 October 1894).

100. Circassians were reportedly primary cultivators of hemp, opium, and tobacco in the subprovince of Tokat; TNA FO 424/122, Richards to Wilson, enclosure 1 in #130 (Sivas, 8 March 1881).

101. TNA FO 424/91, Cooper to Wilson, enclosure 2 in #99 (Kayseri, 27 September 1879).

102. Khutat Family Collection, letter 24, Fuat to Cevat (19 October 1894).

103. Khutat Family Collection, letter 3, Fuat to Cevat (4 July 1892).

104. Khutat Family Collection, letter 27, Fuat to Cevat (20 December 1894).

105. Khutat Family Collection, letter 2, Fuat to Hanife (26 February 1891).

106. Khutat Family Collection, letter 24, Fuat to Cevat (19 October 1894).

107. Khutat Family Collection, letter 21, Fuat to Cevat (12 July 1894).

108. Khutat Family Collection, letter 26, Fuat to Cevat (14 December 1894).

109. Khutat Family Collection, letter 28, Fuat to Hanife (undated, c. March 1895).

110. Khutat Family Collection, letter 29, Fuat to Selim Girey (27 March 1895).

111. Khutat Family Collection, letter 35, Fuat to Cevat (6 February 1896).

112. DLS 19/1/1, ff. 43–44, #29 (*kanun-ı evvel* 1312, December 1896 / January 1897).

113. Khutat Family Collection, letter 38, Fuat to Cevat (5 March 1898); letter 55, Fuat to Cevat (3 May 1902).

114. Khutat Family Collection, letter 35, Fuat to Cevat (6 February 1896); letter 36, Fuat to Cevat (2 December 1897).

115. Khutat Family Collection, letter 46, Fuat to Cevat (17 June 1899).

116. Khutat Family Collection, letter 48, Fuat to Cevat (22 November 1899).

117. Khutat Family Collection, letter 40, Fuat to Cevat (9 July 1898); CDM Defter Salt 5, #31 (15 *şaban* 1315, 9 January 1898).

118. Khutat Family Collection, letter 48, Fuat to Cevat (22 November 1899); letter 49, Fuat to Cevat (27 January 1900).

119. Khutat Family Collection, letter 49, Fuat to Cevat (27 January 1900).

120. Khutat Family Collection, letter 52, Fuat to Cevat (16 November 1900).

121. DLS Defter 19/1/1, ff. 361–62, #98–101 (1898–99).

122. Khutat Family Collection, letter 33, Fuat to Cevat (15 August 1895).

123. The families were Qul, Başkan, Hacı Bayram, Yakubzade, Bud, and Tarkan; Khutat Family Collection, letter 2, Fuat to Hanife (26 February 1891); letter 5, Fuat to Cevat (12 August 1892).

124. CDM Defter Salt 15, #76 (16 *rebiülahir* 1328, 27 April 1910); DLS Defter 32/1/2, ff. 81–82, #74 (*haziran* 1326, June/July 1910).

125. Khutat Family Collection, letters 3, 5, 11–14, 18–20, 25, 35 Fuat to Cevat (1892–96).

126. Khutat Family Collection, letter 56, Fuat to Cevat (27 September 1902).

127. Khutat Family Collection, letter 58, Fuat to Cevat (14 October 1905).

128. Khutat Family Collection, Cevat's Transjordanian passport (1925); correspondence with Salim Khutat (6 February 2023).

129. Khutat Family Collection, Khutat family tree; Hanania, "From Colony to Capital" (2010), 106.

130. Interview with Salim Khutat (10 January 2017).

131. Natho, *Circassian History*, 492, 502–3.

132. Khutat Family Collection, letter 40, Fuat to Cevat (9 July 1898).

133. Khutat Family Collection, letter 43, Fuat to Cevat (21 October 1898).

134. Khutat Family Collection, letter 48, Fuat to Cevat (22 November 1899); letter 49, Fuat to Cevat (27 January 1900).

135. Khutat Family Collection, letter 50, Fuat to Cevat (27 April 1900).

136. Interview with Salim Khutat (10 January 2017).

137. Khutat Family Collection, letter 50, Fuat to Cevat (27 April 1900).

138. Khutat Family Collection, letter 52, Fuat to Cevat (16 November 1900).

139. Khutat Family Collection, letter 52, Fuat to Cevat (16 November 1900).

140. Interview with Salim Khutat (10 January 2017).

141. Yurttaş, "Fuat Bey'in Erzurum Haritası."

142. On the Ottoman Military Academy, see Provence, *Last Ottoman Generation*, 28–29.

143. Rogan, *Fall of the Ottomans*, 26.

144. Interview with Salim Khutat (10 January 2017).

145. Baydar, *Cumhuriyet'in Aile Albümleri*, 190–211.

146. BOA HR.SFR.3 35/7 (25 November 1857); A.DVNSNMH.d 12/276 (29 *zilhicce* 1278, 27 June 1862).

147. Geyikdağı, *Foreign Investment*, 68, 89–90; Özyüksel, *Berlin-Baghdad Railway*, 29.

148. McMeekin, *Berlin-Baghdad Express*, 39–41.

149. Ivanov et al., *Ocherki istorii Ministerstva inostrannykh del Rossii*, 3:203–4; Özyüksel, *Berlin-Baghdad Railway*, 74–77.

150. By 1914, 1,104 Armenians lived in Aziziye District, primarily in Aziziye. Armenians from the district were deported through Gürün and Akçadağ to the killing field of Fırıncılar, and their properties were pillaged; Kévorkian, *Armenian Genocide*, 441–42, 444. According to oral histories, some Armenians survived by hiding in Uzunyayla's Circassian villages, and some Armenian orphans were adopted and raised as Circassians; Doğan, "Circassians in Turkey," 239–42.

151. Miyazawa, "Memory Politics," 102–3.

152. On migration from Uzunyayla to cities, see Temizkan and Çatalkılıç, "Abaza ve Çerkes Köyleri." On Turkish migrations to Germany and back, see Kahn, "Foreign at Home."

153. *Salname-i Vilayet-i Sivas* (h. 1325, 1907), 254–55; Miyazawa, "Memory Politics," 301.

154. Kayseri Büyükşehir Belediyesi website, https://cbs.kayseri.bel.tr/kayseri-ilce-mahalle-muhtar-bilgileri (accessed June 19, 2023).

155. Eiji Miyazawa mentions sixty-two villages in 1997–99; "Past as a Resource," 60. Besleney cites sixty-five villages; *Circassian Diaspora*, 76n3.

Chapter 6: Making the North Caucasian Diaspora

1. "Çerkes Elifbası Hakkında," *Ğuaze* 12 (22 June 1911): 5.

2. Safran, "Diasporas"; see also Clifford, "Diasporas"; Brubaker, " 'Diaspora' Diaspora." On theorizing the contemporary Circassian diaspora, see Besleney, *Circassian Diaspora*, 12–16.

3. On North Caucasian diasporic associations, see Besleney, *Circassian Diaspora*; Chochiev, *Severokavkazskie (cherkesskie) organizatsii*; Arslan, "Circassian Organizations"; Tsibenko, "Faktor natsiestroitel'stva."

4. Kazharov, *Izbrannye trudy*, 36, 321–39; Jaimoukha, *Circassians*, 157–60.

5. "Po osvobozhdeniiu zavisimykh soslovii u gorskikh narodov" (4 June 1866), in Kokiev, *Krest'ianskaia reforma*, 54–60.

6. Gardanov, *Obshchestvennyi stroi adygskikh narodov.*

7. Manning, "Just Like England"; Kazharov, *Izbrannye trudy*, 149–81, 182–87.

8. Jaimoukha, *Chechens*, 85–88; Mamakaev, *Chechenskii taip*, 16–19.

9. Salushchev, "Reluctant Abolitionists," 254–55.

10. Chochiev, "Anatolian Ossetians," 113.

11. For published *'adat* law in the Caucasus, see Leontovich, *Adaty Kavkazskikh gortsev.*

12. Kemper, "Communal Agreements."

13. Kemper, " 'Adat against Shari'a."

14. For example, CDM Defter Salt 6, ff. 118–19 (10 *recep* 1320, 13 October 1902).

15. Jaimoukha, *Circassians*, 166–67.

16. Miyazawa, "Memory Politics," 137–38.

17. *Ğuaze* 22 (19 October 1911), 4; Kırımlı and Yaycıoğlu, "Heirs of Chinghis Khan."

18. Interview with N.Ş., of the Khanuko family descended from the Gerays, in Istanbul (22 September 2014).

19. Kosven, *Etnografiia i istoriia Kavkaza*, 104–26, esp. 106–7; Kazharov, *Izbrannye trudy*, 489–502.

20. Longworth, *Year among the Circassians*, 1:42–44; Pashtova, "Fol'klor cherkesskoi diaspory," 159–70, well-known *khachesh* on 162.

21. Interviews in Amman with M.A. (16 August 2014) and A.J. (21 August 2014).

22. Chochiev, "Anatolian Ossetians," 109.

23. BOA A.MKT.NZD 348/63 (4 *şevval* 1277, 15 April 1861).

24. Fratantuono, "Migration Administration," 202.

25. Yüksel, "Kafkas Göçmen Vakıfları."

26. Cuthell, "Circassian Sürgün," 154–55.

27. Chochiev, "Anatolian Ossetians," 112. On the importance of communal dance for Circassian identity, see Zhemukhov and King, "Dancing the Nation."

28. Khuri-Makdisi, *Global Radicalism*, 35–59.

29. Chochiev, "İttihad Gazetesi," 228–31.

30. BOA Y.EE 149/91 (21 *cemaziyelahir* 1317, 27 October 1899); also, Hanioğlu, *Young Turks in Opposition*, 170.

31. Chochiev, "İttihad Gazetesi," 232–34. In the late Ottoman context, *kavmiyet* referred to ethnic or tribal forms of communal association, sometimes translated as "nationalism."

32. Chochiev, "Reclaiming the Homeland," 626n65.

33. On promises of the Young Turk Revolution, see Campos, *Ottoman Brothers*; and on its disappointments, see Der Matossian, *Shattered Dreams.*

34. Chochiev, *Severokavkazskie (cherkesskie) organizatsii*, 46–52. For biographies of prominent diasporic North Caucasians, see Berzeg, *Edebiyatçılar ve Yazarlar Sözlüğü*; Aydemir, *Muhaceretteki Çerkes Aydınları.*

35. For texts of constitutions of North Caucasian associations, see Berzeg, *Gurbetteki Kafkasya'dan Belgeler*, 10–35; Chochiev, *Severokavkazskie (cherkesskie) organizatsii*, 143–85. The quotes are from "Çerkes İttihad ve Teavün Cemiyeti'nin Beyannamesi" (1908), in Berzeg, *Gurbetteki Kafkasya'dan Belgeler*, 15.

36. "Çerkes İttihad ve Teavün Cemiyeti'nin Beyannamesi," 15.

37. Ibid., 17.

38. Ibid., 15. *Milliyet*, sometimes translated as "nationality," was a new term in late Ottoman usage, derived from *millet*, and could denote either communal identity based on one's ethnicity or the "Ottoman nation"; Schull, *Prisons in the Late Ottoman Empire*, 93–98; Meyer, *Turks across Empires*, 121, 137n32.

39. Chochiev, "Reclaiming the Homeland," 590.

40. "Çerkes İttihad ve Teavün Cemiyeti'nin Beyannamesi," 16–18.

41. Campos, *Ottoman Brothers*, 3.

42. "Çerkes Teavün Cemiyeti'nin Beyannamesi," 20.

43. "Çerkes Teavün Cemiyeti'nin Beyannamesi," 22–23.

44. Chochiev, *Severokavkazskie (cherkesskie) organizatsii*, 40–41.

45. Campos, *Ottoman Brothers*, 136.

46. Different dating exists for Pçehatluk's alphabets. Berzeg, *Adige-Çerkes Alfabesinin Tarihçesi*; Papşu "Çerkes-Adığe Yazısının Tarihçesi."

47. "Çerkes Lisanına Mahsus Elifba," *Ğuaze* 13 (4 July 1911), 6–7.

48. Arslan, "Circassian Organizations," 88–99.

49. The Arabic script–based alphabets for Circassian were proposed by the Adighe Zauil collective in 1915 and by İbrahim Hıdzetl in 1921; and the Latin-based ones by Blenav Batuk Harun in 1918 and by Mustafa Butbay for the Circassian-Abkhazian alphabet in 1919; Papşu, "Çerkes-Adığe Yazısının Tarihçesi."

50. On alphabet choices in the Ottoman and Russian empires, see Kuzuoğlu, "Telegraphy, Typography, and the Alphabet."

51. Soviet authorities adopted the Latin alphabet for Ossetian and Ingush in 1923; Kabardino-Cherkess, or eastern Circassian, and Karachay-Balkar in 1924; Chechen in 1925; Abkhazian in 1926; Adyghe, or western Circassian, in 1927; and Dagestani languages in 1928.

52. Soviet authorities adopted the Georgian script for Abkhazian and Ossetian, in South Ossetia only, in 1938–54 before both were Cyrillized.

53. Zhemukhov and Aktürk, "Toward a Monolingual Nation."

54. KAFFED, "Alfabe konusunda zorunlu açıklama," 3 April 2015, https://kaffed.org/2015/04/03/alfabe-konusunda-zorunlu-aciklama.

55. On contemporary North Caucasian diasporic identities, see my introduction, note 39; also, Hansen, "iCircassia."

56. "Osmanlıca-Çerkesçe Kamus," *Ğuaze* 35, 36, 39, 43 (1912); Arslan, "Circassian Organizations," 97, 239–42.

57. Besleney, *Circassian Diaspora*, 21–22, 54; Chochiev, "Anatolian Ossetians," 113–14.

58. Arslan, "Circassian Organizations," 142, 161–63.

59. Chochiev, "Istoriograficheskaia initsiativa," quote on 237.

60. Oral, " 'Çerkes Tarihi' Yazılması Girişimi."

61. Besleney, *Circassian Diaspora*, 116–21; Zhemukhov, "Modern Circassian Nationalism."

62. Bornu and Wadai were central African states that were later occupied by, respectively, Britain and France and then incorporated into Nigeria and Chad.

63. "Kalimatayn," *İttihad Gazetesi* 1 (1899): 2–4; translated into Russian by Chochiev, "Obshchestvo edineniia cherkesov."

64. A Russian consul in Jedda reported that as late as 1901 enslaved Circassians were sold at markets in a village three hours away from Jedda and in Mecca. Columbia University, Rare Book and Manuscript Library (New York), Bakhmeteff Archive, Sergei Tukholka, "Memoirs of a Russian Consul General" (Paris, date unknown), f. 53.

65. Arslan, "Circassian Organizations," 67–74.

66. "Kölelik aleyhinde 1," *Ğuaze* 1 (2 April 1911).

67. "Kölelik aleyhinde 2," *Ğuaze* 2 (10 April 1911).

68. "Kölelik aleyhinde 4," *Ğuaze* 6 (18 April 1911); "Kölelik hakkında," *Ğuaze* 9 (1 June 1911).

69. Hayriye Melek Hunç, "Beylik kölelik," *Ğuaze* 10 (8 June 1911): 2. On Hunç, see Toumarkine, "Hayriye Melek (Hunç)"; Arslan, "Circassian Organizations," 82–84, 169–85.

70. "Çerkes İttihad ve Teavün Cemiyeti Talimatnamesi" (4 *teşrin-i sani* 1324, 17 November 1908), in Berzeg, *Gurbetteki Kafkasya'dan Belgeler*, 10–14.

71. Güçtekin, "Çerkes Teavün Mektebi."

72. Yıldız, "Strengthening Male Bodies."

73. Jiy Zafer Süren, "Bereketiko'dan Beşiktaş'a," *Jıneps* (1 April 2012).

74. Shkhakhutova, *Istoriia obrazovaniia v Adygee*, 17–18.

75. Marzoeva, "A. Dymov, N. Tsagov."

76. On North Caucasian diasporic politics during World War I, see Chochiev, "Reclaiming the Homeland"; Chochiev, *Severokavkazskie (cherkesskie) organizatsii*, 58–93.

77. See Berzeg, *Kuzey Kafkasya Cumhuriyeti*; Reynolds, *Shattering Empires*, 201, 235–37.

78. Between World War I and the 1950s, North Caucasian diasporic publishing shifted from Turkey, where it was prohibited, to Europe. North Caucasian emigrants' publications included *Kavkazskii gorets* (Prague, 1924–25); *Vol'nye gortsy* (Prague, 1927–28); *Gortsy Kavkaza* (Paris, 1929–34); *Severnyi Kavkaz* (Warsaw, 1934–39); *Kavkaz/Le Caucase* (Paris and Berlin, 1934–39); *Gazavat* (Berlin, 1943–44); *Kavkaz* (Munich, 1951–52); *Svobodnyi Kavkaz* (Munich, 1951–53); *Ob"edinennyi Kavkaz* (Munich, 1953–54); and *Caucasian Review* (Munich, 1955–60); Çelikpala, "Search for a Common North Caucasian Identity," 114–73. North Caucasian emigrants also contributed to *Prométhée* (Paris, 1926–38) and *La Revue de Prométhée* (Paris, 1938–40).

79. On the North Caucasians' struggle for independence after World War I, see Bennigsen, "Muslim Guerrilla Warfare"; Çelikpala, "North Caucasian Émigré Movements"; Reynolds, "Native Sons."

80. On the Circassian Women's Support Association and its school Çerkes Kız Numune Mektebi (1919–23), see Güsar, "İstanbul Çerkes Kadınları Teavün Cemiyeti"; Karakışla, "Çerkes Kadınları Teavün Cemiyeti."

81. Masud, "*Hijra* in Islamic Law."

82. Crews, *For Prophet and Tsar*, 3, 86–89.

83. Gugov, Kasumov, and Shabaev, *Tragicheskie posledstviia*, 223–24.

84. Letter A, Abdurazakov Family Collection. Author unknown, c. 1870s–90s. I am grateful to Zaira B. Ibragimova for facilitating and to R. Abdurazakov for providing access to the collection. See also Ibragimova, "Problema mukhadzhirstva."

85. Letter B, Abdurazakov Family Collection. Authorship attributed to Ghazi Muhammad, c. 1870s–90s.

86. Many Dagestanis also believed that Ghazi Muhammad sent letters calling Dagestanis to support the Ottoman Empire during the Russo-Ottoman War of 1877–78; Institute of History, Archaeology, and Ethnography of the Dagestan Federal Research Center (Institut istorii, arkheologii i etnografii Dagestanskogo federal'nogo issledovatel'skogo tsentra, Makhachkala, hereafter cited as IIAE DFITs RAN) f. 1, op. 1, d. 177, 179 (1877).

87. TsGA RSO-A f. 12, op. 8, d. 27, ll. 3, 90b (10 recep 1283; 18 November 1866).

88. Hamed-Troyansky, "Letters from the Ottoman Empire."

89. Princeton University, Firestone Library Special Collections (Princeton, New Jersey), Garrett 2867Y (Mach 2034), ff. 91b–94a; Kemper, "Khalidiyya Networks," 50–51.

90. Muhammad al-Dagistani al-Kikuni, Najm al-Anam fi Riyadat al-Awamm (Petrovsk: A.M. Mikhailov, 1905); see Ibragimova and Magomedova, "Dagestanskie bogoslovy," 52.

91. "Hicret Mi, Hezimet Mi?" Ğuaze 2 (10 April 1911), 1–2.

92. "Hicret ve 'Avdet," Ğuaze 5 (4 May 1911), 1–2.

93. "Yine Hicret ve 'Avdet," Ğuaze 17 (14 August 1911), 3.

94. "Hicret Mi, Hezimet Mi?" Ğuaze 27 (28 December 1911), 2–3; see also Arslan, "Circassian Organizations," 100–120.

95. Magomet-bek Hadzhetlashe, or Kazi-Bek Akhmetukov, described himself as a Circassian muhajir born near Istanbul in a princely Abzakh family. Bessmertnaya traces his life in the Ottoman Empire, Russia, and France and concludes that he was likely born in a baptized Jewish family in Tiflis and grew up in Odessa and Saint Petersburg before assuming multiple fake identities; "Magomet-Bek Hadjetlaché."

96. Davlet-Girey Khatakokor, "K polozheniiu mukhadzhirov," Musul'manin 15 (1910): 332–34; "Mukhadzhirskii vopros," Musul'manin 2 (1911): 65–67; see Baderkhan, Severokavkazskaia diaspora, 91–95.

97. Ali Kaiaev (1878–1943), born in Kumukh, Dagestan, studied in Cairo's al-Azhar University in 1905–7 and briefly worked in al-Manār, an Egyptian weekly newspaper edited by Rashid Rida. In Russia's Terek Province in 1908, he opened a madrasa in a Balkar village that implemented Jadidist methods, and, in Temir-Khan-Shura in 1913, he edited Jarīdat Dāghistān and opened another madrasa. 'Ali al-Gumuki (Kaiaev), "Limadha yuhajir al-Daghistaniyun ila al-Mamalik al-'Uthmaniyya," Jarīdat Dāghistān 5 (4 February 1913), preserved in IIAE DFITs RAN f. 3, op. 1, d. 253; Navruzov, Dzharidat Dagistan, 117.

98. Meyer, Turks across Empires, 28.

99. Gugov, Kasumov, and Shabaev, Tragicheskie posledstviia, 440n54, 441n69.

100. Bobrovnikov and Babich, Severnyi Kavkaz, 168.

101. My translation of the Russian-language version. Gutov et al., Adygskie pesni, 595–97.

102. On Turkey's North Caucasian diasporic politics, see Besleney, Circassian Diaspora, 83–142; Kaya, Türkiye'de Çerkesler; Taymaz, "Kuzey Kafkas Dernekleri"; Toumarkine, "Kafkas ve Balkan Göçmen Dernekleri."

103. Besleney traces the origins of the Circassian diaspora's dominant ideologies in

Turkey in 1950–89, that of returnism (*dönüşçülük*) to the Association's cultural activism in 1908–13 and of united Caucasianism to its transnational political phase in 1914–18; *Circassian Diaspora*, 183.

Chapter 7: Return Migration to Russia

1. TsGA KBR f. I-6, op. 1, d. 693, ll. 37, 41 (1–18 March 1907).

2. James H. Meyer examined Muslim, especially Crimean Tatar, return migration to Russia in "Russian Muslims in the Ottoman Empire," 20–26. On return migration in Russian-language scholarship, see Badaev, *Chechenskaia diaspora*, 178–202; Dzidzariia, *Makhadzhirstvo*, 235–39, 381–406; Kushkhabiev, *Problemy repatriatsii*, 19–29.

3. Hamed-Troyansky, "Welcome, Not Welcome."

4. E.G. Ravenstein, "The Laws of Migration" (1885), in Gmelch, "Return Migration," 135. For a foray into global return migration history, see Tsuda, *Diasporic Homecomings*; Long and Oxfeld, *Coming Home*. In Middle Eastern historiography, see Khater, *Inventing Home*.

5. Gmelch, "Return Migration," 141–42.

6. Wyman, *Round-Trip to America*, 6, 11.

7. On return migration of Bulgarians, see Pinson, "Demographic Warfare," 154–69; of Greeks, see TNA FO 195/953, Palgrave to Villiers, ff. 27–28 (1869); SSSA f. 5, op. 1, d. 2197 (1872); of Armenians, see *Kavkaz*, no. 224 (22 August 1880): 2; no. 250 (18 September 1880): 2; BOA HR.SYS 2773/19, 23, 27 (1898).

8. See Adelman and Barkan, *No Return, No Refuge*.

9. TsGA RSO-A f. 12, op. 5, d. 30, ll. 72–720b (25 September 1866).

10. TsGA RSO-A f. 12, op. 5, d. 30, ll. 80–81, 86, 108 (1866); d. 32, ll. 28, 31 (1867).

11. TsGA RSO-A f. 12, op. 5, d. 30, ll. 9, 98–99 (1866).

12. TsGA KBR f. I-2, op. 1, d. 652, ll. 2–3 (25 August 1862).

13. TsGA KBR f. I-2, op. 1, d. 652, l. 1 (30 September 1862).

14. TsGA RD f. 126, op. 3, d. 77, ll. 2–3 (15 June 1870).

15. TsGA RSO-A f. 12, op. 5, d. 29, ll. 25–26, 164–67, 170 (1866); op. 8, d. 27 (1867).

16. "Ob areste gortsev, vozvrashchaiushchikhsia iz Turtsii, i ssylke ikh v Sibir' " (9 January 1861), in Kumykov, *Problemy Kavkazskoi voiny*, 1:116.

17. "Pravila otnositel'no vozvrashchaiushchikhsia iz Turtsii kavkazskikh pereselentsev" (June 1861), in Kumykov, *Problemy Kavkazskoi voiny*, 1:124–29.

18. TsGA KBR f. I-2, op. 1, d. 964, l. 2 (13 January 1867).

19. For example, RGVIA f. 38, op. 7, d. 382, ll. 148–510b (29 May 1862); SSSA f. 416, op. 3, d. 1095, l. 1 (2 October 1863).

20. Kumykov, *Problemy Kavkazskoi voiny*, 1:123 (19 May 1861), 2:72 (6 June 1861).

21. SSSA f. 7, op. 1, d. 1352, ll. 67–69 (27 March 1878).

22. SSSA f. 545, op. 1, d. 1664, ll. 1–2 (23 May 1878).

23. SSSA f. 545, op. 1, d. 2836, ll. 2–5 (7 September 1870); "O vrednom vliianii vozvrashchaiushchikhsia iz Turtsii na umonastroenie gortsev," in Kumykov, *Problemy Kavkazskoi voiny*, 1:202–3 (15 August 1863). On individual cases of returnees accused of pro-Ottoman propaganda, see SSSA f. 545, op. 1, d. 469, ll. 5–11 (30 April–1 May 1869); d. 250, ll. 278–79, 367–68 (26 June–5 November 1869).

24. Nikolai Ignat'ev, Russia's ambassador to the Porte, referred to "theories of Pan-Islamism" as a potential threat to Russian rule already in 1874; SSSA f. 5, op. 1, d. 3317, l. 4 (21 November 1874).

25. Aitberov, Dadaev, and Omarov, *Vosstaniia dagestantsev i chechentsev*, 150, 168.

26. In 1911, the military governor of Dagestan Province refused readmitting a returnee who had spent too much time in the Ottoman Empire and "likely witnessed a recent coup there"; TsGA RD f. 2, op. 5, d. 40, l. 60b (3 March 1911). The same governor, in another case, claimed that "witnessing extraordinary political developments" in the Ottoman Empire made one's presence in Dagestan "extremely undesirable"; TsGA RD f. 2, op. 8, d. 39, ll. 22 (25 January 1913).

27. Wyman, *Round-Trip to America*, 151–68.

28. Ottoman Passport Law (14 February 1867), art. 10.

29. MnV f. 5, op. 2, a.e. 24, no. 1615, ll. 147–50 (4 July 1863).

30. MnV, f. 5, op. 2, a.e. 23, no. 1615, ll. 1506–8 (22 July 1863).

31. TNA FO 195/877, Blunt to Lyons, #30, ff. 251–52r (Edirne, 6 June 1867); Kushkhabiev, *Problemy repatriatsii*, 26.

32. For example, BOA A.MKT.MHM 272/18 (1863); Y.A. HUS. 411/97 (1900). On Ottoman policies toward returnees to Russia, see Cuthell, "Muhacirin Komisyonu," 178–85.

33. SSSA f. 545, op. 1, d. 97, l. 61 (27 September 1865).

34. TNA FO 195/1329, #37, Biliotti to Goschen (Çarşamba, 23 August 1880).

35. SSSA f. 5, op. 1, d. 2202, ll. 1–2, 5 (7 August–30 September 1872); Chochiev, "Neskol'ko osmanskikh dokumentov."

36. SSSA f. 545, op. 1, d. 250, l. 240ob (May 1869).

37. SSSA f. 545, op. 1, d. 250, ll. 188–91, 193–96 (25 October–3 November 1868).

38. TsGA RD f. 2, op. 2, d. 93, ll. 8–9 (19 February 1914).

39. BOA Y.PRK.UM 58/42 (18 *muharrem* 1320, 27 April 1902). On Armenian mobility across the Russo-Ottoman border, see Yazıcı Cörüt, *Loyalty and Citizenship*, 145–85.

40. SSSA f. 545, op. 1, d. 90 (1865); Ibragimova, *Emigratsiia chechentsev*, 40–41.

41. RGVIA f. 38, op. 7, d. 382, ll. 15–18 (undated, summer 1861). The Ottomans also preferred to settle muhajirs away from the Russian border to prevent muhajirs' escape to Russia; BOA A.MKT.NZD 398/7 (10 *cemaziyelahir* 1278, 13 December 1861).

42. TNA FO 78/1875, Taylor to Lyons, #1 (Erzurum, 3 November 1865), f. 114.

43. SSSA f. 545, op. 1, d. 97, ll. 66–67 (14 September 1865).

44. SSSA f. 545, op. 1, d. 97, ll. 62–65 (29 September 1865).

45. TNA FO 78/1875, Taylor to Lyons, #2 (Erzurum, 23 November 1865), ff. 118–21r.

46. SSSA f. 545, op. 1, d. 97, ll. 184–89 (Erzurum, 6 November 1865).

47. TNA FO 78/1875, Taylor to Russell, #5 (Erzurum, 25 November 1865), ff. 116–17.

48. SSSA f. 545, op. 1, d. 97, ff. 80–83 (1 November 1865).

49. The expectation that the Russian government would readmit Muslim converts into Orthodox Christianity relied on a precedent. In October 1865, up to 200 Chechens were readmitted after having pledged to convert to Christianity, although, reportedly, no Chechen returnee ultimately converted; Badaev, *Chechenskaia diaspora*, 179–82. In 1864, some Circassian refugees in Trabzon asked the Russian vice-consul permission to return, offering to become Orthodox Christians; SSSA f. 416, op. 3, d. 1114, l. 250b (8 July 1864).

50. SSSA f. 545, op. 1, d. 97, ff. 80–83 (1 November 1865).

51. SSSA f. 545, op. 1, d. 97, ll. 191–96 (15 November 1865); see also Badaev, *Chechenskaia diaspora*, 185–200.

52. RGVIA f. 400, op. 1, d. 49, ll. 34–340b (31 January 1868).

53. SSSA f. 545, op. 1, d. 2786, ll. 40, 75–79, 103–6 (1866–68).

54. SSSA f. 545, op. 1, d. 97, l. 54 (30 October 1865).

55. For the unwritten reimmigration policy, see SSSA f. 7, op. 1, d. 1352, ll. 60–61 (digest, c. 1874), 97–106 (digest, c. late 1871), complemented by my analysis of deportation and readmittance decisions, summarized in table 9. The policy was in place since 1867, when the Terek provincial governor reported that it was impractical to deport those returnees who had already crossed the Caucasus Mountains into his province; SSSA f. 545, op. 1, d. 250, l. 450b (27 July 1867).

56. Based on resolutions of returnee cases in SSSA f. 545, op. 1, d. 250 (1867–70).

57. SSSA f. 545, op. 1, d. 2852, ll. 160–62 (31 May 1871).

58. SSSA f. 5, op. 1, d. 1731, ll. 5–6 (24 December 1871).

59. Kushkhabiev, *Problemy repatriatsii*, 27.

60. SSSA f. 545, op. 1, d. 2852, l. 710b (25 May 1871); f. 7, op. 1, d. 1352, ll. 99–100 (digest, c. late 1871).

61. For the Russian ban on the reimmigration of Karabulaks, see SSSA f. 7, op. 1, d. 1352, l. 100 (12 June 1871).

62. SSSA f. 7, op. 1, d. 1352, ll. 66, 142–43 (1872–78).

63. SSSA f. 7, op. 1, d. 1352, ll. 60–61 (digest, c. 1874).

64. For individual petitions and decisions, see SSSA f. 7, op. 1, d. 1352, ll. 1–57, 116–44 (1872–73); TsGA RSO-A f. 12, op. 3, d. 128–29, 131, 133–38 (1872–80). Ibragimova suggests that almost half of Chechen muhajirs returned to Chechnya by the mid-1870s; *Emigratsiia chechentsev*, 60.

65. SSSA f. 5, op. 1, d. 3011, ll. 3–5 (21 December 1872).

66. TsGA RSO-A f. 12, op. 5, d. 46, ll. 4–5 (30 March 1870).

67. SSSA f. 545, op. 1, d. 2852, l. 71 (25 May 1871). The policy was conceived earlier: in 1865, Zelenyi, a Russian colonel overseeing Chechen emigration from within the Ottoman Empire, petitioned the Caucasus authorities on behalf of three Chechen elders to allow them to return to Russia. The elders assured him they would impress upon Chechens in the Caucasus that "obeying orders by the Russian government was better than dying in Turkey"; TsGA RSO-A f. 12, op. 5, d. 29, l. 10 (15 November 1865). In 1868, the government planned to settle twenty-five Chechen returnees in western Circassia to dissuade local Muslims from emigrating; Kumykov, *Problemy Kavkazskoi voiny*, 2:347–48.

68. TsGA RSO-A f. 12, op. 3, d. 126, quote on ll. 17–180b (21 May 1871).

69. SSSA f. 545, op. 1, d. 2852, l. 770b (25 May 1871).

70. RGVIA f. 38, op. 7, d. 382 (1860–62); SSSA f. 545, op. 1, d. 2852, l. 710b (25 May 1871); Gugov, Kasumov, and Shabaev, *Tragicheskie posledstviia*, 54.

71. SSSA f. 416, op. 3, d. 212, ll. 2–3 (11 October 1871), 5–6 (22 December 1875); TsGA RSO-A f. 12, op. 4, d. 48, ll. 13–16 (2 December 1871), 38–42 (10 December 1874).

72. Dündar, "Pouring a People into the Desert," 279–80.

73. TsGA RSO-A f. 12, op. 5, d. 32, ll. 1–4, 12–13 (1867).

74. SSSA f. 545, op. 1, d. 250, ll. 345–46 (20 October 1869).

75. Dzidzariia, *Makhadzhirstvo*, 372.

76. SSSA f. 7, op. 1, d. 1352, ll. 73–74 (14 June 1878).

77. One collective petition, signed by 300 Abkhazian deputies, was sent to the Georgian exarch of the Russian Orthodox Church. Petitioners complained of being kidnapped and discriminated against for being Christians. They wrote that if they were not allowed to return by Sukhum authorities, they would have no choice but to convert to Islam; *Tiflisskii vestnik*, no. 98 (26 May 1879). In another instance, twenty-four Abkhazians in Samsun complained about their mistreatment in the Ottoman Empire to the Italian and Greek consulates and the Greek Orthodox clergy, and petitioned to return to Russia via the German embassy. They claimed that the Ottoman troops kidnapped them and forced them to convert from Christianity to Islam; SSSA f. 545, op. 1, d. 1466, ll. 19–22 (November 1877); for other claims by Christians, see ibid., ll. 60–62, 68–69, 80, 108, 148, 209, 295 (1877–79).

78. Dzidzariia, *Makhadzhirstvo*, 383.

79. SSSA f. 545, op. 1, d. 1466, d. 2073, ll. 37–40, 78 (1879–80).

80. SSSA f. 545, op. 1, d. 2069, ll. 33, 39, 42 (23–27 July 1880).

81. SSSA f. 545, op. 1, d. 2069, ll. 56–57, 60 (August 1880).

82. SSSA f. 545, op. 1, d. 2069, l. 66 (14 August 1880).

83. TNA FO 195/1329, Biliotti to Goschen, #43 (Trabzon, 9 September 1880).

84. SSSA f. 545, op. 1, d. 2069, l. 86 (18 August 1880).

85. SSSA f. 545, op. 1, d. 2069, l. 126 (4 September 1880).

86. *Kavkaz*, no. 260 (28 September 1880): 2.

87. SSSA f. 545, op. 1, d. 2069, l. 140 (10 September 1880); Dzidzariia, *Makhadzhirstvo*, 388–92.

88. SSSA f. 545, op. 1, d. 2069, ll. 97–103 (17 August 1880), 193–95 (10 February 1881).

89. Dzidzariia, *Makhadzhirstvo*, 396.

90. On return to Stavropol Governorate in 1860–63, see Dzidzariia, *Makhadzhirstvo*, 235; RGVIA f. 38, op. 7, d. 406; SSSA f. 11, op. 1, d. 3239, ll. 176, 217–22. On return to the Kuban and Terek provinces in 1861–65, I take as the base number the estimate of 7,149 returnees to both provinces in 1861–62 by Laipanov, "K istorii pereseleniia", 126, based on SSSA f. 545, op. 1, d. 69; for individual cases: TsGA RSO-A f. 12, op. 5, d. 21–22, 24. To that number, I add returnees to Terek Province in 1863–65, documented in TsGA RSO-A f. 12, op. 5, d. 25–27, 29; op. 6, d. 1276. On return to Grozny District in 1866–78, the estimate of 5,857 comes from Smirnov, *Politika Rossii na Kavkaze*, 224, and includes 3,510 Chechens in 1867–71, 834 in 1872, and 276 (plus 52 Tabasarans) in 1873, documented in SSSA f. 545, op. 1, d. 250; 2852, esp. ll. 79–83; f. 7, op. 1, d. 1352, ll. 1–57, 116–44; some Ingush and Karabulaks returned alongside Chechens; see also TsGA RSO-A f. 12, op. 3, d. 128, 131, 133–38; op. 4, d. 48; op. 5, d. 30, 32. On return to Sukhum Department in 1866–68, see Dzidzariia, *Makhadzhirstvo*, 295; in 1878–81, see Dzidzariia, *Makhadzhirstvo*, 381–406, esp. 396; SSSA f. 545, op. 1, d. 1466, 2069, 2073. The commander of the Caucasus Army cited an even higher number of 4,300 returnees to the Caucasus in 1868; Kushkhabiev, *Problemy repatriatsii*, 27. The estimate for 1881–1914 is approximate, in the absence

of comprehensive lists of returnees. On return after 1881 to Abkhazia, see Dzidzariia, *Makhadzhirstvo*, 396–97; SSSA f. 231, op. 1, d. 308; f. 545, op. 1, d. 2453; to Kabarda, see TsGA KBR f. I-6, op. 1, d. 693, 863; to other Terek districts, see TsGA RSO-A f. 12, op. 3, d. 144; and to Dagestan, see TsGA RD f. 2, op. 5, d. 40; f. 126, op. 3, d. 100.

91. SSSA f. 7, op. 1, d. 1352, ll. 64–65 (7 March 1878), 76–77 (8 July 1878). During the war of 1877–78, Russian authorities even ordered 30 Chechen households to move from the annexed Kars region to Terek Province; ll. 67–69 (27 March 1878).

92. Kanukov, "Gortsy-pereselentsy."

93. SSSA f. 545, op. 1, d. 2983 (1881); f. 231, op. 1, d. 132 (1887).

94. SSSA f. 7, op. 1, d. 1352, ll. 67–69 (27 March 1878).

95. Ibragimova, *Chechenskii narod*, 428–30.

96. TsGA KBR f. I-6, op. 1, d. 589, ll. 90–900b (10 September 1902); Gugov, Kasumov, and Shabaev, *Tragicheskie posledstviia*, 233–34.

97. TsGA RSO-A f. 12, op. 3, d. 144 (1889–93), d. 146 (1891–92), op. 7, d. 515 (1891–92); TsGA KBR f. I-6, op. 1, d. 528 (1900).

98. TsGA RSO-A f. 12, op. 3, d. 144, ll. 97–98 (14 June 1890).

99. TsGA RD f. 2, op. 8, d. 39, ll. 11–110b (6 August 1912).

100. TsGA RD f. 66, op. 5, d. 36, l. 76 (November 1914).

Conclusion

1. I estimate the number of North Caucasian muhajirs by World War I to be under a million, considering high refugee mortality in the 1860s and 1878–80 and slow population growth. The Ottoman population numbered less than 19 million in 1914; Karpat, *Ottoman Population*, 190.

2. Rogan, *Frontiers of the State*, 226–27.

3. Gingeras, "Notorious Subjects"; Yelbaşı, "Exile, Resistance and Deportation."

4. Gingeras, "Sons of Two Fatherlands."

5. On North Caucasians in post-Ottoman Turkey, see Besleney, *Circassian Diaspora*; Çelikpala, "North Caucasian Diaspora in Turkey"; Doğan, "Circassians in Turkey"; Kaya, *Türkiye'de Çerkesler*; Yelbaşı, *Circassians of Turkey*.

6. Circassian troops helped to repel a Wahhabi attack in August 1922 and quell the ʿAdwan revolt in August 1923. Both events were formative for the consolidation of Hashemite rule; Wilson, *Making of Jordan*, 71–72, 77–78; Alon, *Making of Jordan*, 52–57. Mirza Wasfi's son Wasfi Mirza held ministerial portfolios in Jordanian cabinets in the 1950s and 1960s, and his grandson Nasser Wasfi Mirza married into the Hashemite royal family in 1977.

7. Mackey, "Circassians in Jordan," 73–74, 84.

8. White, *Emergence of Minorities*, 51–54; Provence, *Great Syrian Revolt*, 130–31.

9. On Circassians in post-Ottoman Syria, see Kushkhabiev, *Cherkesy v Sirii*, 111–53; Kushkhabiev et al., "Syrian Circassians"; Ismaʿil, *Dalil al-Ansab al-Sharkasiyya*; in Jordan, see Shami, "Ethnicity and Leadership"; Ganich, *Cherkesy v Iordanii*, 87–142.

10. Geller, "Recruitment and Conscription."

11. Şimşir, *Turks of Bulgaria*, 158.

12. On population transfers between 1913 and 1919, see Özsu, *Formalizing Displacement*, 51–69. On Greek emigration from Bulgaria, see Dragostinova, *Between Two Motherlands*, 117–56.

13. Ladas, *Exchange of Minorities*; İğsız, *Humanism in Ruins*.

14. Özsu, *Formalizing Displacement*, 121–23; Robson, *States of Separation*, 72–78.

15. See Kontogiorgi, *Population Exchange in Greek Macedonia*.

16. Robson, *States of Separation*, 54–55; White, "Refugees and the Definition of Syria," 156–63. The Soviet authorities also hoped to resettle Armenian refugees from the Ottoman Empire in Soviet Armenia's countryside; Laycock, "Developing a Soviet Armenian Nation."

17. Skran, *Refugees in Inter-War Europe*, 275–76.

18. On the early Soviet nationalities policy, see Edgar, *Tribal Nation*; Hirsch, *Empire of Nations*; Martin, *Affirmative Action Empire*; and in the Caucasus, see Goff, *Nested Nationalism*.

19. The Circassians' administrative units in the Soviet era were the Adyghe Autonomous Oblast (1922–91); the Kabardino-Balkarian ASSR (1936–44, 1957–91), formerly the Kabardino-Balkarian Autonomous Oblast (1922–36) and the Kabardian ASSR (1944–57); the Karachay-Cherkessia Autonomous Oblast (1922–26, 1957–91), part of it formerly the Cherkess National Okrug (1926–28) and the Cherkess Autonomous Oblast (1928–57); and the Shapsugh National District (1924–45).

20. Catic, "Politics of Genocide Recognition"; Zhemukhov, "Modern Circassian Nationalism," 518–21.

21. On North Caucasian return since 1991, see Shami, "Circassian Encounters"; Erciyes, "Return Migration to the Caucasus."

22. Hamed-Troyansky, "Welcome, Not Welcome," 607.

BIBLIOGRAPHY

Archives

TURKEY

General Staff Military History and Strategic Studies Archive (T.C. Genelkurmay Başkanlığı Askeri Tarih ve Stratejik Etüt Arşivi, ATASE), Ankara

Presidential State Archives of the Republic of Turkey, Ottoman Archives (T.C. Cumhurbaşkanlığı Devlet Arşivleri Başkanlığı, Osmanlı Arşivi, BOA), Istanbul

JORDAN

Center of Documents and Manuscripts (Markaz al-Wathāʾiq wa-l-Makhṭūṭāt, CDM), University of Jordan, Amman

Department of Land and Survey (Dairat al-Arāḍi wa-l-Masāḥa, DLS), Amman

Khutat Family Collection, Amman

Sultan Private Collection, Zarqaʾ

BULGARIA

Central State Archive of Bulgaria (Tsentralen dŭrzhaven arkhiv, TsDA), Sofia

Museum of the Bulgarian Renaissance (Muzeĭ na Vŭzrazhdaneto, MnV), Varna

SS. Cyril and Methodius National Library (Natsionalna biblioteka "Sv. Sv. Kiril i Metodii," NBKM), Sofia

State Archive, Dobrich Branch (Dŭrzhaven arkhiv), Dobrich

ROMANIA

National Archive of Romania, Tulcea Branch (Direcția Județeană Tulcea a Arhivelor Naționale), Tulcea

RUSSIA

Archive of Foreign Policy of the Russian Empire (Arkhiv vneshnei politiki Rossiiskoi imperii, AVPRI), Moscow

Central State Archive of the Republic of Dagestan (Tsentral'nyi gosudarstvennyi arkhiv Respubliki Dagestan, TsGA RD), Makhachkala

297

Central State Archive of the Republic of Kabardino-Balkaria (Tsentral'nyi gosudarstven-nyi arkhiv Kabardino-Balkarskoi Respubliki, TsGA KBR), Nalchik
Central State Archive of the Republic of North Ossetia-Alania (Tsentral'nyi gosudarst-vennyi arkhiv Respubliki Severnaia Osetiia-Alaniia, TsGA RSO-A), Vladikavkaz
Institute of History, Archaeology, and Ethnography of the Dagestan Federal Research Center (Institut istorii, arkheologii i etnografii Dagestanskogo federal'nogo issledova-tel'skogo tsentra, IIAE DFITs RAN), Makhachkala
National Archive of the Russian Federation (Gosudarstvennyi arkhiv Rossiiskoi Federat-sii, GARF), Moscow
Russian State Military Historical Archive (Rossiiskii gosudarstvennyi voenno-istoricheskii arkhiv, RGVIA), Moscow
Abdurazakov Family Collection, Kizilyurt, Dagestan

GEORGIA
National Historical Archive of Georgia (Sakartvelos sakhelmtsipo saistorio arkivi, SSSA), Tbilisi

ARMENIA
National Archives of Armenia (Hayastani Azgayin Arkhiv, HAA), Yerevan

AZERBAIJAN
National Archive of the Republic of Azerbaijan (Azərbaycan Respublikası Dövlət Tarix Arxivi, ARDTA), Baku

UNITED KINGDOM
The National Archives of the United Kingdom, Records of the Foreign Office (TNA FO), London

UNITED STATES
National Archives and Records Administration (NARA), College Park, Maryland

Research Libraries
Bazadugh Private Collection, Zarqaʾ
Caucasus Foundation (Kafkas Vakfı), Istanbul
Caucasus Research, Culture, and Solidarity Foundation (Kafkas Araştırma Kültür ve Dayanışma Vakfı), Ankara
Center for Islamic Studies (İslam Araştırmaları Merkezi), Istanbul
Circassian Charity Association (al-Jamʿiyya al-Khayriyya al-Sharkasiyya), Amman
Columbia University, Rare Book and Manuscript Library, New York
Kabardino-Balkar Institute for Research in Humanities (Kabardino-Balkarskii institut gumanitarnykh issledovanii), Nalchik
North Ossetian Institute for Research in Humanities and Social Sciences (Severo-Osetinskii institut gumanitarnykh i sotsial'nykh issledovanii, SOIGSI), Vladikavkaz
Princeton University, Firestone Library Special Collections, Princeton, New Jersey
Shamil Education and Culture Foundation (Şamil Eğitim ve Kültür Vakfı), Istanbul
State Public Historical Library of Russia (Gosudarstvennaia publichnaia istoricheskaia biblioteka Rossii), Moscow

Newspapers
The Armenian Herald, Boston
Derby Mercury, Derby
Ğuaze, Istanbul
İttihad Gazetesi, Cairo
Jarīdat Dāghistān, Temir-Khan-Shura (Buynaksk)
Jıneps, Istanbul
Kavkaz, Tiflis (Tbilisi)
Kievskaia starina, Kyiv
Levant Herald, Istanbul
Musul'manin, Paris
Österreichische Revue, Vienna
Pravo, Istanbul
Russkii invalid, Saint Petersburg
Tiflisskii vestnik, Tiflis
The Times, London
Tuna, Rusçuk (Ruse)

Published Primary Sources
Abramov, Iakov V. "Kavkazskie gortsy." *Delo* 1 (1884): 62–104.
Aitberov, Timur M., Iu.U. Dadaev, and Kh.A. Omarov, eds. *Vosstaniia dagestantsev i chechentsev v posleshamilevskuiu epokhu i imamat 1877 goda: materialy*. Makhachkala: IIAE DNTs RAN, 2001.
Aristarchi Bey, Grégoire. *Législation ottomane, ou Recueil des lois, règlements, ordonnances, traités, capitulations et autres documents officiels de l'Empire ottoman*. Istanbul: Frères Nicolaïdes, 1873–88.
Bell, James Stanislaus. *Journal of a Residence in Circassia*. 2 vols. London: Edward Moxon, 1840.
Berzeg, Sefer E., ed. *Gurbetteki Kafkasya'dan Belgeler*. Ankara, 1985.
Berzhe, Adol'f P. "Vyselenie gortsev s Kavkaza." *Russkaia starina* 33 (1882): 161–76, 337–63; *Russkaia starina* 36 (1882): 1–32. Reprinted in Nalchik: Izdatel'stvo M. i V. Kotliarovykh, 2010.
Berzhe, Adol'f P., D.A. Kobiakov, and E.G. Veidenbaum, eds., *Akty sobrannye Kavkazskoi arkheograficheskoi komissiei*. 12 vols. Tiflis: Tipografiia Glavnogo upravleniia namestnika Kavkazskago, 1866–1904.
Bliss, Frederick Jones. "Narrative of an Expedition to Moab and Gilead in March, 1895." *Palestine Exploration Fund Quarterly Statement* 27, no. 3 (1895): 203–35.
Chochiev, Georgy. "Neskol'ko osmanskikh dokumentov o poselenii osetin v Anatolii." *Izvestiia SOIGSI* 23, no. 62 (2017): 67–74.
Dimitrov, Strashimir, Nikolai Zhechev, and Velko Tonev. *Istoriia na Dobrudzha*. Vol. 3. Sofia: Bulgarian Academy of Sciences, 1988.
Draganova, Slavka. *Berkovskoto selo v navecherieto na Osvobozhdenieto: statichesko izsledvane spored Osmanskite danŭchni registri*. Sofia: Bulgarian Academy of Sciences, 1985.

————. *Materiali za Dunavskiia vilaet: Rusenska, Silistrenska, Shumenska i Tutrakanska kaza, prez 50-te–70-te godini na XIX v.* Sofia: Bulgarian Academy of Sciences, 1980.

DuBois de Montpéreux, Frédéric. *Voyage autour du Caucase chez les Tcherkesses et les Abkhases.* 6 vols. Paris: Librairie de Gide, 1839–43.

Dulaurier, Édouard. "La Russie dans le Caucase, fin de la guerre de Circassie et dispersion des tribus tcherkesses: L'exode des Circassiens et la colonisation russe." *Revue des deux mondes*, 15 December 1865: 947–82; 1 January 1866: 41–67.

Dzagurov, Grigorii A., ed. *Pereselenie gortsev v Turtsiiu: materialy po istorii gorskikh narodov.* Rostov-Don: Sevkavkniga, 1925.

Dzamikhov, Kasbolat F. *Adygi: bor'ba i izgnanie.* Nalchik: El'-Fa, 2005.

Fisher, Stanley. *Ottoman Land Laws: Containing the Ottoman Land Code and Later Legislation Affecting Land.* London: Oxford University Press, 1919.

Fonvil', A. (Arthur de Fonvielle). *Poslednii god voiny Cherkessii za nezavisimost', 1863–1864 gg.* Kyiv: UO MShK MADPR, 1991.

Gerov, Naiden, ed. *Dokumenti za Bŭlgarskata istoriia.* Vol. 3. Sofia: Bulgarian Academy of Sciences, 1940.

Goodrich-Freer, Adela M. *In a Syrian Saddle.* London: Methuen & Co., 1905.

Gugov, Rashad Kh., Kh.A. Kasumov, and D.V. Shabaev, eds. *Tragicheskie posledstviia Kavkazskoi voiny dlia adygov: vtoraia polovina XIX-nachalo XX veka. Sbornik dokumentov i materialov.* Nalchik: El'-Fa, 2000.

Gurulkan, Kemal, ed. *Osmanlı Belgelerinde Kafkas Göçleri.* 2 vols. Istanbul: Başbakanlık Devlet Arşivleri Genel Müdürlüğü, 2012.

Gutov, Adam M., V.Kh. Kazharov, M.A. Tabishev, and N.G. Sherieva, eds. *Adygskie pesni vremen Kavkazskoi voiny*, 2nd ed. Nalchik: Pechatnyi dvor, 2014.

Haghandoqa, Mohammad Kheir. *Mirza Pasha Wasfi: Kitab watha'iqi, marhala min tarikh bilad al-Sham min khilal watha'iq Mirza Pasha.* Amman: Royal Scientific Society, 1994.

House of Commons. *Papers Respecting the Settlement of Circassian Emigrants in Turkey.* London: Harrison & Sons, 1864.

————. *Parliamentary Papers.* Turkey, no. 6 (1881).

Ivanov, Igor' S., et al., eds. *Ocherki istorii Ministerstva inostrannykh del Rossii, 1802–2002.* 3 vols. Moscow: Olma-Press, 2002.

Kafadar, Cemal. *Between Two Worlds: The Construction of the Ottoman State.* Berkeley: University of California Press, 1995.

Kanitz, Felix. "Die Tscherkessen Emigration nach der Donau: Historisch-ethnographische Skizze." *Österreichische Revue* 3, no. 11 (1865): 227–42.

Kanukov, Inal. "Gortsy-pereselentsy." *Sbornik svedenii o kavkazskikh gortsakh* 9 (1876): 84–103.

Kaufman, Aleksandr A. *Pereselenie i kolonizatsiia.* Saint Petersburg: Biblioteka obshchestvennoi pol'zy, 1905.

Kokiev, Georgii A., ed. *Krest'ianskaia reforma v Kabarde: dokumenty po istorii osvobozhdeniia zavisimykh soslovii v Kabarde v 1867 godu.* Nalchik: Kabardinskoe gosudarstvennoe izdatel'stvo, 1947.

Koliubakin, Boris M. *Russo-Turetskaia voina 1877–1878 gg. na Kavkaze i v Maloi Azii*. 2 vols. Saint Petersburg: Tipo-litografiia A.G. Rozena, 1906–8.

Kondakov, Nikodim P. *Arkheologicheskoe puteshestvie po Sirii i Palestine*. Saint Petersburg: Imperatorskaia Akademiia Nauk, 1904.

Kumykov, Tugan Kh., ed. *Problemy Kavkazskoi voiny i vyselenie cherkesov v predely Osmanskoi imperii, 20–70e gg. XIX v.: sbornik arkhivnykh dokumentov*. 2 vols. Nalchik: El'brus, 2001–3.

———, ed. *Vyselenie adygov v Turtsiiu—posledstvie Kavkazskoi voiny*. Nalchik: El'brus, 1994.

Kundukhov, Musa. "Memuary Generala Musa-Pashi Kundukhova." *Kavkaz / Le Caucase* (Paris): 1–5, 8, 10–12 (1936); 3, 5, 7–8, 10 (1937).

Kushkhabiev, Anzor V., ed. *Istoriia adygov v dokumentakh Osmanskogo gosudarstvennogo arkhiva*. Nalchik: Respublikanskii poligrafkombinat im. Revoliutsii 1905 g., 2009.

Lees, G. Robinson. "Across Southern Bashan." *Geographical Journal* 5, no. 1 (1895): 1–27.

Leontovich, Fedor I. *Adaty Kavkazskikh gortsev: materialy po obychnomu pravu Severnago i Vostochnago Kavkaza*. 2 vols. Odessa: Tipografiia P.A. Zelenogo, 1882–83.

Longworth, John A. *A Year among the Circassians*. London: H. Colburn, 1840.

Loupouleskou. "Russkie kolonii v Dobrudzhe." *Kievskaia starina*, no. 1 (1889): 117–54.

MacGahan, Januarius A., and Eugene Schuyler. *The Turkish Atrocities in Bulgaria*. London: Bradbury, Agnew & Co., 1876.

Magomeddadaev, Amirkhan M., *Mukhammad-Amin i narodno-osvoboditel'noe dvizhenie narodov Severo-Zapadnogo Kavkaza v 40–60 gg. XIX veka: sbornik dokumentov i materialov*. Makhachkala: IIAE DNTs RAN, 1998.

Maksimov, Nikolai V. *Dve voiny 1876–1878 gg*. Saint Petersburg: I.L. Tuzov, 1879.

Mikhailov, Nikolai T. *Spravochnik po Stavropol'skoi eparkhii: obzor gorodov, sel, stanits i khutorov Stavropol'skoi gubernii i Kubanskoi oblasti*. Ekaterinodar, 1911. Reprint, Moscow: Nadyrshin, 2008.

Miliutin, Dmitrii A. *Vospominaniia. 1856–1860*. Moscow: Rosspen, 2004.

Oliphant, Laurence. *The Land of Gilead, with Excursions in the Lebanon*. Edinburgh: W. Blackwood & Sons, 1880.

Ovsianyi, Nikolai R., ed. *Sbornik materialov po grazhdanskomu upravleniiu i okkupatsii v Bolgarii v 1877-78-79 gg*. Vol. 5. Saint Petersburg: Tovarishchestvo khudozhestvennoi pechati, 1906.

Qazan, Salah Yusuf. *'Amman fi Matla' al-Qarn al-'Ashrin: al-Sijill al-Shar'i al-Awwal li-Nahiyat 'Amman, 1319–1326 H / 1902–1908 M, Dirasa wa-Tahqiq*. Amman: Ministry of Culture, 2002.

Salaheddin Bey. *La Turquie à l'Exposition Universelle de 1867*. Paris: Librairie Hachette et C., 1867.

Salname-i Vilayet-i Sivas. Sivas, 1325 H/1907.

Sharafutdinova, R. Sh. *Araboiazychnye dokumenty epokhi Shamilia*. Moscow: Vostochnaia literatura, 2001.

Shavrov, Nikolai N. *Novaia ugroza russkomu delu v Zakavkaz'e: predstoiashchaia rasprodazha Mugani inorodtsam*. Saint Petersburg: Tipografiia Ministerstva Finansov, 1911.

Şimşir, Bilal N., ed. *Rumeli'den Türk Göçleri: Belgeler.* 3 vols. Ankara: Türk Tarih Kurumu, 1968, 1970, 1989.

Taitbout de Marigny, Edouard. *Three Voyages in the Black Sea to the Coast of Circassia.* London: John Murray, 1837.

Todorov-Khindalov, Vladimir, ed. *Godishnik na Narodna Biblioteka v Sofiia, 1926–28.* Sofia, 1930.

Tonev, Velko, et al., eds. *Izvori za istoriiata na Dobrudzha.* Vol. 3, Sofia: IK Gutenberg, 2003; vol. 4, Sofia: Vekove, 2003.

Troinitskii, Nikolai A., et al., eds. *Obshchii svod po Imperii rezul'tatov razrabotki dannykh pervoi vseobshchei perepisi naseleniia.* Saint Petersburg: Parovaia tipo-litografiia N.L. Nyrkina, 1905.

Tukholka, Sergei V. *Russkie poddannye v Turtsii.* Saint Petersburg: Tipografiia V.F. Kirshbauma, 1900.

Secondary Sources

Abdullaeva, Madina I. *Vnutripoliticheskaia situatsiia v Dagestane v 70–90e gg. XIX v. i migratsionnye protsessy.* Makhachkala: IIAE DNTs RAN, 2014.

Abujaber, Raouf Saʿd. *Pioneers over Jordan: The Frontier of Settlement in Transjordan, 1850–1914.* London: I.B. Tauris, 1989.

Adamiak, Patrick John. "To the Edge of the Desert: Caucasian Refugees, Civilization, and Settlement on the Ottoman Frontier, 1866–1918." PhD diss., University of California, San Diego, 2018.

Adelman, Howard, and Elazar Barkan. *No Return, No Refuge: Rites and Rights in Minority Repatriation.* New York: Columbia University Press, 2011.

Adjemian, Boris, and Mikaël Nichanian, eds. "The Massacres of the Hamidian Period." Special issue, *Études arméniennes contemporaines* 10 and 11 (2019).

Ahmed, Feroz. *The Young Turks: The Committee of Union and Progress in Turkish Politics, 1908–1914.* Oxford: Clarendon Press, 1969.

Akçam, Taner. *The Young Turks' Crime against Humanity: The Armenian Genocide and Ethnic Cleansing in the Ottoman Empire.* Princeton: Princeton University Press, 2012.

Akçasu, A. Ebru. "Nation and Migration in Late-Ottoman Spheres of (Legal) Belonging: A Comparative Look at Laws on Nationality." *Nationalities Papers* 49, no. 6 (2021): 1–19.

Akin, Yiğit. *When the War Came Home: The Ottomans' Great War and the Devastation of an Empire.* Stanford: Stanford University Press, 2018.

Akram, Susan M. "Palestinian Refugees and Their Legal Status: Rights, Politics, and Implications for a Just Solution." *Journal of Palestine Studies* 31, no. 3 (2002): 36–51.

Aksakal, Mustafa. *The Ottoman Road to War in 1914: The Ottoman Empire and the First World War.* Cambridge: Cambridge University Press, 2008.

Aksoy, Elbruz. *Benim Adım 1864: Çerkes Hikayeleri.* Istanbul: İletişim Yayınları, 2018.

———. *Beyaz Köleler: Son Sesler.* Istanbul: İletişim Yayınları, 2022.

Alff, Kristen. "The Business of Property: Levantine Joint-Stock Companies, Land, Law, and Capitalist Development around the Mediterranean, 1850–1925." PhD diss., Stanford University, 2019.

Aliev, Bagavudin R. "Severokavkazskaia diaspora v stranakh Blizhnego i Srednego Vostoka: istoriia i sovremennye protsessy (vtoraia polovina XIX–XX v.)." PhD diss., IIAE DNTs RAN, 2002.

Allen, W.E.D., and Paul Muratoff. *Caucasian Battlefields: A History of the Wars on the Turco-Caucasian Border, 1828–1921.* New York: Cambridge University Press, 1953.

Alon, Yoav. *The Making of Jordan: Tribes, Colonialism and the Modern State.* London: I.B. Tauris, 2009.

———. *The Shaykh of Shaykhs: Mithqal al-Fayiz and Tribal Leadership in Modern Jordan.* Stanford: Stanford University Press, 2016.

Amawi, Abla M. "The Transjordanian State and the Enterprising Merchants of Amman." In Hannoyer and Shami, *Amman*, 109–28.

Amrith, Sunil S. *Crossing the Bay of Bengal: The Furies of Nature and the Fortunes of Migrants.* Cambridge: Harvard University Press, 2013.

Amzi-Erdoğdular, Leyla. *The Afterlife of Ottoman Europe: Muslims in Habsburg Bosnia Herzegovina.* Stanford: Stanford University Press, 2024.

Angelova, Daniela. *Demografsko razvitie na Bŭlgarskoto Chernomorsko kraĭbrezhie prez XIX vek (do 1878 g.).* Sofia: Regaliia-6, 2013.

Arendt, Hannah. *The Origins of Totalitarianism.* New York: Schocken, 1951.

al-Arnaut, Muhamed Mufaku. "Islam and Muslims in Bosnia, 1878–1918: Two 'Hijras' and Two 'Fatwās.'" *Journal of Islamic Studies* 5, no. 2 (1994): 242–53.

Arslan, Elmas Zeynep. "Circassian Organizations in the Ottoman Empire (1908–1923)." Master's diss., Boğaziçi University, 2008.

Astourian, Stephan H. "The Silence of the Land: Agrarian Relations, Ethnicity, and Power." In Suny, Naimark, and Göçek, *Question of Genocide,* 55–81.

Avakian, Arsen. *Cherkesskii faktor v Osmanskoi imperii i Turtsii (vtoraia polovina XIX—pervaia chetvert' XX vv.).* Yerevan: Gitutiun, 2001.

Aydemir, İzzet. *Göç: Kuzey Kafkasya'dan Göç Tarihi.* Ankara: Gelişim Matbaası, 1988.

———. *Muhaceretteki Çerkes Aydınları.* Ankara, 1991.

Aydın, Cemil. *The Idea of the Muslim World: A Global Intellectual History.* Cambridge: Harvard University Press, 2017.

Badaev, Said-Emi S. *Chechenskaia diaspora na Srednem i Blizhnem Vostoke: istoriia i sovremennost'.* Nalchik: Respublikanskii poligrafkombinat im. Revoliutsii 1905 g., 2008.

Baddeley, John F. *The Russian Conquest of the Caucasus.* London: Longmans, Green & Co., 1908.

Badem, Candan. *Çarlık Yönetiminde Kars, Ardahan, Atvin.* Istanbul: Aras, 2018.

Baderkhan, Fasikh. *Severokavkazskaia diaspora v Turtsii, Sirii i Iordanii: vtoraia polovina XIX—pervaia polovina XX veka.* Moscow: IV RAN, 2001.

Balistreri, Alexander E. "The Persistence of the Periphery: Domination and Change in the Anatolian-Caucasian Borderland." PhD diss., Princeton University, 2021.

Balkanski, Todor. *Cherkezite v bŭlgarskite zemi: ezikovoarkheologicheski prochit.* Veliko Tarnovo: IK Znak 94, 2011.

Balloffet, Lily Pearl. *Argentina in the Global Middle East*. Stanford: Stanford University Press, 2020.

Banko, Lauren, Katarzyna Nowak, and Peter Gatrell. "What Is Refugee History, Now?" *Journal of Global History* 17, no. 1 (2022): 1–19.

Barakat, Nora Elizabeth. *Bedouin Bureaucrats: Mobility and Property in the Ottoman Empire*. Stanford: Stanford University Press, 2023.

———. "Regulating Land Rights in Late Nineteenth-Century Salt: The Limits of Legal Pluralism in Ottoman Property Law." *Journal of the Ottoman and Turkish Studies Association* 2, no. 1 (2015): 101–19.

Barkan, Ömer Lütfi. "Osmanlı İmparatorluğu'nda bir İskan ve Kolonizasyon Metodu Olarak Sürgünler." *İstanbul Üniversitesi İktisat Fakültesi Mecmuası* 11 (1949): 524–69; 13, no. 1–4 (1952): 56–78.

Barker, Hannah. *The Most Precious Merchandise: The Mediterranean Trade in Black Sea Slaves, 1260–1500*. Philadelphia: University of Pennsylvania Press, 2019.

Barkey, Karen, and Mark von Hagen, eds. *After Empire: Multiethnic Societies and Nation-Building: The Soviet Union and the Russian, Ottoman, and Habsburg Empires*. Boulder: Westview Press, 1997.

Barrett, Thomas M. *At the Edge of the Empire: The Terek Cossacks and the North Caucasus Frontier, 1700–1860*. Boulder: Westview Press, 1999.

———. "'The Land Is Spoiled by Water': Cossack Colonisation in the North Caucasus." *Environment and History* 5, no. 1 (1999): 27–52.

———. "Lines of Uncertainty: The Frontiers of the North Caucasus." *Slavic Review* 54, no. 3 (1995): 578–601.

Bartov, Omer, and Eric D. Weitz, eds. *Shatterzone of Empires: Coexistence and Violence in the German, Habsburg, Russian, and Ottoman Borderlands*. Bloomington: Indiana University Press, 2013.

Baydar, Oya. *Cumhuriyet'in Aile Albümleri*. Istanbul: Tarih Vakfı Yayınları, 1998.

Benbassa, Esther, and Aron Rodrigue. *Sephardi Jewry: A History of the Judeo-Spanish Community, 14th–20th Centuries*. Berkeley: University of California Press, 2008.

Ben-Bassat, Yuval. *Petitioning the Sultan: Protests and Justice in Late Ottoman Palestine*. London: I.B. Tauris, 2013.

Bennigsen, Alexandre. "Muslim Guerrilla Warfare in the Caucasus (1918–1928)." *Central Asian Survey* 2, no. 1 (1983): 45–56.

———. "The Qadiriyah (Kunta Hajji) Tariqah in North-East Caucasus: 1850–1987." *Islamic Culture* 62, no. 2–3 (1988): 63–78.

Berkok, İsmail. *Tarihte Kafkasya*. Istanbul, 1958.

Berzeg, Sefer E. *Adige-Çerkes Alfabesinin Tarihçesi*. Ankara: Şenyuva Matbaası, 1969.

———. *Kafkas Diasporası'nda Edebiyatçılar ve Yazarlar Sözlüğü*. Samsun: Kafkasya Gerçeği, 1995.

———. *Kuzey Kafkasya Cumhuriyeti 1917–1922*. 3 vols. Istanbul: Birleşik Kafkasya Derneği, 2003–6.

———. *Türkiye Kurtuluş Savaşı'nda Çerkes Göçmenleri*. Istanbul: Nart Yayıncılık, 1990.

Besleney, Zeynel Abidin. *The Circassian Diaspora in Turkey: A Political History*. London: Routledge, 2014.

Bessmertnaya, Olga. "Magomet-Bek Hadjetlaché and the Muslim Question: Deceit, Trust, and Orientalism in Imperial Russia after 1905." *Kritika: Explorations in Russian and Eurasian History* 22, no. 4 (2021): 697–727.

Beşikçi, Mehmet. "Başıbozuk Savaşçıdan 'Makbul' Tebaaya: 1877–1878 Osmanlı-Rus Savaşı'nda Osmanlı Ordusunda Çerkez Muhacirler." *Hacettepe Üniversitesi Türkiyat Araştırmaları Dergisi* 23 (2015): 85–123.

Bice, Hayati. *Kafkasya'dan Anadolu'ya Göçler.* Ankara: Türkiye Diyanet Vakfı Yayınları, 1991.

Birdal, Murat. *The Political Economy of Ottoman Public Debt: Insolvency and European Financial Control in the Late Nineteenth Century.* London: I.B. Tauris, 2010.

Blakely, Allison. *Russia and the Negro: Blacks in Russian History and Thought.* Washington, D.C.: Howard University Press, 1986.

Blauvelt, Timothy K. "Military-Civil Administration and Islam in the North Caucasus, 1858–83." *Kritika: Explorations in Russian and Eurasian History* 11, no. 2 (2010): 221–55.

Bloxham, Donald. "The First World War and the Development of the Armenian Genocide." In Suny, Naimark, and Göçek, *Question of Genocide,* 260–75.

Blumi, Isa. *Ottoman Refugees, 1878–1939: Migration in a Post-Imperial World.* London: Bloomsbury, 2013.

Bobrovnikov, Vladimir O. "Mukhadzhirstvo v 'demograficheskikh voinakh' Rossii i Turtsii." *Vostok* 2 (2010): 67–78.

———. *Musul'mane Severnogo Kavkaza: obychai, pravo, nasilie.* Moscow: IV RAN, 2002.

———. "Rossiiskie musul'mane posle arkhivnoi revoliutsii: vzgliad s Kavkaza i iz Bolgarii." *Ab Imperio* 4 (2008): 313–33.

Bobrovnikov, Vladimir O., and Irina L. Babich. *Severnyi Kavkaz v sostave Rossiiskoi imperii.* Moscow: Novoe Literaturnoe Obozrenie, 2007.

Borlakova, Fatima A. "Karachaevo-balkarskaia emigratsiia: etapy formirovaniia i etnokul'turnoi evoliutsii (vtoraia polovina XIX–pervaia polovina XX v.)." PhD diss., Karachaevo-Cherkessk State University, 2009.

Braude, Benjamin. "Foundation Myths of the Millet System." In *Christians and Jews in the Ottoman Empire: The Functioning of a Plural Society,* edited by Benjamin Braude and Bernard Lewis, 1:69–88. New York: Holmes & Meier, 1982.

Breyfogle, Nicholas B. *Heretics and Colonizers: Forging Russia's Empire in the South Caucasus.* Ithaca: Cornell University Press, 2011.

Brisku, Adrian. *Political Reform in the Ottoman and Russian Empires: A Comparative Approach.* London: Bloomsbury, 2017.

Brock, Peter. "The Fall of Circassia: A Study in Private Diplomacy." *English Historical Review* 71, no. 280 (1956): 401–27.

Brooks, Willis. "The Politics of the Conquest of the Caucasus, 1855–1864." *Nationalities Papers* 24, no. 4 (1996): 649–60.

Brower, Daniel. "Russian Roads to Mecca: Religious Tolerance and Muslim Pilgrimage." *Slavic Review* 55, no. 3 (1996): 567–84.

Brubaker, Rogers. "Aftermaths of Empire and the Unmixing of Peoples: Historical and Comparative Perspectives." *Ethnic and Racial Studies* 18, no. 2 (1995): 189–218.

———. "The 'Diaspora' Diaspora." *Ethnic and Racial Studies* 28, no. 1 (2005): 1–19.

Burbank, Jane. "An Imperial Rights Regime: Law and Citizenship in the Russian Empire." *Kritika: Explorations in Russian and Eurasian History* 7, no. 3 (2006): 397–431.

Buzpınar, Ş. Tufan. "The Ottoman Response to Laurence Oliphant's Project of Jewish Settlement in Palestine (1879–1882)." *Journal of Ottoman Studies* 56 (2020): 259–86.

Campbell, Elena I. *The Muslim Question and Russian Imperial Governance*. Bloomington: Indiana University Press, 2015.

Campos, Michelle U. *Ottoman Brothers: Muslims, Christians, and Jews in the Early Twentieth-Century Palestine*. Stanford: Stanford University Press, 2011.

Can, Lâle. "The Protection Question: Central Asians and Extraterritoriality in the Late Ottoman Empire." *International Journal of Middle East Studies* 48, no. 4 (2016): 679–99.

———. *Spiritual Subjects: Central Asian Pilgrims and the Ottoman Hajj at the End of Empire*. Stanford: Stanford University Press, 2020.

Can, Lâle, and Michael Christopher Low, eds. "The 'Subjects' of Ottoman International Law." Special issue, *Journal of the Ottoman and Turkish Studies Association* 3, no. 2 (2016).

Can, Lâle, Michael Christopher Low, Kent F. Schull, and Robert Zens. *The Subjects of Ottoman International Law*. Bloomington: Indiana University Press, 2020.

Casale, Giancarlo. *The Ottoman Age of Exploration*. Oxford: Oxford University Press, 2012.

Case, Holly. *The Age of Questions*. Princeton: Princeton University Press, 2018.

Catford, John C. "Mountain of Tongues: The Languages of the Caucasus." *Annual Review of Anthropology* 6 (1977): 283–314.

Catic, Maja. "Circassians and the Politics of Genocide Recognition." *Europe-Asia Studies* 67, no. 10 (2015): 1685–1708.

Chatty, Dawn. *Displacement and Dispossession in the Modern Middle East*. Cambridge: Cambridge University Press, 2010.

———. "Refugees, Exiles, and Other Forced Migrants in the Late Ottoman Empire." *Refugee Survey Quarterly* 32, no. 2 (2013): 35–52.

Cherkasov, Aleksandr A., Vladimir G. Ivantsov, Michal Smigel, and Violetta S. Molchanova. "The Demographic Characteristics of the Tribes of the Black Sea Region in the First Half of the XIX Century." *Bylye gody* 40, no. 2 (2016): 382–91.

Chirikba, Viacheslav A. "Rasselenie abkhazov i abazin v Turtsii." *Dzhigetskii sbornik* 1 (2012): 21–95.

Chochiev, Georgy. "Caucasian Newspaper in the Late 19th-Century Cairo: 'İttihad Gazetesi.' " *Folklor/Edebiyat Dergisi* 20, no. 2 (2014): 225–37.

———. "Evolution of a North Caucasian Community in Late Ottoman and Republican Turkey: The Case of Anatolian Ossetians." In *Diasporas of the Modern Middle East: Contextualising Community*, edited by Anthony Gorman and Sossie Kasbarian, 103–37. Edinburgh: University of Edinburgh Press, 2016.

———. "General Musa Kundukhov: nekotorye fakty zhizni i deiatel'nosti v emigratsii." *Kavkazskii sbornik* 3 (35) (2006): 65–86.

———. "Istoriograficheskaia initsiativa cherkesskoi elity v Osmanskoi imperii (1883–1884 gg.)." *Voprosy istorii* 12, no. 4 (2019): 233–47.

———. "Obshchestvo edineniia cherkesov i ego pechatnyi organ gazeta 'Ittihad' (Kair, 1899 g.)." *Vestnik Instituta Tsivilizatsii* 6 (2005).

———. "On the History of the North Caucasian Diaspora in Turkey." *Iran and the Caucasus* 11, no. 2 (2007): 213–26.

———. "Rasselenie severokavkazskikh immigrantov v arabskikh provintsiiakh Osmanskoi imperii (vtoraia polovina XIX–nachalo XX v.)." In *Osmanskaia imperiia: sobytiia i liudi*, edited by Mikhail S. Meier and Svetlana F. Oreshkova, 94–127. Moscow: Gumanitarii, 2000.

———. "Reclaiming the Homeland: The Caucasus-Oriented Activities of Ottoman Circassians during and after World War I." In *War and Collapse: World War I and the Ottoman State*, edited by M. Hakan Yavuz and Feroz Ahmad, 588–632. Salt Lake City: University of Utah Press, 2016.

———. *Severokavkazskie (cherkesskie) organizatsii v Turtsii (1908–1923 gg.)*. Vladikavkaz: SOIGSI, 2009.

Chochiev, Georgy, and Bekir Koç. "Migrants from the North Caucasus in Eastern Anatolia: Some Notes on Their Settlement and Adaptation (Second Half of the 19th Century—Beginning of the 20th Century." *Journal of Asian History* 40, no. 1 (2006): 80–103.

Chokobaeva, Aminat, Cloé Drieu, and Alexander Morrison, eds. *The Central Asian Revolt of 1916: A Collapsing Empire in the Age of War and Revolution*. Manchester: Manchester University Press, 2020.

Clifford, James. "Diasporas." *Cultural Anthropology* 9, no. 3 (1994): 302–38.

Cohen, Julia Phillips. *Becoming Ottomans: Sephardi Jews and Imperial Citizenship in the Modern Era*. Oxford: Oxford University Press, 2014.

Colarusso, John. *Nart Sagas from the Caucasus: Myths and Legends from the Circassians, Abazas, Abkhaz, and Ubykhs*. Princeton: Princeton University Press, 2002.

Crews, Robert D. "Empire and the Confessional State: Islam and Religious Politics in Nineteenth-Century Russia." *American Historical Review* 108, no. 1 (2003): 50–83.

———. *For Prophet and Tsar: Islam and Empire in Russia and Central Asia*. Cambridge: Harvard University Press, 2009.

Cuthell, David Cameron Jr. "The Muhacirin Komisyonu: An Agent in the Transformation of Ottoman Anatolia, 1860–1866." PhD diss., Columbia University, 2005.

———. "The Circassian Sürgün." *Ab Imperio* 2 (2003): 139–68.

Çadırcı, Musa. "Türkiye'de Muhtarlık Teşkilâtının Kurulması Üzerine bir İnceleme." *Belleten* 34 (1970): 409–20.

Çatalkılıç, Didem. "Kafkasya'dan Uzunyayla'ya Taşınan Hafıza Mekanları: Köy Toponim ve Sülale Tarihleri." *Karadeniz Araştırmaları* 18, no. 69 (2021): 71–120.

Çelikpala, Mitat. "From Immigrants to Diaspora: Influence of the North Caucasian Diaspora in Turkey." *Middle Eastern Studies* 42, no. 3 (2006): 423–46.

———. "North Caucasian Émigré Movements between the Two World Wars." *International Journal of Turkish Studies* 9, no. 1–2 (2003): 287–314.

———. "Search for a Common North Caucasian Identity: The Mountaineers' Attempts for Survival and Unity in Response to the Russian Rule." PhD diss., Bilkent University, 2002.

308   BIBLIOGRAPHY

Çiçek, Nazan. " 'Talihsiz Çerkesleri İngiliz Peksimeti': İngiliz Arşiv Belgelerinde Büyük
Çerkes Göçü (Şubat 1864—Mayıs 1865)." *Ankara Üniversitesi Siyasal Bilimler Fakültesi
Dergisi* 64, no. 1 (2009): 57–88.

Datta, Arunima. *Fleeting Agencies: A Social History of Indian Coolie Women in British
Malaya*. Cambridge: Cambridge University Press, 2021.

David-Fox, Michael, Peter Holquist, and Alexander N. Martin, eds. "Subjecthood and
Citizenship." Special issue, *Kritika: Explorations in Russian and Eurasian History* 7, no.
2–3 (2006).

Dawud, Jurj Farid Tarif. *al-Salt wa Jiwaruha*. Amman: Jordan Press Association, 1994.

Dazey, Theresa. "Trial and Error: Cultural Negotiation and the Circassian Diaspora in
the Shariah Court Records of Ottoman and Inter-War Jordan, 1878–1939." PhD diss.,
Indiana University, 2020.

Der Matossian, Bedross. *Shattered Dreams of Revolution: From Liberty to Violence in the
Late Ottoman Empire*. Stanford: Stanford University Press, 2014.

Deringil, Selim. "Legitimacy Structures in the Ottoman State: The Reign of Abdülhamid
II (1876–1909)." *International Journal of Middle East Studies* 23, no. 3 (1991): 345–59.

———. " 'They Live in a State of Nomadism and Savagery': The Late Ottoman Empire
and the Post-Colonial Debate." *Comparative Studies in Society and History* 45, no. 2
(2003): 311–42.

———. *The Well-Protected Domains: Ideology and Legitimation of Power in the Ottoman
Empire, 1876–1909*. London: I.B. Tauris, 2011.

Dobreva, Margarita. "Bulgaristan'ın İvraca ve Rahova Kazalarında Yaşayan Çerkeslerin
Nüfus Yapısı ve İktisadi Etkinlikleri (1860–1870)." *Journal of Caucasian Studies* 1, no.
2 (2016): 43–74.

———. "Circassian Colonization in the Danube Vilayet and Social Integration (Preliminary Notes)." *Journal of the Center for Ottoman Studies* 33 (2013): 1–30.

———. "Çerkes Tehcirinin Medyaya Yankısı: Takvim-i Vekayi Gazetesi." *Yeni Türkiye* 74
(2015): 779–88.

———. "Remarks on the Circassian Settlements in the Kaza of Lom and Belogradçik."
In *Prouchvaniia po stopanska istoriia i istoriia na sotsialno-ikonomicheskata sfera v Iugo-
zapadna Bŭlgariia*, edited by Petar Parvanov and Boryana Dimitrova, 106–30. Blago-
evgrad: UI Neofit Rilski, 2015.

Doğan, Setenay Nil. "Formations of Diaspora Nationalism: The Case of Circassians in
Turkey." PhD diss., Sabancı University, 2009.

Dolbee, Samuel. "Empire on the Edge: Desert, Nomads, and the Making of an Ottoman
Provincial Border." *American Historical Review* 127, no. 1 (2022): 129–58.

———. *Locusts of Power: Borders, Empire, and Environment in the Modern Middle East*.
Cambridge: Cambridge University Press, 2023.

Dragostinova, Theodora. *Between Two Motherlands: Nationality and Emigration among
the Greeks of Bulgaria, 1900–1949*. Ithaca: Cornell University Press, 2011.

Dumanov, Khasan M. *Adygskaia i karachaevo-balkarskaia zarubezhnaia diaspora: istoriia
i kul'tura*. Nalchik: El'-Fa, 2000.

Dündar, Fuat. *Crime of Numbers: The Role of Statistics in the Armenian Question, 1878–
1918*. New Brunswick: Transaction Publishers, 2010.

————. "How Migration Institutions 'Think'? The Ottoman-Turkish Case." *Anatoli* 9 (2018): 165–83.

————. *İttihat ve Terakki'nin Müslümanları İskan Politikası (1913–1918)*. Istanbul: İletişim Yayınları, 2001.

————. *Modern Türkiye'nin Şifresi: İttihat ve Terakki'nin Etnisite Mühendisliği (1913–1918)*. Istanbul: İletişim Yayınları, 2008.

————. "Pouring a People into the Desert: The 'Definitive Solution' of the Unionists to the Armenian Question." In Suny, Naimark, and Göçek, *Question of Genocide*, 276–86.

Dzidzariia, Georgii A. *Makhadzhirstvo i problemy istorii Abkhazii XIX stoletiia*. Sukhumi: Alashara, 1975.

————. *Vosstanie 1866 goda v Abkhazii*. Sukhumi: Abgosizdat, 1955.

Eden, Jeff. *Slavery and Empire in Central Asia*. Cambridge: Cambridge University Press, 2018.

Edgar, Adrienne Lynn. *Tribal Nation: The Making of Soviet Turkmenistan*. Princeton: Princeton University Press, 2004.

Emgili, Fahriye. *Yeniden Kurulan Hayatlar: Boşnakların Türkiye'ye Göçleri, 1878–1934*. Istanbul: Bilge Kültür Sanat, 2012.

Erciyes, Jade Cemre. "Return Migration to the Caucasus: The Adyge-Abkhaz Diaspora(s), Transnationalism and Life after Return." PhD diss., University of Sussex, 2014.

Erdem, Ufuk. *Osmanlı'dan Cumhuriyet'e Muhacir Komisyonları ve Faaliyetleri (1860–1923)*. Ankara, 2018.

Erdem, Y. Hakan. *Slavery in the Ottoman Empire and Its Demise, 1800–1909*. Houndmills: Macmillan, 1996.

Eren, Ahmet Cevat. *Türkiye'de Göç ve Göçmen Meseleleri*. Istanbul: Nurgök Matbaası, 1966.

Erkan, Süleyman. *Kırım ve Kafkasya Göçleri (1878–1908): Tatarlar, Çerkezler, Abhazlar, Gürcüler, Ahıskalılar, Dağıstanlılar, Çeçenler, Diğerleri*. Trabzon: KTÜ, 1996.

Etkind, Alexander. *Internal Colonization: Russia's Imperial Experience*. Cambridge: Polity Press, 2011.

Fadeev, Anatolii V. "Ubykhi v osvoboditel'nom dvizhenii na zapadnom Kavkaze." *Istoricheskii sbornik* 4 (1935): 135–81.

Fahmy, Khaled. *All the Pasha's Men: Mehmed Ali, His Army and the Making of Modern Egypt*. Cambridge: Cambridge University Press, 1997.

Fahrenthold, Stacy D. *Between the Ottomans and the Entente: The First World War in the Syrian and Lebanese Diaspora, 1908–1925*. Oxford: Oxford University Press, 2019.

Ferrara, Antonio, and Niccolò Pianciola. "The Dark Side of Connectedness: Forced Migrations and Mass Violence between the Late Tsarist and Ottoman Empires (1853–1920)." *Historical Research* 92, no. 257 (2019): 608–31.

Firro, Kais M. *A History of the Druzes*. Leiden: Brill, 1992.

Fischbach, Michael R. *State, Society, and Land in Jordan*. Leiden: Brill, 2000.

Fisher, Alan W. "Emigration of Muslims from the Russian Empire in the Years after the Crimean War." *Jahrbücher für Geschichte Osteuropas* 35 (1987): 356–71.

Fishman, Louis A. *Jews and Palestinians in the Late Ottoman Era, 1908–1914: Claiming the Homeland*. Edinburgh: Edinburgh University Press, 2020.

Fortna, Benjamin C. *The Circassian: The Life of Eşref Bey, Late Ottoman Insurgent and Special Agent*. Oxford: Oxford University Press, 2016.

Frank, Matthew, and Jessica Reinisch, eds. "Refugees and the Nation-State in Europe." Special issue, *Journal of Contemporary History* 49, no. 3 (2014).

Frary, Lucien J., and Mara Kozelsky, eds. *Russian-Ottoman Borderlands: The Eastern Question Reconsidered*. Madison: University of Wisconsin Press, 2014.

Fratantuono, Ella. "Migration Administration in the Making of the Late Ottoman Empire." PhD diss., Michigan State University, 2016.

———. "Producing Ottomans: Internal Colonization and Social Engineering in Ottoman Immigrant Settlement." *Journal of Genocide Research* 21, no. 1 (2019): 1–24.

———. "State Fears and Immigrant Tiers: Historical Analysis as a Method in Evaluating Migration Categories." *Middle East Journal of Refugee Studies* 2 (2017): 97–115.

Frost, Linda. *Never One Nation: Freaks, Savages, and Whiteness in U.S. Popular Culture, 1850–1877*. Minneapolis: University of Minnesota, 2005.

Gammer, Moshe. *Muslim Resistance to the Tsar: Shamil and the Conquest of Chechnia and Daghestan*. London: Frank Cass, 2005.

Ganich, Anastasia A. *Cherkesy v Iordanii: osobennosti istoricheskogo i etnokul'turnogo razvitiia*. Moscow: ISAA MGU, 2007.

Gardanov, Valentin K. *Obshchestvennyi stroi adygskikh narodov (XVIII–pervaia polovina XIX v.)* Moscow: Nauka, 1967.

Garsaev, Leichii M., and Khodzha-Akhmed M. Garsaev. *Chechenskie mukhadzhiry i ikh potomki v istoriii i kul'ture Iordanii: istoriko-etnograficheskie ocherki*. Grozny: Groznenskii rabochii, 2019.

Gatrell, Peter. *The Making of the Modern Refugee*. Oxford: Oxford University Press, 2013.

———. "Refugees—What's Wrong with History?" *Journal of Refugee Studies* 30, no. 2 (2017): 170–89.

———. *A Whole Empire Walking: Refugees in Russia during World War I*. Bloomington: Indiana University Press, 1999.

Gatrell, Peter, Anindita Ghoshal, Katarzyna Nowak, and Alex Dowdall. "Reckoning with Refugeedom: Refugee Voices in Modern History." *Social History* 46, no. 1 (2021): 70–95.

Geller, Randy. "The Recruitment and Conscription of the Circassian Community into the Israel Defence Forces, 1948–58." *Middle Eastern Studies* 48, no. 3 (2012): 387–99.

Genov, Georgi P. *Bulgaria and the Treaty of Neuilly*. Sofia: H.G. Danov & Co., 1935.

Geyikdağı, V. Necla. *Foreign Investment in the Ottoman Empire: International Trade and Relations in the Late Nineteenth Century*. London: I.B. Tauris, 2011.

Gingeras, Ryan. "Notorious Subjects, Invisible Citizens: North Caucasian Resistance to the Turkish National Movement in Northwestern Anatolia, 1919–23." *International Journal of Middle East Studies* 40, no. 1 (2008): 89–108.

———. "The Sons of Two Fatherlands: Turkey and the North Caucasian Diaspora, 1914–1923." *European Journal of Turkish Studies* (2011): 2–17.

———. *Sorrowful Shores: Violence, Ethnicity, and the End of the Ottoman Empire, 1912–1923*. Oxford: Oxford University Press, 2009.

Gmelch, George. "Return Migration." *Annual Review of Anthropology* 9 (1980): 135–59.

Goff, Krista A. *Nested Nationalism: Making and Unmaking Nations in the Soviet Caucasus.* Ithaca: Cornell University Press, 2021.

Goff, Krista A., and Lewis H. Siegelbaum, eds. *Empire and Belonging in the Eurasian Borderlands.* Ithaca: Cornell University Press, 2019.

Gould, Rebecca. *Writers and Rebels: The Literature of Insurgency in the Caucasus.* New Haven: Yale University Press, 2017.

Grant, Bruce. *The Captive and the Gift: Cultural Histories of Sovereignty in Russia and the Caucasus.* Ithaca: Cornell University Press, 2009.

Grassi, Fabio L. *Una nuova patria: L'esodo dei Circassi verso l'Impero Ottomano.* Istanbul: Isis Press, 2014.

Gratien, Chris. "'The Mountains Are Ours: Ecology and Settlement in Late Ottoman and Early Republican Cilicia, 1856–1956." PhD diss., Georgetown University, 2015.

———. "The Ottoman Quagmire: Malaria, Swamps, and Settlement in the Late Ottoman Mediterranean." *International Journal of Middle East Studies* 49, no. 4 (2017): 583–604.

———. *The Unsettled Plain: An Environmental History of the Late Ottoman Frontier.* Stanford: Stanford University Press, 2022.

Greble, Emily. *Muslims and the Making of Modern Europe.* Oxford: Oxford University Press, 2021.

Gutman, David. *The Politics of Armenian Migration to North America, 1885–1915: Sojourners, Smugglers and Dubious Citizens.* Edinburgh: Edinburgh University Press, 2019.

———. "Travel Documents, Mobility Control, and the Ottoman State in the Age of Global Migration, 1880–1915." *Journal of the Ottoman and Turkish Studies Association* 3, no. 2 (2016): 347–68.

Güçtekin, Nuri. "Çerkes Teavün Mektebi (1910–1914)." *Yakın Dönem Türkiye Araştırmaları* 12, no. 1 (2013): 1–21.

Güler, Ali. *Osmanlı Devletinde Azınlıklar.* Istanbul: Turan Yayıncılık, 1997.

Güsar, Vasfi. "İstanbul Çerkes Kadınları Teavün Cemiyeti." *Kafkasya Kültürel Dergi* 48, no. 2 (1975): 21–26.

Habiçoğlu, Bedri. *Kafkasya'dan Anadolu'ya Göçler.* Istanbul: Nart Yayıncılık, 1993.

Hacısalihoğlu, Mehmet, ed. *1864 Kafkas Tehciri: Kafkasya'da Rus Kolonizasyonu, Savaş ve Sürgün.* Istanbul: BALKAR & IRCICA, 2014.

———. "Borders, Maps, and Censuses: The Politicization of Geography and Statistics in the Multi-Ethnic Ottoman Empire." In *Comparing Empires: Encounters and Transfers in the Long Nineteenth Century,* edited by Jörn Leonhard and Ulrike von Hirschhausen, 171–216. Göttingen: Vandenhoeck & Ruprecht, 2012.

———. "Negotiations and Agreements for Population Transfers in the Balkans from the Beginning of the 19th Century until the Balkan Wars of 1912–1913." *Journal of Balkan and Black Sea Studies* 1, no. 1 (2018): 31–75.

Hacker, Jane M. *Modern 'Amman: A Social Study.* Durham: Durham Colleges in the University of Durham, 1960.

Haghandoqa, Mohammad Kheir. *The Circassians: Origin, History, Customs, Traditions, Immigration to Jordan.* Amman: Rafidi Print, 1985.

Halaçoğlu, Ahmet. *Balkan Harbi Sırasında Rumeli'den Türk Göçleri, 1912–1913.* Ankara: Türk Tarih Kurumu, 1995.

Hamarneh, Mustafa B. "Amman in British Travel Accounts of the 19th Century." In Hannoyer and Shami, *Amman*, 57–70.

Hamed-Troyansky, Vladimir. "Becoming Armenian: Religious Conversions in the Late Imperial South Caucasus." *Comparative Studies in Society and History* 63, no. 1 (2021): 242–72.

———. "Circassian Refugees and the Making of Amman, 1878–1914." *International Journal of Middle East Studies* 49, no. 4 (2017): 605–23.

———. "Imperial Refuge: Resettlement of Muslims from Russia in the Ottoman Empire, 1860–1914." PhD diss., Stanford University, 2018.

———. "Letters from the Ottoman Empire: Migration from the Caucasus and Russia's Pan-Islamic Panic." *Slavic Review* 82, no. 2 (2023) 311–33.

———. "Population Transfer: Negotiating the Resettlement of Chechen Refugees in the Ottoman Empire (1865, 1870)." In *Russian-Arab Worlds: A Documentary History*, edited by Eileen Kane, Masha Kirasirova, and Margaret Litvin, 60–68. Oxford: Oxford University Press, 2023.

———. "Welcome, Not Welcome: The North Caucasian Diaspora's Attempted Return to Russia since the 1960s." *Kritika: Explorations in Russian and Eurasian History* 24, no. 3 (2023): 585–610.

Hanania, Marwan D. "From Colony to Capital: Reconsidering the Socio-Economic and Political History of Amman, 1878–1928." *Middle Eastern Studies* 55, no. 1 (2019): 1–21.

———. "From Colony to Capital: A Socio-Economic and Political History of Amman, 1878–1958." PhD diss., Stanford University, 2010.

Hanioğlu, M. Şükrü. *Preparation for a Revolution: The Young Turks, 1902–1908*. New York: Oxford University Press, 2001.

———. *The Young Turks in Opposition*. New York: Oxford University Press, 1995.

Hanley, Will. *Identifying with Nationality: Europeans, Ottomans, and Egyptians in Alexandria*. New York: Columbia University Press, 2017.

———. "What Ottoman Nationality Was and Was Not." *Journal of the Ottoman and Turkish Studies Association* 3, no. 2: 277–98.

Hannoyer, Jean, and Seteney Shami, eds. *Amman: Ville et société*. Beirut: CERMOC, 1996.

Hansen, Lars Funch. "iCircassia: Digital Capitalism and New Transnational Identities." *Journal of Caucasian Studies* 1, no. 1 (2015): 1–32.

Harris, John. *The Last Slave Ships: New York and the End of the Middle Passage*. New Haven: Yale University Press, 2020.

Hassan, Mona. *Longing for the Lost Caliphate: A Transregional History*. Princeton: Princeton University Press, 2016.

Hillis, Faith. *Utopia's Discontents: Russian Émigrés and the Quest for Freedom, 1830s–1930s*. Oxford: Oxford University Press, 2021.

Hirsch, Francine. *Empire of Nations: Ethnographic Knowledge and the Making of the Soviet Union*. Ithaca: Cornell University Press, 2005.

al-Hmoud, Noufan Raja. " 'Amman fi Awakhir al-'Ahd al-'Uthmani: Dirasa fi Tatawwur Awda'iha al-Idariyya wa-l-Ijtima'iyya wa-l-Iqtisadiyya." In Hannoyer and Shami, *Amman*, 72–88.

———. *'Amman wa Jiwaruha khilal al-Fatra 1864–1921.* Amman: Business Bank Publications, 1996.

Hoerder, Dirk. "Migrations in Slavic, Tsarist Russian and Soviet History." Special issue, *Journal of Migration History* 3, no. 2 (2017).

Holquist, Peter. "To Count, to Extract, to Exterminate: Population Statistics and Population Politics in Late Imperial and Soviet Russia." In *A State of Nations: Empire and Nation-Making in the Age of Lenin and Stalin,* edited by Terry Martin and Ronald Grigor Suny, 111–44. Oxford: Oxford University Press, 2001.

Hotko, Samir H. "Importance of the Russian-Turkish War of 1877–1878 for the Circassian History." In *The Ottoman-Russian War of 1877–78,* edited by Ömer Turan, 221–26. Ankara: Middle East Technical University, 2007.

Hunt, Catalina. "Changing Identities at the Fringes of the Late Ottoman Empire: The Muslims of Dobruca, 1839–1914." PhD diss., Ohio State University, 2015.

Hütteroth, Wolf-Dieter. "The Influence of Social Structure on Land Division and Settlement in Inner Anatolia." In *Turkey: Geographic and Social Perspectives,* edited by Peter Benedict, Erol Tümertekin, and Fatma Mansur, 19–47. Leiden: Brill, 1974.

Iakimov, Georgi. "Vŭzrozhdenskiiat pechat za cherkezite v bŭlgarskite zemi prez 60-te–70-te godini na XIX v." *Istoriia* 4–5 (2004): 71–78.

Ibragimova, Zaira B. "Problema mukhadzhirstva v dagestanskikh pamiatnikakh epistoliarnogo zhanra kontsa XIX–nachala XX vv." *Voprosy istorii* 4 (2012): 152–56.

Ibragimova, Zaira B., and Zeinab A. Magomedova. "Dagestanskie bogoslovy o pereselencheskom dvizhenii musul'man Kavkaza v kontse XIX–nachale XX veka." *Manuskript* 12, no. 12 (2019): 50–53.

Ibragimova, Zarema Kh. *Chechenskaia istoriia: politika, ekonomika, kul'tura. Vtoraia polovina XIX veka.* Moscow: Evraziia +, 2002.

———. *Chechenskii narod v Rossiiskoi imperii: adaptatsionnyi period.* Moscow: Probel-2000, 2006.

———. *Emigratsiia chechentsev v Turtsiiu (60–70 gg. XIX v.).* Moscow: Maks Press, 2000.

İğsız, Aslı. *Humanism in Ruins: Entangled Legacies of the Greek-Turkish Population Exchange.* Stanford: Stanford University Press, 2018.

İnalcık, Halil. "The Policy of Mehmed II toward the Greek Population of Istanbul and the Byzantine Buildings of the City." *Dumbarton Oaks Papers* 23/24 (1969/1970): 229–49.

Iordachi, Constantin. *Liberalism, Constitutional Nationalism, and Minorities: The Making of Romanian Citizens, c. 1750–1918.* Leiden: Brill, 2019.

İpek, Nedim. "Göçmen Köylerine Dair." *Tarih ve Toplum* 25, no. 150 (1996): 15–21.

———. *Rumeli'den Anadolu'ya Türk Göçleri (1877–1890).* Ankara: Türk Tarih Kurumu Basımevi, 1994.

Isma'il, Muhammad Kheyr. *Dalil al-Ansab al-Sharkasiyya: Dirasa fi Asl al-Sharkas wa Tarikhuhum wa Ansabuhum wa Amakin Tajammu'akum fi al-Jumhuriyya al-'Arabiyya al-Suriyya.* Damascus: Dar al-Salam, 1993.

İzbırak, Reşat. "Uzunyayla'da Coğrafya Araştırmaları." In *Uzunyayla: Rapor ve Belgeleri,* edited by Muhittin Ünal, 2:74–93. Ankara: Kaf-Dav, 2008.

Jagodić, Miloš. *Naseljavanje Kneževine Srbije 1861–1880.* Belgrade: Istorijski Institut, 2004.

———. "The Emigration of Muslims from the New Serbian Regions 1877/1878." *Balkanologie* 2, no. 2 (1998).

Jaimoukha, Amjad M. *The Chechens: A Handbook*. London: Routledge Curzon, 2005.

———. *The Circassians: A Handbook*. Richmond: Curzon, 2001.

Janib, Musa 'Ali. *Muwatin Sharkasi Yatahaddath 'an Masqat Ra'sihi*. Amman: al-Mu'allif, 2006.

Jersild, Austin. *Orientalism and Empire: North Caucasus Mountain Peoples and the Georgian Frontier, 1845–1917*. Montréal: McGill-Queen's University Press, 2002.

Kabuzan, Vladimir M. *Naselenie Severnogo Kavkaza v XIX–XX vekakh: etnostatisticheskoe issledovanie*. Saint Petersburg: BLITS, 1996.

Kahn, Michelle Lynn. "Foreign at Home: Turkish-German Migrants and the Boundaries of Europe, 1961–1990." PhD diss., Stanford University, 2018.

Kale, Başak. "Transforming an Empire: The Ottoman Empire's Immigration and Settlement Policies in the Nineteenth and Early Twentieth Centuries." *Middle Eastern Studies* 50, no. 2 (2014): 252–71.

Kane, Eileen. *Russian Hajj: Empire and the Pilgrimage to Mecca*. Ithaca: Cornell University Press, 2015.

Karaca, Ali. *Anadolu İslahatı ve Ahmet Şakir Paşa (1838–1899)*. Istanbul: Eren, 1993.

Karakışla, Yavuz Selim. "Çerkes Kadınları Teavün Cemiyeti." *Toplumsal Tarih* 88 (2001): 39–43.

Karamürsel, Ceyda. " 'In the Age of Freedom, in the Name of Justice': Slaves, Slaveholders, and the State in the Late Ottoman Empire and Early Turkish Republic, 1857–1933." PhD diss., University of Pennsylvania, 2015.

———. "Transplanted Slavery, Contested Freedom and Vernacularization of Rights in the Reform Era Ottoman Empire." *Comparative Studies in Society and History* 59, no. 3 (2017): 690–714.

Karataş, Ömer. "Çerkeslerin Sivas-Uzunyayla'ya İskanları ve Karşılaştıkları Sorunlar (H. 1277–1287/M. 1860–1870)." PhD diss., Ege Üniversitesi, 2012.

Kark, Ruth. "The Contribution of the Ottoman Regime to the Development of Jerusalem and Jaffa, 1840–1917." In *Palestine in the Late Ottoman Period: Political, Social, and Economic Transformation*, edited by David Kushner, 46–58. Jerusalem: Yad Izhak Ben Zvi, 1986.

Karpat, Kemal H. "The Hijra from Russia and the Balkans: The Process of Self-Definition in the Late Ottoman State." In *Studies on Ottoman Social and Political History*, 689–711.

———. "Jewish Population Movements in the Ottoman Empire, 1862–1914." In *Studies on Ottoman Social and Political History*, 146–68.

———. "Nation and Nationalism in the Late Ottoman Empire." In *Studies on Ottoman Social and Political History*, 544–55.

———. "The Ottoman Family: Documents Pertaining to Its Size." In *Studies on Ottoman Social and Political History*, 235–42.

———. "Ottoman Immigration Policies and Settlement in Palestine." In *Studies on Ottoman Social and Political History*, 783–99.

———. *Ottoman Population, 1830–1914: Demographic and Social Characteristics*. Madison: University of Wisconsin Press, 1985.

———. "Ottoman Urbanism: The Crimean Emigration to Dobruca and the Founding of Mecidiye, 1856–1878." In *Studies on Ottoman Social and Political History*, 202–34.

———. *The Politicization of Islam: Reconstructing Identity, State, Faith, and Community in the Late Ottoman State*. New York: Oxford University Press, 2002.

———. "The Status of the Muslim under European Rule: The Eviction and Settlement of the Çerkes." In *Studies on Ottoman Social and Political History*, 647–75.

———. *Studies on Ottoman Social and Political History: Selected Articles and Essays*. Leiden: Brill, 2002.

Kasaba, Reşat. *A Moveable Empire: Ottoman Nomads, Migrants, and Refugees*. Seattle: University of Washington Press, 1999.

Kasumov, Alii Kh., and Khasan A. Kasumov. *Genotsid adygov*. Nalchik: Logos, 1992.

Katav, Ahmet, and Bilgay Duman. "Iraqi Circassians." Report 134 (2012). Ankara: ORSAM.

Kaya, Ayhan. *Türkiye'de Çerkesler: Diaspora'da Geleneğin Yeniden İcadı*. Istanbul: İstanbul Bilgi Üniversitesi Yayınları, 2011.

Kazharov, Valerii Kh. *Izbrannye trudy po istorii i etnografii adygov*. Nalchik: Pechatnyi dvor, 2014.

Keely, Charles B. "The International Refugee Regime(s): The End of the Cold War Matters." *International Migration Review* 35, no. 1 (2001): 303–14.

Kefeli, Agnès Nilüfer. *Becoming Muslim in Imperial Russia: Conversion, Apostasy, and Literacy*. Ithaca: Cornell University Press, 2014.

Kemper, Michael. " 'Adat against Shari'a: Russian Approaches towards Daghestani 'Customary Law' in the 19th Century." *Ab Imperio* 3 (2005): 147–74.

———. "Communal Agreements (Ittifaqat) and 'Adat-Books from Daghestani Villages and Confederacies (18th–19th Centuries)." *Der Islam* 81 (2004): 115–51.

———. "Khalidiyya Networks in Daghestan and the Question of Jihad." *Die Welt des Islams* 42, no. 1 (2002): 41–71.

———. "The North Caucasian Khalidiyya and 'Muridism': Historiographical Problems." *Journal of the History of Sufism* 1–2, no. 5 (2007): 151–67.

Kern, Karen M. *Imperial Citizen: Marriage and Citizenship in the Ottoman Frontier Provinces of Iraq*. Syracuse: Syracuse University Press, 2011.

Kévorkian, Raymond. *The Armenian Genocide: A Complete History*. London: I.B. Tauris, 2013.

Khalid, Adeeb. *The Politics of Muslim Cultural Reform: Jadidism in Central Asia*. Berkeley: University of California Press, 1998.

Khammash, Ammar. *Notes on Village Architecture in Jordan*. Lafayette: University Art Museum, University of Southwestern Louisiana, 1986.

Khater, Akram Fouad. *Inventing Home: Emigration, Gender, and the Middle Class in Lebanon, 1870–1920*. Berkeley: University of California Press, 2001.

Khodarkovsky, Michael. *Bitter Choices: Loyalty and Betrayal in the Russian Conquest of the North Caucasus*. Ithaca: Cornell University Press, 2011.

———. *Russia's Steppe Frontier: The Making of a Colonial Empire, 1500–1800*. Bloomington: Indiana University Press, 2002.

Khorava, Bezhan. *Mukhadzhirstvo abkhazov 1867 goda*. Tbilisi: Artanudzhi, 2013.

Khoury, Dina Rizk, and Sergey Glebov, eds. "Citizenship, Subjecthood, and Difference in the Late Ottoman and Russian Empires." Forum, *Ab Imperio* 1 (2017).

Khoury, Philip S. *Urban Notables and Arab Nationalism: The Politics of Damascus, 1860–1920*. Cambridge: Cambridge University Press, 1983.

Khuraysat, Muhammad 'Abd al-Qadir. *al-Masihiyun fi Qada' al-Salt: al-Salt, al-Fuhays, al-Rumaymin, 1869–1920*. Amman: Ministry of Culture, 2012.

Khuri-Makdisi, Ilham. *The Eastern Mediterranean and the Making of Global Radicalism, 1860–1914*. Berkeley: University of California, 2010.

King, Charles. *The Ghost of Freedom: A History of the Caucasus*. New York: Oxford University Press, 2008.

———. "Imagining Circassia: David Urquhart and the Making of North Caucasus Nationalism." *Russian Review* 66, no. 2 (2007): 238–55.

Kipkeeva, Zarema B. *Karachaevo-balkarskaia diaspora v Turtsii*. Stavropol: SGU, 2000.

———. *Severnyi Kavkaz v Rossiiskoi imperii: narody, migratsii, territorii*. Stavropol: SGU, 2008.

Kırımlı, Hakan. "Emigrations from the Crimea to the Ottoman Empire during the Crimean War." *Middle Eastern Studies* 44, no. 5 (2008): 751–77.

———. *Türkiye'deki Kırım Tatar ve Nogay Köy Yerleşimleri*. Istanbul: Tarih Vakfı Yurt Yayınları, 2012.

Kırımlı, Hakan, and Ali Yaycıoğlu. "Heirs of Chinghis Khan in the Age of Revolutions: An Unruly Crimean Prince in the Ottoman Empire and Beyond." *Der Islam* 94, no. 2 (2017): 496–526.

Klein, Janet. "Making Minorities in the Eurasian Borderlands: A Comparative Perspective from the Russian and Ottoman Empires." In *Empire and Belonging*, edited by Goff and Siegelbaum, 17–32. Ithaca: Cornell University Press, 2019.

———. *The Margins of Empire: Kurdish Militias in the Ottoman Tribal Zone*. Stanford: Stanford University Press, 2011.

Klier, John. *Russians, Jews, and the Pogroms of 1881–1882*. Cambridge: Cambridge University Press, 2011.

Knysh, Alexander. "Sufism as an Explanatory Paradigm: The Issue of the Motivations of Sufi Resistance Movements in Western and Russian Scholarship." *Die Welt des Islams* 42, no. 2 (2002): 139–73.

Kocacık, Faruk. "Balkanlar'dan Anadolu'ya Yönelik Göçler (1878–1890)." *Osmanlı Araştırmaları* 1 (1980): 137–90.

Koç, Bekir. "Tuna Vilayeti Göçmenleri ve Midhat Paşa." *Journal of Caucasian Studies* 2, no. 4 (2017): 55–70.

Kontogiorgi, Elisabeth. *Population Exchange in Greek Macedonia: The Rural Settlement of Refugees, 1922–30*. Oxford: Oxford University Press, 2006.

Kosven, Mark O. *Etnografiia i istoriia Kavkaza*. Moscow: Izdatel'stvo vostochnoi literatury, 1961.

Koyuncu, Aşkın. "Tuna Vilayeti'nde Nüfus ve Demografi (1864–1877)." *Turkish Studies* 9, no. 4 (2014): 675–737.

Kozelsky, Mara. "Casualties of Conflict: Crimean Tatars during the Crimean War." *Slavic Review* 67, no. 4 (2008): 866–91.

Kreiten, Irma. "A Colonial Experiment in Cleansing: The Russian Conquest of Western Caucasus, 1856–65." *Journal of Genocide Research* 11, no. 2–3 (2009): 213–41.

Kudaeva, Svetlana G. *Ognem i zhelezom: vynuzhdennoe pereselenie adygov v Osmanskuiu imperiiu (20–70 gg. XIX v.)*. Maikop: Adygeiskii Gosudarstvennyi Universitet, 1998.

Kumykov, Tugan Kh. *Sotsial'no-ekonomicheskie otnosheniia i otmena krepostnogo prava v Kabarde i Balkarii (1800–1869 gg.)* Nalchik: Kabardino-Balkarskoe knizhnoe izdatel'stvo, 1959.

Kurt, Ümit. *The Armenians of Aintab: The Economics of Genocide in an Ottoman Province*. Cambridge: Harvard University Press, 2021.

Kurtynova-D'Herlugnan, Liubov. *The Tsar's Abolitionists: The Slave Trade in the Caucasus and Its Suppression*. Leiden: Brill, 2010.

Kushkhabiev, Anzor V. *Cherkesskaia diaspora v arabskikh stranakh: XIX–XX vv.* Nalchik: KBNTs RAN, 1997.

———. *Cherkesy v Sirii*. Nalchik: Vozrozhdenie, 1993.

———. *Ocherki istorii zarubezhnoi cherkesskoi diaspory*. Nalchik: El'-Fa, 2007.

———. *Problemy repatriatsii zarubezhnykh cherkesov: istoriia, politika, sotsial'naia praktika*. Nalchik: KBNTs RAN, 2013.

Kushkhabiev, Anzor, Naima Neflyasheva, Murat Topçu, and Oytun Orhan. "Syrian Circassians." Report 130 (2012). Ankara: ORSAM.

Kuzuoğlu, Uluğ. "Telegraphy, Typography, and the Alphabet: The Origins of Alphabet Revolutions in the Russo-Ottoman Space." *International Journal of Middle East Studies* 52, no. 3 (2020): 413–31.

Ladas, Stephen P. *The Exchange of Minorities: Bulgaria, Greece and Turkey*. New York: MacMillan, 1932.

Laipanov, Kh.O. "K istorii pereseleniia gortsev Severnogo Kavkaza v Turtsiiu." *Trudy Cherkesskogo NII* 5 (1966): 111–31.

Lampe, John R., and Marvin R. Jackson. *Balkan Economic History, 1550–1950: From Imperial Borderlands to Developing Nations*. Bloomington: Indiana University Press, 1982.

Laycock, Jo. "Developing a Soviet Armenian Nation: Refugees and Resettlement in the Early Soviet South Caucasus." In *Empire and Belonging*, edited by Goff and Siegelbaum, 97–111. Ithaca: Cornell University Press, 2019.

Layton, Susan. *Russian Literature and Empire: Conquest of the Caucasus from Pushkin to Tolstoy*. Cambridge: Cambridge University Press, 1994.

Lewis, Norman. *Nomads and Settlers in Syria and Jordan, 1800–1980*. Cambridge: Cambridge University Press, 1987.

Lohr, Eric. *Russian Citizenship: From Empire to Soviet Union*. Cambridge: Harvard University Press, 2002.

Long, Lynellyn D. and Ellen Oxfeld, eds. *Coming Home? Refugees, Migrants, and Those Who Stayed Behind*. Philadelphia: University of Pennsylvania Press, 2004.

Lorenz, Fredrick Walter. "An Empire of Frontiers: Between Migrant and State in the Late Ottoman Empire, 1835–1911." PhD diss., University of California, Los Angeles, 2022.

———. "The 'Second Egypt': Cretan Refugees, Agricultural Development, and Frontier Expansion in Ottoman Cyrenaica, 1897–1904." *International Journal of Middle East Studies* 53, no. 1 (2021): 89–105.

Mackey, Bruce Douglas. "The Circassians in Jordan." Master's diss., Naval Postgraduate School, 1979.

Magomeddadaev, Amirkhan M. *Emigratsiia dagestantsev v Osmanskuiu imperiiu: istoriia i sovremennost'.* Vol. 2. Makhachkala: IIAE DNTs RAN, 2001.

Magomedkhanov, Magomedkhan M. *Dagestantsy v Turtsii.* Makhachkala: IIAE DNTs RAN, 1997.

Makdisi, Ussama. *The Culture of Sectarianism: Community, History, and Violence in Nineteenth-Century Ottoman Lebanon.* Berkeley: California University Press, 2000.

———. "Ottoman Orientalism." *American Historical Review* 107, no. 3 (2002): 768–96.

Malkki, Liisa H. "Refugees and Exile: From 'Refugee Studies' to the National Order of Things." *Annual Review of Anthropology* 24 (1995): 495–523.

Mamakaev, Magomet A. *Chechenskii taip (rod) v period ego razlozheniia.* 1934. Reprint, Grozny: Checheno-ingushskoe kn-vo, 1973.

Mamsir Batsaj, Muhammad Khair. *al-Mawsu'a al-Tarikhiyya li-l-Umma al-Sharkasiyya "al-Adigha": Min al-Alf al-'Ashir ma qabla al-Milad ila al-Alf al-Thalith ma b'ada al-Milad.* 6 vols. Amman: Dar al-Wa'il, 2009.

Manasek, Jared. "Protection, Repatriation and Categorization: Refugees and Empire at the End of the Nineteenth Century." *Journal of Refugee Studies* 30, no. 2 (2017): 301–17.

Mandel, Neville J. "Ottoman Policy and Restrictions on Jewish Settlement in Palestine: 1881–1908: Part I." *Middle Eastern Studies* 10, no. 3 (1974): 312–32.

———. "Ottoman Practice as Regards Jewish Settlement in Palestine: 1881–1908." *Middle Eastern Studies* 11, no. 1 (1975): 33–46.

Manning, Paul. "Just Like England: On the Liberal Institutions of the Circassians." *Comparative Studies in Society and History* 51, no. 3 (2009): 590–618.

Marrus, Michael Robert. *The Unwanted: European Refugees in the Twentieth Century.* Philadelphia: Temple University Press, 2002.

Martin, Terry. *The Affirmative Action Empire: Nations and Nationalism in the Soviet Union.* Ithaca: Cornell University Press, 2001.

Marzoeva, T. Kh. "A. Dymov, N. Tsagov—osnovateli Baksanskogo prosvetitel'skogo tsentra." *Vestnik KGU* 2 (2007): 25–27.

Massad, Joseph A. *Colonial Effects: The Making of a National Identity in Jordan.* New York: Columbia University Press, 2001.

Masud, Muhammad Khalid. "The Obligation to Migrate: The Doctrine of Hijra in Islamic Law." In *Muslim Travellers: Pilgrimage, Migration and the Religious Imagination,* edited by Dale F. Eickelman and James Piscatori, 29–49. London: Routledge, 1990.

Mays, Devi. *Forging Ties, Forging Passports: Migration and the Modern Sephardi Diaspora.* Stanford: Stanford University Press, 2020.

McCarthy, Justin. *Death and Exile: The Ethnic Cleansing of Ottoman Muslims, 1821–1922.* Princeton: Darwin Press, 1995.

McKeown, Adam. "Global Migration, 1846–1940." *Journal of World History* 15, no. 2 (2004): 155–89.

McMeekin, Sean. *The Berlin-Baghdad Express: The Ottoman Empire and Germany's Bid for World Power.* Cambridge: Harvard University Press, 2012.

Meshcheriuk, Ivan I. *Pereselenie bolgar v iuzhnuiu Bessarabiiu, 1828–1834 gg.: iz istorii razvitiia russko-bolgarskikh druzheskikh sviazei.* Kishinev: Kartia Moldoveniaske, 1965.

Methodieva, Milena B. *Between Empire and Nation: Muslim Reform in the Balkans.* Stanford: Stanford University Press, 2021.

Meyer, James H. "For the Russianist in Istanbul and the Ottomanist in Russia: A Guide to the Archives of Eurasia." *Ab Imperio* 4 (2008): 281–301.

——. "Immigration, Return, and the Politics of Citizenship: Russian Muslims in the Ottoman Empire, 1860–1914." *International Journal of Middle East Studies* 39, no. 1 (2007): 15–32.

——. "Speaking Sharia to the State: Muslim Protesters, Tsarist Officials, and the Islamic Discourses of Late Imperial Russia." *Kritika* 14, no. 3 (2013): 485–505.

——. *Turks across Empires: Marketing Muslim Identity in the Russian-Ottoman Borderlands, 1856–1914.* Oxford: Oxford University Press, 2014.

Minkov, Anton. "Ottoman *Tapu* Title Deeds in the Eighteenth and Nineteenth Centuries: Origin, Typology and Diplomatics." *Islamic Law and Society* 7, no. 1 (2000): 65–101.

Mirkova, Anna M. *Muslim Land, Christian Labor: Transforming Ottoman Imperial Subjects into Bulgarian National Citizens, 1878–1939.* Budapest: Central European University Press, 2017.

Mitchell, Timothy. *Colonising Egypt.* Berkeley: University of California Press, 1991.

Miyazawa, Eiji. "Memory Politics: Circassians of Uzunyayla, Turkey." PhD diss., School of Oriental and African Studies, University of London, 2004.

——. "The Past as a Resource for the Slave Descendants of Circassians in Turkey." In *The Past as a Resource in the Turkic Speaking World*, edited by Ildikó Bellér-Hann, 59–84. Würzburg: Ergon-Verl., 2008.

Moon, David. "Reassessing Russian Serfdom." *European History Quarterly* 26, no. 4 (1996): 483–526.

Morack, Ellinor. *The Dowry of the State? The Politics of Abandoned Property and the Population Exchange in Turkey, 1921–1945.* Bamberg: University of Bamberg Press, 2017.

Morrison, Alexander. *Russian Rule in Samarkand 1868–1910: A Comparison with British India.* Oxford: Oxford University, Press, 2008.

Mostashari, Firouzeh. *On the Religious Frontier: Tsarist Russia and Islam in the Caucasus.* New York: I.B. Tauris, 2006.

Motadel, David, ed. *Islam and the European Empires.* Oxford: Oxford University Press, 2014.

Mousa, Suleiman. "Jordan: Towards the End of the Ottoman Empire 1841–1918." In *Studies in the History and Archaeology of Jordan*, edited by Adnan Hadid, 385–91. Amman: Department of Antiquities, 1982.

Muchinov, Ventsislav. *Migratsionna politika na Osmanskata imperiia v Bŭlgarskite zemi prez XIX vek (do 1878 g.).* Sofia: Regaliia-6, 2013.

——. "Ottoman Policies on Circassian Refugees in the Danube Vilayet in the 1860s and 1870s." *Journal of Caucasian Studies* 2, no. 3 (2016): 83–96.

Mufti, Shauket (Habjoka). *Heroes and Emperors in Circassian History.* Beirut: Librairie du Liban, 1972.

Mugerditchian, Thomas K. *The Diyarbekir Massacres and Kurdish Atrocities*. London: Gomidas Institute, 2013.

Mundy, Martha, and Richard S. Smith. *Governing Property, Making the Modern State: Law, Administration and Production in Ottoman Syria*. London: I.B. Tauris, 2007.

Murphey, Rhoads. *Exploring Ottoman Sovereignty: Tradition, Image and Practice in the Ottoman Imperial Household, 1400–1800*. London: Continuum, 2008.

Murtazaliev, Akhmed M. *Literatura dagestanskoi diaspory Turtsii: vtoraia polovina XIX– XX vek*. Makhachkala: IIaLI DNTs RAN, 2006.

Nashkhu, Jawdat Hilmi. *Tarikh al-Sharkas (al-Adigha) wa-l-Shishan fi Liwa'i Hawran wa-l-Balqa' (1878–1920)*. Amman: Lajnat Tarikh al-Urdun, 1998.

Natho, Kadir I. *Circassian History*. New York, 2009.

Navruzov, Amir R. *'Dzharidat Dagistan'—araboiazychnaia gazeta kavkazskikh dzhadidov*. Moscow: Mardzhani, 2012.

Norman, Theodore. *An Outstretched Arm: A History of the Jewish Colonization Association*. London: Routledge & Kegan Paul, 1985.

Ochsenwald, William. *The Hijaz Railroad*. Charlottesville: University Press of Virginia, 1980.

Oral, Mustafa. "Sultan II. Abdülhamit Döneminde bir 'Çerkes Tarihi' Yazılması Girişimi." *Çağdaş Türkiye Tarihi Araştırmaları Dergisi* 7, no. 16–17 (2008): 71–88.

Orat, Julide Akyüz, Nebahat Oran Arslan, and Mustafa Tanrıverdi. *Osmanlı'dan Cumhuriyet'e Kafkas Göçleri (1928–1943)*. Kars: Kafkas Üniversitesi, 2011.

Ozavcı, Ozan. *Dangerous Gifts: Imperialism, Security, and Civil Wars in the Levant, 1798– 1864*. Oxford: Oxford University Press, 2021.

Özbek, Nadir. "Philanthropic Activity, Ottoman Patriotism, and the Hamidian Regime, 1876–1909." *International Journal of Middle East Studies* 37, no. 1 (2005): 59–81.

Özcan, Azmi. *Pan-Islamism: Indian Muslims, the Ottomans and Britain, 1877–1924*. Leiden: Brill, 1997.

Özel, Oktay. "Migration and Power Politics: The Settlement of Georgian Immigrants in Turkey (1878–1908)." *Middle Eastern Studies* 46, no. 4 (2010): 477–96.

Özsu, Umut. *Formalizing Displacement: International Law and Population Transfers*. Oxford: Oxford University Press, 2015.

Öztan, Ramazan Hakkı. "Point of No Return? Prospects of Empire after the Ottoman Defeat in the Balkan Wars (1912–13)." *International Journal of Middle East Studies* 50, no. 1 (2018): 65–84.

Özyüksel, Murat. *The Berlin-Baghdad Railway and the Ottoman Empire: Industrialization, Imperial Germany and the Middle East*. London: I.B. Tauris, 2016.

———. *The Hejaz Railway and the Ottoman Empire: Modernity, Industrialisation and Ottoman Decline*. London: I.B. Tauris, 2014.

Palairet, Michael R. *The Balkan Economies c. 1800–1914: Evolution without Development*. Cambridge: Cambridge University Press, 1997.

Papşu, Murat. "Çerkes-Adığe Yazısının Tarihçesi." *Nart* 51 (2006): 1–6.

Pashtova, Madina M. "Fol'klor cherkesskoi diaspory: lokalizatsiia traditsii, funktsional'nost' tekstov." Habilitation thesis, Institute of Humanities Research of the Republic of Adygea, 2021.

Pastor, Camila. *The Mexican Mahjar: Transnational Maronites, Jews, and Arabs under the French Mandate.* Austin: University of Texas Press, 2017.

Peçe, Uğur Zekeriya. "An Island Unmixed: European Military Intervention and the Displacement of Crete's Muslims, 1896–1908." *Middle Eastern Studies* 54, no. 4 (2018): 575–91.

Peirce, Leslie P. *The Imperial Harem: Women and Sovereignty in the Ottoman Empire.* New York: Oxford University Press, 1993.

Penslar, Derek Jonathan. *Zionism and Technocracy: The Engineering of Jewish Settlement in Palestine, 1870–1918.* Bloomington: Indiana University Press, 1991.

Perović, Jeronim. *From Conquest to Deportation: The North Caucasus under Russian Rule.* Oxford: Oxford University Press, 2018.

Petrov, Milen. "Tanzimat for the Countryside: Midhat Paşa and the Vilayet of Danube, 1864–1868." PhD diss., Princeton University, 2006.

Pinson, Mark. "Demographic Warfare: An Aspect of Ottoman and Russian Policy, 1854–1866." PhD diss., Harvard University, 1970.

———. "Ottoman Colonization of the Circassians in Rumili after the Crimean War." *Études balkaniques* 3 (1972): 71–85.

———. "Russian Policy and the Emigration of the Crimean Tatars to the Ottoman Empire (1854–1862)." *Güneydoğu Avrupa Araştırmaları Dergisi* 1 (1972): 37–55; 2–3 (1974): 101–14.

Pletn'ov, Georgi. *Midkhat Pasha i upravlenieto na Dunavskiia vilaet.* Veliko Tarnovo: Vital, 1994.

Polovinkina, Tamara V. *Cherkesiia: bol' moia i nadezhda.* Nalchik: Izdatel'stvo M. i V. Kotliarovykh, 2014.

Provence, Michael. *The Great Syrian Revolt and the Rise of Arab Nationalism.* Austin: University of Texas Press, 2005.

———. *The Last Ottoman Generation and the Making of the Modern Middle East.* Cambridge: Cambridge University Press, 2017.

Quataert, Donald. "The Age of Reforms, 1812–1914." In *An Economic and Social History of the Ottoman Empire,* edited by Halil İnalcık and Donald Quataert, 2:759–944. Cambridge: Cambridge University Press, 1994.

Radovanović, Jelena. "Contested Legacy: Property in Transition to Nation-State in Post-Ottoman Niš." PhD diss., Princeton University, 2020.

Randolph, John, and Eugene M. Avrutin, eds. *Russia in Motion: Cultures of Human Mobility since 1850.* Urbana: University of Illinois Press, 2012.

Reynolds, Michael A. "Buffers, Not Brethren: Young Turk Military Policy in the First World War and the Myth of Panturanism." *Past & Present* 203, no. 1 (2009): 137–79.

———. "Native Sons: Post-Imperial Politics, Islam, and Identity in the North Caucasus, 1917–1918." *Jahrbücher für Geschichte Osteuropas* 56, no. 2 (2008): 221–47.

———. *Shattering Empires: The Clash and Collapse of the Ottoman and Russian Empires, 1908–1918.* Cambridge: Cambridge University Press, 2011.

Richmond, Walter. *The Circassian Genocide.* New Brunswick: Rutgers University Press, 2013.

———. *The Northwest Caucasus: Past, Present, Future.* London: Routledge 2011.

Riegg, Stephen Badalyan. *Russia's Entangled Embrace: The Tsarist Empire and the Armenians, 1801–1914*. Ithaca: Cornell University Press, 2020.

Robarts, Andrew. *Migration and Disease in the Black Sea Region: Ottoman-Russian Relations in the Late Eighteenth and Early Nineteenth Centuries*. London: Bloomsbury, 2017.

Robson, Laura. *States of Separation: Transfer, Partition, and the Making of the Modern Middle East*. Oakland: University of California Press, 2017.

——. *The Politics of Mass Violence in the Middle East*. Oxford: Oxford University Press.

Rodogno, Davide. *Against Massacre: Humanitarian Interventions in the Ottoman Empire, 1815–1914*. Princeton: Princeton University Press, 2011.

Rogan, Eugene L. "Aşiret Mektebi: Abdülhamid II's School for Tribes (1892–1907)." *International Journal of Middle East Studies* 28 (1996): 83–107.

——. *The Fall of the Ottomans: The Great War in the Middle East*. New York: Basic Books, 2015.

——. *Frontiers of the State in the Late Ottoman Empire: Transjordan, 1850–1921*. Cambridge: Cambridge University Press, 1999.

——. "Incorporating the Periphery: The Ottoman Extension of Direct Rule over Southeastern Syria (Transjordan), 1867–1914." PhD diss., Harvard University, 1991.

——. "The Making of a Capital: Amman, 1918–1928." In Hannoyer and Shami, *Amman*, 89–107.

——. "Turkuman of al-Ruman: An Ottoman Settlement in South-Eastern Syria." *Arabic Historical Review for Ottoman Studies* 1–2 (1990): 91–106.

Romaniello, Matthew P. *The Elusive Empire: Kazan and the Creation of Russia, 1552–1671*. Madison: University of Wisconsin Press, 2012.

Ross, Danielle. *Tatar Empire: Kazan's Muslims and the Making of Imperial Russia*. Bloomington: Indiana University Press, 2020.

Rosser-Owen, Sarah A.S. Isla. "The First 'Circassian Exodus' to the Ottoman Empire (1858–1867), and the Ottoman Response, Based on the Accounts of Contemporary British Observers." Master's diss., School of Oriental and African Studies, 2007.

Rothman, E. Natalie. *Brokering Empire: Trans-Imperial Subjects between Venice and Istanbul*. Ithaca: Cornell University Press, 2012.

Safi, Polat. "History in the Trench: The Ottoman Special Organization—*Teşkilat-ı Mahsusa* Literature." *Middle Eastern Studies* 48, no. 1 (2012): 89–106.

Safran, William. "Diasporas in Modern Societies: Myths of Homeland and Return." *Diaspora* 1, no. 1 (1991): 83–99.

Sahillioğlu, Halil. "A Project for the Creation of Amman *Vilayet*." In *Studies in Ottoman Economic and Social History*, edited by Halil Sahillioğlu, 175–88. Istanbul: IRCICA, 1999.

Saliba, Najib E. "The Achievements of Midhat Pasha as Governor of the Province of Syria, 1878–1880." *International Journal of Middle East Studies* 9, no. 3 (1978): 307–23.

Salushchev, Sergey. "Reluctant Abolitionists: Slavery, Dependency, and Abolition in the Caucasus (1801–1914)." PhD diss., University of California, Santa Barbara, 2022.

Saraçoğlu, M. Safa. *Nineteenth-Century Local Governance in Ottoman Bulgaria: Politics in Provincial Councils*. Edinburgh: Edinburgh University Press, 2018.

Saydam, Abdullah. *Kırım ve Kafkas Göçleri, 1856–1876*. Ankara: Türk Tarih Kurumu, 1997.

———. "Osmanlıların Siyasi İlticalara Bakışı ya da 1849 Macar-Leh Mültecileri Meselesi." *Belleten* 61, no. 23 (1997): 339–86.

Schayegh, Cyrus. *The Middle East and the Making of the Modern World*. Cambridge: Harvard University Press, 2017.

Schilcher, Linda S. "The Hauran Conflicts of the 1860s: A Chapter in the Rural History of Modern Syria." *International Journal of Middle East Studies* 13, no. 2 (1981): 159–79.

———. "Violence in Rural Syria in the 1880s and 1890s: State Centralization, Rural Integration and the World Market." In *Peasants and Politics in the Modern Middle East*, edited by Farhad Kazemi and John Waterbury, 50–84. Miami: Florida International University Press, 1991.

Schull, Kent. *Prisons in the Late Ottoman Empire: Microcosms of Modernity*. Edinburgh: Edinburgh University Press, 2014.

Schweig, Alex. "Tracking Technology and Society along the Ottoman Anatolian Railroad, 1890–1914." PhD diss., University of Arizona, 2019.

Seikaly, Sherene. "The Matter of Time." *American Historical Review* 124, no. 5 (2019): 1681–88.

Shami, Seteney. "Circassian Encounters: The Self as Other and the Production of the Homeland in the North Caucasus." *Development and Change* 29, no. 4 (1998): 617–46.

———. "The Circassians of Amman: Historical Narratives, Urban Dwelling and the Construction of Identity." In Hannoyer and Shami, *Amman*, 303–22.

———. "Disjuncture in Ethnicity: Negotiating Circassian Identity in Jordan, Turkey and the Caucasus." *New Perspectives* 12 (1995): 70–95.

———. "Ethnicity and Leadership: The Circassians in Jordan." PhD diss., University of California, Berkeley, 1982.

———. "Historical Processes of Identity Formation: Displacement, Settlement, and Self-Representations of the Circassians in Jordan." *Iran and the Caucasus* 13, no. 1 (2009): 14–59.

———. "Prehistories of Globalization: Circassian Identity in Motion." *Public Culture* 12, no. 1 (2000): 177–204.

al-Sha'r, Hind Abu, and Noufan Raja al-Hmoud. *'Amman fi al-'Ahd al-Hashimi*. 2 vols. Amman: Greater Amman Municipality, 2004.

Sharkey, Heather. *A History of Muslims, Christians, and Jews in the Middle East*. Cambridge: Cambridge University Press, 2017.

Shaw, Stanford J., and Ezel Kural Shaw. *History of the Ottoman Empire and Modern Turkey*. 2 vols. Cambridge: Cambridge University Press, 1976–77.

Sherry, Dana. "Imperial Alchemy: Resettlement, Ethnicity, and Governance in the Russian Caucasus, 1828–1865." PhD diss., University of California, Davis, 2007.

———. "Social Alchemy on the Black Sea Coast, 1860–65." *Kritika* 10, no. 1 (2009): 7–30.

Shkhakhutova, Zarema Z. *Istoriia obrazovaniia v Adygee (konets XIX veka–20-e gody XX veka)*. Moscow: Direkt-Media, 2015.

Siegelbaum, Lewis H., and Leslie Page Moch. *Broad Is My Native Land: Repertoires and Regimes of Migration in Russia's Twentieth Century*. Ithaca: Cornell University Press, 2014.

Sigalas, Nikos, and Alexandre Toumarkine, eds. "Demographic Engineering." Special issue, *European Journal of Turkish Studies* 7 (2008), 12 (2011), 16 (2013).

Skran, Claudena M. *Refugees in Inter-War Europe: The Emergence of a Regime.* Oxford: Clarendon Press, 1995.

Smiley, Will. "The Burdens of Subjecthood: The Ottoman State, Russian Fugitives, and Interimperial Law, 1774–1869." *International Journal of Middle East Studies* 46 (2014): 73–93.

———. *From Slaves to Prisoners of War: The Ottoman Empire, Russia, and International Law.* Oxford: Oxford University Press, 2018.

Smirnov, Nikolai A. *Politika Rossii na Kavkaze v XVI–XIX vekakh.* Moscow: Izdatel'stvo sotsial'no-ekonomicheskoi literatury, 1958.

Stein, Sarah Abrevaya. *Family Papers: A Sephardic Journey through the Twentieth Century.* Farrar, Straus & Giroux, 2019.

Sunata, Ulaş. *Hafızam Çerkesçe: Çerkesler Çerkesliği Anlatıyor.* Istanbul: İletişim Yayınları, 2020.

Sunderland, Willard. *Taming the Wild Field: Colonization and Empire on the Russian Steppe.* Ithaca: Cornell University Press, 2006.

Suny, Ronald Grigor. "Eastern Armenians under Tsarist Rule." In *Armenian People from Ancient to Modern Times,* edited by Richard G. Hovannisian, 2:109–37. New York: St. Martin's Press, 2004.

———. *Looking toward Ararat: Armenia in Modern History.* Bloomington: Indiana University Press, 1993.

———. *The Making of the Georgian Nation.* Bloomington: Indiana University Press, 1994.

Suny, Ronald Grigor, Norman Naimark, and Fatma Müge Göçek, eds. *A Question of Genocide: Armenians and Turks at the End of the Ottoman Empire.* New York: Oxford University Press, 2015.

Swietochowski, Tadeusz. *Russian Azerbaijan, 1905–1920: The Shaping of National Identity in a Muslim Community.* Cambridge: Cambridge University Press, 1985.

Şahin, İlkay, ed. *Uzunyayla Çerkesleri: Topluluk, Aydiyet ve Kimlik.* Konya: Çizgi Kitabevi, 2018.

Şaşmaz, Musa. "Immigration and Settlement of Circassians in the Ottoman Empire on British Documents, 1857–1864." *OTAM* 9 (1999): 331–66.

Şimşir, Bilal N. *The Turks of Bulgaria, 1878–1985.* London: K. Rustem & Brother, 1988.

Taki, Victor. *Tsar and Sultan: Russian Encounters with the Ottoman Empire.* London: I.B. Tauris, 2016.

Taymaz, Erol. "Kuzey Kafkas Dernekleri." In *Türkiye'de Sivil Toplum ve Milliyetçilik,* edited by Stéphane Yerasimos et al., 451–60. Istanbul: İletişim Yayınları, 2001.

Tejel, Jordi, and Ramazan Hakkı Öztan, eds. "Forced Migration and Refugeedom in the Modern Middle East." Special issue, *Journal of Migration History* 6, no. 1 (2020).

Tell, Tariq. *The Social and Economic Origins of Monarchy in Jordan.* New York: Palgrave Macmillan, 2013.

Temizkan, Abdullah, and Didem Çatalkılıç. "Bir Hafıza Mekanı Olarak Uzunyayla'nın Pınarbaşı İlçesine Bağlı Abaza ve Çerkes Köyleri." *Karadeniz Araştırmaları* 17, no. 66 (2020): 423–55.

Terzibaşoğlu, Yücel. "Land Disputes and Ethno-Politics: Northwestern Anatolia, 1877–1912." In *Land Rights, Ethno-Nationality, and Sovereignty in History*, edited by Stanley L. Engerman and Jacob Metzer, 153–80. London: Routledge, 2004.

———. "Landlords, Nomads, and Refugees: Struggles over Land and Population Movements in North-Western Anatolia, 1877–1914." PhD diss., Birkbeck College, University of London, 2003.

Ther, Philipp. *The Outsiders: Refugees in Europe since 1492*. Princeton: Princeton University Press, 2019.

Todorov, Nikolai. *The Balkan City, 1400–1900*. Seattle: University of Washington Press, 1983.

Todorov, Petŭr. *Agrarnite otnosheniia v Iuzhna Dobrudzha 1878–1944 g.* Veliko Tarnovo: Kiril i Metodii, 1982.

Toksöz, Meltem. *Nomads, Migrants and Cotton in the Eastern Mediterranean: The Making of the Adana-Mersin Region, 1850–1908*. Leiden: Brill, 2010.

Toledano, Ehud R. *As If Silent and Absent: Bonds of Enslavement in the Islamic Middle East*. New Haven: Yale University Press, 2007.

———. *The Ottoman Slave Trade and Its Suppression, 1840–1890*. Princeton: Princeton University Press, 1982.

———. *Slavery and Abolition in the Ottoman Middle East*. Seattle: University of Washington Press, 1998.

Toumarkine, Alexandre. "Entre Empire ottoman et État-nation turc: les immigrés musulmans du Caucase et des Balkans du milieu du XIXe siècle à nos jours." PhD diss., Université Paris IV, 2000.

———. "Hayriye Melek (Hunç), a Circassian Ottoman Writer between Feminism and Nationalism." In *A Social History of Late Ottoman Women*, edited by Duygu Köksal and Anastasia Falierou, 317–38. Leiden: Brill, 2013.

———. "Kafkas ve Balkan Göçmen Dernekleri: Sivil Toplum ve Milliyetçilik." In *Türkiye'de Sivil Toplum ve Milliyetçilik*, edited by Stéphane Yerasimos et al., 425–50. Istanbul: İletişim Yayınları, 2001.

———. *Les migrations des populations musulmanes balkaniques en Anatolie (1876–1913)*. Istanbul: Isis, 1995.

Troutt Powell, Eve M. *Tell This in My Memory: Stories of Enslavement from Egypt, Sudan and the Ottoman Empire*. Stanford: Stanford University Press, 2012.

Tsibenko, Veronika. "Faktor natsiestroitel'stva v sisteme mezhdunarodnykh otnoshenii na primere deiatel'nosti cherkesskikh organizatsii v Turtsii (XIX–XXI vv.)." Habilitation thesis, Diplomatic Academy of the Ministry of Foreign Affairs of the Russian Federation, 2022.

Tsuda, Takeyuki, ed. *Diasporic Homecomings: Ethnic Return Migration in Comparative Perspective*. Stanford: Stanford University Press, 2009.

Tsutsiev, Arthur. *Atlas of the Ethno-Political History of the Caucasus*. New Haven: Yale University Press, 2014.

Tuna, Mustafa. *Imperial Russia's Muslims: Islam, Empire, and European Modernity, 1788–1914*. Cambridge: Cambridge University Press, 2015.

Ünal, Muhittin. *Kurtuluş Savaşı'nda Çerkeslerin Rolü*. Ankara: TAKAV, 2000.

Üngör, Uğur Ümit. "Seeing Like a Nation-State: Young Turk Social Engineering in Eastern Turkey, 1913–50." *Journal of Genocide Research* 10 (2008): 15–39.

Üngör, Uğur Ümit, and Mehmet Polatel. *Confiscation and Destruction: The Young Turk Seizure of Armenian Property*. London: Continuum International, 2011.

Walz, Terence, and Kenneth M. Cuno, eds. *Race and Slavery in the Middle East: Histories of Trans-Saharan Africans in Nineteenth-Century Egypt, Sudan, and the Ottoman Mediterranean*. Cairo: American University in Cairo Press, 2010.

Watenpaugh, Keith David. *Bread from Stones: The Middle East and the Making of Modern Humanitarianism*. Oakland: University of California Press, 2015.

———. "The League of Nations' Rescue of Armenian Genocide Survivors and the Making of Modern Humanitarianism (1920–1927)." *American Historical Review* 115, no. 5 (2010): 1315–39.

Werth, Paul W. *The Tsar's Foreign Faiths: Toleration and the Fate of Religious Freedom in Imperial Russia*. Oxford: Oxford University Press, 2014.

White, Benjamin Thomas. *The Emergence of Minorities in the Middle East: The Politics of Community in French Mandate Syria*. Edinburgh: Edinburgh University Press, 2012.

———. "Refugees and the Definition of Syria, 1920–39." *Past & Present* 235 (2017): 141–78.

White, Richard. *"It's Your Misfortune and None of My Own": A New History of the American West*. Norman: University of Oklahoma Press, 1993.

Williams, Brian Glyn. *The Crimean Tatars: The Diaspora Experience and the Forging of a Nation*. Leiden: Brill, 2001.

———. "Hijra and Forced Migration from Nineteenth-Century Russia to the Ottoman Empire: A Critical Analysis of the Great Crimean Tatar Emigration of 1860–1861." *Cahiers du Monde Russe* 41, no. 1 (2000): 79–108.

Wilson, Mary C. *King Abdullah, Britain, and the Making of Jordan*. Cambridge: Cambridge University Press, 1987.

Wyman, Marc. *Round-Trip to America: The Immigrants Return to Europe, 1880–1930*. Ithaca: Cornell University Press, 1993.

Yaşar, Murat. *The North Caucasus Borderland: Between Muscovy and the Ottoman Empire, 1555–1605*. Edinburgh: Edinburgh University Press, 2022.

Yavuz, M. Hakan, and Isa Blumi, eds. *War and Nationalism: The Balkan Wars, 1912–1913, and Their Sociopolitical Implications*. Salt Lake City: University of Utah, 2013.

Yavuz, M. Hakan, and Peter Sluglett, eds. *War and Diplomacy: The Russo-Turkish War of 1877–1878 and the Treaty of Berlin*. Salt Lake City: University of Utah Press, 2011.

Yazıcı Cörüt, Gözde. *Loyalty and Citizenship: Ottoman Perspectives on Its Russian Border Region (1878–1914)*. Göttingen: V&R Unipress, 2021.

Yel, Selma, and Ahmet Gündüz. "XIX. Yüzyılda Çarlık Rusyası'nın Çerkesleri Sürgün Etmesi ve Uzunyayla'ya Yerleştirilmeleri (1860–1865)." *Turkish Studies* 3, no. 4 (2008): 949–83.

Yelbaşı, Caner. *The Circassians of Turkey: War, Violence and Nationalism from the Ottomans to Atatürk*. London: I.B. Tauris, 2019.

———. "Exile, Resistance and Deportation: Circassian Opposition to the Kemalists in the South Marmara in 1922–1923." *Middle Eastern Studies* 54, no. 6 (2018): 936–47.

Yelbaşı, Caner, and Ekrem Akman. "From 'Brothers in Religion' to 'Bandits': Chechens in Mardin in the Late Ottoman Period." *Middle Eastern Studies* 58, no. 4 (2022): 504–19.

Yıldız, Murat Cihan. "Strengthening Male Bodies and Building Robust Communities: Physical Culture in the Late Ottoman Empire." PhD diss., University of California, Los Angeles, 2015.

Yılmaz, Hüseyin. *Caliphate Redefined: The Mystical Turn in Ottoman Political Thought.* Princeton: Princeton University Press, 2018.

Yüksel, Hasan. "Kafkas Göçmen Vakıfları." *Ankara Üniversitesi Osmanlı Tarihi Araştırma ve Uygulama Merkezi Dergisi* 5 (1994): 117–26.

Yurttaş, Hüseyin. "Fuat Bey'in Erzurum Haritası." *Atatürk Üniversitesi Türkiyat Araştırmaları Enstitüsü Dergisi* 15 (2000): 49–71.

Zelkina, Anna. *In Quest for God and Freedom: The Sufi Response to the Russian Advance in the North Caucasus.* London: Hurst, 2000.

Zhemukhov, Sufian. "The Birth of Modern Circassian Nationalism." *Nationalities Papers* 40, no. 4 (2012): 503–24.

Zhemukhov, Sufian, and Şener Aktürk. "The Movement toward a Monolingual Nation in Russia: The Language Policy in the Circassian Republics of the Northern Caucasus." *Journal of Caucasian Studies* 1, no. 1 (2015): 33–68.

Zhemukhov, Sufian, and Charles King. "Dancing the Nation in the North Caucasus." *Slavic Review* 72, no. 2 (2013): 287–305.

INDEX

Abaza, 12, 261n146. *See also* Abazins;
Abkhazians
Abazins: emigration, 49, 261n146;
identity, 12–13, 163, 201; Ottoman
settlement, 73–74, 159–61, 165. *See also*
Abaza
'Abbad, 140, 144–45
Abdülaziz, Sultan, 69, 160
Abdülhamid II, Sultan, 65, 69, 160, 196,
203–4
Abdülmecid I, Sultan, 69
Abkhazia: conquest of, 26; destruction
of archive in, 49; geography of, 12–13;
governance in, 39, 216–17, 237; Ottoman recapture of, 112, 234; uprising in,
40, 92, 223, 234
Abkhazians: Christian, 14, 231, 235–36;
culture, 161, 191; emigration, 36, 40, 49,
53, 261n146; identity, 12–13, 202, 213;
language, 288n51, 288n52; Ottoman
settlement, 73–74, 92, 97, 153–54;
petitioners, 109–10, 236, 294n77;
return to Russia, 216, 225, 231, 234–39,
294n90; slavery, 11, 39, 52, 100, 192. *See
also* Abaza
abolition. *See* slavery: abolition of
abolitionism: Ottoman, 101; Ottoman-
Circassian, 203–5; Russian, 39

Abzakhs: in Amman, 125, 129, 133; as
Circassian subgroup, 12–13, 190;
emigration, 30, 49, 208; in Na'ur, 146;
Ottoman settlement, 74, 92; in Uzun-
yayla, 159; in Wadi al-Sir, 145, 148–49.
See also Adyghe; Circassians
Adana, 151, 153–55, 167, 177
'*adat*, 35, 138–39, 191–92
'Adwan, 140, 144–45, 279n93, 295n6
Adyghe: Autonomous Oblast, 296n19;
Khabze, 191; language, 187, 202,
248, 288n51; as self-designation, 12;
as Soviet nationality, 248. *See also*
Circassians
'Afashat, 147–48
Afshars, 164–67, 169–70, 183
agriculture: barley, 107, 127, 134, 136–37,
141, 145; cotton, 91, 156, 282n16; land
scarcity and, 57, 91, 96–100; muhajir labor and, 77, 96–97, 127, 233;
Ottoman plans for, 59, 76–77, 121,
233; refugee regime and, 76–77, 247;
Russian plans for, 29, 37, 42, 233; trade
and, 133, 136, 141, 144–45, 176, 199. *See
also* wheat
'Ajarma, 140, 144–45, 147, 279n93
aliyah, 11, 71, 82
alphabet, 187–88, 200–201, 288n51, 288n52

329

Russia: consuls of, 44–45, 93, 216, 225,
234–35; emigration from, 29–32, 35–36,
38–44, 47–49; expansion of, 25–28, 33;
immigration in, 34, 37–38; migration
policies of, 5–6, 24, 29–33, 37–38, 42–
47, 221–23, 228–34; return migration
to, 215–34, 237–42. *See also* Russo-
Ottoman
Russian: imperialism, 25–33, 248–49;
nationalism, 32–33, 37–38; settler colonialism, 6, 29–30, 37–38, 42; subjecthood, 45–47, 84, 222
Russo-Ottoman: agreement of 1860, 29–
30; agreement of 1865, 40, 121, 226–28;
migrations, 10, 33–35, 216–17, 246–47;
policies compared, 6, 102, 244; wars,
25, 34; war of 1877–78, 64, 80, 110–13

Salt: court, 134, 138–39; land registry, 127–
29, 134, 139; merchants from, 130–32,
138–40, 146–48, 176; town of, 124,
145
Sayetkhan, 117, 134–40, 176, 249
sectarianism: in the Balkans, 110–12; definition of, 91; Ottoman collapse and,
4, 85, 90–91, 99; Ottoman settlement
and, 80–85, 93; in Russo-Ottoman
migrations, 6, 10, 33–35
sedentarization, 36, 78–79, 84, 153, 164–65
Serbia: immigration in, 115; independence
of, 28, 64, 113; muhajir settlement in,
2, 92–93
serfdom, 11, 38–39, 98, 102–3
settlement, North Caucasian: geography
of, 2, 73–74, 79, 91–93, 120–24, 153–54;
infrastructure for, educational, 194,
205–7; infrastructure for, religious,
145, 147, 193–94; model villages for,
74; objective of, anti-nomadic, 78–80,
122, 140–41, 153, 163–65; objective of,
economic, 76–77, 121; objective of,
sectarian, 80–82, 84–85, 93; Ottoman
models of, 74–75

Shamil, Imam, 27, 191, 196, 209. *See also*
Ghazi Muhammad
Shapsughs: in Amman, 125, 129, 133, 146,
148–49; attempt to return, 224; as
Circassian subgroup, 12–13, 163, 190,
202; emigration, 30, 41, 49; National
District, 296n19; Ottoman settlement,
74, 92; as Soviet nationality, 248. *See
also* Adyghe; Circassians
shariʿa: in Caucasus Imamate, 27, 51, 191;
courts, 17, 128, 138–39, 149, 176; as
reason for migration, 50
sheep, 104, 106, 164
Sivas Province: immigration in, 153–54,
158–61, 281n10; railways in, 182–83;
slavery in, 171–74
slave: Chechen, 172–73; Circassian, 103–4,
136–37, 219–20, 234; as legal status,
102–3, 172, 220; manumission of,
39, 103–4, 171, 220, 234; market, 11,
100–101; petition to Ottoman Empire,
103; petition to Russia, 230–31; revolts,
103–4, 172, 204; testimony to British
consul, 172–73
slaveholder: emigration from Russia, 39–
40; petition to Ottoman Empire, 103;
petition to Russia, 171
slavery: abolition of, 39–40, 101, 154,
171; activism against, 203–5; agricultural, 102, 170–73; black, 39, 101; in
the Caucasus, 38–39, 190; harem, 11,
100–101, 204; in Ottoman Empire, 11,
40, 52, 100–102, 170–73; Ottoman vs.
Caucasus, 102
smallpox, 1, 61, 119
smuggling, 157, 174, 225, 234, 240
Sochi, 31, 248
Society for Circassian Unity, 195–96,
203–4
South Caucasus: conquest of, 26; emigration from, 33; governance in, 35, 39,
216–17, 229; immigration in, 34, 38. *See
also* Abkhazia

Printed in the USA
CPSIA information can be obtained
at www.ICGtesting.com
CBHW032003280124
3814CB00009B/682